WRESTLING
WITH LOVE

WRESTLING WITH LOVE

HOW MEN STRUGGLE WITH INTIMACY

WITH WOMEN, CHILDREN, PARENTS

AND EACH OTHER

SAMUEL OSHERSON, Ph.D.

FAWCETT COLUMBINE   NEW YORK

Grateful acknowledgment is made to the following
for permission to reprint previously published material:
FARRAR, STRAUS & GIROUX, INC. AND FABER AND FABER LIMITED:
Excerpts from "Follower" and "A Kite for Michael and Christopher" from
Selected Poems 1966–1987 by Seamus Heaney, Copyright © 1990 by Seamus Heaney.
Reprinted by permission of Farrar, Straus & Giroux, Inc. and Faber and Faber Ltd.
HARPERCOLLINS PUBLISHERS, INC.:
Excerpts from "Passing It On" from Climbing Into the Roots by Reg Saner.
Copyright © 1976 by Reg Saner.
Reprinted by permission of HarperCollins Publishers.
HOLY COW! PRESS: Excerpts from Brother Songs: A Male Anthology of Poetry (1979)
edited by Jim Perlman. Reprinted by permission of Holy Cow! Press (Duluth, MN).
THE NEW YORKER: Excerpts from "My Mother in Old Age" by Eric Ormsby,
originally appeared in The New Yorker. Copyright © 1989 by Eric Ormsby.
Reprinted by permission.
CAROLE OLES AND POETRY:
Excerpts from "The Interpretation of Baseball" by Carole Oles,
originally appeared in Poetry. Copyright © 1988 by The Modern Poetry Association.
Reprinted by permission of Carole Oles and the Editor of Poetry.
RANDOM HOUSE, INC.:
Excerpt from "Return" from The Selected Poetry of Robinson Jeffers.
Copyright 1935 and renewed 1963 by Donnan Jeffers and Garth Jeffers.
Reprinted by permission of Random House, Inc.

Library of Congress Cataloging-in-Publication Data
Osherson, Samuel, 1945–
    Wrestling with love : how men struggle with intimacy with women,
children, parents, and each other / Samuel Osherson.
        p.   cm.
    Includes bibliographical references and index.
    ISBN 0-449-90550-0
    1. Men—Psychology. 2. Men—Family relationships. 3. Love.
4. Intimacy (Psychology. I. Title.)
HQ1090.0853 1992   91-57970
155.6'32—dc20   CIP

Text design by Holly Johnson

Manufactured in the United States of America

First Edition: April 1922
10 9 8 7 6 5 4 3 2 1

To my wife, Julie.
My true companion, and wrestling partner.
With love and admiration.

CONTENTS

ACKNOWLEDGMENTS

First and foremost, this book could not have been written without the men and women who have over the years talked openly and honestly with me about their lives: participants in my research, those who've taken my workshops and seminars, students in my courses on men's lives, gender issues, and changing sex roles at Harvard, The Fielding Institute, MIT and elsewhere, and clients in therapy. Names and identities have often been disguised for the sake of confidentiality, but I hope all those I have come to know in the course of writing this book will accept my thanks, and gratitude for letting me learn from their lives.

I am also fortunate to know many enthusiastic, thoughtful, creative colleagues, friends, and students who have been willing to respond generously with their time and energy to my half-formed thoughts, drafts of chapters, or need for encouragement. In particular I want to thank: Don Bell, Shepherd Bliss, Robert Bly, Michael Blumenthal, Colin Browne, Nia Chester, Nancy Downing, Ted Englander, Marshall Forstein, Betty Freidan, Anne Gray, George Hermanson, Bill Hodgetts, Nick Kaufman, Alison Krupa, Judith Lazerson, Jim Leone, Ron Levant, Mark Lipman, Nathaniel Michelson, Eric Nichols, my brother, Dan Osherson, Joe Pleck, Bob and

Cindy Raines, Lillian Rubin, Sheila Weinberg, Peter White, and Jackie Zilbach.

One of the origins of this book lies in wonderful, provocative discussions over the years with two colleagues: Dr. Anne Alonso and Dr. Steve Krugman. I have come to treasure our conversations, and much of what we have learned together has found its way into this book. The errors and misunderstandings in what follows are entirely mine, but I want to acknowledge my debt and gratitude for their friendship and stimulation.

I also wish to thank my colleagues at the Harvard University Health Services for many useful discussions and for their encouragement in writing about the complicated subject of men's lives, particularly Dr. Randolph Catlin and Dr. Win Burr. And my thanks also to the faculty and staff at The Fielding Institute, fellow mavericks and free thinkers all.

My editor at Ballantine, Ginny Faber, has been a trusty, invaluable companion in this process, providing constant encouragement and honest feedback. The same is true for David Laskin, whose editorial consultation on this book was invaluable. Both have been willing to take the time with me to think through hard questions, and both Ginny and David provided graceful editorial suggestions that have very much improved this book. We formed a rewarding threesome, and through successive drafts I found that both genders have something to learn from the other's reaction to the same experience!

My agent, Jim Levine, saw the value of the book I wanted to write and has helped give it shape at every stage of the process. Jim's willingness to give freely of his time, and to enter into my vision of this book both intellectually and personally, has been a source of great support, particularly during the unavoidable moments of doubt and crisis in working on a book when the writer wants to change careers immediately!

For support, encouragement, and reminders of being loved, I am constantly grateful to my family: my wife, Julie Snow Osherson, and my children, Toby and Emily. So much of this book draws on what I've learned from them. To each I want to say: My gratitude is not only for all those summer mornings you allowed me to peddle my bicycle down the road to write, but also for all that I've learned about wrestling with love from each of you. And I can say the same for my parents, Louis and Adele Osherson: Thank you for your encouragement and loving willingness to constantly provide what's needed.

Once again, I've relied on the generosity of my friends in New Hampshire to provide me writing spaces over the summers, packing up my computer from Cambridge in search of the rich, timeless forests and sturdy stone walls of New Hampshire that reassure this writer in the midst of his creative confusion and self-doubt. My thanks for their valued friendship to Barry and Karen Tolman, Beth Williams and Mike French, Mike Iselin, Betsy Taylor, Richard Artese, Russ Thomas, and Kathy and Ray Bollerud.

WRESTLING
WITH LOVE

INTRODUCTION

TALKING TO MEN ABOUT LOVE

ATTACHMENT BATTLES

Twenty-five men, mostly in their thirties and forties, are gathered in a comfortable room at a rural retreat center. Our chairs form a large circle across the comfortable carpeted floor. The building sits atop a mountain ridge, and several large windows open out on a gorgeous view of the valley below, ablaze with the colors of a sunny fall day. Hardly anyone looks out the window, though. The men, most fathers themselves and all sons, are listening to each other. We are there for a weekend to talk about "Men and Their Fathers: Unfinished Business."

At one point Tim, a surgeon, leans forward in his chair to describe the painful alienation he feels from his teenage son. Tim is a big man, about fifty, his hair beginning to gray. His size suggests a football linebacker, and a weariness about him hints that he's taken his share of shots from life, on and off the field. He looks down at the floor, concentrating, as he speaks.

"My son says I'm a starched collar; he can't get close to me."

"Are you?" inquires another man.

"I've put a lot of pressure on him, about career choices and all. He talks to his mother, but not all that much to me."

3

Suddenly a sense of urgency breaks through Tim's restrained demeanor.

"He's going off to college next year. I don't want him to leave the way my father and I separated, with antagonism between us. He's my son. I love him. He hardly knows me, and he's going off to college, mad at me."

Tim looks up, his eyes tentatively scanning the group; he looks ashamed at having acknowledged his need for his son.

Then Tim regrets that the boy is not at the weekend retreat as well, so the two of them could work out some of their conflicts.

"What if he was here?" another father wonders.

Caught off guard, Tim blurts out: "Oh, thank God he's not. What would we say to each other if he had come?"

Tim's inner struggle immediately comes into focus: wanting his son there but relieved at his absence; wanting contact with the boy but not wanting to have to talk to or confront him directly.

Tim's words vividly illustrate what I have dubbed "attachment battles": men's lifelong struggles with intimacy, with expressing and responding to feelings for those we love. An attachment battle is an inner conflict between our need to connect and our reluctance to connect. It occurs, often unseen and unnoticed, in relationships with women, children, parents, colleagues, and other men. I believe this is one of the most important issues facing men today. Often we fight with those we love, or become sullenly detached or abusive because we are unable to deal with the ambivalent yearnings that love creates for us as men.

Attachment battles can take place with others and within ourselves. I will be considering both kinds of battles around intimacy, but it is the internal one that I'm going to emphasize in this book.

The Male Paradox. My experience working with other men, and as a man myself, leads me to believe that men today face a paradox. Many of us are successful and competent, or at least have learned to act that way. Yet, along with our sense of success and competency, many of us are pained by a sense of failure or disappointment or absence as husbands and lovers, as fathers, as sons to aging parents, as mentors and protégés at work, and as friends to each other. We hardly have words for either our competencies or our ineptnesses in the domain of love.

At root, an attachment battle is really a struggle with different parts of ourselves. We all strive to think of ourselves as single-minded, and of a single voice. Yet men today, like women, struggle with competing parts of themselves.

Tim, the surgeon at the father weekend, wants to be like the stolid "starched" father he knew in his childhood *and* at the same time Tim wants to be more responsive to his son, to get off his high horse and find some common ground with this boy, soon to be off in college. Just as Tim needs to honor and accept both these parts of himself, we all need to listen to the competing voices, the conflicting parts of ourselves that demand expression in intimate moments.

A myth about men is that they are emotionally remote and uninterested in relationships, autonomy minded and well defined. Like many myths, this one has an element of truth, but it is also seriously misleading.

If we pay attention only to men's wish to run away from relationships, then we miss their attempts to connect, and I think many current portraits of men omit their struggles to connect with those they love. Often the desire to connect and the impulse to shun intimacy arise at the same time. This is the essence of an attachment battle, and in the pages that follow we'll see this battle fought in many different guises by many different kinds of men.

In Hiding. One night I was having dinner with an old friend named Ed whom I hadn't seen in several years. He was telling me about "the worst part of these last five years: the breakup of our marriage."

He had been divorced for two years, yet the fact that things hadn't worked out with his wife was still so painful that several times he blinked back tears.

His wife, Peggy, had gone back to her nursing career as their children entered high school. Despite having been supportive of her work, even encouraging, Ed felt "lonely" as the house became emptier. "Part of me just clammed up and shut her out," Ed mused.

"When do you know things are really over in a relationship?" he wondered aloud to me, looking out the window of the restaurant. "For us I guess it came on a camping trip in the Adirondacks, just my wife and I. We had left the kids with my wife's parents and took several days to be alone together. I guess we hoped we'd talk things out."

Ed then went on to describe how resolutely he resisted his wife's entreaties to go for a hike and talk. He looked sheepish as he explained: "Well, the weather was lousy—lots of rain. But that wasn't the real problem. Peggy kept saying we needed to walk and talk. I stayed inside the tent most of the time. Which is amazing, because we were there almost a week."

Perplexed, I asked: "What did you do all that time in the tent?"

"I was reading a how-to book on relationships, keeping a journal, trying to figure stuff out. It was a little like I was hiding."

My friend then went on to explain more about the hiding. "I felt so confused, our marriage in trouble, nothing I did seemed right, inside I was furious one minute, felt like crying the next, and I couldn't face Peggy."

Finally he spoke of his deepest fear:

"I was so afraid I was going to lose her; I didn't know what to do."

Here is a man with considerable personal resources describing an attachment battle: how to face his wife and protect himself from her at the same time? Ed was angry at Peggy and needy of her simultaneously, all the while burning with embarrassment because his marriage was in trouble. Despite the fact that we live in a supposedly "liberated" age and think of ourselves as "nontraditional," it is still very hard for many men to deal with their need for women's support and availability in the home, or the painful inadequacy of not knowing how to heal a wounded marriage.

It doesn't take a divorce to stir up these difficult, ambivalent feelings. Many men are supportive of a working wife and say they want more egalitarian marriages, but then are caught by surprise at the anger, envy, and loss they feel when their wives become more independent. They find themselves struggling both to connect with their wives and to get away from them, and to all the world they look like sullen, preoccupied, or uncaring husbands.

Locked in his attachment battle, Ed was struggling with the tension between his anger at Peggy for not being there for him and his love for her. In the deepest sense Ed was hiding from himself in the tent that week, from angry and powerless parts of himself. It can be very hard for a man to acknowledge—much less talk about—anger, love, and hopelessness, especially how they all get intertwined. Often we feel we might as well just shut up, or go off and try to "solve" all these difficult feelings on our own.

Shame, Anger, and Love. Intimate moments confront men with devalued and difficult parts of themselves. We feel on the spot, exposed and vulnerable, struggling with shame. As might be expected, when we feel cornered, we often get angry, start a fight, or we flee from or ignore the relationship. This deeper struggle in men often gets overlooked amid the fighting, the silence, or the competent or disinterested poses that men assume when they feel threatened.

There is a flood of books today telling us that men can't love, that men long to escape intimacy and responsibility, that women love men who can't love them, and that women alone are the guardians of relationships.

This doesn't fit with my own experiences, or what I have seen and heard from other men's struggles.

Over the past twenty years I've had the opportunity to talk to many different men in a number of settings. I direct the Adult Development Project at Harvard, a longitudinal study of men from their college days in the mid-1960s to mid-life.[1] I am also a psychotherapist and teach a number of courses and workshops around the country on topics such as "Men's Identities and Changing Sex Roles."

The men I have heard are often trying to find ways of talking about love and relationships after a lifetime of assuming that work and "independence" were going to be their major preoccupations.

I am in some ways a child of the women's movement, in that I was born in 1945 and came of age during the 1950s and 1960s, when women were beginning to question the traditional beliefs about what it meant to be a wife and mother. My father was a retail businessman, and for him earning the family's income was part of the traditional father's role. I watched my mother, happily married, take part-time jobs and bring in outside income. And I observed the difficulties that caused in the home, even among loving and well-meaning spouses, who stayed committed to each other.

I was in college in the 1960s when Vietnam dominated the curriculum. Many men, including myself, protested the war, yet in my confused inner logic it seemed as if antiwar feelings were more "womanly." For years I identified men with war, women with peace; men with the status quo, women with change; men with stolidness and career, having to "give up your adolescence," as one mentor advised me, women with vitality, questioning, changing. Men seemed stolid, women passionate.

Yet by marrying, becoming a father, aging into my middle years, and talking and learning from other men, I've found that passion about love, and mastery in relationships, is not the sole domain of women. Most of the important work I've done, both professionally and as a husband, father, son, and friend, is to help other men and myself find ways to talk about love without flinching.

MASCULINE COLIC

Working as a therapist with men often feels like being in a battle. A man will come in for counseling because he is feeling "stuck," or "dead-ended," or "bored" in his life, and he may begin to make connections to his sadness and grief about how things went with his father or mother, or his yearnings to have children or be a better father, or his wish to have a richer relationship with his wife.

Then a new, subtle note will appear in the office: The therapy will begin to feel like a struggle between patient and therapist. The patient wonders if therapy "really gets us anywhere," or he gets more silent and resentful. Suddenly work becomes very important and he doesn't have time for counseling.

Often what is happening here is that the man is feeling tender or needy and suddenly powerless or vulnerable and he gets angry or yearns to withdraw from the therapy, as he has withdrawn from other relationships in his life.

Part of my work as a therapist has been to learn how to understand and defuse the battles that men start when they get in touch with their intimacy needs, so that we can focus on their longings for connections, not just their wishes to remain aloof. At the heart of attachment battles are men's attempts not to see, to mask and hide—from themselves as much as from others—the passionate yearnings under the surface.

The Principal. A fifty-five-year-old high school principal once came for counseling because he contemplated early retirement. His teenage kids were going off to college and, as he put it, "All my life I've worked hard, but I've never really been sure where I'm going." His successful career as an educator had distracted him from his loneliness.

His commitment to his career had gotten him through several painful losses. A beloved daughter had died in childhood, and his own father had died ten years before he came to see me. His father almost seemed to stand behind us while we talked. His father, who had been wounded in World War II, had worked most of his life with a crippled leg, never complaining but also never really connecting with his kids. "My father just did what had to be done: He went to work every day; we didn't see all that much of him, but he was an honorable man who took care of his family."

Finally one day the principal's loneliness became manifest. He talked about how painful it was to take care of work, without much emotional return. Talking about his father, he began to cry. His voice trailed off, and tears ran down his cheeks. He looked at me, squinting through his wet bifocals. A simple truth: He misses his father. Like many men he didn't get enough of his father when growing up and he still yearns for a father today to reassure and help him.

Those who've been in therapy know the moments when the patient and therapist seem connected, understanding flowing freely between them. It's a bodily sensation of safety and comfort. Such a moment occurred as the principal wept for his father. Then something happened. The principal pulled back. Suddenly the talk turned to scheduling difficulties and how busy he was.

"I'm not sure I can come in next week," he said abruptly. He had some meetings at work he had to prepare for. Important meetings: He was worried about losing the respect of his younger staff if he wasn't prepared.

"I want respect," he announced defiantly, as if my granting it were in question. The principal's dilemma was poignant. He was in my office for help, yet he wanted to be respected, by himself and by me, in "manly" ways, through his intellect and achievements. Who can blame him for wanting to retreat from tears and irrational anger and embarrassment? He was a busy educator and didn't have time for such feelings.

The words of a wise, older colleague came to mind. One day she exclaimed to me, with obvious good humor, "When men talk about their pain, they remind me of colicky babies. If you try to pick them up and comfort them they resist and try to squirm away; if you put them down they twist around in obvious distress, seeking comfort."

Like many men, the principal wanted help, comfort, and an ally in the process of finding new answers in his life, but he didn't want to expose his confusing internal mix of anger, shame, and sadness. So, with hardly any time left in the hour, he attempted the coup de grace.

"I don't know if I can come in next week; I'll call you." He looked hard and steely, jaw set, lips tightly closed—the way men get when they've put their armor on. Don't call me, I'll call you.

My own inner "manly" voice, angry and defensive, counseled me: *Tell him, Okay, fine. See you. Bye-bye, on to the next patient. No problem, no commitment.*

For a few moments we both thrashed around—patient and therapist—with what Phillip Roth calls that "masculine clumsiness" about intimacy. The subtext of the principal's words were: This is all too hard for me. Too much pain for me to expose to you. Real men get on with the real work, they don't get mired down in these sad, hopeless feelings.

It would be easy to lose this subtext in the male posturing the two of us were engaged in. He was halfway out the door and I was having trouble staying with his feelings.

Thankfully, I had my wits about me enough that day to look beyond the principal's anger and wish to disconnect, to remember the underlying intimacy needs that left him irritated and feeling threatened by me.

A crucial male lesson, one that men learn throughout their lives, is that if you let your guard down you'll be hurt. A vulnerable man is in danger. This lesson is driven home on the playgrounds and battlefields of men's lives. The corollary: It's much easier and safer to be the one who leaves relationships than the one who stays. Power lies in leaving, not waiting. Leaving, which may seem only a loss, also puts men in a one-up position. By leaving we are no longer the passive, helpless ones.

So I tried a different approach.

"Your pain has validity and meaning—we'll find a way to talk about it."

He wasn't sure. "I just don't think I can be here next week." The principal stood up and started to put on his coat, clearly relieved the hour was almost over.

My unpleasant inner voice urgently counseled me to bail out. *Don't get too vulnerable here, don't get into the one-down position.* Instead, I gritted my teeth and took a risk: "I'll be here next week and it's important that you be here too. I hope you will join me."

The educator looked at me in a curious way, tightened his lips even more, and walked out the door.

You're going to just wait for him? my inner accuser intoned with shock. *You're going to look like a fool!*

A week later I opened the door to my waiting room and the principal was there. He walked in, looked at me, and exclaimed, "The fact that you said you'd be here is the most important reason I am." As we talked he revealed that our session the week before was the first time a man he respected made him feel that his loneliness was a legitimate emotion that he could take seriously.

I relate this incident less to applaud my therapeutic skill than to underline a point about men: If we attend only to their wishes to disconnect we overlook their wishes to connect. It is vitally important to understand how men experience intimacy and how we connect with those we love.

SEPARATION AND CONNECTION IN MEN'S LIVES

A strong need to connect with others is a basic fact of being human. Erik Erikson, the great analyst who wrote about the "8 ages of man," reminds us that adult life involves a widening social radius, and teaches that the central task of mid-life is to find a greater generativity and nurturance in our lives. George Vaillant, in his study of men's lives, *Adaptation to Life*, found that the central tasks of adulthood involve the ability to master relationships. In his study of the "intimacy motive," psychologist Dan McAdams found that while women score higher than men on the need to be close and responded to, the difference between the genders is not huge and many men have strong intimacy needs.[2]

Indeed, most observers of human growth and development put our needs for connectedness and relationship at the very center of development. According to the curiously labeled but influential theory of "object relations," human beings from day one have needs for connectedness—attention, cooing, the sound and feel of loved ones—that rival our needs for food and other basic elements of survival.

This goes for boys as well as girls, men as well as women.

Yet boys and men have particular difficulty in recognizing and acknowledging their needs for connection with and response from those they love. This difficulty with love stems from our earliest struggles as boys to hold on to and let go of those we love first: our parents.

So much of the boy's development is marked by the push to separate: to let go of mother and identify with father. This is a far more difficult process than we realize, for even as they separate boys struggle to connect with their fathers and hold on to their mothers.

Freud directed our attention to the importance of separation in the boy's development. His description of the drama of masculine development pivots on the "oedipal struggle" and the boy's need to renounce mother and identify with father. Freud portrayed the relationship between father and son in very competitive terms. He helped us understand that the father's and son's competition for mother is mutually threatening and can alienate one from the other. Freud also described the yearnings between mother and son in very sexual terms, highlighting the boy's wish to be close to mother as a wish to possess her sexually. Feminists such as Nancy Chodorow, Carol Gilligan, and Lillian Rubin have criticized Freud's work, among others, for being "male centered." They remind us that Freud's model does not adequately capture the relational struggle of the little girl.[3]

However, there is also a relational struggle in the boy's life. We are just beginning to see that the boy's early ambivalence about separating from mother and father can create wounds that last a lifetime. A boy doesn't only compete with his father, he also wants to be close to and depend on him. Boys yearn to be like their fathers and loved by them. Similarly the boy has normal and natural wishes to be close to and like his mother, and to feel beloved of her. Many boys, and men, rarely feel affirmed in these relational yearnings, and so shame comes to surround their wishes for connection with those they love. Psychologist Fred Wright observes that "most men have had a major separation-induced trauma inflicted on them in early life, and carry a serious shame and humiliation based handicap with them forever after."[4]

This vulnerability can coexist with personal competencies and enormous strength. We need to honor both in understanding men and we need to respect the pain that such discrepancies between our moments of mastery and moments of vulnerability can create.

There is often a double separation for the boy: He knows he can't be like mother all his life, can't linger in her skirts too long, yet he often isn't sure how close he can get to father. The worst thing in the world is to be called a "mama's boy," yet how do you get to be "daddy's man"? How do you overcome your boyish fears of and competitiveness with your father? Fathers are mysterious figures for boys; they often come and go, leaving home early and returning late, like the tide.

Many men grow up yearning for more connection with mother and father, yet have to renounce both in order to feel manly. As Nancy Chodorow points out, becoming a male entails the "denial of relation and connection (and denial of femininity)."[5] Attachment needs thus create a great deal of inner sadness and anger and embarrassment, which can continue into adulthood.

For males a struggle with competence, independence, stoicism, and public performance evolves from separation issues; and this struggle obscures our desire to feel responded to and responsive to those we love. We want to be able to prove our competence and demonstrate self-reliance on the basketball court or in the living room, in the boardroom or the bedroom. Yet even as we achieve competence and mastery, the urge to connect doesn't disappear. What's striking about men in these days of changing sex roles is not our remoteness from relationships, but rather how much we are seeking to find a language for intimacy, to understand more about what we need, emotionally, and what we have to offer those we love.

In the next section I explore more fully what I mean by finding "a language for intimacy."

MISLED BY THE PINSTRIPES

For the past five years I've been leading workshops on "Men and Their Fathers: Unfinished Business." Men come from all over the country to talk about their fathers and the other important relationships in their lives. They may come with a wary eye, or out of desperation, or because their wives have bought them tickets as a birthday present, but they come nonetheless.

A prestigious private school in the Southeast has contacted me because parents and teachers are concerned about some of the lessons their boys are learning about what it means to be a man. They have reason to be: Several of their sons were recently caught setting off a bomb on a local golf course. "They blew up the eighteenth tee as a joke," the headmaster explained grimly over the phone. The explosion on the golf course is symptomatic of a larger problem: The teenagers seem so "wound up tight" and cut off from their elders. The headmaster asked me to lecture the students on "Being a Man: Challenges and Opportunities." I suggested instead working with the fathers in a day-long event on "Fathers and Sons: Unfinished Business."

"Interesting idea," mused the headmaster, in a tone that suggested unspoken reservations. "Do you suppose fathers will attend, particularly if we offer it on a weekday, as we must?"

The school went ahead and offered it, and then had to limit the event to the first fifty fathers who signed up, since there wasn't room to accommodate everyone. These men came in their power suits, pinstripes and ties, willing to take a day away from their busy law practices, government offices, and banks to talk about themselves, their fathers, and their children.

The headmaster arranged for a room far from telephones: "Otherwise," he explained, "people would be walking in and out at awkward moments to call their brokers."

Standing in the dark-paneled room with stained-glass windows— manly tradition bred into the stiff-backed chairs—I found, as I have at other events of this sort, that one of my first challenges was to get past my own blinders and stereotypes. I had to allow these men to be human, had to acknowledge that, despite appearances, these sleek, powerful men didn't have the answers and knew they didn't, that they were as puzzled or struggling as men anywhere. I had to strive not to be misled by the pinstripes.

Very quickly, as often happens with men at workshops, the boundaries between themselves, their sons, and their own fathers got blurred.

We wound up talking about how we learned to be men and what we were trying to teach our sons and daughters. Fathers will talk about their love for and anger at their kids. One father, talking of his approach to discipline, said: "I bark at my kids, it keeps me from biting them." It became clear that this man's bark was worse than his bite. Then he lamented: "But how do I draw them closer if I only know how to bark?" Another man wondered: "I didn't get all that much from my father, how much am I supposed to give to my kids?"

An architect with a busy practice and three children noted sadly that "women just don't understand the loneliness of men, our need to stake a claim in the world and prove ourselves."

Usually men come to these events because they perceive that one of their relationships is not working well, or is not as satisfying as they wish. Often the men will be alienated from, angry at, or hungry for a deeper relationship with their fathers, wives, or children. A surprising number of men deep down don't feel a happy or confident sense of manhood, despite being "successful" at work or home. The architect's words about women not understanding men's loneliness seem particularly poignant, except that neither men nor women may realize how lonely many men feel. Loneliness and shame can spiral together, each intensifying the other. Feeling lonely, we feel ashamed. Too often we take our loneliness, our yearnings for richer relationships with parents, lovers, children, or friends, as signs of personal failure and inadequacy. Also, failure can lead to loneliness. We may try to "tough out," proudly and independently, moments of loss and difficulty, passing by moments of connection with others that might heal the wounds we feel.

The stereotypical image of men's groups is a bunch of guys drumming and chanting and wrestling as they strive to find the "inner warrior" and other mythic aspects of masculinity. Yet these activities don't represent what generally happens in men's groups: At most groups men talk about basic, simple life issues. Expectant fathers wonder about what kind of father they're going to be after the birth of their first child. Dads of teenagers come in stumped as to how to defuse the tensions with their kids. Men may worry that their fathers or mothers will die before things are worked out. For some men fathers *have* died before things have been worked out; a man will come to the workshop wondering how to put matters to rest, perhaps feeling he's been left holding the bag. Men will complain they don't feel like a real man in the family. Or they're scared their wives will leave them before they've worked things out.

Who comes to these events? I've surveyed two hundred participants from these events around the country, using both questionnaires and in-depth interviews. A typical attendee is a forty-three-year-old married man, in a professional career such as medicine, social work, management, or high-tech, never divorced, with children at home.

"That's not striking," a friend of mine said after I reported these findings to her. It sounded as if she would find it more interesting if these events were peopled by far-out types—Woodstock refugees who've never grown up, or "Mr. Moms."

Yet a single profile doesn't capture the interesting mix of backgrounds and ages and experiences of men at these events. Participants range in age from the late teens to the seventies. A third of the men are under forty, while another third of them are over fifty.[6]

One-third of the men I surveyed at these events have been divorced at some point in their lives; one-third have never married.

About 95 percent of the participants identify themselves as heterosexual, while about 5 percent identify themselves as gay or bisexual. Histories of abuse are difficult to gauge; typically about one-third of the men at these events will identify themselves as victims and/or perpetrators of physical or sexual abuse.

One-third of the men who come have never been fathers, while one-third have three or more children. About 7 percent of the participants are new fathers, with only children under five in the home, but almost a third of the men are "veterans," with adolescent children, and another third of the fathers are "empty nesters," whose children have all left home.

Financially, these are "mainstream"-type men. About 41 percent of the men I've surveyed had incomes between $50,000 and $100,000 in 1990 dollars, while another 48 percent earned between $20,000 and $50,000.

Just the opportunity to talk across generations and life experiences is a most helpful part of the event, reminding us how little access men have to the experience of other men. The majority of the men I meet at these events have never been in a men's group before and have never attended a weekend event on men's issues. Yet over 90 percent of the men at the end rate the event as "positive" experience.[7]

Attendance at these workshops is not limited to the white middle- and upper-class elite. Of the twenty-five participants at a recent weekend workshop sponsored by an urban adult education center, the majority of men were white professionals, but there was also a black minister, an Irish Catholic priest, a Hispanic high school teacher, and the owner of a garage, as well as several blue-collar workers, including a carpenter, an electrician, and a man who had worked for twenty years on the assembly line at General Electric.

So, there is no single "type" of man who attends these events. Participants are more likely to be in professional and managerial careers, but their concerns are likely to be shared by blue-collar and working-class men.

Having said this, I must add that I make no claim that the men I have come to know and the stories they tell in this book are representative of all men. This group is special in some ways, perhaps most special for the fact that these men have identified issues of intimacy in their lives and are trying to articulate them and take active steps to resolve them. Just by coming to a weekend event, they have singled themselves out as individuals struggling with the true cutting-edge issues for men in our culture and time: shame, sorrow, love, anger, reclaiming greater vitality and wholeness in one's emotional life and relationships. Clearly race and class and ethnic differences interweave with these issues in different ways, but my emphasis in this book is on identifying the *core issues* we share as men.

I feel privileged to be part of these communities of men and to watch their struggles to connect. For me, to observe a group of men trying to legitimate appropriate feelings and provide counsel and support to each other is a moving experience. Without trying to romanticize, it feels important to rediscover that men too, however clumsy, can be nurturant and life-giving.

Seeing Men Whole. My emphasis on connective struggles in men, their often unseen and unacknowledged desires to connect, may feel odd and disturbing to both men and women. This aspect of men runs counter to the experience of many women—and many men. I also know that women are often mistreated by men, and that men can act in infuriating, puzzling, and abusive ways, both to others and to themselves. I do not intend to whitewash men.

However, there *are* many men out there who are struggling in honorable and legitimate ways with the puzzling opportunities and problems that intimacy creates in today's world. The men who come to workshops, those I've interviewed in other research projects and seen in therapy, may be further along in their development just by virtue of the fact that they've identified something wrong in their lives and are taking active steps to change. Yet I believe that they also reveal dynamics true for all men that we easily miss in the ordinary confusion of everyday life.

I have also been impressed by the possibilities within men when they feel relatively "safe" from accusation, blame, and exposure. For me the issue today for men is not power and control but *powerlessness*, an internal disconnection from self, triggered by normal, common moments we experience as fathers, husbands, sons, and friends when we feel out of control and vulnerable. Men, like women, don't like to come out of situations feeling painfully worse about themselves. But men don't have many opportunities to sort out what they feel and believe about being a father, husband, lover, friend, son, or worker. Men often feel an internal powerlessness when confronted by their own feelings and the dilemmas of growing up and being a man. When we try to sort out who we really are, to see ourselves clearly, we often feel on the spot, judged, and found wanting by a well-meaning wife, friend, or boss—or by ourselves.

"It's hard to connect with others when I can't even connect with myself," a friend recently commented ruefully. Our confusing, abusive, or disappointing behavior often comes out of that internal battle to connect, and I've been impressed by men's ability to understand and begin to deal with their inner struggles when they don't feel too exposed or on the spot, whether in a marriage, a friendship, or at a weekend workshop. My experience tells me that men are not just traditional or nontraditional, good or bad, open or closed—we are multipotentialed.

Sometimes women will attend these events, eager to understand more about men's experience, wanting to empathize more with their husbands or lovers, or to understand their own fathers. One woman, a social worker who counsels men, remarked after an event: "I'm struck by how much more men understand about relationships than they say; they're often much more savvy than women think, but they stay so silent."

It can be eye-opening for a woman to realize that men have inner conflicts around intimacy. We often miss men's passions about love and attachment because men silently shift them into the arena of work.

Working on Love. Traditionally men have expressed their love for others through their performance, by what they do. We're used to thinking of men as "providers," "breadwinners," preoccupied primarily with work or careers. We are all familiar with "workaholic" men who try to lose themselves in their offices. Work often seems "a jealous mistress"; it can become a solution for living, as Eliza Kazan once described Robert DeNiro's seemingly single-minded devotion to his acting career.

What often happens though, is that men try to solve problems of love and intimacy in their work. When dilemmas seem intractable at home, we take them to the office.

A father who feels that he failed his children may strive to become a mentor, a better father, to the young at work. His children may know nothing of their father's yearning for connection or his ability to be "fatherly" to his subordinates.

When a wife becomes pregnant a man often strives harder at work, creating a "parallel pregnancy." An expectant father once referred to a new business project as "my baby," implying a fertility to match his wife's.

Dramatic career changes at midlife may even originate in a man's sense of disappointment or failure as a husband, father, or son to aging parents.[8]

MUST MEN BECOME WOMEN?
EXPRESSIVENESS VERSUS RESPONSIVENESS

"The image of the ideal man today is the perfected woman," poet Robert Bly commented to me over dinner one evening. I suspect that part of the reason men become silent about love is that they fear that in order to be good enough in relationships they have to turn into women. Men feel bombarded by the demand to become more expressive, to "show their feelings more." However, just pouring out feelings is not necessarily valuable or good. Certainly in relationships constantly talking about one's feelings or displaying them can be as oppressive to a partner as silence or the repression of feelings. Men don't have to be expressive in the way women are to be intimate. What is important in intimacy is responsiveness.

Responsiveness is the ability to respond to and enliven ourselves and those we cherish. Responsiveness is not the same as expressiveness, nor is it the same as problem solving. It is not an arcane or mysterious talent. Responsiveness involves the ability to listen carefully—and to really hear. Responsiveness is an emotional resonance with ourselves and others. Often responsiveness doesn't involve many words: It is a way of really looking, or seeing, or providing encouragement or contact with an empathic gesture, a touch, a word of reassurance or advice. We may feel responded to more by the way a person listens than by what he or she says.

A crucial adult challenge for men is to become more responsive to their own heart's yearnings, as well as responsive to their children, wives and lovers, and friends.

From my work I've concluded that there is a process to men's struggles to become more responsive and connected, with themselves and others. It is not a simple, easy one. It involves a journey through shame, anger, and the normal grief of manhood toward greater self-acceptance and personal empowerment and renewal. This is the process I want to describe in the chapters that follow.

This book focuses on how the struggle for intimacy is played out in crucial areas of men's lives: as husbands and lovers, fathers and sons, as friends to other men, and in the workplace. It draws not only on my professional background as a researcher and psychotherapist, but on my personal experience. It presents a sort of road map, identifying key crises and markers of change, as well as pathways toward personal renewal and growth that are manageable and realistic. Once we understand the normal course of change in men, we can reclaim intimacy in our lives.

Women will find much in this book they can identify with. Why focus on men? Because there is a male "twist" to these struggles with intimacy. It is important to understand the normal and predictable difficulties boys and men have in coming to terms with their love for their mothers and fathers, the common ways by which men wind up on the emotional periphery of their families, and the particular ways that shame and anger become intertwined with love for males. In order to do this, though, we must also consider why it is so hard for many of us to look at and hear men's struggle to connect.

OF WIZARDS AND MEN

Most of us naturally resist hearing about men's pain, their tenderness, or their ability to love. In America, we like our genders clear-cut and straight (no pun intended). Seeing men whole creates anxieties for both genders.

First, there is our wish for heroes. We all want to feel that someone out there is strong and sturdy and understands the world. Freud's observation that a boy has no stronger need than "the need for his father's protection" is true for daughters as well, even if Freud couldn't say it. It's comforting to believe that there is a good father who can protect and defend us from the awful uncertainties of the world.

This very need to idealize men can be the source of conflict for a lot of men and women. Most of us protest that we want to fight our own battles. Yet we all want protection, just as we need comfort. Both genders romanticize men as fulfillers of that wish. We ask men to be like the Rock of Gibraltar. As one family therapist observed, "Some women want men hard as rocks and they wind up in marriages cold as stones."

Gloria Emerson, in her book, *Some American Men*, observes the mixed cultural expectations men live with today: "At a time when women, with good reason, are asking men to make known their most guarded feelings, when we want them to love and raise babies and remember our birthdays, it is also required that they be the ones to rescue people in a burning building, and startle the dragons when they are heard in the dark."[9]

There is a cost, along with enormous gain, for women when men become more involved in relationships. A husband who is more open about his vulnerabilities and hopes may lead a wife to wonder nervously if she can depend on him for traditional male duties of protection and security. In addition, men's greater participation in the area of intimacy can confront women with their need to be in charge of relationships. A man who becomes more empowered around the home as a husband and father, for example, may leave the woman unsure of whether she is living up to the traditional ideals of wife and mother.

There is also our need for enemies. We usually feel better when we can locate evil out there, in others. Numbers of books today trash men, blaming them for most relationship problems. Men often believe in the inherent evilness of masculinity as well. Many men, strongly identified with their mothers, wonder whether they have anything as men to contribute to relationships. One of the biggest obstacles to understanding themselves is the belief that men are incapable of real love and nurturance. Why understand more about one's own inadequacy?

It is easy to look at men as the repository of all that's wrong in the world, and to polarize gender. At a pro-choice rally in Washington, Molly Yard, the president of NOW, speaking of male opposition to abortion, proclaimed defiantly, "We won't accept the tyranny of men." Which men? There were many men in the demonstration. How did they feel when they heard that? It is reassuring to assume that the enemy is external. Molly Yard, for example, makes no mention of the women who oppose abortion.

It is convenient for both genders to locate the problem out there and act as if the opposite sex were the source of our pain and difficulties in life.

Finally, some men and women don't want to hear about men's struggles because they feel disappointed in and rejected by men. So they give up on men. Women can feel profoundly wounded by their inability to hold on to the love and attention of important men in their lives, a feeling that begins with the normal childhood "deidealization" of their fathers.

Women's disappointment in and anger at men brings to mind the film *The Wizard of Oz*. At the end of the tale, the unseen wizard has made a number of promises to Dorothy that he hasn't kept. All Dorothy knew of the wizard was his booming voice and the impressive spectacles that accompanied all his pronouncements. But then Dorothy becomes aware that the *real* wizard is hiding behind a curtain and operating the special effects. When she pulls aside the curtain, what does she find? Not a magnificent wizard but a small, balding man.

Infuriated that the wizard hasn't lived up to his promise, Dorothy scolds him: "You're a bad man!"

Dorothy's words echo the refrain of so many sons and daughters whose hearts have been broken by their fathers' inability to keep promises.

The wizard, though, unlike many fathers, stands his ground:

"No," he explains. "I'm a good man, just a bad wizard."

To understand men, we have to forgive them for being bad wizards and allow them to be good men. Let's see how that happens.

PART ONE

FRAGILE

CONNECTIONS

1

SHAME IN MEN'S LIVES

TOP SECRET

The roads were nearly empty as I drove to the public school near my home early one Saturday morning for the second day of a weekend workshop I was leading called "Men and Intimacy." My family was still asleep; I had tiptoed out of the house minutes earlier to rejoin the group.

A lazy winter fog hunched over the ugly brick school building. I felt a familiar fog inside me as well; my mind felt dense and thick. Part of me wanted to be home: Why was I doing this on a day I could spend with my wife and kids? Teaching intimacy instead of doing it. What's that line about academics? *Those who can do, those who can't teach.*

The school building, a three-story dirty brick building, looked as if it dated back to the time of Attila the Hun. Many of my high school teachers would have felt perfectly comfortable in it. I pushed open the big iron doors. Cavernous echoes in the empty school building awakened an ancient dread I remembered feeling on my way to organic chemistry class as I wondered how to stand up in front of the entire class and explain to an impatient, demanding teacher that my homework wasn't complete.

Instead of my organic chemistry teacher, though, the first person I confronted as I walked in was Allan, one of the forty participants in the workshop. We are meeting in the school because he is the superintendent of schools and has arranged for this community-sponsored event to be held there. Tall, balding, with a wife and several grown children, he doesn't look like Attila the Hun. In fact, he's a nice guy. He had revealed the evening before that he had come because his youngest child had recently gone off to college, leaving him with feelings of both freedom and relief as well as some loss and confusion. "I've spent so much time taking care of my wife and kids that I've never really thought about what I want from life, and what it means to me that my kids are now grown up."

As Allan and I putter around setting up cups and coffee, the iron door behind us creaks open to let in a new arrival, Mack, who had missed the night before. He has a tentative look on his face.

"Excuse me, I'm looking for a workshop on men and intimacy," says Mack, sounding as if he is trying to solicit something illegal.

"Come on in," Allan says encouragingly, holding the door open for Mack. "You're in the right place. In fact, here's the instructor." Allan points to me, standing there in my fog.

"Oh, hi," says Mack, looking warily at me. "Gosh, you seem so young," he remarks.

I am *too young for this!* part of me agrees silently. Too young for the plans I have for this morning: I want to invite us as a group to begin to find a way to talk about shame in men's lives. I have planned a written exercise, Top Secret, in which each of us must reveal a particularly embarrassing moment in our lives. But Top Secret right now is my secret, since we haven't talked about the agenda for this morning.

Soon the room has filled with the forty men. We all mill around chatting and nibbling on doughnuts, as if we were in a train station in a foreign country, perhaps refugees of war, or businessmen trying to get the last train out. Some men sit hunched over and tense, sipping coffee, not talking to the others. Having never taken a whole day to talk about themselves or other men, they're not sure what's ahead. One man chews his doughnut angrily, as if mulling over how he got involved with this. Some other men cluster together talking about their work. There are jokes and laughter as well.

We're trying as a group to do something difficult and different for men: talk about parts of our lives that aren't working well. We're trying to understand and get help with opportunities and problems with wives, parents, children. Mack's wife has threatened to leave him because he seems so unresponsive emotionally. Another man's parents died suddenly in a car accident, and, as he puts it, "I never had a real chance to say good-bye and I want to try and do that now." A distinguished-looking man, a journalist, talking over half-moon glasses, told us last night, "I'm sixty-two. How many years do I have left? Ten, twenty, none? I want to understand more about the choices I've made and will make." Across from him sits a fisherman from Maine who drove two hundred miles for this event because although he came from a family with four brothers, "I feel as if I have no family—I haven't talked to any of them in twenty years; I need to find some way to heal the alienation I feel from them." Another man seems only able to fight with his daughter and can't understand why. Haltingly, a doctor in his thirties says that he is there because "I've always admired the intimacy that happens between my wife and her friends, they can talk about infertility and problems and I want some of that comfort in my life." It emerges that he has recently found out that he is infertile, the only son in his large family unable to father children.

The very act of coming to this event welds together hope and embarrassment. Acknowledging need, confusion, and uncertainty violates the strong, silent ideals of manhood that all of us to some extent learn from the day we first put on pants. A savvy, experienced older man once provided me his idealized image of manhood: "There's a tradition that a man is a strong silent person who doesn't fool around with what he's feeling. He goes ahead and does what has to be done. Sounds like an old movie, doesn't it? *Beau Geste* or *Bridge On the River Kwai*. Remember Alex Guinness in that one? Or any of the private eyes. Bogart, for instance. Yes, Bogart! He looks around and he sees what has to be done and he just forges ahead."

I know what I have to do, but it scares me nonetheless. Playing Top Secret is like being the exact opposite of Bogie. In *Casablanca*, when faced with the loss of the most beautiful, adoring woman in the world, Bogie steeled himself and told Ingrid Bergman that he and she would do what they had to do. He was like the Rock of Gibraltar, helping her elude the Nazis and get on the plane with her heroic husband, saying good-bye without betraying a tear. Then after she goes, he makes a joke and walks off with his best buddy. He doesn't look back, and whatever pain he feels he keeps secret. Later he'll be back at Rick's bar, drowning his pain—but never talking about it.

I'm about to ask the men assembled in this room on a Saturday in the winter not only to look back but also to reveal some secrets. I'm going to ask them to talk about how they're not Bogart.

We sip our coffee, waiting to begin, as I wonder how long it's okay to let the small talk last. Anything's better than Top Secret. We face an important and impossible task together: We need to find a way to talk about our fears of being inadequate without *feeling* too inadequate. Might as well try to dance *Swan Lake* on top of eggshells without breaking any.

I have found that attending first to our embarrassment around intimacy is particularly helpful. It helps us get past the silence, withdrawal, and fighting posture we are most familiar with. It moves us toward our normal sorrow, anger, hope, and more unfamiliar wishes for connection.

Yet to talk about shame among men often feels like violating a taboo. I feel embarrassed just raising the subject. Part of me drifts away. *There must be better things to do,* a cowardly sprite within me counsels. *Why spend a nice weekend mired in those feelings?*

The morning session begins. We start with business matters about where lunch is, how new participants can register.

Then we run out of things to talk about. The men look to me expectantly. I'm impelled by a wish to keep talking—to make sure everyone knows where lunch is, ask for their questions, lecture some more.

But I gather myself together and walk over to a nearby piano on which our gear is stored. Trying to look as nonchalant as Bogie, I pick up a stack of three-by-five lined index cards.

"I'd like to propose that we talk some about shame in men's lives. This is a very important and little-understood part of our experience. To get at it I'd like to begin with an exercise. Anyone here ever played Top Secret?" I ask, trying to keep my voice from faltering.

Maybe this will be old hat for everyone so we can skip the whole thing. All I get back are blank stares or friendly head shakes indicating no.

The instructions are simple. I will distribute the index cards, and then each of us will take a few moments to write down a particularly embarrassing or humiliating memory, preferably something we've never told anyone else. After everyone has finished I'll collect the cards, shuffle them up, and we'll read out the memories anonymously.

The group at first recoils at the exercise, feeling put on the spot. One man rolls his eyes, another giggles, and there is furtive talk between two men in the back, like schoolboys observing what a pain this new teacher is. Yet there is also curiosity.

I walk around the circle of seated men handing a card to each one, like a dealer in Vegas playing blackjack with forty gamblers. Mark takes his card as if handling a vial of deadly poison, others look as if they're facing their last cigarette before the firing squad. They want to do it with *beau geste*.

Soon the room is quiet with thought and the sound of writing. I am repeatedly touched by the generosity and trust of men willing to dredge up their memories and put them into words in this way. After a while I collect the cards, shuffle them, and redistribute them: Each man gets another man's card to read aloud.

We sit in a circle, and one by one the cards are read. Comments and interruptions are saved for afterward.

> I was called into my boss's office and he advised me that I was being fired, without prior warning. I felt dreadful going home and telling my wife and kids and eventually my parents. The fear of rejection has always been very strong, and that was the ultimate rejection. . . .

> I left my wife a year ago, and feel a lot of shame. I left, showing I was a quitter, wondering how my children were doing, whether this could happen again with another woman. . . .

> In my twenties I got into a fight with another guy at a baseball game, and lost. He knocked me down, and everyone else was looking at me as I lay there, afraid to get up.

> When I argue with my wife in front of my children, I yell and feel like a complete clown. . . .

> I can't do this exercise. I want to, something is there, but I feel too ashamed to write it down in front of the group. Sorry. . . .

> In college one night my date poured water over another guy's head at a bar, and then she expected me to defend her honor. I didn't want a fight to start and tried to cool things down, but felt afraid inside.

Not being able to make love to my wife. I have an or-
gasm in about six seconds flat. . . .

Climbed into the back seat of my car with date—both of
us quite drunk. My opportunity to lose my virginity but too
drunk to perform. Then the next day having to ask her what
happened. . . .

Often memories go way back, to moments of shame and embarrassment with parents. Often men recall pangs of shame surrounding
moments with their fathers:

Riding in a streetcar for hours rather than going home
to tell my father the draft board had classified me 4F during
the Second World War. . . .

I had to stand between my father and mother. He came
home drunk as usual and he lunged toward her to strike her.
I picked up a dining room chair and said, "Leave her alone!"
He stopped, smirked and said "Oh." I felt I had betrayed
him, had taken his place by protecting her. . . .

Watching the abuse my father took from the company
where he worked. . . .

My father asked me to go for a walk, when he was not
well. I refused and said no. I remember watching him walking away by himself. I was thirteen and he died shortly after
that.

As the last man reads his card the room is hushed, each of us
bearing witness to the stories men have to tell. One man is weeping;
most of the rest of us seem both drained and relieved. "I never knew
other men struggled with this," offers one man.

The game has allowed us to get to what is really on men's minds,
something deeper, a part of ourselves we don't talk about much. The
exercise requires us to really listen to each other's pain, not to argue
or intellectualize or shift the focus. Top Secret brings men closer to
their feeling life.

"I never realized shame is something I felt. That there is a word
for these experiences!" exclaims another man.

Often in these groups Top Secret triggers a vivid discussion of the pain of not living up to expectations. Men talk about how awful it feels to be exposed and goofy for all to see, the pain of trying hard to have "the right stuff" and wondering if you truly are living up. They talk about how shame keeps bubbling up through the normal dilemmas of love that men struggle with as fathers, husbands, sons, and friends. From what I have heard from men in these group discussions and private interviews, I have reached a sharper understanding of the link between intimacy and shame in men's lives.

The morning session at the brick schoolhouse is ending. It is near lunchtime and we are eager for a break, and hungry too. As we wind up, one man, Jesse, raises his hand with a question: "What shall we do with the index cards we read out loud?"

There's a momentary silence as we all consider the question.

"Burn them," suggests one man.

"Yeah, like plague germs," says the man next to him, laughing.

"Could you keep them?" several men ask me, as if I were a toxic waste dump.

Mark raises his hand.

"Can I keep the card I read? I would like to hold on to this man's story, even though I don't know whose it is."

INTIMACY AND SHAME

To connect intimacy to shame in men's lives is an unusual idea. Even though most men grow up struggling with shame, we don't easily think about shame as a powerful part of men's lives. And we don't normally associate it with intimacy. But the link, though hidden, is there.

The core, bottom line feeling in shame is that we feel defective, worthless, without value. It's a visceral feeling—we feel "disgusting," "slimy," "pathetic," "smaller than a piece of dust," or "mortified, like I wanted to die."[1]

Shame is one of the hardest feelings for men to talk about, precisely because the feeling of being defective cuts so much at our hardwon sense of ourselves. When we feel ashamed, we get foggy, angry, feel suffocated or bored. We want to get away. We don't want to look, we don't want others to see, so we hide or withdraw or provoke fights to cover up our pain. Thus our ability to be intimate with ourselves and with others suffers.

I've found it helpful to focus on three ways that intimacy creates shame for men:

1. When we feel we are failing at "manly" tasks, and our self-worth plummets.

2. When we get flooded by powerful feelings, usually anger, sorrow, or love, that feel "unmanly" or "ugly" or "defective."

3. When we get in touch with yearnings for connection and contact that seem counter to what a man should feel and how he should behave.

At these times intimacy creates shame as we confront the painful chasm between our internal idealized images of men as big, competent, autonomous, protective of the weak, and the reality of our human needs and wishes.

GETTING SMALL: PERFORMANCE FAILURES

Asking for Help. Ted and Alice are a midwestern couple who went away for a week-long vacation on their fifteenth wedding anniversary. They left the children with Ted's parents and spent the week traveling in Quebec. It was a wonderful time of replenishment and reconnection. They had never been to Quebec and they found that the French-speaking province rekindled some of the romance they had forgotten amid the normal and chronic emergencies and routines of raising a family. The only glitch in an otherwise special time was the tension that arose in the car whenever Ted and Alice set off to a new destination.

"He would not ask anyone for directions," Alice lamented. "We'd get lost and spend an hour wandering a superhighway with direction signs in French whizzing by, which neither of us speak, and he"—gesturing at her husband—"refused to stop and ask for help."

"Look, it's true I don't speak French and I had never been to Quebec before," acknowledged Ted, "but I just hate to stop and ask for directions when I travel. It's my pride, I suppose. I feel I should be able to figure out my way."

"Do you know," he continued, "what it is like to walk up to a strange gas station, filled with mechanics talking a language you don't understand, and have to ask directions? *I felt like a little kid going to the street corner guys—telling them I was lost.*"

Ashamed at feeling small and failing to live up to his romantic ideal of a husband, Ted became tense and controlling whenever he and his wife were in the car. As a man it can feel awful to not know the answer, to need help, to lose control of one's own destiny, to be helpless and adrift and *needy*. Such feelings violate the inner ideals or code that says that men are strong and independent and in control. It's at moments like these that men can return to early feelings of being small, childlike, and ashamed.

Ted's description of asking the street corner guys for help reminds us how much the little boy struggles with the pain of being smaller, more helpless than the "big boys," and how much acting big and competent offers salvation for the boy, helping him rise above his shameful smallness and inadequacy. We underestimate at our own peril the importance to a man of seeming "big" and the humiliation of getting deflated or becoming small and "defective."[2]

Guilt and Shame. Guilt and shame are often confused. Guilt refers to the uncomfortable feeling of *violating* an inner standard or taboo. Shame means the *failure to live up* to one's inner ideals.

Often we talk about guilt when we're feeling shame. It may be that men are less likely to talk about or know they're experiencing such an "unmanly" emotion. Guilt is manly, it involves struggle, bigness, power: Yahweh and Moses having it out on the mountaintop. Shame involves dissolution and surrender, feeling small and powerless, feelings women may feel more comfortable admitting to.

Guilt, too, brings with it the chance for penance: We can undo our guilty act or thought by atoning for it. Shame offers no way out; we are left feeling naked and tiny and worthless. There is an old joke that guilt is the gift that keeps on giving; it might more appropriately be said of shame.

Three Levels of Shame. I find it useful to define three levels of shame. There is "primary shame," which is the initial, usually childhood, feeling of inadequacy—the times, for example, when Ted as a boy wasn't sure or needed help, and was left feeling inept or embarrassed. Then there is "secondary shame," or the pockets of embarrassment and humiliation from the past that we reexperience as adults. For Ted that is what happened when he contemplated stopping at a gas station and felt again like a lost little kid going to grown men for help. And finally there is "tertiary," or third-level, shame, which is the embarrassment of feeling seen or exposed or reminded of our inadequacy by the people around us. This third level is a sort of "shame of shame," in that the shame of our shortcomings is sometimes as painful as the shortcomings themselves. Ted, for example, feels embarrassed that he's so flustered about a simple matter of asking directions. He knows that his desire to protect himself from his little-boy feelings is in one way silly, and Alice, by offering perfectly reasonable suggestions that Ted resists, is unknowingly making her husband more shamed. By witnessing Ted's struggle about whether to get help, Alice is inadvertently kindling this third kind of shame. Women often don't realize that the anger or sullenness of the men they love is the result of this "third level" of shame.

We usually protest that as grown-ups we have outgrown childhood preoccupations with competence and adequacy and saving face. Yet my experience tells me that within all of us there are residues of the young boy's struggles to get help with difficult problems of living. In this book I invite you to consider the difficulty many boys and men have in asking for help at times when they do get lost, and the painful shame that asking for help generates.

We normally and naturally lose our way at times as husbands, fathers, sons, and friends. In this chapter, I'll be looking at when and why men get lost in shame. Later chapters explore how men find their way in these tricky moments of relationship.

Performance Failures. A group of men are gathered at a workshop on fathering, sitting together and talking about becoming a man. There are eight of us, all strangers to each other, and we've been relating some of our experiences as young boys, as adolescents on dates, as fathers ourselves now. One man, Bill, has been particularly quiet. He seems reserved, as if he's not certain whether to really be a part of the group. It is only after the conversation has turned to shame that he talks. And what he talks about is "the most humiliating moment of my life." He tells us about the death of his youngest son ten years earlier. The boy died tragically of a rare form of leukemia at age twelve. Bill and his wife had searched heroically for bone marrow donors, because an operation might have cured the cancer. With energy and optimism they had organized community blood drives, searching for possible donors around the country. But they were unable to locate a donor and the boy died. Bill related all this, the loss still obviously weighing on him, and then he made a remarkable comment: "The most humiliating aspect of this was that I couldn't prevent this from happening, that despite all my efforts I couldn't save this boy I loved above all else." Deep down he felt he should have been able to protect and save his son, that if he was a real man he would have been able to lick the cancer, protect and defend his loved one. His very loss bred shame: *I should have done better. I failed.*

Until Bill could give voice to his sense of failure, that shame had isolated him from the group. As we sat and talked, he felt like the only true failure among us, the only one struggling with sorrow, anger, and loss.

Bill went on to tell us how painful and shaming it was to see the strong, competent medical staff, mostly male, around him. "I felt smaller still because they paraded around without feelings; they gave us little support."

In other words, the male doctors seemed to get through all this ordeal by relying on technique and rationality and their medical training to stay emotionally distanced. There was no male in the situation to legitimize the agony and the loneliness and the sense of helplessness Bill felt. "My wife spoke to a woman down the street who had lost a child, but there was no one I could talk to." So his very feeling of sadness, loss, and anger became a source of shame because all the "real" men around him seemed so controlled and in charge. Ironically, the doctors couldn't save the boy either, but the stolid "docs" became reminders of the male ideal of protectiveness and competence while Bill was left feeling small and unmanly in his helplessness and sorrow.

As men we can shame each other just by our appearance of stolidity, our rationality, our business suits: At moments when we feel helpless, less than manly, or needy, these tokens of "real" masculinity remind us of how we "should" behave according to an ideal of manliness that is hard to shake.

For Bill, the shame of not living up to the manly ideals of protectiveness and performance ate at his ability to be intimate. Angry at his wife because her very presence reminded him of their loss and his shame, Bill withdrew from his family into a guarded posture or into working harder to prove his manhood. In the group of men that day, Bill was similarly constrained by his shame. His comments about "competent docs" give the clue. He saw all of the rest of us men as competent fathers, real men, who don't feel as if they've failed. For him to talk to us about the disappointment and failure he feels as a man and a father means to take a big risk: Would he be ignored by us, attacked, humiliated for not living up to the manly ideals he struggles with?

What did happen was that Bill's courage in talking about his painful sense of inadequacy opened that topic up for all of us. Bill was able to see that the reality and fear of failing as a man was something that was shared.

Bob, who had been fired recently from his job during an economic downturn in the state economy, talked about how humiliating it was to go home and tell his family, *who depended on him*, that he wasn't able to bring home the paycheck. From the shared connection in our group that day we all learned, too, that disclosing intimate pain, sorrow, and disappointment as men can bring us closer to others, not just leave us vulnerable.

For Bob and for many other men, working hard and providing materially for their families is the major way of expressing love. We measure our adequacy as men by how much we provide materially rather than emotionally to our families.

Divorce can stir up the same sort of humiliating feelings of having failed as a man, of not having the toughness to cope with the demands of the family, of having cut and run. Alex, a fifty-five-year-old high-tech engineer, spoke of his embarrassment after a divorce: "Dropping off my teenage daughter every Sunday night at her mother's house reminded me of the failure of the marriage, and of how much I had let down my girl, and myself." This very shame isolated Alex. Hurrying through those Sunday night separations, he left his daughter, Pam, wondering whether she was important to him at all. As he quickly dropped her off, seeming preoccupied and rushing to get somewhere else, Pam, too, struggled with shame: *I don't seem to matter very much to my father.* Alex, of course, was merely trying to avoid his own shame: *I can't even succeed at being a father!* But in the very attempt to avoid shame, Alex was creating more shame.

Warren, at age sixty-four, revealed that the bedroom squabbles between himself and his wife reflected in part his difficulties sustaining an erection as he aged. "The most difficult moment for me is getting into bed with my wife; after years of feeling sexually proficient now I feel like a little kid who can't get it up."

Warren related a recent fight between himself and his wife, Carol, that was based in shame.

It was the first time in weeks that they had some relaxed time together in bed. So they were watching TV and one thing led to another and soon they were making love.

"We were kissing and all, and Carol reached over to turn off the TV," reported Warren. "Except that I wanted to keep the baseball game on."

Carol was furious: "Watching a baseball game is more interesting than making love to me!"

Then a fight erupted and the lovemaking was forgotten.

What emerged as Warren spoke of this highly charged moment was how much shame he felt as he struggled with the fear of not being able to perform sexually, of being unable to have an erection and satisfy his wife. The baseball game on TV served to dilute the intensity of his fear. It served to buffer Warren from his shameful anxiety about whether he would be able to get an erection.

Shame arising from sexual failure or sexual need and powerlessness can constrict our ability to be intimate. We talked in our group about feeling at the mercy of our sexual and aggressive impulses as kids: standing up in high school to answer a question in class with a book in front of our pants to hide an erection, or feeling "impotent" on the playground when picked on by other kids, or learning how to look and act cocky even if you didn't feel it. Mark talked of his humiliation at not being able to perform at age seventeen when he went out with a date and fell asleep drunkenly in the back seat. Getting drunk was a way out of that awful pressure to perform, but then he was left with the shameful sense of failing at this most masculine of initiation rites: sexuality. Mark told us how much he felt protective of his ability to perform ever since that day, how he defined intimacy with his wife and children by how "competent" he was, often cutting him off from more "playful" moments with his family.

Often just having been unable to "do it," to master and cope, is the source of great shame for men, and it underlies our resistance to being helped.

Yet I think there's more going on when men talk about being unable to "perform," sexually or otherwise. Men are also revealing how little faith they have that women will help them if they are truly needy. Warren, feeling on the spot sexually, is worried that if his need is exposed—if he needs to take his time in bed, needs to go slowly, needs his wife to be patient and understanding—he's not sure that will happen. The shame here is: *If I really show you how needy I feel, you won't be there for me.*

Those who counsel men—therapists, mentors in the business world, ministers and other helping professionals, and even well-intentioned wives trying to be supportive—often make the big mistake of overlooking how ashamed a man may feel just acknowledging that things are not going well in his life. Often a counselor, male or female, wants to "help" by getting the man to "admit" or "face" problems, which is in itself shaming for many men. So the man gets more and more silent or hostile while the counselor gets angrier and angrier at this "resistant" client or employee or spouse. Often this resistance helps the man manage moments in which he is in danger of being flooded by shame. It is important for the counselor to join with the man he or she is trying to help in acknowledging how risky it can be to admit difficulty and ask for help, how much it puts a man on the spot. We often overlook the courage it takes for a man simply to face, however hesitantly, the parts of himself and his life that are not working as well as he hoped.

The One-Down Position. Women may not appreciate the fear men feel of being looked down on. Relationships may seem "tilted" against us when we're asked to express uncomfortable feelings, putting into words vulnerabilities and hopes men have traditionally kept to themselves. When a woman seems more adept at expressing feelings, a man may feel shamefully helpless and inadequate.

Men can also feel painfully small and diminished when trying to deal with the women they love. Being in the one-down position with a wife or lover can painfully pierce the male ideal of independence and autonomy.

After ten years in a dual-career marriage in which both partners maintained traditional gender roles at home, Paul's wife, Mary, told him that she wanted more. Paul was a stockbroker and Mary an elementary school art teacher. Yet Paul still made most of the decisions about where they lived and how they spent their money, while Mary was the expert decorator of the home, the social ambassador who took care of entertaining, and a great conversationalist. As they reached mid-life it was not enough for Paul to play "Strong Pa" and for Mary to be the colorful one who deferred to him on important decisions. Mary wanted more sharing. She entreated Paul to talk about their home life, how he viewed her, what they wanted together as a couple. Feeling lost in a new territory, Paul lamented: "I just don't know what she wants of me. I just wish the family was back the way it was."

Being caught without the answer, unable to satisfy his wife, Paul struggled with his deepest fear: "I'm afraid she'll leave before we can work this out. It embarrasses me to say that." He is ashamed to admit his need for her.

When Paul was a youngster his mother survived a painful and frightening bout with breast cancer. He, of course, worried about growing up without a mother, and throughout his life the fear of losing the woman he loves has haunted him. Being the stolid, hard-working man of the house has reassured him of his ability to protect Mary, but it also has protected him from his fears of loss and abandonment.

At age forty-five, Paul now finds himself confronting a whole new ball game: His wife wants him to be "more open," so that his major competencies at work don't count anymore, and he is swamped by old childhood insecurities about losing the love of the woman in his life. Both of these pressures feel shameful to Paul, who has prided himself on his ability to be the competent man of the house. Now he mainly feels exposed and self-conscious.

"I walk in the door and I know Mary wants something from me," he confesses. "I want to run and get a newspaper to hide behind. I feel so goofy when she looks at me."

It strikes me that our feeling of goofiness or ineptness often comes in part from our inability to acknowledge or identify our struggles with the normal difficulties of love. When we in response withdraw and sulk or become manipulative or angry, then we actually *are* inept, goofy, or incompetent. My hunch is that women will trade the wish for answers for emotional responsiveness: access to men's feelings, feeling heard and responded to.

My own experience and my impression from working with men show me that much of our sense of having the right stuff flows from the ability to handle ourselves in the public world of performance, whether it's the classroom, the football field, the office, or a restaurant when dealing with a maître d' on your first date. We don't like to look inept or goofy.

The feeling of shame can be even more acute when we are out of the public eye. Women often don't realize that men can feel very much on the spot in the privacy of their homes. If, as psychologists tell us, women live so much within the web of relationships, they may not understand how exposed and inadequate men feel when there is a problem or normal difficulty in a relationship.

Men can feel shamed when they feel they are being asked to "open up" after years of doing just the opposite: shutting down and getting the job done. We may feel embarrassed even that there is a relationship problem at all; it can feel unmanly just to have difficulty in the house you can't seem to solve on your own.

Often we see reflected in other people's reactions—brief glances, tones of voice, or passing comments—our own *internal* shame and embarrassment. Unable to recognize or bear the inner shame, we wind up starting fights with those we love.

Most of all, men can feel painfully small or inadequate when awash in the many conflicting feelings that intimacy can create. This shameful sensation of being flooded emotionally is what I would like to consider next.

EMOTIONAL FLOODING

Intimacy not only leaves us feeling exposed or inadequate, it can also disorganize us. We may be flooded with anger, sorrow, hope, or despair and then feel as if something is wrong with us for being so torn or uncertain, or we may fear fragmenting or falling apart under the pressure of feelings that overwhelm our capacity to contain them.

This is the essence of intimate shame: feeling that our cherished sense of self is coming apart or is damaged by feelings too strong for us to have or that seem not to fit the mold. We may feel like the figure in Samuel Hoffenstein's poem who declares: "Wherever I go / I go also / And spoil everything."[3]

A wife goes to work after twenty years of being dependable and necessary as a homemaker and support for her husband; he may want to help and support her *and* at the same time punish her for upsetting the cozy home life he has come to take for granted. We may want to be available and present with our children *and* to be off on our own without responsibilities. We may feel that we want to be the apple of our bosses' eye and yet also outcompete them, defeat them.

Mixed feelings are a normal and natural part of being an adult, yet a man may not acknowledge this if he is used to keeping things private, striving to be in control and certain of what he knows.

Often we need to know that there are no simple answers to the dilemmas of love in a time of changing sex roles, and that it is normal and natural for men to feel a mixture of love and hate, sorrow and hope. Otherwise, we may feel out of control, or less than normal, defective. We feel the slimy finger of shame pointing at us.

The experience of shame has a disruptive effect on men that women may not appreciate. We do, after all, pride ourselves on our self-control and sense of self. These can feel like the essence of manhood for many of us. It can be disconcerting to say the least to have all these *feelings* pressing in on us.

When Paul walks into his home and feels "goofy" it is because he is flooded with feelings he can't work out. What husband can't identify in part with Paul's inner turmoil? He wants "things back the way they were" because he wants to again feel loved by his wife. Suddenly vulnerable to his wife's judgment, he feels angry at her demands for things he's not sure he can give, and maybe worst of all, he doesn't know how to get her attention without driving her away.

In other words, Paul is overwhelmed by feelings he hasn't had much practice in identifying and labeling: love, anger, hope, vulnerability. Many men have spent much of their childhood trying to master and get in control of their feelings. Being flooded by them brings a shameful sense of falling apart, of being a "sissy," "wimp," or "faggot."

Asking a man "What are you feeling?" is in itself a shaming question, because it stirs up inner turmoil (*"I don't know what I feel, I just feel like gritting my teeth!"*) or emptiness (*"I don't feel anything— how's that for inadequacy!"*) or self-hatred (*I feel like a cretin because you're unhappy, okay?"*), all of which leaves us feeling defective.

It's taken me a long time as a man and a therapist to realize that men *do* have lots of feelings but they're often embarrassed or disgusted or overwhelmed by them. Men will often say they want to talk about what they're feeling, be grateful to be asked, but when they struggle to put their feelings into words it's as if they're talking about something that is *wrong* with them. This is true of anger, sorrow, love, and that bugaboo word for men—*dependency*.

Anger. Oscar, for example, once sat silently in a group for hours until he finally said, "I feel like a blast furnace inside, and I want to open it up just to peep, then to slam it shut." A *blast furnace*? It is pretty hot and destructive inside there, and it became clear that he was also asking a question: Dare I show you how angry I am? Will you throw me out of the group? Will you destroy me? Or will my anger destroy the group, burn it up?

Oscar's anger was itself shameful to him. Sitting in the group he had an experience of shame I suspect is common to men: *Everyone here looks so calm, cool, and collected, while I burn inside. What kind of monster am I? How can I possibly show myself to you? I could do something really destructive here, or be destroyed myself.*

As Oscar opened up, he talked about the pain of not having gotten very much from his dying father, and he wondered if he was entitled to demand anything from this man whose life had ended in suffering. The anger felt both legitimate and illegitimate, and in telling us about the blast furnace Oscar made a place for himself. But first he had to give voice to how ashamed he felt of the fire within him, to test out how safe it was to show. Like Oscar, many men have not felt much safety or legitimation around their normal male anger, and they withdraw this "defective" part of themselves, becoming aloof from relationships, hidden and silent.

Sorrow. This emotion, too, can flood a man. One such man, Jose, who had coped with numerous losses in his life, described himself as "like an iceberg, all frozen." He meant that he had become cold and numb to his own pain, that he felt "frozen inside." As he talked and felt heard by other men, his sorrow began to emerge, and he joked about icebergs that are towed to warmer climates. Then he *really* began to worry and talked about whether the greenhouse effect could melt the polar icecaps and flood countries. It became clear that his own frozen sorrow felt as huge to him as the polar icecaps and he worried, ashamed, about how the group might view his tears. Would his tears flood the group? Would his need to grieve be welcomed—or flatly rejected? Around the sorrow lay shame: *My tears are too big for this room; they'll flood everything.*

Another man, Hank, stimulated by the imagery, reassured Jose: "You know men may have put a lot of feelings in cold storage, but they are there and available to be thawed out." *No one* is there to help many boys master and integrate some of the real and normal sadness of manhood. And when the boy becomes a man, he has long since learned to put his sorrow and grief in cold storage, having discovered early on that it is too much for him, or those he loves. So too with his "dependency."

Dependency. "I don't want to become too needy, too dependent," a man will explain when apologizing for holding himself aloof from relationships. What's often happening here is that we get attachment and dependency mixed up, and in moments of intimacy we fear we're going to rely too much on the relationship. Normal wishes for connection then feel too dependent and breed embarrassment.

After spending so many years learning to renounce connection and maintain control, a man may get flooded by his yearnings to connect with a woman, a friend, or a parent. Sometimes a man fears being dependent because he has so little experience at being *inter*dependent that any attempt to rely on others for advice, support, or reassurance takes him into a shameful, unfamiliar territory. A man may need to experiment with asking for help by taking time to be with his wife; by talking to someone he trusts about the expected, darker sides of marriage, parenting, or work; or by actively seeking new answers via counseling or at a weekend workshop far from home.

The poet John Dryden's comment that "men are but children of a larger growth" captures this embarrassment: One minute I feel like a man, the next a child. "Do you know what it's like to feel like a competent adult one minute and then have all these *feelings* the next?" challenged one executive. "Who am I?" he wondered.

A Lack of Feeling Or a Lack of Words? Men often are ashamed because they have no language for talking about the parts of the self that press at them. It may even seem as if women *feel* more than men about intimate matters. I'm not sure that I agree. Men may have equally strong feelings but be less adept at attending to them, or putting them into words. Women may have greater facility with and access to words for feelings, and thus have learned ways to articulate their feelings in ways men have not.

Our very sense of inarticulate struggle in the presence of strong feelings of love, anger, or sorrow may become a sign of our defect and inadequacy.

Shame can grow in a husband when his wife flashes her superior ability to express and label feeling. He is left, stumbling and awkward, feeling once again as if there is something *defective* about himself. This very shame at being emotionally flooded can leave the husband eager to get out of sight—or to strike back. Yet on the other hand, few things are more liberating than finding the words for shameful feelings that we have been secretly and inarticulately harboring inside us for years.

The following story about a couple named Larry and Marie provides an example:

A Battle on Main Street. Larry and his wife, Marie, had been married several years before the birth of their first child. Becoming a father had been particularly intense for Larry, at age thirty-five. As Larry explains: "I felt this pressure to be perfect, that I had to do it better than my own father, be a different, better father. And on top of that my wife and I had less time for each other, and I felt left out."

Larry and his wife went for marital counseling. As Larry put it, they found "a terrific counselor; we both feel we're getting what we need." However, this was a new situation for Larry, the youngest of three brothers, who came from a farm in North Carolina. "Therapy was the last way anyone in my family would try to solve their problems."

In therapy Larry began to look at his own childhood and how lonely he had felt. During one session a particularly painful memory came back. Larry recalled a time when he was eight, working with his father in the family garage. His father, born in Italy, asked for a tool in Italian. Larry didn't understand the word, was afraid to ask again, and brought the wrong tool. His father whacked him over the shoulders with it. A painful memory of humiliation. Just bringing up this memory was shameful for Larry, reminding him of when he was a helpless little boy scared of a more powerful father.

On top of that, Larry wondered what kind of father he might

be: "Would I treat my children as harshly as my father treated me? Does the anger I feel as a father make me abusive?"

This was too much. "A lot to talk about and I wasn't sure how," Larry stated. Suddenly he felt awkward and stumbling in front of his wife in the counseling session. He was used to feeling in charge, and he had come to therapy with the secret belief that it might help Marie. Suddenly he himself felt aware of painful inner turmoil; he was no longer there to help Marie but needed some help himself.

Yet Marie's very facility with words was shaming to Larry. His wife tried to help but "the more she talked the quieter I got. This all seemed too much for me. I wanted to slow things down."

And always there was the counselor, a male, who seemed so composed while Larry floundered around with his painful feelings. The fact that the counselor was present to witness his inept struggle left Larry with tertiary shame, the shame of shame.

"We left the counseling session and I knew something was unresolved," Larry recounted. "We went to the theater that night and so never dealt with it. The next day we had planned to spend the day together shopping for furniture. Nothing went well from the moment I awoke. *She* couldn't drive right, *she* couldn't make a decision, et cetera. . . . As we sat in the car in front of the first furniture store, I went into a rage and stormed away from her.

"We were sitting in downtown Raleigh and here I was, thirty-five years old, arguing about stupid stuff with my wife in front of everyone.

"I felt so angry, and the only way to deal with it was by attacking Marie. I can see now that I tended to assume Marie would leave if I really depended on her." Larry was experiencing the shameful sense that if he turned for help, his loved ones would disappear. In addition, he wanted to get away from the shame of being seen by Marie in his confused, boyish struggle.

Larry couldn't stay in the car. He got out, went into the furniture store, walked around, got back into the car.

"The worst thing was having all these feelings in front of other people, the people on the sidewalk, my wife. I felt that I should have had this down by now, that I was a fool for acting this way, storming around." Larry was experiencing *emotional flooding*, the feeling of being overwhelmed or becoming fragmented in the face of powerful feelings that threaten to swamp the self. The bottom line is the feeling of defect: *Real men don't have all these feelings. We're supposed to love our families, protect women, not feel angry and resentful as fathers and husbands.*

As Larry stormed around, Marie sat there, calmly.

"Finally I realized that I had to get out of the public eye, away from the main street where I had acted so foolishly. I told Marie that and we drove around the corner a few blocks, to a place where no one could see us and I felt safer and we talked." Free from the eyes of the world—really his own painful self-consciousness—Larry could deal more effectively with what was happening.

"I told Marie about the memory of my father," said Larry, "and how painful it was, and I told her how stupid and ashamed I felt for being so out of control."

Marie replied: "You're not stupid, and I love you, Larry."

Larry concluded: "We talked and we both cried together in the car. I felt that we had worked something important out. I had seen my pain, Marie had seen it, and the world didn't end. We went out afterward and had a great day together."

MALE SHAME AND THE WISH TO CONNECT

As men age two of the key markers of healthy growth are a widening awareness of relationships and a desire to connect with others. By mid-life we want to feel more "generative," rather than just successful in careers; we search for reconciliation with parents, not just "independence"; we want to have wisdom to offer the younger generation, not become faceless "grown-ups." Yet after years of denying needs for connection in the race to "be a man," men are often stymied by their shame. Simply to acknowledge their long-buried yearnings for more from relationships is shaming.

Psychologists often talk about whether men or women are more "shame prone." That is, are men or women more likely to feel ashamed of themselves? That's the wrong question. It is more helpful to talk about what kinds of experiences lead each gender to feel shame. Men seem to feel more ashamed when they feel intimate and attached; women when the attachment bond is threatened.

Shame involves the failure to live up to inner ideals. If, as so many psychologists and writers have pointed out, women are oriented to relationships and have internalized an ideal self that has to do with taking care of relationships—being a good mother and wife who takes care of others—then to the extent that they go out into the world and become powerful and autonomous they will feel shame. Men, on the other hand, who have internalized ideals of being the hero, strong and independent and able to protect and defend those they love, will feel ashamed when they experience relationships more fully and become aware of wishes to hold on to those they love.

At one workshop, Henry and Dan, a father and son, come together, sitting warily next to each other within the circle of men. Henry, aged seventy, is a doctor; Dan, aged forty-five and with a family of his own, is also a doctor. Why have they taken a weekend together, away from their busy lives, to attend an event titled "Fathers and Sons: Unfinished Business"? Because as they age both father and son feel a need to sort out the past with each other and find some common ground and reconciliation. Both father and son want to restore their relationship after a moment of shame and alienation seventeen years earlier.

The father used a dancing image: "We are slow dancers and want to learn how to dance together, my son and I. The women in our family are graceful dancers, they know about intimacy, they talk together. We men are more awkward at this dance and we needed some place to learn how to dance together without feeling embarrassed."

The father and son have spent years at family events and holidays, being together and never talking. Now as Henry nears seventy and Dan is at mid-life, divorced and remarried, a father now himself, they want to talk. The women in the family find talk so easy—they just do it—but it's harder for the men to know how to break the ice. Even for these two men to reveal their clumsiness at this new dance of intimacy is hard. Men are supposed to lead at dancing, not be clumsy about it.

The shame for the father here is how to let his son see his need for him, how to get past the veneer of paternal performance, to show his son the other sides of himself. The father wants to find some connection with his son, to know that he is okay, that his son sees and values him as he ages. To do that he has to put down his familiar repertoire of jokes, poses of authority, and male rituals of competition and talk straight to his son. He has to let his son really see him—to see both how he has failed his son and how he has come through for him.

As they age, many fathers fear looking at the defective, "ugly" sides of themselves, the ways they have let their families down, not been there emotionally, have "failed" materially or psychologically. As they try to come to terms with the past, they may wonder if there is any forgiveness or healing possible.

The doctor had been absent a lot in his son's life, working hard to support his family, but both father and son felt the other's absence. The father wonders if he can acknowledge what was lost be-tween them even as they turn toward each other now.

So, too, the son at his father's side wonders whether to really look at his father or to turn away in his shame. "I wasn't sure whether to come or not," Dan admits. "I was scared Dad would just start acting like, well, like *Dad*, and put people off and I'd come away feeling ashamed and frustrated."

Dan wonders whether this attempt at reconciliation will turn out like other attempts he made to talk to his father only to wind up feeling angry and frustrated as his father got puffed up or pompous. In his anger the son turned away.

Then Dan talks of a pivotal moment in the relationship seven-teen years ago. "It was right after the end of my first marriage," Dan recalled. "I went up to my father wanting to talk during a Thanks-giving holiday, and he went and turned on a football game on the TV." The son had felt rebuked by his father just at the moment he needed a response from him. In his feeling of hurt, he also felt shame. At the time of his breakup—a painful, embarrassing moment in his life—the son had needed some affirmation from the father that he was still okay. Dan wanted his father to reassure him that despite everything he was still a beloved son.

For his part the father had also felt shame: "I didn't know how to respond to him that Thanksgiving Day. I was so angry that he had walked out of the marriage, and wondered if it were my fault somehow. Yet I knew he needed me and I was so angry and knew at some level I had failed him but didn't know how to respond and make it better."

Shame had driven father and son apart, and male clumsiness around intimacy had left them alienated. Now at the weekend, they struggle to talk about shame and clumsiness, about how important they are to each other. And they ultimately succeeded. Both in the group and later alone together in their shared dormitory room, Dan and Henry spoke directly about the love and disappointment and anger that unites them as father and son. "Seeing a real father and son, both grown up, talk so openly to each other was one of the most inspirational parts of the weekend," observed one participant later.

We do many dances of intimacy as men, when we try to get closer to those we love as fathers, husbands, sons, and friends. And at each point one of our partners in the dance is the shame we feel when trying to be intimate.

How Hard to Work? Career Success and Shame. There are several male struggles around connection and shame in the context of work. First, our wish for heroic "success" can clash with our desire to feel safe and secure, one of the gang. And secondly, success at work can separate us from our fathers and create a shameful sense of loss for the man who may seem to "have everything." John, at age forty, a busy movie producer, illustrates both of these problems.

When we first began our interview John told me at length about a very exciting career move he had recently made, leaving his position with a major studio in order to become an independent producer and agent.

Toward the end of our interview, though, John became more thoughtful. Leaning back in his chair, he reflected: "There is another side to all this, harder to talk about." He began by apologizing: "There's no question that this was the right move, financially. I'm making about twice as much money as before and I'm my own boss. But the hardest part is that I miss the way things were at the studio. There was a whole gang of people there, I'd see them all the time, we'd make decisions together. Here, I'm the boss, I'm in charge, everyone looks to me as the authority, and that separates me from them. It gets lonely here." Then John gestured around his lovely office, stopped, and looked at me.

"This feels weird, but sometimes I wonder if the money is worth it and maybe I should go back to the studio to be part of the group again."

What's weird or shameful for John about the yearning to be with "the gang" again is that it clashes with his heroic, independent vision of himself. It leaves him feeling boyish, not manly. We can underestimate the cost of manly success; a man may have little way to articulate a shameful yearning to remain safe and sheltered and valued, to return to more "boyish" times. Feeling ashamed and trapped in their own success, some men may become resentful and sabotage their careers, or take out their pain on their families.

The Guard at the Door. Career success too can threaten the connection to our fathers. My interview with John was almost over. He had other appointments waiting, and I needed to leave. There was good feeling between us as I packed up my notes and tapes. John wasn't quite finished, though. Coming around his coffee table, he recalled whimsically the building he used to work in:

"I mean, the guard at the door knew me and we'd joke together at the beginning of the day."

A crack in John's voice surprised him. We sat down and talked some more. John's comment illustrates how we often slip into a discussion almost parenthetically some of our most heartfelt desires. The guard, it turned out, was an elderly gentleman whom John had come to know over the years and with whom he joked briefly every day when he arrived at and left the studio. He mentioned the man so briefly that it was tempting to overlook him. Yet it emerged that John, who had lost his own father when young, treasured these brief moments of connection with this older man. The guard evoked and satisfied John's yearnings for gentle encouragement from a father figure. One of the things that was lost in this career shift was the manly blessing and affirmation he felt each day from the guard at the door as he went about the difficult task of "being creative and supporting my family." The brief joke, breezy hello, friendly tap on the shoulder, each was a bit like touching the father John had lost too early.

On the way home from my interview with John I thought more about the way our very career success can shamefully separate us from our *real* fathers as well. In becoming successful, we may "leave" our fathers by outstripping them. A man may not know how to reconcile in his own mind his success and his father's struggles. I recalled the laments of many men who felt as if they had shamefully "buried" their fathers in their own success. These men felt their fathers couldn't understand their adult choices about career, or marriage and children. The shame of these grown sons centered on a feeling of failure to get their father's blessing, and of not being able to thank their fathers for the sacrifices they had made. In that silence lived the shame of grown men who felt either they or their fathers were defective and ungrateful.

Shame can also become entwined with work when careers demand the sacrifice of our wish to be connected to our families. Many men at mid-life with whom I talk express a wish to spend more time with their families, even just to bring less work home with them, yet often this wish is accompanied by a sense that such yearnings are not really "manly." The sense of shame that surrounds love haunts fathers, many of whom want to be less of a remote authority around their children, yet worry that their wishes to be more emotionally available will undermine their sense of manliness. For many fathers and husbands the wish to be more emotionally available is entwined with shame. On the other hand, to become competent at work, making a business or a profession or a job succeed, often means putting aside yearnings to be at home, to play with the kids, to spend time with one's wife. Here again is a situation in which male shame and the lack of words for these feelings get in our way.

Of course, there is great joy and satisfaction at the sense of mastery and competence that comes from such effort, as Robert Weiss indicates in his book *Staying the Course: The Social and Emotional Life of Men Who Do Well at Work*. Reflecting on these men, Weiss reminds us: "For the most part, [they] function well, emotionally and socially, in the work sector and in other sectors of their lives. Most of the time they are psychologically comfortable, free from painful thoughts and memories, able to relax, and able to maintain a reasonably good mood. They are able to feel good when good things happen. They are hopeful enough about the future to want to plan for it. They have enough energy for the tasks of the day. They meet ordinary social expectations."[4]

However, success and accomplishment at work can also, paradoxically, bring some residual sense of loss and alienation: "I've worked so hard, and what have I gotten?" Once I gave a talk at the twenty-fifth reunion of an Ivy League college class from the 1960s. The topic was healthy development in the mid-life years. The large group of men and women was quite interested in the discussion of work and family at mid-life. However, it was only after the public talk, as I made my way off the stage, that the true energy for this topic emerged. A knot of men who had questions formed around me. One distinguished-looking alumnus took the lead and asked: "Look, how hard do you really have to work to feel successful, how hard?"

I suspect that many men ask themselves the same question. We may wonder what we have to give up to be a successful man, what we have lost. Can men lament even decisions that seem right and that they feel good about or must they stoically bear the cost of succeeding?

Loneliness and Shared Pain. When I've talked with men about the sacrifices of success and what has to be endured as a man, there is often relief and compensation just to know that this is a shared burden. It lessens the load we carry, leaves us feeling less deviant and defective. Often the shameful sense of defect men carry around lies in feeling: *I'm the only man who feels this way. Other men just go about achieving, mastering, being competent. They don't experience the confusion, uncertainty, sorrow, and hope that I struggle with.*

When talking with men I often come away astonished both at the competencies and mastery men display and, paradoxically, at how much our image of men as well-defined and autonomous creatures, who get their identities along with their college diplomas, is a misleading myth.

Psychologist Robert May writes: "Once one slips beneath the

surface of social presentation and ritual, the internal . . . world of the 'adult' is quite as chaotic as that of the adolescent."[5] *Men are not supposed to be chaotic,* part of me protests when I read May's words.

One place where chaos can reign beneath the surface is in a group in which we get in touch with our "shameful" wishes to be more connected with people. You can see this in the weekend workshops when men express both great relief and anxiety at being part of such a group. Men speak of how nice it is to be together, to feel the reassurance and calmness that comes from feeling "part" of something. And then the good mood is abruptly broken by a wish to "get somewhere." "This is all well and good but what about my son back in Oregon?" someone will ask. As if connection and "being part of" something creates anxiety for the adult man just as it does for the little boy who wants to go back to mommy or daddy for safety, a tousling of the hair, some gentle touch, but who worries that doing so means admitting he is not really the adventurer or conqueror of his dreams.

One of the most important lessons I've learned as a therapist, often the hard way, is to remember that male clients are often struggling with shame that arises from their wishes for connection, and acting that out in ways that distract them from their goal. Male patients will respond with stunned silence when I stumble about trying to find a way to talk about their heartfelt yearnings to feel affirmed and responded to. For example, a smart twenty-eight-year-old graduate student named Marty I was seeing recently complained that he wasn't getting very much out of therapy anymore and perhaps we had covered all the ground. He was a rising star in his department at the university, a favorite of the faculty because he was so brilliant. However, he had come to see me because the closer he came to finishing his degree the more frightened he felt, realizing that he had all his life used his intellect as a competitive weapon both to defend himself against a demanding father and to gain his love. His intellect was like a sword: The more he polished it the better he could hold off his father's verbal abuse and also get recognition from this man, who so valued quickness of thought. The problem was, as Marty said sadly, "I'm going to graduate and have a great career, but I feel very lonely and alone."

We did a lot of productive work in several months' time. Then one day Marty started our session by expressing his indignation when undergraduates showed up late for appointments with him. He himself hated to be late, Marty told me. It was a sign of respect to be on time; indeed, he had hurried to get to my office on time this very day. As Marty talked I wondered how "respect" fit in here in my office. Why, I wondered, after months of working together, were we talking today about being "respected"? Had I been late for an appointment, left him feeling disrespected, as if I didn't put much value on our sessions?

I expressed this question aloud to Marty, once again tussling internally with a shameful sense that I was making more of myself than I should.

"I wonder if I've left you feeling disrespected in here," I said to him. *You're making far too much of yourself,* a shrill internal voice scolded me. *What makes you think you're so important anyway?*

The debate with my own inner voice of shame was interrupted by Marty's hesitant reply.

"Well, yes," he began. Timidly, he went on: "The last two weeks, you know, you've begun our sessions three minutes late." He stopped, looking almost as if he wanted to apologize, but he found the courage to go on.

"I suppose I have been wondering if what I have to say has been boring you."

Suddenly I realized that Marty and I were struggling with shame, and his shame was leading Marty to want to withdraw from our relationship. Beneath his veneer of proud accomplishments, Marty's sense of self-worth was low. He had gotten very little affirmation from his father, and really thought little of himself. He carried around a shameful sense of being inadequate and unworthy. In our work together Marty had opened himself up to me, revealing much of his loneliness and uncertainty. Now he was very vigilant to any sign that I, like his father, might not think much of what he truly was feeling. My being late was for Marty an affirmation of his own low self-worth, a sign that I, deep down, didn't respect his loneliness and vulnerability. If I really valued him, I'd be on time.

Shame is the underside of low self-esteem. Marty was asking me about self-worth, his own worth, as he had asked his father and father-surrogates throughout his life. *Does the part of me that feels unsure, discouraged, lonely, matter to you, or is it defective?* Marty was asking for some reassurance: Am I okay as I question some of the most treasured assumptions of my life? Am I okay realizing now that I want more from my life than the same old weaponry I've relied on all these years? It's as if Marty were saying: "I've exposed all these parts of me that don't fit the mold, are you disgusted or turned off by them?'' Marty needed to hear me tell him that his loneliness and wish for more from his life were appropriate and normal, and of course my lateness might lead him to wonder if I found his struggles worthless or boring. When he heard me say that he visibly relaxed.

My shame was leading me to disconnect too: *Don't make yourself so important, don't act like you count for much, keep a low profile, don't get in the way!* For me an early shame is embedded in these words I often hear just when those who depend on me are asking me to respond—as a therapist, certainly, but also as a father, husband, son, and friend. When my son and daughter need me to reassure them, to tell them it's okay, to provide some help at mastery or competence, and I don't hear it, it's as if I were deaf to how people talk about need for each other, as if I were convinced at some level that I don't have much to offer to others emotionally and so I turn away: "Sorry, kids, I just don't speak that language."

The inner voice of shame that drowns out our responsiveness is one that we learn early as men: we believe there is something defective and worthless about our wishes to feel beloved and important as people, not just as paychecks—or as "providers" or "problem solvers" or "performers"—but as people whose emotional presence, attention, and regard are important gifts and treasures to give and receive. It's hard to be emotionally responsive to your wife, children, and others you love, or to yourself and your own needs, when you're not supposed to count as a person.

One of the most important lessons I've learned in my professional and personal life is to pay attention to that "deafness" so many men have to cries for affirmation, support, and connection. Let's consider, for example, the difficulty men have in openly saying good-bye.

Departures and Disruptions. In any group meeting—workshop, seminar, or at the office—it often happens that someone has to leave the meeting early or unexpectedly. Perhaps to avoid disrupting the meeting, the person usually just gets up and leaves without excusing himself or saying good-bye.

However, leaving a group such as this is never a simple act emotionally, even though we often gloss over what its impact is. What do the remaining men feel and do when someone leaves? In a teaching situation or workshop this is an excellent opportunity to discuss how people deal with being left, and with loss. This is particularly true at a weekend workshop where we've spent three days talking together about the most intimate matters. On Sunday morning, as our time is coming to an end, a man may put on his coat and gather his things and leave the room. No one says anything and the conversation continues even as he's leaving.

"What are people feeling right now?" I might ask, if I have my wits about me.

Often just asking that question provokes bemused looks from the participants: "What do you mean? He left, what do you mean what do I *feel?*"

"What does it feel like to have someone leave without saying anything, not even good-bye?" I'll persist, feeling like a pesky teacher forcing pupils to learn a lesson they don't want to. Sometimes I feel as if I'm treading on old bruises that go way back, muffled cries of pain, some early shame around being left as a boy that I'm not supposed to ask about.

Usually someone will say, "Well, I wondered how come Jim left just as I was talking: I suppose I might have wondered if it was something I said."

Or: "I'm sorry he left without saying good-bye. I liked him and wanted a chance to wish him well."

If I truly have my wits about me and ask my pesky question *before* the person actually leaves, the man will often turn around when he is half way out the door and respond with relief: "I wanted to say good-bye and tell people how much this mattered to me, how much I cared about what I heard, but I didn't want to interrupt things. I didn't know if I ought to interrupt, or how to."

In other words, *those who are left want to feel affirmed by and affirm those who are leaving, and those who are leaving want to speak to those who are staying, and no one can acknowledge or speak of those desires and needs.*

It feels crazy at times: After spending a day together going through all this, how could we not care about each other? Yet that feels very hard to talk about, and it fills us with shame.

At these moments in our group we are reliving shame from long ago. As we change from boys to men we get numb to our wishes for connection, we get filled with shame, and we come to take exclusion, brief hellos and stiff good-byes and all the wounds they create, for granted. And then in turn we act out our shame with those we love, becoming experts in the quick hello and the mumbled good-bye, creating shame in those we love, making them wonder if they have any real value to us, just as we wonder about our value to those we love.

This is, after all, what causes us great pain: not being able to talk about connection and love with those we care about, not being able to communicate with those we love or feel truly beloved by ourselves. I think this often happens because we have learned not to attend to our wishes for connection. We turn away from them in our shame.

THE TWO LANGUAGES OF SHAME: ANGER AND THE SILENCE OF LOVE

Shame around intimacy often leaves us wanting to flee, get away, or withdraw, to escape from the public eye. Shame is often *most* apparent not from what men say but from what they do. Shame for men is a feeling so profound that it is often not articulated. We reveal our shame in other ways.

Silence is one language of shame; anger is another. Much of what we explore in this book pivots on how men become vague or silent or combative at moments when they are struggling with wishes to be more responsive emotionally. Silence and anger help us manage our shame. Here's an introduction to the silent and angry languages of shame.

The Peacock's Tail. Poet Robert Bly illuminated men's silence when he wondered why his voice trails off when he recites his poetry in public. Often we become inaudible when we speak most directly from the heart. Shame silences us. In his poem "The Night We Missed the Wedding," shame leads Bly to doubt and to turn away from his passion:

> When I recite a line,
> I allow the voice to
> fall off. I speak strongly
> as I climb the line, and then
> leave the last word
> to trail down, so that
> no one can hear it.
> Doubt enters then, just when
> there should be something fierce—
> when the throat should come in
> lifting up what it knows,
> what it feels, what it *wants*.
>
> Why shouldn't the voice spread
> its peacock tail in which the eyes

of the universe are open?
This failing of breath
is the shamed boy
who hides in his room at night. . . ?"[6]

The spreading of a peacock's tail brings to mind the wish to be seen, admired, and treasured, to be loved and loving ourselves. Men often hide their peacock tails; they leave their wishes to be loved and loving unspoken. Shame around love—shame aroused by the yearning to be valued by and valuing of others—often makes men unwilling to see or to speak or to hear in intimate situations; we want to avert our awareness from what seems humiliating.

So, Warren struggling with sexuality and performance, lying in bed with his wife, withdraws into the TV set and a baseball game, seeking reassurance and support from the male images on the screen. My friend Ed, whom we met in the first chapter, isolates himself in his tent as his marriage is in trouble and he "burns" inside. Marty wonders about leaving therapy as he imagines himself "boring" in my eyes. We become quiet and preoccupied, silent or withdrawn, just at the moments that we yearn most deeply for a response.

My Inquisitor. We can also hide behind anger and accusation. I saw this clearly one day when within five minutes of beginning a workshop a man once expertly put me on the spot, in just the way he himself felt on the hot seat. I was talking about fathers and their importance in children's lives when Alfred, a thirty-five-year-old accountant, raised his hand, innocently. "I just want to ask, how many men in this country have these difficulties with their fathers?" He proceeded to press for exact numbers and precisely quantified details.

Quoting studies and statistics mollified him a little, but over the course of the day he became my inquisitor. Alfred clearly had work to do: His own father had been a demanding man whom he had never been able to really please; he had died before there was any real reconciliation. Yet it seemed all Alfred wanted to do was argue: about statistics, about the fine details of research and the grand details of theories. *I* began to feel shamed. I tried to shut him up; I tried to ignore him. All to no avail.

Finally I realized the unasked, embarrassed question underneath Alfred's niggling: *Is it okay to miss my father, and to feel alienated from him? Does that make me different, abnormal, less manly, or does every man feel that way?*

He wanted some reassurance from me, too, about whether I was trustworthy or just a "con." It's as if Alfred were pleading: *Where are the facts? Make your case, Dr. Osherson, so I can be sure I'm not being sold some ridiculous bill of goods."*

Alfred's anger and accusation were a way of asking for help, a way of connecting with me through the shame he felt at his very need to be in this workshop, which was potentially so embarrassing to him.

Facts are helpful, but the evidence of our hearts is the most persuasive.

"It's embarrassing how much we needed our fathers, isn't it?" I finally said.

To which Alfred started to cry.

André Malraux once observed: "What is a man? A miserable pile of secrets." Men are, of course, much more than that. Often the misery and secrets, however, grow out of longings for attachment and connection.

Making the secrets known can be very helpful, as can telling our stories so that the loneliness and hunger of being a man becomes more of a shared opportunity rather than a private, solitary mark of shame.

Where do we learn that our yearnings for connection are shameful? Let's examine the origins of this male struggle in the boy's normal divided love for his mother and father.

2

DIVIDED LOYALTIES

MEN'S LONELINESS AND THE

MYSTERY OF OUR PARENTS

A SKINNED KNEE

"I can remember the moment I gave up on hugs," recalled Barry, a thirty-eight-year-old unmarried graphic artist in an advertising agency outside Baltimore. "It was when I was five years old." He then described a poignant moment when he felt torn between his mother and father:

"I was playing in front of our house in upstate New York, by myself. There was a big rock in front of the barn, which I liked to climb. That day I had scrambled up to the top of the rock, but had tripped and fallen off it. Not a very big rock, but I scraped my knee." The injury to his pride was worse than to his knee.

"So I ran into the house. This was right after dinner time and my father was watching TV. My mother was sitting across the room, knitting.

"I ran right up to my father, in front of his chair. I can still remember him looking down at me. I was crying and put my arms up to him.

"I wanted him to pick me up and put me in his lap, to hug me. Instead he looked down at me and exclaimed:

'You're too old for that!'

"It was as if he had slapped me. I turned away from him, trying not to cry, feeling so humiliated and hurt. My mother put down her knitting on the sofa and put out *her* arms. She smiled at me and said, 'Come here.' "

At age five Barry faced a dilemma: Does he listen to Dad and toughen up or does he go to Mom for that hug? Either way, he loses: He's got the choice of being a mama's boy or a Marine.

That's a choice you could struggle with and maybe work out, finding some compromises, if you were aware that those were the choices. But the young Barry is not aware; he is shamed by his wish for comfort. To toughen up for Dad means to renounce Mom's offer of solace: To go to Mom means to be a sissy in Dad's eyes.

An important lesson is being negotiated among father and son and mother in this living room. Here is a boy facing a moment of disappointment: One minute he's climbing a rock, feeling big and powerful, a manly rock climber/explorer; the next minute he's a little boy, hurt and needy. He's struggling with a realization that haunts us throughout our lives: *I'm not as big and powerful as I hoped.*

In his disappointment the boy yearns for a moment of reassurance from his father. Instead, his father leaves his son standing there feeling humiliated and exposed in his "unmanly" yearning for affirmation. He reaches for reassurance, a hug, and he's told to be separate, to get himself under control. The son's need for connection is not reflected back in the response he gets. In fact, just the opposite.

Heinz Kohut, a psychoanalyst, makes the important point that we need to have our feelings reflected back or "mirrored" to us by those we love in order to know that what we feel is appropriate and safe.[1] When we are not "joined" in a feeling we may come to feel it is inappropriate or a sign of our own defect.

When a man says he gives up on hugs, he means that he gives up asking for reassurance and comfort. But he also gives up on his ability to provide these treasures to himself or others. These parts of our lives become surrounded by shame and we renounce what we once wanted, what we continue to want as men.

Many of the struggles with love and attachment in men's lives are rooted in the boy's struggles to feel loved and affirmed by both his parents.

This is not an attack on parents. I believe that there are normal and perhaps unavoidable misunderstandings and difficulties that plague the relationships between sons and their parents, and that as a result one task for us as grown men is to come to terms with the mystery of our mothers and fathers.

All children have a desire for and need to connect with both their mother and father. In both cases, and in different ways, there is great potential for boys to become ashamed of that connection with each parent.

There is a crucial dilemma for the boy: To develop an adequate sense of self as a man he must loosen the bond to mother and develop a sturdy and trustworthy identification with his father. The task is different for girls. A girl's first identification is with the same-sexed parent, her mother, and achieving a sense of female identity does not entail renouncing her. A boy's first identification is with the opposite-sexed parent, and developing a secure sense of self means turning away from his mother and toward his father. This is a much more difficult task than we realize.

Families differ, and not all mothers and fathers present as dramatic alternatives to their sons as Barry's parents did. Sometimes the images are more subtle, and in some families the roles are reversed, with fathers offering solace and mothers pushing their sons toward independence. However, normal tensions in both the mother-son and father-son relationship introduce shame into the boy's earliest yearnings for connection.

Let's look first at how shame enters into the relationship with mother, and then how fathers and sons do a dance with connection and distance.

THE LOST ROMANCE WITH MOTHER

Every boy is in love with and wants to be loved by his mother. This is one of the necessary conditions of growth and attachment, and it's one of the normal precursors of shame. At some point, usually intensifying around ages three to five, we have to give mother up, or allow this bond to mature into a different kind of relationship. Psychologists refer to a process of "disidentification" from mother, in which the young boy begins to renounce parts of himself that seem too "motherly" or "feminine."

A mother often notices the embarrassment of her son when she shows up at his primary school classroom bringing a lunchbox he forgot, or when she displays too much maternal warmth to him on the playground, or when she calls him in earlier than the others at night when he is out playing with his friends. On the other hand, what young son also doesn't want to linger a little while longer in his mother's lap, or feel her tousle his hair and comfort him, or spark a gleam of love in her eye with his glorious adventures ("Look Ma, no hands!")? Many boys (and men) struggle with their wishes to hold on to mother's warmth and nurturing.

Many mothers are like the "designated hitters" in baseball, assigned specific tasks and responsibilities in the family; mothers are often the "designated feelers," the emotionally expressive or nurturant parent.

The notion of disidentification from mother is a sad one, implying that to become men boys have to give up tender yearnings and abilities that they may have learned from their mothers.[2] Happily, I think that this "disidentification" is a less clear-cut phenomenon than our neat theories imply. Boys identify with both parents, and adulthood is often a normal time of finding and connecting with generative, life-giving parts of our mothers and fathers. Unfortunately, too many men feel conflicted about their yearning for their mothers. The task for the boy is how to deal with the parts of himself that feel like mother, that are rooted in a relationship with her, but that seem too "hot" to handle and thus become embarrassing or devalued.

Feelings as Feminine. A girl can look at her mother and see herself and her future; but when a boy looks at mother he sees "the other." So feelings may come to be seen as the province of women, while self-control or distance may seem more manly.

Nurturing Ourselves and Others. What of the mother within us? The capacity to soothe ourselves during times of stress, to return to an inner peacefulness and sense of security and relative optimism when things are not going well or when life seems demanding, is partly dependent on the "mother" that we have taken into ourselves. When we need to, we can reassure ourselves with a visceral, bedrock feeling or being beloved and worthwhile, even as the outer world seems to be indicating otherwise, or when the internal voice of shame hisses at us. This internal confidence is rooted in our earliest experiences of a trustworthy mother's calming voice, touch, smell. For many men, though, the "mother inside" is withered or silent.

"I'm too old to be missing my mother," lamented one forty-year-old man, obviously embarrassed at talking about his memories of her warmth, which he'd had to give up too quickly.

Yet it is precisely in our warm memories of our mother's closeness that we can find part of our capacity to nurture as men. The memories of how good it felt to linger longer in mother's arms or to return to her and feel her touch and caring is at the roots of our capacity to provide these emotional necessities to ourselves, our wives, our children, and others we love. When mother was too forbidding and emotional warmth was absent or undependable, a man may end up feeling small and vulnerable at the very moments when he tries to be tender.

The Comfort of Women. Women often don't understand the enormous power they have in men's lives. Having rarely found emotional support and help from other men, many of us come to look upon women as the sole repositories of safety, security, comfort, and support. Unable to obtain a friendly smile, soft touch, or gentle words of encouragement or kindness from men, a man may become an expert in finding such reassurance from women friends, or his wife. If he feels that the need for close touch and contact are not "manly," a man may turn to sex with women as the only available experience of touching and bodily comfort. I have known many single men who walk about wanting to "score" on a weekend night by picking up a woman to sleep with. It sounds as if their goals are sexual, but in truth what they really want is to find a person to share their bed with, to reduce the loneliness of their apartment, to feel the warmth and touch of another person sleeping next to them, not to wake up alone the next morning. Even if we don't pursue sex in this way, many of us can only really let our guard down around women. Only with our wives or women friends will we allow ourselves to seek comfort and help, and feel warmed by another person's kindly attention.

The Power of Women. Given the early importance of mothers and women in the home, child care, and the schools, some boys feel controlled by women. A little boy may feel doomed to live in a feminine world while trying to connect to the world of men. When the boy becomes a man he may experience a sense of suffocation in the presence of women, of wanting room to breathe, of being impotent or reduced by a powerful woman to the status of a little boy. It is only in the outside world of work that a man can truly live free—free of the shaming domination of women.

Men's need for and distrust of women can extend into the workplace as well. At age thirty-eight, Jason is a corporate executive who is sympathetic to women yet also carries around a resentment toward them. Although he works well with female bosses, he is very prickly at moments when he feels they have too much power. At such times he likes to flaunt his independence in ways that may undermine his effectiveness with them. One day, sitting in his busy office, he mused about his mother: "I really idealized her. I can even recall the smell of her perfume when she entered the room before going out to dinner with my father." But there was a painful sense of being too much an appendage of his mother, of having to give up his father in order to hold on to his mother. Swinging his chair away from me, almost as if to mask the sadness and embarrassment he felt, Jason told me a different version of the skinned-knee story:

"For years I would kiss both my father and mother at bedtime. Then when I was about eleven years old I remember coming down to the kitchen table before bedtime for a kiss. Both my parents were sitting talking and I stood between them and went to my father for a kiss. My mother said to my father, 'Isn't he too old for that?'

"My father drew back, and that was the last time we kissed."

The mother's power here was enormous, and it reflects the boy's sense of being his mother's property.

As an adult, Jason's efforts at intimacy with women often leave him feeling in danger of being emasculated, of feeling like a little boy who lives at the whims of his mother. He carries around a lingering sensitivity and resentment of women whom he feels have too much power over him. This struggle was crystallized for him one morning when he was working at his office on a day he had planned to take off. Responsible executive that he is, he came in to the firm on his own time to take care of some pressing business. Since he hadn't planned to see anyone at work he was dressed in blue jeans and a workshirt, rather unusual workday attire for this prestigious Chicago firm. While sitting at his desk he got an unexpected call from the female president of the firm asking if he could come in that afternoon for an interview with an executive vice president of the firm for an exciting new position, one that Jason had applied for.

"I knew the interview appointment was a coup for me," said Jason, "and that it meant I had an inside track on the position. But I sat there angry at the president for not arranging it earlier—'Am I at her beck and call?' part of me fumed.

"I'd have to go home and change my clothes, and part of me was tempted to go to the meeting in my blue jeans, which would have been disastrous for my chances. I ultimately went home, changed, came to the meeting, and all went well, but I know part of me was tempted to be provocative just to show my independence from this woman boss who had so much power over me."

Jason understood the point without creating an embarrassing situation for himself: Mother had too much power in his life, and he has spent too much time working hard to please women. His sense of shame at the office grew out of the deeply rooted humiliation he felt as a boy that his mother had such power that she could strip him of his father, dictate to the men in the house what kind of closeness they could have, and *both he and his father went along with it.* It was a feeling of shame he carried with him all his life.

When a man feels too strongly the shameful and wonderful sense of being "mama's son" without a corresponding sturdy knowledge that he is also "papa's boy," then his capacity for intimacy with both women and men suffers. For many men the yearnings for their mothers are such a source of shame that they strive to prove their manliness by denying any need for her.

Part of the reason that boys struggle with their love for their mothers stems from the absence of their fathers. Let's take a closer look now at the father-son bond.

LOST TREASURES: THE SEARCH FOR FATHER

A group of men at a workshop titled "Men and Intimacy" is sitting in a circle, and I go over to get my index cards. The men roll their eyes—no more shame, please! Instead we are going to play The Treasure Game. "Write down a gift that you got from your father, something you hold dear to your heart."

The instructions cause some confusion. "You mean something he did for me?"

"Possibly," I reply, deliberately trying to be ambiguous. I want us to search our memories without too much instruction. "It may be something he gave you, a moment together, a tool, a saying, a song, a picture. Whatever you got that you treasure from your father."

Again the men go along, willing to try, although often reluctantly, as if exploring a wound they wished they didn't feel.

"No copying off your neighbor," I admonish, striving for a ray of humor amid a task that few find funny. Again we pour our hearts out onto little index cards. The cards are collected and shuffled, then redistributed so that everyone has a card to read out anonymously.

When I was eight years old we sat in the woods fishing. We caught some fish and cooked it over the fire. It started snowing. He pulled me between his legs, put his coat over me, and that's how we had lunch. It is the best memory of my entire life. . . .

Dad taking me with him to his chemistry lab on a Saturday morning and he and I weighing things like a strand of hair, grain of sugar, or a dot on a piece of paper on the balances in the lab. Sometimes we'd blow glass into intricate shapes. It felt good to share his work world in this way and for him to want me there. . . .

He bought us a rowboat with a six-horsepower motor, so just the two of us could go fishing. . . .

Throughout childhood, sitting with my father in church, to his left. Reaching into his left-hand coat pocket for cellophane-wrapped candy. Opening the candy quietly, which was hard to do, sucking on the candy and falling asleep, leaning my head on his arm. . . .

I cannot remember a thing I treasure from my father. . . .

My tenth birthday. My friend had a bike, and I had a second-hand broken-down one from an older sister. My parents couldn't afford a new bike for me, and there was no bike. I cried sadly. My father went out that very afternoon, borrowed the money, and brought home a new bike. That bike said to me, "I love you, son". . . .

My father helping me to learn how to throw a football in a perfect spiral. . . .

Our fathers' love for us was often encoded in their actions. They gave us deeds, not words, and we had to read between the lines. Often great feeling thundered beneath the quiet, unspoken, often unnoticed, moments when fathers could express their love for their sons, sons could lean on fathers, depend on them to teach mastery (throwing a football), model vitality as a man (in the lab), and blanket the son with warmth, protecting him from the cold.

One man doesn't know what to say. "There's an emptiness there," he says sadly. "I wish I had more from him." The treasures the other men have described are often too small, too fleeting to fill up the larger sense of emptiness that they feel too.

My work with men and my examination of my own life and struggles convince me that in our society, we take for granted a father's absence—psychological and/or physical—from his family. And we also take for granted the pain this causes.

The essence of a boy's dilemma is that it is very hard for him to truly feel what his heart most yearns for: that he is his father's beloved son. The wound transmitted from father to son is one of shame and grief: feeling unimportant, devalued, worthless to each other as *real people*, seen and accepted as we are, with warts and all.

This is not an indictment of fathers. There are a number of common impediments that keep fathers from being available to their children.

First, fathers through the ages have defined their participation in the family primarily in terms of being the protector and the provider. They still do. "If love is understood by what I do, then of course I loved my children," says one bemused father trying to understand his children's complaint that he wasn't really "there" for them. Many fathers don't fathom how hungry their children are to excite a gleam of love in their eyes. The father who considers his major mission as being an authority figure, limit setter, breadwinner, and model of "manly" values may be blind to the simple moments of emotional responsiveness and loving attention that nurture a child's self-esteem.

After all, we all go on the basis partly of what we received from our own fathers, and many fathers don't feel particularly treasured by their own fathers. Our fathers may have felt defective themselves, and this shame is transmitted through the generations.

For years I felt angry about my father's inability to communicate more of a sense of confident manhood in our home. But my anger abated when, at age thirty-nine, I learned that my grandfather, who died before I was born, had been a cavalry man in the czar's army. "A man's man," my father shyly described him. "I never really felt that I was good enough for him." Suddenly I began to see the fear of inadequacy my father had been masking behind his distant pose.

Here lies a difference for sons and daughters. Having a son confronts a father with the burden of being a good enough man to raise healthy, "masculine" boys. The father may strive to mobilize his manliness, to have "the right stuff" for his son in a way that he will not feel with daughters. As a corollary, he may expect his son to have the same stuff, to the detriment of creating a more responsive, human bond of warmth between them. With a daughter, the father may be attuned to her developing "femininity" and feel less pressure about his own masculinity. A father of a daughter may in turn be able to feel more playful, "softer," and less oppressed by standards of "masculinity" to which a father of a son holds himself and his son. A father's concern, however, that his daughter be "feminine" enough can become oppressive to both parent and child.

Furthermore, in many families mothers and children bond together to exclude father. The mother is the "family expert." When the father returns home from work he is off balance even before he sets foot in the door by the fact that his wife knows better than he what went on during the day. She may even have set the father-child agenda for him ("Wait till your father comes home!"). A father's shame may also lie in the inadequacy he feels to be a particularly forceful presence in the home. "How much should I love Daddy?" can become a distressing question for a son. It may seem not worth the gamble of alienating mother by putting one's faith and trust in father. The hidden shame that our fathers deliver to us is: "I am not really able to hold the attention of those I love."

And let's not forget the son's role in this dance. Children have normal mixed feelings toward their fathers. No matter how small and inept a father may feel, he is a giant to his son, larger, more muscular, with a deeper voice and more body hair. Boys with their smooth skin and high voices are, in some way, closer in appearance to their mothers than their fathers. Sons often want to dethrone and undercut these larger-than-life figures at the same time that they want to cozy up to them and cuddle safely and securely in their laps. The boy's fear or awe of his father's "power" and "magic" may create barriers that are hard for fathers to know how to climb.

DAEDALUS AND ICARUS: MEN FLYING HIGH AND FALLING

The Greek myth of Icarus and Daedalus is instructive in this regard. Daedalus, a legendary inventor and creator, makes sets of artificial wings for him and his son Icarus to use to escape from the prison of King Minor on the island of Crete. Daedalus cautions his son not to fly too high because the heat from the sun will melt the wax used to construct the wings. During their escape, Icarus ignores his father's warnings and, to Daedalus's horror, flies too high, melting the wax. Icarus falls to his death in the Aegean Sea, while his father watches, unable to help. "The father cried, 'Icarus, Icarus, where are you?'

At last he saw the feathers floating on the water, and bitterly lamenting his own arts, he buried the body."[3]

The story of Daedalus and Icarus has always touched me because it seems a fitting metaphor for the way fathers and sons fail each other in basic lessons about human limits. Icarus's fate is a lesson in the sadness and difficulties of staying closer to reality, rather than losing oneself in impossible exploits. The son wants to fly high, higher even than his father is willing to go. It is the soaring past the reach and beyond the hearing of his father that leads to Icarus's fall. The father's words of caution fall on deaf ears, in part because *the son will not listen.* What son doesn't partly want to disregard his father—to fly high, to dazzle the old man, outreach him? In that way we really don't want to hear whatever lessons our fathers can teach us.

The story of Daedalus and Icarus points to what fathers *don't* teach sons, and to what sons don't want to hear (at least until they're older) about the limitations of manhood, about the hard work and sadness, as well as joy, of flying safely close to earth rather than losing oneself in wild dreams of conquest and artifice. Many of us as sons don't want to accept our fathers' limitations. We want them to be greater, to fly higher—and when they don't, we fly high and away from them, blind to the love and sorrow inherent in the struggle of their lives.

The myth holds a moral to both fathers and sons. The father's skills and invention become deadly in the impetuous, unrestrained hands of his son. The son is unwilling to listen to caution from his father, and the father places too much trust in his son's ability to fly on his own. Each is deaf to the cries of the other.

Despite the distance between them, though, fathers and sons are often engaged in an active yet silent negotiation about life and love. Let's explore how fathers are constantly teaching sons about intimacy, often with unintended consequences.

THE NEGOTIATION OF LOVE BETWEEN FATHER AND SON

Although Icarus flies away from his father, most boys at first fly *toward* them. In our fathers' response to us, and how we observe them behaving toward others, reside important lessons for sons about how men deal with intimacy.

When asked about our boyhood moments with father, many of

us first remember a wish to connect to our father and then being dismissed, in his workshop, in the backyard, or in the TV room.

These memories often come out in the Top Secret game, in which men write down particularly painful memories on index cards to be read aloud anonymously. Often men will remember ancient, shameful attempts to make contact with father.

Listen to the boyhood memories these men summoned up in a game of Top Secret conducted at a recent workshop:

> I went down into the basement shop where my father was working with his tools, and wanted to nail some boards down the way he was doing. I must have been about six years old. My father saw me and yelled, "Get out of here, you'll knock over the nails!"

> Puberty. I have just started shaving. Am in the bathroom, my father standing at the door. I ask him why I need to use hot water to shave. The reply was that with a beard like mine, so puny, I didn't need hot water.

> In fourth grade there was a show-and-tell in which everyone was supposed to bring a pet and/or a parent. My father promised to leave work early and bring my cat. He never did, nor did he call. The teacher thought it would be a good idea for me to act as the host, escorting other parents around to the exhibits. I was the only one without a parent. I felt as though I were put on display for being fatherless.

> Age fourteen or fifteen. There I was with my peer group and one girl in particular whom I liked a lot. I had left a chore undone back at the house and I planned to finish it later. Having a great time talking, laughing, flirting back and forth. Whoa! Father appears! Dad has had a few! He's a loud, garrulous guy to begin with—all eyes turn to Dad as he spots me and heads toward our group! He shouts my name to get my attention—calls me a "little bastard," then *smack* across my face. I go numb, try to act nonplussed. Escaping from him, I get back to the car ASAP. Exit car. Kids watching. End of scene, but it still hurts and I'm forty-three years old! . . .

> My mother always tried to impress on us that it's the thought that counts; as a child I had very little money to

use for gifts. One year when Father's birthday came around I went to Mom to ask advice on what to give. She said, "Even if you only give a candy bar it's okay." So I bought a candy bar and approached my father gingerly as he sat in his chair dozing off. He mumbled his thanks in a very insincere fashion. I lingered for a minute, hoping for something more but didn't get it, so I ran off, shamed and feeling like I had done something wrong, but not really knowing what. The gift was very inadequate and I knew it, but I couldn't tell what to do next. I tried again with a pack of cigarettes with the same results. I don't give gifts to men very often. When I do it involves troublesome worries over inappropriateness. . . .

In these memories the fathers have failed to recognize or connect with the inner worlds of the children. When a boy goes to his father in his workshop he wants to gain love and recognition in his father's eyes. Instead the boy is told to watch out for the nails, and he leaves feeling shamed. His self-esteem suffers, as he learns the bitter lesson that he is less important than metallic objects, that men's appropriate concerns are for tools, not for feelings. The shame lies in his sense of being a nuisance, unimportant to a father. He may feel: *If I were more of a man my father would be more interested in me.*

This may not be what the father intends. The father may just want a few minutes of peace in his workshop, away from the family after a hard day's work. When Barry's father scolds his son that he is too old for hugs, he may not wish to reject him but rather to try to teach him an important lesson about being a man: *You can't keep running to me crying when you're hurt. If you do you'll be in big trouble on the playground.* The trouble is that, in learning this lesson, Barry also learned the collateral lesson that affection is not manly. Neither father nor son fully understood the other. Both came away feeling hurt and confused.

The son who brings a present to a father who does not respond may come to feel that he has little to offer. But who knows what his father felt? Unworthy of receiving presents because of his own failure? Exhausted and deprived? These parts of our parents' emotional lives remain mysteries to the child, who feels shamed. The shame for the boy lies in the feeling of not being able to get the validation and love he craves from his father. We men in general may then come to reflect our own shame and low self-esteem, as we withhold gifts to men (our love? our help? our appreciation?) for fear that what we have to offer is not good enough.

There are often important dialogues going on between fathers and children in these moments that seem so random and chaotic. Since our father is the first man in our lives, as children we idealize him, just as we do our mother. Inevitably we make our fathers potent figures who we are and will become.

A boy standing in front of the bathroom sink with his daddy, holding a real or pretend razor and asking about shaving, is also inquiring about his emergent manliness and hopes of being big and strong like his father. The father can confirm or diminish the boy's hopes of someday having a big, hairy beard just like Daddy, being big and strong and manly.

The father who storms in and humiliates his adolescent son while he is trying to master that most important of adolescent male tasks— flirting with girls—is negotiating several lessons around shame with his son. The son is humiliated by his father's "out-of-control" and angry behavior and he may come to fear his own anger. Identifying with his father, the son may come to see both his anger and his "weakness" as shameful parts of himself. Many of us as men have really never come to terms with our aggression, in large part because we had little opportunity to really wrestle with our fathers. Our fathers were either "nice guys"—too gentle and self-sacrificing to get mad at—or they came on like gangbusters when angry and left us with a bubble of humiliation.

Children constantly see themselves in their parents. The father is a particularly important figure in helping the son come to terms with his internal world of feelings. When fathers hold themselves aloof by not taking time with their sons, or by being too remote or austere, or so "heroic" and all-knowing as to be unapproachable, then the son is denied the father's help in learning about and mastering what he is feeling. Often sons need to "wrestle" with fathers emotionally simply to learn that their feelings are okay.

So, too, boys look to fathers for cues about sexuality and women, starting with their mothers. Fathers play an important role in helping their sons "make sense" of their love for women and of their sexual feelings. When the boy doesn't feel that father mirrors back his own love for and interest in his mother, he may end up feeling that he must divide his affection between mother and father.

"My father and I used to go fishing," recalled Wilson, "and we would spend whole weekends in the backwoods fishing and talking about rods, reels, tackle, bass, salmon, pickerels. They were wonderful moments, and my father would get so excited showing me how to repair a busted reel or how to bring in a tricky pickerel fish. I saw his gusto there. Once, though, I remember on the way home I said how much I loved Mother and he looked across at me from driving. He mumbled something, and then he continued talking about fishing."

Wilson's father may have had little vocabulary for talking about love. If he had said, "What you're feeling for your mother is love; I feel it too—I love her a lot," he would have given his son words and a language for speaking of love. Without this language, the boy develops black/white put-down ways of talking about girls, love, and connection, a forerunner of what happens between adult men and women.

And as a result of never hearing his father talk openly about his love for his mother, a man may grow up with a residue of shame surrounding his natural love for and affection toward women. The man may come to feel: *If I show my love and affection and interest in women too much I'm not really a man in Father's eyes.*

In becoming fathers ourselves we relive some of the same childhood struggles we had with our own fathers. Becoming a father may trigger questions about how much like our fathers we ourselves are. We'll explore in later chapters how fatherhood allows the grown son to undo some of the painful lessons of the past.

FATHER LESSONS

What do men learn from their fathers about love?

The "Real" World Is Where Men Live. For many men growing up, the "real" world for men existed outside the home: the backyard, the garage, the office. The workshop became the place where real men live, for our fathers spent hours there. Home is the place where women live. The home can become a shameful place where strong men become weak, under the power of women, a place where our fathers failed.

As boys we learned that real men did their work not in the household but rather "out there" in the "real," public world.

Coming and Going. Men's most treasured memories of their fathers often center on a brief, special moment of shared connection, when the boy felt he really had his father's attention. "Saturdays were special times for my father and me," one man recalled. "We'd go to the town dump with our trash together in the truck. Just the two of us. Sometimes we'd talk, sometimes we'd just drive along in silence, but I loved those trips to the dump."

There's often an intermittent, brief quality to interactions with father. Time with father often is special, but it may have a number of interruptions, moments when it may be difficult for the child to comfortably hold father's attention. When a father returns home from work, he may play with the children, then dinner will follow, and perhaps bedtime. Play with father may have a tentative quality to it, as father wants to also relax, get a drink, change his clothes, talk to his wife, or attend to some household task. Fathers have been described as bringing a "kamikaze" quality to their play with children, raising the children's energy level, then going on to some other activity.[4] For the child, it may feel as if a father cruises through family life like a boat under full sail, with little time for "children" matters. The lesson that the son may take away from this is that men do not stay very long with commitments of intimacy: We move on as other tasks preoccupy us. When we become fathers, an "antsy" feeling may accompany our time with our children, as if we ought to go someplace, be *doing* something, instead of just hanging out with our kids.

Love Unspoken. Often special moments when a father really stood up for or affirmed us as a person will involve few words. "After a party when I was sixteen I came home drunk and fell asleep on the front porch," Jim remembered at age forty-five with special pleasure. "My father got up and helped me to bed and tucked me in and never said a word about it to my mother." It turned out that his father never said a word about it to Jim either. Between fathers and sons much often remains unspoken, and it can feel confusing and embarrassing as a man to try to find ways to express what our fathers kept silent. We may be left wondering whether father even dealt with an incident that was so crucial to us.

Objects Replace People. Often treasured memories will involve connection that is mediated by an external object or activity: going to the dump, having a game of catch, working with tools. The close connection is made possible by having something *else* to focus on, something outside oneself, out there, something apart from inner feelings and the inner world.

The son who remembered trips to the dump with a special joy recalls picking through trash while his father commented on what was worth keeping and what was better thrown away. The fact that father may have actually been talking about life itself was never expressed directly to the child. It wasn't until age forty-eight that the grown son suddenly put this together: "It occurs to me that my father was showing me much of what he loved about life in those trips to the dump: about taking the time to be careful with things others would throw away, about sorting through our experiences, and also just spending time with me. But I didn't realize that at age twelve!"

The lack of an external object to focus on in moments of emotional intensity can leave men feeling very exposed and embarrassed. Often women don't realize that their demands that men express their feelings directly—"Put down that book" or "Turn off the TV so we can talk"—can make a man feel that he is in alien territory where he is too much in the spotlight.

Father's silence in his workshop or at the office, or the shared moments without words when father is working in the backyard, may communicate to a boy that men do not talk during moments of emotional complexity.

Of Cars and People: Alex's Dialogue with His Father About Love. "My father worked very hard to get me interested in things, not people," recalls Alex. "When my grandmother died, I was fourteen and my father was fifty. He never really got over that loss, and gradually withdrew more and more into work. He wasn't there really for me except that he used to try to involve me in his construction projects.

"And cars. Of all that I inherited from my father, what I treasure most is his Model T Ford—it's the first car my father ever got, and it's still in my garage. I was sixteen, just got my license, and I kept asking him about it," remembers Alex, describing his attempts to resurrect his grieving father. "It felt like his mother's death had taken the wind out of his sails, and I'd ask him about this car he loved. He called it Eloise, and I'd say, 'I wonder if Eloise will start.' The car was miles away in his mother's barn and I'd want to go get it with him."

Alex's hope was that he and his father would return to the ancestral family home, get the car, and fix it up together. In that way he would restore his father to health as well. The father didn't pick up on this overture, except that one day he turned to his son as they sat in the living room and said: "I don't know about Eloise, I don't have time for it, I'll give it to you," and tossed the keys to his son. Alex at age sixteen went and retrieved the car and fixed it up, and to this day, years after his father's death, he keeps the car in excellent shape.

Father and teenage son are having a dialogue here, in which the son is trying to find the empowered, enlivened father. He is search-ing for a way to involve his father in his life, teach him how to separate from mother and feel more manly himself. Asking about his father's beloved car is a way for Alex to try to rouse some excitement in a father who appears too tied to his own mother without either one of them losing face.

The father responds by sending Alex on a quest, an errand out-side the home, away from the real source of his heartache (his father) and toward an object (Eloise). For Alex the search for his manhood, really a father-quest, goes on outside the home and is connected to cars, mechanics, trying to find in the world of machinery the lost sense of manhood tied to his father's gradual decline. The message here is one many men struggle with: the belief that their sense of grief and loss and shame is solved outside the home, outside the painful family relationships.

Father directs his son's attention to the world of cars and sheet metal and engines, but he can't affirm the son's youthful, impetuous wish to talk to his father of grief, to restore his father, to feel his father's strength and confidence, not just his melancholy and mourn-ing. Most of all, the son needs to bring his anger at his mother, whom he saw as overcontrolling and too dominant, into the rela-tionship with his father. Instead Alex is turned to objects and activ-ities as a way of mastering his hope, love, sorrow, and anger.

Alex is now an excellent probation officer in the Baltimore court system because he is attentive to what is not said between men. With great skill and sympathy he told me of how he handled a difficult situation with a nine-year-old truant boy whom both the school and counseling systems had given up on. "He trusted me," said Alex. "I knew where he was coming from. His mother was overwhelmed and his father was gone, and I got him involved in the same kind of construction project that my father had spent time with me on."

Many fathers, like Alex's, are good at showing affection for ob-jects or things—garbage dumps, fishing tackle, cars—but are not able to reveal their affection and love for other human beings. Psychia-trist Harold Searles refers to this as a turn toward the "nonhuman" environment."[5] Boys, following their fathers' lead, often move away from the world of people and relationships and toward activities, things, and objects as expressions of love because the bond of love between them and others is not directly nurtured.

"Manly" time, in other words, focuses on an external goal, is less language-oriented, and doesn't directly acknowledge the impor-tance of connection between people.

Treasured memories with mother are very different. Mothers are often remembered as "always there for me," or as having "provided the basic security in my life." Memories of mother have a timeless, pervasive quality whereas memories of father tend to highlight special and finite moments of connection with shadowy figures who come and go in our lives. "Even though she made my life miserable, I always knew my mother was there," reported one man. "Too much mother, not enough father," lamented another, who then wondered: "Everyman's story: What's unusual about that?"

Not much, but the point is not the uniqueness of the story but the core of sadness and humiliation that remains alive inside many men.

THE FATHER-SON SACRIFICE

The notion of abandonment and sacrifice between father and son goes to the very roots of our culture. The first version of Dr. Spock, the Bible, which is really a guide to how the generations should get along, is very clear about this. For example, the Abraham and Isaac story in the Old Testament captures the special significance of sons to fathers. In this story God asks Abraham to sacrifice his beloved son Isaac as proof of his religious fidelity. Abraham starts up Mount Moriah with Isaac.

The son, curious as ever, wonders what is to be sacrificed.

"Where is the sheep, Father?" asks the child.

"God will see to the sheep, my son," replies the steadfast father.

Abraham does not actually sacrifice his son. God sees his willingness, is proud, and tells the father to go home with his son.[6] Yet the message is clear: Fathers must be willing to give up their sons, to let go of their love for them, to sacrifice them. To what? Manhood, higher ideals, the state.

The Christ story too is a powerful tale of shame and a father's abandonment of his son. Christ's last words are "Father, why have you forsaken me?" At this moment of greatest suffering and need He is unable to gain a response from His father; He is abandoned. In His suffering, of course, Christ is reunited with His father.

Themes of being forsaken, abandoned emotionally or physically amid great yearning for contact, run through many father-son stories.

THE FATHER PUZZLE

Fathers are puzzles that boys try to solve, and in so doing we often misunderstand them. Children don't know about existential pressures on fathers, or generational legacies, or "sex role socialization." We are egocentric when we are young: We interpret what happens with reference to ourselves. So boys will interpret father's distance or inattention or absence or failure as evidence of something wrong with them: We come to experience ourselves as defective, and it is in the capacity for love that such defects show themselves.

This is the wounded quality that many carry around with them. No wonder some Jungian scholars argue that the Greek god Hephaestus is a potent image for modern man.[7] Hephaestus, who must win an award for the most unpronounceable name, was the God of tamed fire, the protector of the earth and of family life around it. He was the son of Hera and Zeus, and when he angered his father, Zeus hurled Hephaestus from Olympus. He spent an entire day falling, and when he hit the earth at Lemnos both his legs were broken—wounds of rejection that shaped his life.

However, while we may feel thrown away by our fathers, often the rejection is unintentional. The very privacy of the father's experience makes him relatively inaccessible to his son. Sons are not privy to the emotional lives of their parents. Fathers often feel far more than they can say to their children, and sons often talk of trying to "read between the lines," to "construct an image" of their fathers.

Becoming a father myself made most clear to me the father's dilemma: how much you want to say to a son about love and being a man and how difficult it is to communicate that. Your son wants independence from you and wants to depend on you; you want to provide both gifts to him but aren't sure how to do that. After all, these are lessons we struggled with as boys ourselves. Every step your son takes may remind you of one of your own. How do you avoid confusing yourself with him but also make sure you're there for him when he needs you?

Spreading your peacock tail as a father can be tricky: You want to enliven and excite your boy, but not cast a shadow over him. Many fathers struggle to embody both authority and tenderness for their sons. A father sees himself in his son, wants so much for him, and fears him as well. The son, after all, can both carry a father's dreams forward and dash or surpass them as well.

In his poem "Graham," poet Sid Gershgoren writes: "My dear

son whom I put to bed each evening I am almost frantic with love for you." Charles Wright wonders in his poem "Firstborn": "You lie here beside me now, / Ineffable elsewhere still. / What should one say to a son?"[8]

Here again is a burden that women may not understand. It is possible for daughters to charm their fathers long past the age when most boys can. Many daughters can cuddle up close to dad, can get him to express warmth and closeness by what they say and how they act, right into adulthood. This can be a trap for many women who never stop trying to be cute for dad, or it can provoke a painful struggle to combine femininity and power. For boys the struggle may be reversed: trying to live up for dad and yet combine tenderness and power as a man. Men often have no way to express their love for their fathers except through performance and hard work, just as they have no way to express their love for their mothers except by protecting and providing for their wives and children.

We may have a shameful feeling of being unable to win dad's love except through how well we perform. One man recalled with some bitterness: "My father wanted me to go to military school because everyone in our family had done that through the generations. I hated it, but when I called home miserable after the first semester he said, 'Tough it out.' I did, for him, and at graduation when everyone threw their hats in the air to celebrate, I was the only one who didn't."

THE FATHER HUNGER OF MEN

Many men feel considerable grief at the absence of father in their life. In "Father Song," singer Fred Small gives voice to this yearning: "There's a man I hardly remember / Who would hold me in his arms without flinching / And tell me it's all right."[9]

The yearning for a strong daddy who will make everything right can feel very humiliating for the grown man. As men we're supposed to be adult and independent, not needing a strong, supportive father around to affirm and protect and explain to us. We're supposed to be that protecting father. Yet what man doesn't at times feel the yearning to return to father's strong arms?

A powerful example comes from one of the survivors of the Titanic disaster, Frank Goldsmith. He was nine years old when the ship went down in 1912. As it sank his father put him in a lifeboat, handing him to his mother, who held him close to her to make sure, of course, that he would not fall into the water. His father's last words to his son were "See you later, Frankie." So Frankie bid good-bye to his father, who like most of the men, stayed on the boat and went down with it. Frank Goldsmith lived to be seventy-eight, and when he died a few years ago, he asked in his will that his ashes be spread over the spot in the North Atlantic where the Titanic had sunk all those years ago. He wanted to be reunited with his father.[10]

The hunger for father can have significant historical conse-quences. In his book Citizens: A Chronicle of the French Revolution, historian Simon Schama begins his story by pointing out that when Lafayette came to the aid of the American Revolution he was not working out of democratic ideals as much as a profound identification with George Washington as the father he never had. Lafayette's father had been killed in battle years earlier, and Washington looked extraordinarily like this fallen warrior. Lafayette and George Wash-ington developed such a close relationship that Washington was the godfather of Lafayette's children and the elder statesman took almost a paternal interest in the younger Frenchman.[11]

Father Quests. Many men go on quests to find surrogate fathers in bars, on the streets. The wish is to find a father who will affirm us and explain life to us, legitimate what we want and need. One man I know, Eric, told me once of walking down the street and seeing a man walking ahead of him, and being convinced that it was his long-dead father come back, that he had found this father he had been so hungry for. Eric hesitated as the man crossed the street in front of him. When the man turned around Eric was saddened to see that it was not his father. The shame for Eric was in becoming aware of his yearning for his father, of becoming aware of how alone he felt without his father. In a way, Eric was like the boy in the school show-and-tell who felt put on display for being without a father. Each felt shame that his aloneness and *difference* were exposed for all to see. Here lies the power of shame. Neither Eric nor the boy in school were truly exposed. It's likely that no one walking down the street knew of Eric's father hunger or his disappointment when the stranger turned his head. And in a busy class a little boy's missing his father is easily overlooked. However, at such moments of self-recognition and disappointment, when our need and feeling of powerlessness are strong, we may *feel* as if all eyes are upon us, as if we are an open book that others can read. We have no way of covering up the wound we feel. Many men fear being ashamed—in front of other men or the women they love—for their yearning for a better, healed, healthy father to come back and help them make sense of the world.

OBJECT HUNGER IN MEN

Given the normal difficulties with connection, many boys and men have a profound "object hunger": a wish for connection with others and the sense of not being able to achieve it. The hunger itself becomes a mark of shame, as often in intimate situations men are flooded with visceral feelings of wanting to touch, to be hugged, and to be accepted by father or father substitutes.

Feeling hungry is no fun; feeling starved is worse. We think of being hungry for food, but men and women are often hungry for affirmation, support, a kind word. The phrase "starved for affection" captures the kind of father hunger some men feel. When you're really hungry, it can be hard to share, and that difficulty can be a source of considerable shame for men.

One father I know got into several fights with his wife about their son's high school graduation. The boy wanted a big party and the man's wife did too. This man, Jose, who loved his son very much, found himself quite resentful of how much money the graduation party was going to cost. "A band, why does he need a band on top of everything else!" he exclaimed to me one day over lunch. As we talked, Jose revealed something I never knew: His father had died unexpectedly during his high school years. He had never seen Jose graduate high school or college, watched him marry and become a father, or shared in the joy he felt about his own children.

Jose knew he'd missed a lot. "I was gypped," he exclaimed ruefully, as we contemplated the twenty-five years since his father's death, years filled with happiness but also with a yearning for his father. Then with considerable embarrassment and shame Jose realized what some of the fighting about his son's high school graduation was about: "When you feel gypped yourself, it's hard to give to someone else."

Jose's hunger for his own father often left him feeling depleted, without a lot to give at a moment when his son demanded a lot from him, materially and emotionally. Yet our talk must have helped: Jose went home and asked his son what kind of band he wanted at his graduation. He found his son merely wanted him to pay for some friends to play, and Jose found the inner resources to give his son the affirmation he wanted.

Jose's story touched me because it left me wondering what we do as men with our hunger for contact, affirmation, help, and affection from our fathers and other men. Men often fill these human needs by substituting the nonhuman: work, hobbies, activities. These are profound and important sources of satisfaction, but there are some times in our lives when intimacy and relationships can become particularly important: For example, when we become fathers and need to learn more about that from other men, or when changes in our marriages demand that we turn to or give more to our wives. These times may make us feel propelled back to early moments when we walked into daddy's workshop for help and were told to get out or when we wanted to turn to mother and felt too old for that. We experience shame around our very need for others.

Authority figures and bosses at work often stimulate men's wishes for a warm and tender father to show them how to be a real man and to give them love. And yet all too often shame and anger cloud our need for these figures. We yearn for what we didn't get and at the same time want to pay back those who didn't give it.

Inadequate Fathers. A man's wound may also come out of his unspoken feeling: *If my father had been more of a man, then I'd feel more manly.* Many fathers seemed inadequate in the home; mother had a secret, or not-so-secret, power that seemed hero-breaking. One man remembered: "After hearing my mother yelling and arguing with my father, he left in silence and retreated into the bedroom, and my mother yelled after him, 'You never stand up and fight back.' " This man yearned for a father to stand up to his mother, so as to allow the boy himself to be strong. If his father had asserted himself more, he felt, then he would be free both of the shameful feeling of being controlled by his mother and of being too strong for his own father. This man is filled with a sorrowful sense of his own inadequacy. Angry at his own father's inability to model male strength, he spends a lot of his work time showing his bosses how much they have failed him.

Never Die Young. Fathers who die young or abandon the family can leave an unspeakable sense of shame alive in their sons. A man whose father died when he was two years old, and whose mother never remarried, recalled the "mark" he felt when other fathers brought their children to Little League. To cover his embarrassment he would ask a friend's father if he could go with him. The absence of a father can become shameful in itself, as if exposing for all the world to see the boy's fear that *his father is not there because he is not good enough.*

I hope it doesn't seem glib to say that many of our fathers "die" too young, and this is a great source of shame for men. I don't mean that they literally pass away, but they may seem burdened by life, by the demands of working, or by providing for the family, and as a result they fall into an abiding melancholy at mid-life or older. The son may have a powerful wish to "heal" or "fix" his father and feel great helplessness at his inability to do so. A son may strive through his work to redeem his father; such a son's competitiveness is not just a wish to defeat his old man, but also an attempt to deny the sorrow he feels at his father's aging or decline. By competing at work he sidesteps his own grief that his father turned out not to be the godlike hero he once hoped for but rather an ordinary, wounded mortal man.

WOUNDED FATHERS, WOUNDED MOTHERS

After a morning session at a men's weekend retreat I am walking through the woods to the cafeteria for lunch. Big, lazy snowflakes saunter toward the ground on this cold January day. Marv walks up behind me hurriedly, catching his breath. He is here because he is bothered by the fact that he works so hard and spends less time than he'd like with his family. Working and being an authority are the major ways he feels comfortable in his family as a father and a husband—"giving things to my children instead of being with them," as he puts it.

Marv catches his breath as he walks alongside me, both of us enjoying the view through the woods, our appetites sharpened by the chill winter air. He has a question he doesn't want to ask in public. Intensely, sounding a bit like Joe Friday on "Dragnet" interrogating a suspect, he asks me: "Look. What do men really feel? I mean all my life I've worked hard and done everything a man is supposed to do. My father showed me how a man is supposed to *act*. But what is a man supposed to *feel*?"

"Gee, that's a good question," I reply, trying to sound bright. Yet I'm puzzled: "Why don't you bring that question up inside so we can all talk about that together."

Marv looks shocked. "Talk about it with the whole group of men—they don't know either!"

What can happen to some boys who disconnect from their fathers is that they "misconstruct" men. We identify masculinity with what we see around us: strength, size, power, and the attempt to live up. This is a misinterpretation because we don't see other parts of our fathers and other men. Failing to see men as sources of emotional nurturance, we turn away from our own gender and look to women as the major source of emotional caretaking.

We carry around as men a "wounded father" inside: a distorted sense of manhood and ourselves as defective, empty, or angry and demanding, judgmental and critical; a belief that manhood has little to give emotionally, rooted in the experience of our fathers; a conviction that women alone can give and receive love directly. When a man has turned too often to women for help without also finding support from men, he may naturally come to feel that women are the repositories of affection and caring.

We get split between a belief that men are powerful and action-oriented and that women are caretakers and supporters. We also have a "wounded mother" alive within us as men. The wound is rooted in our experience of mother as having the "goodies" in the family, or as truly having the power, especially to reduce us to little boys over and over again by virtue of our very need for her. The mother wound lies in our sense of women's power and our own helplessness in the face of it. We "misconstruct" women just as we do fathers. The mother inside us may be needy and helpless, leaving us trying to protect her from loneliness or judgment. Or she may be critical and judgmental, leaving us feeling at her mercy. As a result, our ability to provide warmth and comfort to ourselves or others remains unavailable or undiscovered. Many men lack the inner sense of being able to rely on and turn to either mother or father for the help, comfort, and support they want to receive and to give.

Sometimes when I, a father myself, listen to men's memories of their fathers, I cringe; one moment of failure and this is what a son remembers! I protest in part because I can see myself in much of what I hear about the fathers of others. It's a lot easier to be critical of fathers when you're only a son, not also a father. Yet I think that these memories crystallize not single moments of difficulty with father but a lifetime of being unable to feel really affirmed as a male. Fathers become the lightning rods for a deeper disappointment.

Often men's feeling of disappointment in their fathers reflects the deeper dilemma of yearning to feel like a beloved part of the male community. We know whether we're heterosexual or homosexual, but ironically either way we may not feel really accepted by other men, or clear about what it means to be a man except, as one man told me, "to work hard and pay your bills."

Many boys' anger and sadness about their fathers is expressive of their inability to get a trustworthy blessing from the male community. Boys search for affirmation of their maleness from football coaches, teachers, camp counselors, older males of many stripes. When boys become men this search for affirmation and understanding goes on in bars, hunting groups, men's lodges.

Often we find a sense of worth as men only in living up, proving we are smart enough for teachers, tough enough for coaches, and loyal enough for bosses.

Since many men don't get a blessing from the male community, they aren't always sure if they really and truly have the right stuff. This is the core sense of male shame.

Sounds pessimistic. But my experience is that things *can* be different for us as grown men. Much of what men are trying to do as they age is to locate new parts of themselves. As human beings we constantly struggle with these inner voices and divided loyalties, confronting moments when we feel defective and unsure whether to withdraw into the role of the wounded man of our memory or to open our hearts and become the fuller, more responsive fathers we are each capable of being.

Much of men's strongest desire today is to understand more deeply what they feel, what is appropriate for them to feel about themselves and those they love. Often this is what is being shared and negotiated in myriad ways when men get together in men's groups, when they arrive for a first-time men's retreat, or simply when they talk to their friends.

MASTERY AND CARE: FINDING THE MOTHER AND FATHER WITHIN

In the powerful movie *Field of Dreams*, the hero, Ray Kinsella, by dint of his extraordinary efforts, magically resurrects his youthful father, the one who existed before he aged so badly, before he became alienated from his son. It's one thing for Kinsella to build a ball field where his dead childhood hero Shoeless Joe Jackson can return to play ball. It's quite another when, at the end of the movie, Kinsella's innocent, vital, youthful father appears. That's the point at which many men (and many women, with legitimate father struggles of their own) burst into tears in the dark: it captures so movingly the wish to get back that youthful father of our dreams. There is hardly any talk between the two men during their reunion; instead, they play catch outside the farmhouse where Ray lives. Note also that it's the youthful father who returns, not the aged man with whom

Ray might actually work out the pain of the past. In this detail the film truly captures some of the men's divided feeling for their fathers: Do we want to try to come to terms with the "real" father or rather keep trying to resurrect the lost, ideal father we never really knew?

Many of us wait for our fathers to change or for a better father to come and to change us. But by doing so we fail to identify the more pressing questions: How do we father and mother each other and ourselves? And what does it mean to be a "good-enough" father and mother to ourselves and each other?

I am not talking about men turning into women, or vice versa. This line of thought reflects errors in the way we conceptualize mothering and fathering.

One error is that we take basic human needs and tie them to gender, partly because of the role divisions we experience in our parents growing up.

How to think about "mothering" and "fathering" as things we *all* do, within the limitations of living within a male or female body?

Barry's parents certainly had the conventional role divisions down pat: one offering care, the other remembering mastery. Barry's mother offered comfort to her son, extending her arms and encouraging him to come to her. As children and grown-ups, we all need to feel reassured, affirmed, to have the comfort of a helping hand or tender touch during a difficult moment. Such affirmation restores our optimism and confidence, reminds us that we are special to someone, provides us with a place to retreat to when we need to get emotionally refueled and resupplied. Mother's lap or skirts are the prototype of these crucial supplies. There is a kind of inward pull, an enfolding and "snuggling in" implicit here.

Let's call this "mothering" but not make it an attribute solely of women. Men are certainly capable of providing these things, and in some families the husband/father is better at this mothering than the wife/mother.

But this kind of mother-comfort is also not enough, as one eight-year-old boy recently reminded his mother. He had been telling her about his worries about not doing well enough in school. She tried to reassure him for the umpteenth time by telling him how wonderful he was and how much she loved him. He replied: "Oh, Mom, mothers always say that!" He was reminding her that yes, it was nice to hear how much she loved him, but that he also needed someone to teach him how to do advanced multiplication and spelling.

So in addition, there is *mastery*, which Barry's father remembers, albeit clumsily. He is telling his son that he can't stay in Mommy's

lap all the time, being supported and told he is wonderful and special. You also have to master difficulty. Putting aside your wound and
facing your fear, you have to be able to go out there and climb the
rock. There is a kind of outward thrust here, a pull into the outer
world of accomplishment and mastery.

Let's call this "fathering" but not make it an attribute solely of
men. Women are very capable of teaching mastery, and wives and
mothers can be as good as or better than their husbands and fathers
at this.

Another error we often make in thinking about adult life is to
assume that "mothering" and "fathering" are things that only parents do to children. As adults we are constantly in situations where
we are called upon to provide care for and seek mastery from each
other. Husbands and wives, mentors and protégés, bosses and subordinates, teachers and students, male and female friends are often
groping to find ways to "mother" and "father" each other, without
realizing that this is what they are doing.

Ideally we combine *both* mastery and support for ourselves and
others when we need it. Sometimes we need to sit in the lap a bit
longer, sometimes it's necessary to get up and climb the rock again.
Problems occur when mastery and care get split. Men's struggles
often are rooted in the fact that they were pushed toward mastery
without being able to hold on to comfort. In that case, treasures can
get lost.

We need to provide both to ourselves. Men often encounter
times when they are at their wit's end. A job is going badly, a career
feels burnt-out, there is trouble in the marriage, our kids are driving
us crazy. Often we get ourselves exhausted and in more trouble because we try so hard to become instrumental and competent without
also knowing how to provide ourselves inner reassurance, tenderness,
a sense that it's okay to feel dispirited and dejected. We lack the
basic optimism and trust that we can turn to others and to ourselves
for help.

We're as hard on ourselves as we are on others. It strikes me
that we men often struggle to know how to provide "mothering" to
those who need us. It comes more naturally to us to be overly competent and try to "solve" problems, but we don't know how to address deeper needs for reassurance and support. You can hug a person
without ever touching him with a kind word, gesture, moment of
attention, or empathic gesture—and it often seems to me that this is
what men are trying to learn.

In later chapters I will explore how men try to combine "mothering" and "fathering," providing opportunities for mastery and care to themselves and those they love, as husbands, fathers, sons, at work, and with friends.

Yet I am getting ahead of myself. Often to a man "mastery" and "care" are the last things on his mind. Rather, men are often just trying to make connections without feeling too exposed and vulnerable.

Usually the way men try to do that is, paradoxically, to intimidate or act tough and independent. We mask our gentle touch inside an armored glove. Adulthood offers us numerous opportunities to heal and resolve male dilemmas about love, shame, and hope. But to follow the roads to healing, we first need to understand aggression, intimidation, and connection in men's lives. In the next chapter we will explore how acting strong, in charge, aloof, even angry and dominating, allows men to connect with those they love without losing their self-esteem as men.

3

ANGER AND OTHER

ATTEMPTS TO CONNECT

The wind was howling across the parking lot when I arrived at the computer company on a cold day in the late spring. I was there to speak at a "men's day" sponsored by the company itself. Would anyone show up for this lunchtime talk? I wondered, as I made my way toward the long, low building housing the administrative offices of the company. This company, one of the biggest employers in its state, has a progressive reputation and regularly sponsors "outreach" events focusing on the work-family and life-style concerns of its employees.

A senior executive had driven me from town to the plant. Along the way he provided background for the event. "We've had women's days, days for employees of color, and other kinds of issues," he explained. "Some of the male employees, and many of the women, felt we needed a day to talk about the experiences and concerns of the men." An apologetic note entered his voice. "A lot of people wondered why we are sponsoring this. Men have all the power in the company anyway, they say; why have a men's day? But I think we're missing some real pain and confusion on the part of men these days about work and family life."

The talk, in the company cafeteria, was well-attended, and we followed up with a meeting with fifteen men in a "focus group" to talk over more specific concerns.

Fold-out plastic walls were drawn across part of the cafeteria to provide some privacy; in the rest of the cafeteria, company employees went about the business of getting lunch.

The fifteen of us struggled to connect in our special room, while the easygoing laughter and busy hubbub of lunchtime conversations went on tantalizingly just beyond our flimsy walls.

To my left, about six seats away, sat an intense, well-dressed young man who looked increasingly frustrated as time went on. He clearly wanted to say something, but nothing came. I later learned that he was project manager of a new, highly touted software product; he was a rising "star" at the company.

Another man was relating that both he and his wife worked and it felt like there was really no time for them as a couple in the marriage.

"That's a hard one," I agreed.

Whereupon the silent manager's voice cut across the room: "So, they don't have all the answers at Harvard, huh?" Several people looked aghast at this comment, particularly the personnel manager, who was serving as my host. Nervous laughter and coughing followed, as happens when family members realize someone is being rude to an invited guest.

Yet there seemed a familiar kind of male greeting embodied in the manager's words.

My first impulse was to launch a returning salvo, perhaps to reply: "Not all the answers—just the right ones." Something "friendly" like that. My mental computer whirred through other "response options," such as putting a beatific smile on my face ("Nothing disturbs me") and ignoring the guy. Yet this man had been present throughout the entire event, and had been listening to everything that was said. Could he be trying to find his way into the group by blasting his way in? Blasting back didn't seem the best way to help someone open up and talk about what was really on his mind.

So I holstered my pistol and instead blurted out the truth: "Certainly not. I need all the help I can get these days."

Several men, including my interrogator, then talked about how inexpert they felt. One man described how his wife seemed so confident working these days, while he—after twenty years on the job—felt over the hill. Precisely because she seemed so "up" when he felt "down," he didn't feel he could talk about this with her. Another man revealed that he felt his male bosses were far more sympathetic to the needs of female subordinates than those of male ones. "They can charm the boss, be a good little girl for daddy: I don't like to play good boy for him."

During a moment of silence the watchful manager turned to me and revealed: "What I said before about having the answers? I was just looking for the chink in your armor."

Which led another man to put his finger on the truth about a lot of us: "You wanted contact and didn't know how to get in." A chink implies a way in; it's a way for two people to touch. Now that's hard stuff for men to talk about: the wish to get close to a father figure who seems to have answers, not just to get answers but to have warm contact from a man who might be on our side, reassure us, leave us feeling good about ourselves.

Mr. Manager saw me as the expert and wanted answers from me. More important, he wanted to get close to me—but how do you cozy up to daddy and still feel like a man? What if daddy tells you you're an idiot, or worse, doesn't pay attention to you and leaves you feeling like you hardly count at all? There's that male dilemma again. Men's deepest struggle often centers on the wish to be seen and heard, to feel valued and worthwhile to—even beloved by—those who matter to us. Wanting to connect, to be seen and to contribute, but also not wanting to feel exposed and shamed, we often hide both impulses in an aggressive gambit. The manager, for instance, struggled with the question of how to get my attention that day. He was a rising star, used to having the answers and being seen as competent. Now here he was sitting in the company cafeteria wanting to ask a question about a part of life in which he didn't have the answers: how to balance the demands of work and family life. He wanted to connect with me—to ask a question, feel heard, talk about these matters. Sounds simple, perhaps—just raise your hand and speak! But what if I didn't respond, what if I just passed him by, or what if he asked a "stupid" question in front of his peers? So he poked at me, which gets my attention, connects me to him, and also pushes me away.

So whose armor did he really see? Usually we're really struggling with our own. The more powerful I seemed and the more needy he felt, the more armored up and closed he became to protect himself. My hunch is that he put on his armor to protect himself from his own feelings and then felt trapped in it.

Mr. Manager wanted to connect with me, so he punched me, verbally. If we're not careful we only attend to the aggression and miss the attempt to connect. We're so used to thinking of male aggression as violent and destructive that it's hard to think of it any other way. It challenges us to see men's anger as an attempt to protect a threatened relationship, and it strains us even more to understand how a combative stance toward love may help boys manage difficult moments with intimacy growing up.

The fact is that a number of male behaviors imply distance but are really attempts to connect or to maintain relationships in the face of shame. Things are not always what they seem.

This chapter explores how anger, rituals of wounding, masks, shields, and distractions all serve to help men connect with themselves and with those they love even as these behaviors threaten to disconnect us. We will see that anger and aggression can often become the ways boys and men grapple with a question: how to connect without feeling too ashamed and unmanly?

AGGRESSION AS AN EXPRESSION OF LOVE

Aggression and connection are intimately intertwined in men's lives, often very enjoyably. As they grow up, boys commonly use verbal wordplay and physical sparring and intimidation as ways to experience closeness. In high school we used to call it "sounding": a group of us would sit around the lunch table and lovingly taunt each other. One lunchtime, a friend announced that his father was going that very day to buy his first really fancy new car—obviously he was proud of his father's accomplishment. Next to me, the wealthiest kid retorted: "In my family we go in a Cadillac to buy a Cadillac." We all laughed, congratulating him on his "sound," even though none of us owned a Cadillac. Obviously, there's cruelty here, but also a drawing closer. We all (even the "soundee") felt the camaraderie of the group. We basked in our shared humor (albeit at the expense of another) and the exhilaration of verbal combat. Backslapping, loving and mocking glances, and chuckles circulated among us. All of these were moments of connection, feeling cherished and affirmed by each other. We were also learning and teaching some valuable lessons about dealing with public put-downs, keeping your wits about you when caught off guard, and handling assaults on your self-esteem when you reveal too much.

In many families aggression and closeness are bound up together. For example, wrestling with dad or taunting or provoking him may be the best way to get his attention. Many men try to enliven dad by poking at him. "Enlivening" means to get a heartfelt response, to feel acknowledged with a smile, a touch, an interested question. The five-year-old who jumps on a tired father who has just walked in the door; the fourteen-year-old who berates his father about world events; the twenty-five-year-old who tries to beat his father on the tennis court! Each act is not just a competitive aggressive attack on father but also an attempt to enliven or vitalize him, to get him out of his bubble of adult preoccupations. A wrestling match with dad—in whatever form it takes—is a way of wrapping oneself up in the father's arms and still feeling okay about oneself as a male.

One man once told me: "The only way I could get my father's active attention was to argue with him about whether Franklin Roosevelt was a good president or not; I couldn't have cared less about FDR, but I knew that taunting my father would produce a good fight with him."

Few sons don't yearn to feel that they carry around inside them a powerful father who can help them feel like a real man when dealing with work, women, and other men. Often sons will try to energize their real fathers in order to enliven the "inner father," the one they carry around inside them. Many men continue to use verbal or physical pokes or provocations as ways to try to jump-start others when they feel left out or ignored.

Stand Up for Me! Here's an example of how aggression expresses love for a man, with results that backfire. Tony is a thirty-five-year-old man who has been alienated from his father for a number of years and is closely allied with his mother. He is the middle brother in an Italian family, not very athletically inclined. Tony's father focused more attention on the other brothers, while the more studious Tony became his mother's favorite. Then, when Tony was seventeen, his father became seriously ill with cancer and the robust man began to fail. Tony faced the possibility of never really working things out with his father, never feeling "really blessed by the old man." What a dilemma for the teenager trying to achieve his manhood: Once his father was gone there would be no one there to help him loosen the bonds that tied him to his mother.

Then came a climactic moment, when aggression and love became confused for Tony. Father, son, and mother were sitting around the dinner table finishing their meal when his mother asked Tony to clear the table.

"No way," Tony responded, with just enough insolence in his voice to raise eyebrows at the table.

The father rebuked the son:

"Don't talk to your mother like that!"

"Oh yeah?" demanded Tony. "Who's going to stop me?"

The father jumped up, the son did too, and soon the two men were wrestling on the floor. Years later Tony expressed the wish that his father had wrestled him to the ground, had been a strong and loving father who could help him separate from mother by feeling his own manhood. Instead, the son pinned his dying father to the ground. The attempt to resurrect his father had failed.

Tony carries around the shame of having humiliated his dying father. A good Catholic, Tony has been to confession many times since that day years ago. He's done his penance, but the fiery grip of shame remains. If guilt is forgiven, how is shame healed? It is much harder for him to come to terms with his continuing feeling of not being manly enough, of not feeling like the beloved-enough son of his father, of not having a father strong enough to loosen the hold his mother has over him.

Tony, through his provocation, was appealing to his father: Stand up for me! The provocation was an attempt at connection, although neither father nor son could see it. An adolescent needs his father's affirmation, and Tony's surly question was really a plea. *See me, respond to me, be there for me, help me deal with Mom!* In the next chapter we'll see how as an adult Tony continues to use provocation as a way to get closer to father figures at work—with disastrous results.

Tony's anger also served to mask the shame he felt. At the dinner table, instead of acting like a needy little boy going to his father to help him separate from mommy, Tony got angry and "chippy" to make himself feel more like a man. Tony's plight illustrates one of the central dilemmas for men: the way men convert neediness and shame into their opposites—attempts to act big, tough, and aggressive. And why not? If shame disorganizes us and cuts to the core of our well-being, then anger mobilizes us, pumps us up, and helps us feel powerful and big. It can momentarily wipe out shame and sadness and neediness.

So what if in the process of buckling on our six-shooters to blast our way out of our greatest need, we wind up shooting ourselves in the foot most of the time? For many men that may seem a small price to pay to avoid the debilitating feelings of shame and grief.

THE ENERGY OF DIFFERENCES

Men often *do* connect, and then need to manage the anxiety that actually getting closer creates. Finding differences or starting fights with those we truly feel close to is one way of dealing with the tension that intimacy brings.

At the beginning of one day-long workshop on fathering, the group began by talking about their experiences with their own fathers. One man recalled being disciplined by his father in the oddest way:

"When I was a teenager I said some nonsense word like *zottletoast* back to my father when he asked me to do something, and he told me never to say that word again. He was obviously upset, but I didn't even know what it meant to him and he never explained how come he got so angry."

The group was obviously amused and touched by the puzzlement of the now grown son and the mystery of the father's reaction. Another man spoke of how much he worked to please his father and how he was never sure if he succeeded: "My father worked all his life in the steel mills; he became a patternmaker, one of the most skilled jobs in the plant. But at home he seemed to lose all his energy. After he died the one thing I wanted most was his toolbox, because that was what he seemed to love most: a two-by-two-foot wooden box he made himself, without any nails. I keep it in my study, near my computer." Then he added: "I hope I can love my kids as much as he loved that toolbox."

In the group we all felt a sense of playfulness and goodwill. We were developing the camaraderie and closeness that sometimes comes when people speak freely and truly about their deepest passions. The group no longer felt like such a lonely or anonymous place; clearly, we were feeling more intimate and safe.

Maybe too intimate; suddenly the sense of playfulness was punctured. A doctor from Philadelphia abruptly exclaimed: "Oh, this is all well and good, but what am I going to do about my fourteen-year-old son who won't talk to me?" The atmosphere changed dramatically. Several people felt attacked. Some got angry and attacked the doctor for being so "goal-oriented," while others defended him and wanted him to have "an opportunity to get what he needs here."

My heart jumped when he spoke, feeling challenged myself. Partly of course, he was trying to enliven me: *"Okay, Dr. Osherson, all this intimacy is fine but are you the expert or not? Give me some answers."*

A familiar male tactic: By pulling me in as the expert and forcing me to display my authority, he deflects the intimacy. People are less willing to talk and expose themselves. When things get too hot, provoke an argument.

Rather than rising to that challenge, I kept my peace. What became obvious was that sorting ourselves into different camps and arguing about the doctor felt more comfortable and manly than talking about our disappointments and hopes in regards to our own fathers. One man observed: "Perhaps we need the energy of combat to keep us together here."

Without that combative energy the closeness of the group felt too threatening. Relaxing with everyone and openly showing our feelings seemed too much like sitting in mother's lap. So we found something else to talk about. The doctor was helping the whole group contain their anxiety and shame when he suggested we talk about his son, someone or something outside of that room! We needed to separate in order to stay together.[1] And we did stay together: After a period of arguing and distancing, we were able to return to the reality of our own intimate struggles as fathers and sons.

RITUALS OF WOUNDING: COMBAT AND THE LEGITIMATION OF MALE TENDERNESS

We often make the mistake of assuming that men love sports because of their aggressive, competitive needs. But on the football field, at fraternity hazings, in the law school class or factory assembly line, as well as in corporate offices, the assertion of toughness allows men to feel tender. On the football field a brawny fullback plows into the line and a bunch of sweaty, beefy men tromp all over each other. Yet when the play ends, the players put their arms around each other, pat each other, and often express deep affection out of the shared pain and sacrifice of their bodies.

As boys grow up, much of their tactile contact with other males is in the context of competition and physical endurance. Most male rites of passage, when they exist at all, are organized around some affirmation of the ability to endure pain and display toughness. These rituals allow for tenderness and care, even as they disavow it by reminding us of toughness and mastery.

The Grog. An army officer once described the envy he felt when reading an account of the incredible sense of closeness among some units in the Vietnam War. "We don't have that anymore, the grief of combat," he lamented. In a peacetime army, few opportunities arise for soldiers to express their affection for one another.

Another army officer spoke of the "dining in" ritual in which the new recruits are asked unanswerable questions by the commander; when they fail they have to drink "the grog," an unspeakable mixture of putrid liquids. With a sweet smile the officer concluded: "Then they became one of us."

Of course the grog expresses the aggression of the elders toward the young, a kind of warning that the young must not become too uppity or try to overtake the elders. But after draining the aggression, the group is able to express its tenderness, the love that a father has for a son, the welcome he wants to provide to the youngster, and the hopes he has for him. So first comes the scarring, the sacrifice, then comes the tenderness.

The grog is a kind of masculine mother's milk; it is the milk of manhood, bitter and harsh. Having swallowed that, the recruits can be admitted into the tenderness of men.

A Ritual Wounding by Committee. This doesn't just happen in the military. Recently I attended a graduate dissertation defense. This is a public meeting in which the new doctor of psychology discusses his dissertation and answers questions about it. (*Defense* is an interesting word here, implying attack rather than discussion.) The three members of the man's dissertation committee were there, two female professors and the chairman of the committee, an older male professor.

The graduate student, Bill, was himself an older student, about forty. He described his research, which involved a fair amount of statistical analysis. Bill did a fine job of presenting it, the questions went well, and there was a celebratory air in the room, a happy welcoming of this man for the achievement of writing a dissertation and completing graduate school at age forty, while carrying on a busy professional career, maintaining his marriage, and fathering his two children. We were all proud of what he had accomplished, and so was the chairman, who was actually Bill's mentor and had taken considerable time to help him juggle the contradictory demands of work, graduate study, and family.

Outside the room an informal potluck reception waited, organized by several other students, and inside the room both of Bill's young children, dressed in ties and jackets, played with toys on the floor while their father discussed his weighty doctoral dissertation. They looked at their father with pride, even if they didn't really understand what he had done.

Suddenly the chairman surprised the group: "I have one more question to ask." Mentioning an unpronounceable statistical theory, he intoned: "Tell me, Bill, from the point of view of their theory, what is the major flaw in your work?"

Bill squirmed in his seat, trying to get the answer, obviously unsure.

The chairman sat and watched Bill, who smiled weakly back at him, searching for the answer.

Tension suddenly filled the room; the festive moment had turned into the College Bowl and Bill looked stumped. The two female professors looked at each other aghast, and one nudged the chairman. "Oh, come on, Dan, what's the answer?" Her voice had a maternal, soothing tone to it. A tone that only seemed to make matters worse. The chairman resisted, her words only eliciting a cryptic smile from him. He looked at Bill and waited.

I was seized by an impulse to take the young children from the room, as if to prevent them from seeing their father bleed. Yet I also felt curiously at ease in this tension; it felt very familiar.

Bill finally admitted, "I don't know. We've talked over the results so often and you've never mentioned this theory."

The professor eventually relented: "Oh, it's just a small point, I wondered what you'd make of it." He then explained the "minor point," and the meeting adjourned.

We all headed for the food with a palpable sense of relief, as if the chairman had pulled a knife out of Bill. There was some conversation over paper plates that evening about the chairman's behavior. Several people were outraged at his "sadism," while some laughed at the man's need to one-up a younger graduate student.

Yet I suspect more was going on. Certainly the chairman's comments served to distance him from the warmth of the moment enfolding him and Bill. Yet given the maternal air in the room, the concerned female professors who clearly had real affection for Bill, the presence of family and good food waiting beyond the door, the chairman's nasty question may also have reflected a wish to bring some masculine element to this event, lest it become too "soft." The chairman wanted to make it tough enough to feel like a male event. It's as if he were saying, "Let's make sure there's not too much mommy in this room; make room for daddy." The chairman wanted to make sure that Bill could really take care of himself, so he tested his mettle under fire. He brought to mind the combat veteran of Vietnam who said to me, "The most important thing I want to know about a friend is that he is dependable, that he will cover my ass when a firefight breaks out."

The chairman was saying that Bill didn't need to be coddled so much. In that sense it wasn't sadism or distancing going on there, it was connection. The chairman was loving Bill in the only way he knew how: by making things very difficult, by testing the young person to toughen him. In this male initiation, like the downing of the grog, some wounding must accompany the welcome.

There was a grown-up Ph.D. who was still "sounding" on others in the cafeteria as a way of getting close. No wonder the scene felt familiar to me.

TENDER BRUTES AND UNCOMFORTABLE FEELINGS

Talking to a friend who is telling me about some difficulty, I make a friendly-sarcastic comment. He replies affectionately: "Ah, Sam, you have sharp elbows." He means that I poked at him even as I went to comfort him. I felt relief that the elbows are affirmed, that they connect as well as distance. But how close do you get when you feel an elbow poking into you? Perhaps that's the point—the sarcasm, the aggression, the taunt, the roughhouse keep us from feeling too womanly and maternal at the very time we're getting closer and more loving, feelings that many of us must disavow or suppress as we grow up.

In the novel *Red Storm Rising*, author Tom Clancy provides an amusing glimpse of the way that aggression serves to legitimate male affection and tenderness. Ed Morris is the commander of a destroyer during World War III, a fictional nonnuclear confrontation between NATO and Russia. Morris's boat is badly damaged by a Russian torpedo and there are many casualties. His boat is ignominiously towed back to its home port by a salvage tug.

As captain, Morris has the task of informing the families of the deaths of their husbands, fathers, and sons. Understandably, Morris is consumed by grief and shame, and his feelings come to a head when he has to break the sad news to the small daughter of one of his men. He almost weeps as he tells the little girl that she will never see her father again, and later berates himself for not being able to cry in front of strangers.

Morris suffers nightmares reliving the submarine attack, and savagely blames himself for not having spotted it sooner, though he was truly not at fault. An able officer, he is soon given command of another antisubmarine boat, and sent back out to sea to escort a convoy bound for Europe. As he prepares to depart, he seems preoccupied and unsure of himself. One of his new officers, Jerry O'Malley, realizes that unless the captain can grieve, the entire ship is in danger.

So O'Malley takes Morris out one night to a bar. O'Malley produces a bottle of Irish Whiskey. The officer skillfully and tenderly gets his captain to open up and cry, finally releasing the painful sense of frustration and helplessness he feels. There is a tender moment between the two war veterans in their booth at the back of the darkened bar as Morris sobs while O'Malley sits across from him and comforts him. After a while O'Malley gently helps his grieving captain toward the door of the bar.

Then what happens? The mood changes: a near-fight occurs! A taunting seaman provides O'Malley a chance to display his masculinity.

" 'What's the matter, Navy, can't take it?' "

Tom Clancy informs us that O'Malley is "a man of considerable strength." His left arm supports Morris, and with his right arm O'Malley grabs the taunting seaman by his throat.

" 'You got anything else to say about my friend, Dickweed?' O'Malley tightened his grip."

The seaman whispers an apology. O'Malley lets the man go and walks out the door, still supporting Morris.

Here is another moment of connection for men that must be welded to violence. O'Malley cannot be a male "mother," unless he is also a tough guy. We can all sleep tight, knowing that with one arm O'Malley can hold up the needy, and with the other can defeat the wicked. Masculinity demonstrated, O'Malley and his buddy can continue their exploits. No wimps here. The strong arm, the bar, and the booze all serve to reassure us.

Imagine how naked a man can feel with just the tenderness and no opportunity to prove his manhood along with it.

THE HARSH MILK OF MANHOOD:
IDENTIFICATION WITH THE AGGRESSOR

What is it about growing up male that results in these circuitous connections—provocation, dominance, control—that don't reveal the true nature of our desire? Let's examine the dynamics whereby our attempts to connect become welded to an aggressive posture.

Let's return to Barry, the man who as a little boy skinned his knee and ran to his parents for comfort, only to be told by his father that he was "too old for that," while his mother smiled at him from across the room, put out her arms, and said "Come here."

He sat stiffly as he recounted that moment thirty-five years earlier. Picturing him standing there, exposed and ashamed, I wondered: "What did you do?"

Without hesitation he replied: "I ran out of the house."

"Well, what did you do then?"

He stopped, surprised that I would ask. Barry thought for a moment and then his eyes lit up: "I went into our garage, next door to the house, and found my father's toolbox. He had a wonderful old toolbox that he kept very clean and organized. It was on his workbench in the garage. I got a hammer out of the box and took it onto the driveway and found some large rocks on the ground and sat there, smashing the rocks until I felt better."

The young Barry has used aggression to master an overwhelming situation. He smashed rocks, the original source of his humiliation, and he used one of his father's tools to do it. His father told him to toughen up, and he obeyed.

The concept of "identification with the aggressor" means that in situations in which we are abused or frightened we side with power rather than vulnerability and take on the attributes of our oppressors. Gregory Rochlin suggests in his book *Man's Aggression* that identifying with the aggressor is a means of overcoming the feelings of being helpless, weak, and dependent—feelings intolerable for the young boy—by assuming the stature of strength.[3] Anna Freud writes: "By impersonating the aggressor, assuming his attributes or imitating his aggression, the child transforms himself from the person threatened into one who makes the threat."[4] Rather than feeling abused, intruded upon, abandoned, or violated—experiences all men (and women) have growing up—we search for positions of strength, power, and dominance. The harsh milk of masculinity that all boys must drink flows from the normal losses, sorrow, and yearnings for intimacy of boyhood and from the way that aggression comforts even as it distances us.

Consider Barry. He has not just withdrawn into aggression. For that any hammer would do. Instead he gets his *father's* hammer. He has drawn himself closer to his father by getting an object of his father's. And he derives some comfort and soothing from the repetitive, forceful smashing of the rocks. For the young boy who has just struggled with the fragmenting shame of feeling caught between his parents, the repetitive smashing helps to restore the sense of self. Notice too that the self-soothing through aggression occurs in a private, ritualistic way. He becomes a little "worker" channeling his anger, hurt, and shame into smashing the rocks. In the same way adult men calm and soothe themselves through work and other private, individualistic, repetitive activities that restore self-esteem and the sense of self.

A university professor boxing at a gym on the West Side of New York advised me how wonderful the speed bag was because it "washed clean the frustrations of the day." The repetition of large muscle activity, the aggression of swinging and smashing, restores the sense of self. This too is one of the functions of anger. Aggression restores the sense of self, while excessive vulnerability undermines it.

I truly dislike jogging in the morning, much preferring to run in the afternoon. I remember only once running early in the day, getting up at dawn and putting on an extra layer of clothes beneath my sweatsuit in order to run on a dark, cold, winter morning. In several hours I would be facing an especially challenging university presentation. My first teaching job depended on this presentation, and I felt a queasy uncertainty about how well I'd handle it. I swallowed my distaste and ran that morning because the sense of my own muscular ability and the wake-up of blood pulsing through my veins reassured me at a time when I wanted to be most in touch with my manhood. With this cold, hard, lonely effort I was reassuring myself, connecting with a comforting inner vitality: *I am a man, I am big and strong, I can handle this situation.*

The notion of "identification with the aggressor" is a neat way of understanding men—perhaps too neat. For it is too easy to assume that men are most interested in power and control, and thus fail to see the connective wishes underneath. Men also hold on to their warmer, gentler, responsive sides.

"You know, stones are not so cold as they appear," ruminated one man, who at first had seemed as cold and hard as a piece of New Hampshire granite in winter. "You can tell a lot from a stone—if it is smooth or craggy, whether it feels soft or brittle. You can rub your hand over a stone and warm it, or you can hide behind it yourself." He was inviting me, and himself, to look beneath the surface to see a warmer, more responsive part of himself than he was able to show or to put into words, even to himself. The feeling of having to protect and nurture a very vulnerable part of themselves is very profound in men, and often the only way to do it is to withdraw or become very watchful or very dominating.

The Harsh Warmth of Our Fathers. Often fathers and sons miss their attempts to connect and vitalize each other, so that we come to experience the aggression in our fathers and not the love. We saw in the last chapter that fathers often offer sons a cold lesson in love—directing our attention away from the direct expression of feelings, working hard to get us interested in things, not people.

Often, though, it's a father's own masculine clumsiness, rather than bad intentions, that lead the boy to see masculinity as critical or judgmental. Arnold remembered telling his father at age fifteen that he worried about his friend Steve, who was drinking a lot. "I wanted to talk about how scared I felt about drinking, and that my best friend was drinking too much. My father in an attempt to be helpful said later, 'Oh, Steve is just an alcoholic.' I felt humiliated and unheard, because I was worried about Steve and about myself, not wanting to feel judged." What Arnold really wanted to talk to his father about was his own shyness and worries about drinking too much in order to find courage. His father's quick judgment of "alcoholics" left Arnold feeling humiliated.

Years later, looking through a family scrapbook together, Arnold's father reminisced with his son, now aged thirty-eight, about those teenage years: "I was worried about you then, wanted to help you when you were struggling so much with drinking and didn't know how to help." The only way his father could offer "help" was to put down Steve, using judgment and criticism as a way to offer advice about "what not to do."

This struggle to live up is a tough lesson that men learn from their fathers. Our fathers' bitterness conceals both the love and sorrow in their lives.

By their silence or stoniness or absence, many of our fathers communicate the sense of renunciation and loss that they knew all too well: *To be a man I have to be ready to go out and endure great hardships for my family and give up those I love in order to provide and protect, and no one ever sees the sacrifices I have made.*

"Being a man is a dreadful obligation—that's how I see it," admitted a friend to me one day.

Poet Seamus Heaney testifies to this burden in his poem "A Kite for Michael and Christopher." A father is flying a kite with his young boys on a lovely afternoon. The father's wish that his boys hold the soaring, dipping kite before it falls becomes a metaphor for the grief transferred from men to men: "Take in your hands, boys and feel / the strumming, rooted, long-tailed pull of grief. / You were born fit for it. / Stand in here in front of me / and take the strain."[5]

The father *wants* his sons to feel grief. He wants his sons to know what he has gone through—the soaring and falling of a father's hopes as he ages—he wants to show them the way a man's spirits can flag, the way life can bring us down. He wants to prepare them for that strain, to make their hands and hearts ready to hold the straining rope of manhood. This is really a lesson in love from fathers to sons, communicated in silent ways that may leave boys feeling more hurt, damaged, or confused than loved.

We Were Born Fit for It, Boys. Often members of the male community—our fathers and others—wound their young in trying to communicate that strain. They leave us as boys preferring to get into the dominate position rather than the vulnerable, grieving one. Instead of grief we learn about aggression—the lesson backfires.

Here's an example. Ben, at age thirty, told me that on the day of his high school graduation, while cooking hamburgers on their suburban backyard barbeque grill during the family celebration, his father pulled him aside from the festive group. Ben found himself standing alone with his father in front of the fiery grill. While the guests milled happily around the yard, the father's tone changed, and he spoke almost in a whisper to his son.

What did he tell the proud, jubilant eighteen-year-old graduate? He revealed a family secret, something the boy had never known about his father—that he had spent several years in a Japanese prison camp during World War II.

While the guests ate hamburgers and hot dogs, the father told the son, in low, mournful tones, about terrible deprivation and humiliation: having one bowl of rice a day, crawling with maggots; of being beaten up by guards when he complained about the food, then being forced to sleep in a tiny cell without being able to leave for days, even to go to the bathroom.

Ben, years later, described his reaction: "I felt myself *harden* that at this time of my joy he told me about his greatest pain and deprivation."

Then Ben paused and said:

"It's only recently that it's occurred to me that he was trying to tell me about his suffering and what he hoped wouldn't happen to me."

In other words, the father was trying to connect with his son: Here was a man who almost died a horrible POW death during World War II—he likely thought he'd never survive. His pain and the degradation of his imprisonment had been a family secret. Now he found himself not only alive but witnessing his only son's graduation from high school. He likely felt overwhelmed by his happiness, pride, envy ("I wish I had my youth back"), and sadness at what he had to endure at a similar age. *Suddenly he wanted to be seen and recognized by his son, he wanted to communicate his love for his son and likely wanted to hear his son's love for him. He was flooded by all that he had survived and sacrificed just to get to this moment.* But he couldn't say that—so instead he blurted out a painful secret that his son experienced as an aggressive attack and a pitiful memory at the same time.

The son came away not with a deeper awareness of male vulnerability and grief but rather "hardened," with a deeper appreciation of the value of being the one who surprises rather than the one who is surprised, of being the attacker rather than the target. As a boy Ben learned the value of being private, keeping himself from being too open to his own or other people's pain. It wasn't until years later that he appreciated that underneath his father's apparent aggression was an urgent need to connect.

THE HARSH INTERNAL VOICE OF LOVE:
THE RETURN OF THE SWOONING COWBOY

As a boy on the verge of adolescence, I had my own experience of how love and anger become melded together in the process of hardening oneself to the burdens of manhood.

When I was a little child watching cowboys slug it out on TV, I was always embarrassed for the cowboy who got punched out. Once two cowpokes were fighting in a barn and one of them socked the other into a wall; the loser hit the wall and was knocked out. He slid down the wall, slid down onto his butt, and slumped there unconscious, his head lolling off to one side. Then in a final touch, a horse harness fell off its peg and onto his shoulders, framing him for all the world to see. Unconscious, exposed, and defenseless, he might have been dead for all the youngsters watching the show knew. On national TV. That seemed the height of humiliation: to be vulnerable in public.

Sometimes I wanted to help and would imagine holding a sheet in front of the guy who had lost so no one could see his disgrace. Usually, though, I wanted to have nothing to do with the incompetent boob. The victor seemed so much more thrilling, standing there big and strong with the energy of conquest flowing in his veins.

Over the years I learned to be a man in my own personal version of the cowboy shows, at home and in school, on the city street and at summer camp. My buddies and I struggled with the core wisdom that boys transmitted in brief, unexplained nuggets of insight such as: "Don't get caught with your pants down," "Don't be a mama's boy," "Buck up," and "Learn to take it." The lonesome, swooning cowboy in the barn came to embody a basic truth about being a man: *Don't get caught with the horse collar around your neck.*

Then there was the day at summer camp, when I was about eleven years old, that I actually became the swooning cowboy. I remember that summer as the year I looked forward to graduating from intermediate to senior. Becoming a senior implied to me a kind of grown-up status—becoming an "older brother" in the family of the camp—that I very much wanted yet truly didn't feel ready for. Deep down what I wanted was to *have* an older brother, rather than to be one.

Back home, I already *was* the oldest brother, with all the rewards and disadvantages that implied. One disadvantage I knew well—it meant that I didn't have an older brother to show me how to snag hard grounders at second base or to cram for a biology exam, or more important, to encourage and reassure me, to give me a clear image of what it meant to go from boyhood to manhood. Not that I was so great at providing that to my younger brother, who often seemed to me a potential usurper threatening to reveal how little I *really* knew about baseball, girls, and taking care of yourself amid the peer group. Deep down I wished that someone would set me straight about that. My father was going through very demanding business difficulties just when I reached early adolescence: He had his own demons to fight. We weren't able then to be there for each other.

One hot July day that summer we took a long bus ride to another camp for a day of sports competition. This was new turf, with lots of older kids around, and I wanted to prove myself even as I felt out of my element. Even the pine needles smelled different from the ones on the trees back at my camp.

These older kids, by virtue of their extra year on me, seemed to know secrets I could only wonder about. In front of one bunkhouse, a cluster of boys was gathered around a punching bag, a full-length "body bag," taking swings at it. Dust rose as the kids danced around it, punching away for all they were worth. I walked up to watch. To my surprise and pleasure a space appeared for me right up front.

Maybe, I ventured to hope, I could be a part of all this. Several older kids bunched around behind me, and I could feel the closeness at my back. Perhaps there were potential friends in the group, maybe an "older brother" or two for me. Under the press of bodies I edged nearer to the bag, while the kid on the other side kept punching away. The warmth of the day, the press of the kids, the rhythm of the activity lulled me into a sleepy unguardedness.

Suddenly out of nowhere I felt an explosion in my stomach; the boy had punched the bag with all his strength and sent it flying into my stomach. I doubled over, a fire in my gut. Some recess of my mind went onto automatic pilot: What had just happened? Was this an accident? I didn't know, but the laughter at my pain confirmed my suspicion. I resolved to buck up, to suck in my gut and take it, to not show the humiliation, the hurt, the sense of betrayal and anger I felt.

Someone offered help, but I was intent on showing that I wasn't hurt. Looking like the hunchback of Notre Dame, I steadfastly limped away down the path toward my own campmates.

As I limped away, I truly needed that older brother. I needed *someone* to do what I couldn't—provide some comfort and reassurance, tell me that I was okay. I needed someone to stand by me, speaking to me in a soothing and reassuring voice that would restore my self-esteem. To tell me, *"You're all right, you're a great kid, these things happen."* So I tried to fashion this voice. I can remember it—angry and demanding. My own, it hissed: *"You stupid, glasses-wearing shmuck! Never let that happen again!"*

At age eleven this was the best I could do to connect with my own self-esteem. With the wind kicked out of me, I wanted to provide love and protection but I was also ashamed of myself. The aggression turned inward, and I hated my own need and vulnerability. So partly ashamed, partly loving, in my mixed-up way I poked at and prodded myself to provide comfort.

My hunch is that boys and men often talk to themselves internally with this mix of anger and love, attempting in a harsh, angry way to connect with a reassuring part of themselves. This demand that we *live up and do better and protect ourselves* is our internalization of what it means to be a man. The harsh voice is not just the voice we use on other people, but also the voice we use on ourselves when we try to connect with our neediness. It's often the only voice we have to console ourselves with in moments of defeat, uncertainty, or pain.

Here again is the harsh milk of manhood. Love and comfort and connection are provided with a slap or wounding that masks the very object of our desire. Boys and men alike use aggressive behavior to protect and shield themselves from their vulnerability when they desire connection. We do it to others, and we do it to ourselves.

Let's explore some of the other ways in which men cloak their bids to be attended to and valued in an aggressive or provocative posture, one that often winds up alienating the very people they're trying to draw closer.

MASKS, SHIELDS, AND DISTRACTIONS: FROM SHAME TO ANGER AND POWER

As men we are all attempting both to stiffen up and to reach out at the same time. We demand of ourselves that we be tough and live up to stern images, but we also seek to become more nurturing and tender, to put into words and actions the feelings of love and responsiveness that our fathers and generations of men could not.

When men become hostile or remote in relationships, they often are trying to shift the focus off the self so that they can silently satisfy their needs without feeling too painfully exposed. We treat ourselves with the same roughness and tentativeness that we treat others.

Have you ever seen what a young boy does when his pride is injured? Consider a five-year-old boy riding his bike in the park for the first time without training wheels. He is in the full bloom of heady, prideful achievement. His parents give him a push and he wobbles down the concrete path, imagining perhaps that everyone mistakes him for a hairy biker on a Harley-Davidson. There's a curve ahead and the bike lists to one side. His mother runs up to him to give him a hand and then—disaster! The bike tips and down he goes, with a crash of metal on concrete. The boy jumps up and points an accusing finger at his mother:

"Mom," he yells, "that was your fault!"

We know what the boy wants to do: he wants to cuddle up next to his mommy or daddy and be comforted, but not at the cost of his newly found and exhilarating sense of masculinity. Having established for all the world that (a) his mom's at fault, and that (b) he's still big and tough, he can then let her look at his scrapes and hug him and help him get back on the bike. The boy wants to return to mother for comfort without losing the ability to venture forth and conquer the world. He is saying to her: *Be here for me, but don't get too close!*

With his forceful accusation of his mother, the boy is doing something else as well: He has become the aggressor instead of the victim. No longer the little five-year-old who has fallen off his bike, he has transformed himself into the avenging angel, a wrathful superhero screaming accusation and virtue at the offending hordes. By virtue of his anger, his intolerable sense of smallness and powerlessness has been transformed into a sense of bigness and power.

There's a little bit of the five-year-old boy alive, thank goodness, in all of us. No one, no matter how grown up, likes to have his efforts at independence and achievement fail or see them called into question. No one wants to be the object of public ridicule. If men early on feel in their bones that there is something ridiculous or inadequate about their wish for connection or comfort, if they come to believe that they have little to contribute emotionally as husbands, fathers, friends, and sons, then in any highly charged emotional situation they will invariably shift the focus off the self. They will work harder and seem withdrawn; they will become silent about love and "let actions speak louder than words," or attack when they feel bogged down in the vulnerable, murky, "feminine" world of feelings, love, and the family.

Thus unseen and protected, we can go about the task of healing ourselves in silence and in private. So what if that very psychological isolation serves to reinforce the shame and sense of inadequacy, the sense that: "I must be the only man in the world who feels like I'm not really living up"? When you're up to your neck in the alligators of shame, it doesn't help to remember that your original goal was to drain the swamp of inadequacy.

We want to protect or buffer the self from exposure, but also to connect with those we love, to give to them or to communicate our pain or need, to get warmth back into our lives. The use of aggression is one of the only ways for men to feel as if they actually have value and that people can see them and respect them. This is often a misguided notion, but it remains alive in the minds of men nonetheless, and is often reinforced in their lives.

There are a number of creative strategies that men use at work and home to handle disowned feelings of shame, grief, and anger, strategies that affect the contradictory goals of connecting with others and hiding the self from further exposure. Sometimes the balance is toward self-protection, at other times toward connection and self-exposure or responsiveness. In all cases, though, the anger and distancing allow us to express connective impulses too difficult to reveal more directly. Let's take a look at these strategies now.

HYPERMASCULINITY

First, there is *the hypermasculine pose in the face of diminishment*. If you feel in danger of being diminished, it can help to swell up and show the world how big you are, or would like to be. A busy corporate executive I know named Bob had routine access to a company jet to facilitate meeting with subordinates around the country. But for years Bob had left the jet unused, preferring to make conference calls to communicate with his workers. Then he began encountering more and more difficulty with his family as his daughter and son reached their teens, and his wife began to break away from her dependence on him.

Bob's wife, Sally, had worked only part-time in the public schools while the children were young. Recently, however, Sally had gone back to graduate school and was now working as a school administrator. Their home suddenly felt much emptier to Bob. Sally often had meetings at night, and was no longer as available to her husband when he got home from work as she once was. "The house just seemed lonelier than I can ever remember it," Bob observed. Bob's adolescent children also tested him in a new way, particularly his seventeen-year-old son, Steve. Steve strained his father's emotional resilience, waffling for a long time about college applications, studying just hard enough to pass his courses but not to graduate with the honors his father hoped for, yet at the same time clearly wanting his father's attention.

Bob struggled with the father's dilemma of how to be available to his son without taking over and dominating him. He struggled with the husband's challenge of supporting his wife while also dealing with his own sense of abandonment after years during which his reliance on her presence was masked.

Much of this undermined Bob's sense of his own manhood and self-worth. In fact, he was plunged back into memories of how much he had relied on his mother as a child, and how empty the relationship with his *own* father had been during his adolescence. Trying to be available as a father to his son left him with an emptiness as he recollected the wish that his own father had been there for him. "What do I have to give to my son?" he mused one day. "My own father absented himself from my life when I was twelve—I depended on my mother for most things."

All this was very difficult for Bob, who had learned to think of himself as a high-powered executive. Having so long thought of his contributions mainly in terms of providing and protecting, Bob wondered if he still had anything worthwhile to offer his family.

As his own sense of "manliness" and self-worth became diminished, he found himself spending more time on the corporate jet. He spent much of his week flying around the country in the jet, Nixon-like, attending important meetings and doing highly competitive "manly" work.

On the one hand Bob isolated himself from his wife and children by his travel, and also created a larger-than-life male persona with his busy schedule and use of the company jet. All these travels and meetings filled some of the internal "emptiness" he felt from the changes at home.

Yet there was also a desperate emotional message in his frantic efforts: *I am a man, I work hard and take care of important business.* The connective impulse in his seemingly isolating behavior lay in his wish that his family notice him and see how hard he worked, how hard he worked for them. It's as if he was asking them to tell him that he was *capable and worthwhile*, at a time when he felt so diminished and unsure of himself in the arena of family love.

However, the hypermasculine work focus and style only distracted him from his own feelings of inadequacy and cut him off from his children at a pivotal and needy time in their own lives.

Herein lies some of the frustration men often engender. When we see someone swaggering around we may feel like saying "You idiot!" yet that may be the only way the guy can feel that he's an adequate man, worthy of our attention and his own self-esteem.

I often sense a "puffed-up" quality to those men for whom a pipe, a newspaper, and a briefcase are the major props in their self-presentation to the world. The connective impulse underneath these props lies in our sense that without these "puffed-up" attributes our yearnings to be in contact would be too risky: Others might see us as little boys, or we'd feel too unsure of ourselves, or seem "ugly" or "pathetic" or "inappropriate."

Recently I received a hurried phone call from a younger male colleague named Todd. He called to tell me that he wanted to set up a symposium on fathering. As he talked I could hear a baby crying in the background. Todd mentioned that he was calling from home, where he was taking care of his newborn. Todd rushed to tell me details of the thousands of mailings he hoped to put out, of all the people he wanted to invite, of the numbers of topics to be covered. "We'll talk about what it's like to become a father, how it changes your relationship with your wife, coming to terms with your own father." All worthy topics, but there was an urgency to his voice that caught my attention, particularly given that he hoped to make this major effort happen rather soon, without having much prior background in carrying off such an event.

"How come you're doing this?" I wondered aloud to him. There was a momentary break as Todd went to change his daughter's diaper.

When he returned to the phone Todd talked of "fathering issues" and "recent advances" in research, "how fathers are the last frontier in family research," and so on. As he talked and became more and more academically puffed up, I started to puff up myself, and soon we were into a discussion of an obscure research report in an obscure journal.

I was still confused as to why he was going to all this effort now. He had a newborn at home, his wife worked too, they both seemed overloaded. Why take on such a demanding task as this conference he proposed?

Perhaps I seemed fatigued enough from being a father myself, something in my tone must have felt inviting, because Todd explained: "It does feel like a lot to do right now, with a new baby and all, but you know this is our first child—and *I feel so lonely*. I don't talk to a lot of other fathers, I'm so busy and all."

Todd, understandably, felt lonely and somewhat isolated as a new father. Wanting contact with other men, he decided to sponsor a lengthy, weighty conference. This strategy both connected and disconnected him from his family. It separated him from the engulfing nature of new parenthood, giving him an important work goal outside the home. But it also connected him with other men, giving voice to the part of him that felt: *I've got to talk to other men about this, I've got to sort out the confusing mix of sadness, joy, despair, and love I feel as a new father.* Of course this connective impulse was masked by his need to organize a conference to accomplish connection. Why not just call up some other fathers and talk about what it's all like? For many of us that's not so easy to do. The mix of feelings, the uncertainty about what's appropriate, our desire not to look too out of control or needy might engender an unconscious need to "puff up" somewhat. It's an acceptable, if ultimately self-defeating, way to hide from the doubt and uncertainty we feel.

The problem with hypermasculine strategies of connection is that they can lead to competitive frenzies with others. Once you've puffed up, it can be hard to unpuff. And as those around us feel diminished by our attempts to assert our fragile manhood, we become more isolated. Our proof of manhood leads others to prove theirs in a vicious cycle of male competition.

For instance, recently I was invited to a day-long gathering of male academics, helping professionals, and others interested in understanding more about "current issues in men's lives, having to do with work, family, and changing sex roles." About forty of us arrived and sat together in a large room, waiting to begin. The conference organizers then started by complimenting all of us: "This is an esteemed group of men, it is remarkable to find this august collection of men together to talk about these issues." One of the organizers went on to note that this event was important enough that several of the participants made time in their busy schedules to fly into Boston from across the country in order to be here.

Well, by the time this introduction was finished, we'd all become so "august" that many of us feared not living up, and began working very hard to be "important." It was hours before we could stop being so puffed up and "august" and become real people who could just talk together about the issue of the day: What is it really like to be a man today?

THE ASSERTION OF AUTONOMY

Another connective strategy is *the assertion of autonomy in the face of interdependence.* Tom is a single father in his mid-forties. One day he told me that his son's high school graduation was the next week and he had not yet been given a ticket by his son. Tom cared very much for the boy and has raised him since the divorce, fifteen years earlier. The boy's mother had been invited, but no ticket had been given to Tom.

Tom is a big man, bearded, who runs a garage. His face seemed a mask of rage and vulnerability, etched in stone, as he described the dinner he had the night before, alone with his son, both men cooking stew and rice, making salad, sitting at the table to eat, and then cleaning up together, without the father mentioning the graduation. Throughout the meal Tom thought about the event, but he would not ask for a ticket. Instead he asserted autonomy:

"It's his decision who to invite to his high school graduation; I'm not going to demand that he give me a ticket," he explained proudly to me, his arms limp at his side. He looked tired and defeated as he spoke. The conflict seemed to leak out of every pore in his body: wanting to go, feeling proud of his son's accomplishments, but also too proud to ask. Tom felt that fathers shouldn't be vulnerable to their children, but he could only imagine himself "crawling" to the boy in asking.

Tom's assertion that his son had the right to make his own decision was a way of protecting himself against the pain of being turned down. What if he asked for a ticket and was refused?

Carol Gilligan, noting that men tend to give a logical interpretation to events, concludes that we "value justice over relationships."[6] I suspect rather that our attention to autonomy serves to help us control moments in relationships that feel out of our control. Tom's haughty proclamation of autonomy was a way of disavowing the need he felt for his son's love and validation, symbolized by the graduation ticket.

Listening to Tom's attempts to isolate himself, I felt that what Tom needed was some self-respect. That at some level he didn't feel *entitled* to be at his son's graduation, as if he really wasn't good enough to say what most fathers would automatically say to their boy at this rite of passage: "I don't need a ticket, I'll be at your graduation, my son!" As it turned out, the ticket *did* symbolize self-worth for both father and son. Tom screwed up his courage late one evening at home and, stopping on the threshold of his son's room, asked the boy for a ticket. His son eagerly exclaimed: "I was waiting for you to ask!"

The isolation and nonengagement of both of these men reflected their struggles with self-worth and shame. The father and son were both asking how much they were worth to each other, and whether they would get a thank-you or an acknowledgment of the sacrifices of love from the other. What stood between them was the sacrifice of the mother to the divorce and all that Tom had given up in choosing to be with his son and all that the son had given up in living with his father rather than his mother. The ticket became the vehicle expressing the struggle. How does a man find self-respect at age forty-five, to know that his presence is important and valued, not just as a provider, but as an emotionally engaged participant? How does a father come to know that it's important to affirm a child's worth, even if it means swallowing his own pride? And how does a young adult come to realize that it is equally important to affirm his parents, that to separate is one mark of maturity, but to connect is the other? And, too, how do men overcome their accumulated resentment, grief, shame, and disappointments in order to find the kernel of love and affirmation that their hearts seek?

THE PREEMPTIVE STRIKE

The preemptive strike in the face of loss is another useful way to avoid feeling too exposed and needy in close relationships. Often, when men feel in danger of being humiliated by women or other men, they will attempt to strike the first blow, thus forestalling their own vulnerability.

A thirty-five-year-old college professor repeatedly gets involved with women, then feels vulnerable to his inability to really hold their attention and provokes a fight to end the relationship. The roots of his behavior go back to an early perception of himself as not really worthy of another's attention. His mother was exceedingly important to him, and a lot of his self-worth has always come from enchanting and holding on to women; his father was a more gruff, demanding figure. Becoming involved in a relationship was a scary event for this man, who wanted to make a woman love him but also became scared of losing that love. The more aware he became of the importance of women, the angrier he got at their "suffocating presence." The bitter fights that he provoked expressed his wish both to escape and to get even for his thwarted neediness.

And too there is a connective impulse. In this case it may be more masked and self-protective, but the wish for connection is there. He alludes to it when he speaks of "suffocation": *You become so important to me I can't breathe, I have to throw you away.* As a panicked child will toss away the very blanket that keeps him warm yet also stifles him. It's as if in rejecting her, he's asking the woman in his life: *Do you know how awful it feels to love someone and fear you can't hold them, to fear that you'll fail in their eyes and your own?*

Another man posed this question: What do you do after the first date? He always made a big play for the woman, but then he worried whether she'd find anything interesting in him after that. So a fight developed, and he'd become angry and rejecting. The street talk of his native Brooklyn peppered his description of this recurrent pattern: "I like to blow them off, before they walk out on me."

Walking down the street after interviewing this man I contemplated the virtues of anger, the way it carries us far above the awful swamp of sadness and loss. There is an Icarian flush to anger, sweeping us up and helping us forget that we will soon come tumbling down.

I recalled the time my cherished girlfriend and I decided to call our relationship quits when I was in graduate school in 1970. She was my first real love, but we just could not make the relationship

work and the loss was very real. Sharon was the pivotal person helping me make it through a painful year when, at age twenty-four, I
was doing my internship at a VA hospital, avoiding the draft, and
trying to counsel psychotic, furious twenty-four-year-old Vietnam
veterans. I remember choking my way through my notes about a
Vermont farmer's young, mute son who had a leg blown off in 'Nam
and looked at me with eyes that bled rage and impotence. "You've
got to talk about the phallic implications of that wound!" my supervisor told me bluntly. Yeah, well I tried, but I had to deal with my
own "phallic implications" of not having gone into the army at all,
and I wondered if I was any sort of man to listen to the boy's fury.
It was the love between Sharon and me that probably got me through
that year. Her love was my safe haven as we sat together in front of
the TV in my apartment, watching "Upstairs, Downstairs" and taking refuge in a world of order and simple, understandable values.

The differences between us were greater than the similarities.
Neither of us was ready for a "permanent" commitment, and the
relationship ended painfully for both of us. The day came for her to
move her things out of my house, and the last item was that TV set.
The car was loaded outside in the driveway, and Sharon, as beautiful
as the day I met her, turned in the front doorway to look around. A
kerchief covered her blond hair and sunglasses hid the fact she had
been crying earlier. Then she spotted the TV, really her TV.

"What about our TV?" she wondered.

Looking at her, thinking of the TV, all that I was about to lose
flooded in on me. I was forced to confront my failure: that I could
not keep this person I loved. All of the inadequacy and failure of
these years threatened to come tumbling out right there: the fact
that Sharon and I couldn't really respond fully to each other, the
terror that intimacy and sexuality opened up for me at age twenty-
four, the wound that Vietnam inflicted on me as well as my patients,
the grief I felt at not being able to live up. All of this might have
come tumbling out, and if it had I might have saved the relationship;
I certainly would have saved myself from years of stifled grief and
mourning for her and for myself. But it felt like too much: I had not
the words, the time; I had not the certainty in myself to take the
risk of falling apart in front of the person I loved then.

"Take the fucker!" I blurted out, gesturing at the TV. Sharon
recoiled as if she had been hit, and she exclaimed. "Oh, Sam, I want
you to keep it." It was her final gesture of caring, and she hurried
off to the car, the anger too much for both of us.

My anger at that moment was also an attempt to hold on to her as we said good-bye. Lashing out at the TV drained some of my anger and expressed the futility I felt. It also carried a deeper message: *Back off, give me space, don't strip me of my defenses too quickly here.* Because in pointing to the TV Sharon had touched on my wound—the loss of all the comfort I felt from her, and the memory of our times together I most treasured. What I most wanted to say I could hardly give voice to: *Let's find a way to say good-bye, but not in a way that rubs my face in grief.* So the anger spoke for me.

Many men, I suspect, haven't found the words to talk about loss and change and hope. So at moments when we are confronted by the departures of those we love, we feel so helpless and on the spot that we encode our negotiations in angry gestures, tones, and words that drive us farther apart than we wished.

DISDAIN AND RIDICULE

Disdain and ridicule often help us give voice to devalued parts of ourselves. Assaulting others and shifting the focus or the blame to them can help us manage our own shame. We become the accusers, piercing others with a glance of moral certainty. There's tremendous power in catching others with their pants down; it's better than the other way around.

Get the focus off the self and onto others. A man may attack others for being needy, vulnerable, a mama's boy, or "sentimental." He harbors these shameful feelings himself, but he masters them by taking the one-up position.

Ricardo is a housepainter, charming and friendly, who in his late forties did a remarkable thing: He stopped smoking and drinking and opened himself to a loneliness he had been struggling with since childhood.

He sought me out one day, and sat down wearily in a chair in my writing studio. "I'm a mess," he confessed. "I'm depressed and upset, like I have no energy. I've stopped drinking and smoking over the past year, and now I feel worse than ever." Ricardo had been a pack-a-day smoker and a six-pack-a-day drinker of beer. No wonder he was down: He had none of his accustomed means of soothing himself. "I had to give up the smoking as well as the beer: I didn't want to substitute one addiction for another."

Ricardo was just beginning to recognize how isolated he had been all his life. "I feel like I'm just seeing how lonely I feel, how scared I am to make any commitments to my girlfriend Kathy. Here

I am forty years old: Am I going to spend the rest of my life living in a little cabin in the woods? Sometimes I feel like a polar bear living on an ice floe. But I don't want to go into therapy. I can't stand all those theories: Freudian, Jungian, New Age. I don't want to be objectified."

Ricardo reminded me what a challenge it is for men to look at themselves, to ask for help. He had been a competent, hardworking man all his life, and now he needed another person to help him. All around him men seemed to be making it by relying on cigarettes and alcohol or work. He had taken the first step of acknowledging that he couldn't do it all by himself. But he didn't know how to take the second step. He wanted help, and yet he still felt compelled to "disown" the needy part of himself. He didn't want to be too "dependent." He worried that if others, such as Kathy, saw how needy he felt they'd walk out on him.

Where can he find a place to lean? How can he expose the loneliness without driving people away? In this visit, he was checking out with me whether or not what he was feeling was appropriate and acceptable.

"You need a place you can talk," I offered to Ricardo.

He looked at me warily. "Well, I've gone to some AA meetings, but . . ."

Then Ricardo gathered himself up and in the most disdainful voice, exclaimed: "I don't want to sit with a bunch of drunks."

Through this disdain Ricardo gave voice to his deepest feelings of shame and inadequacy. It's as if he were wondering: Maybe all I am is a pathetic drunk. Ricardo used ridicule and disdain to protect himself from his sense of inadequacy. And he gave me a direct message: Don't suggest I'm a failure, or am pathetic. Be careful what you say. I don't want to walk out of here feeling worse about myself!

Therapy, AA, Kathy, talking with a good friend: whichever he chose was not the point. Ricardo needed a place to talk, to feel responded to, and to explore the loneliness eating away at him. But he couldn't quite accept this need yet.

Ricardo left me thinking about male patients in therapy. A man in therapy can easily feel spooked and on the spot when he talks about painful, confused parts of himself. Very quickly he may feel as if a private wound has been made too public, leaving him looking pathetic or unmanly. At these moments therapists who work with male patients often find themselves the objects of disdain and ridicule. When the patient gets in touch with his intimacy needs he may become angry and disdainful of the therapist.[7] In the most withering tones, the patient may inform the therapist: "You're just an intellectual, effete, soft, wimpy person—not like me." The man is giving voice to his fears about himself, but he projects them onto the therapist.

One man I worked with in therapy for several years became more and more furious at me as he revealed his love for a rejecting father. The more aware Harvey became of wanting to hold on to my love and attention the angrier he got. Therapy was "useless" and I was just a "sentimental fool," Harvey observed over and over in the most dismissive tone. One day when Harvey was out of town on business and had to miss an appointment, he sent a letter to my office, furiously assaulting me for all my inadequacies. The stamp on the envelope was unusual: It said "Love."

Harvey arrived for his next appointment and asked if I had gotten his letter. "Yes," I replied and, deciding to take a chance, I continued: "And I got your message too." I pointed to the stamp.

Harvey replied: "I can't believe you noticed that! I sent a stamp like that to my girlfriend and she didn't even notice it."

The anger and disdain softened. Harvey was finally able to make connection and let himself feel the pain of talking about love with someone you fear will reject you. Listening to Harvey, I was struck by how easy it is for men to pick up on anger and try to defend themselves while they ignore or overlook attempts to be loved and loving. This ebb and flow of disdain and connection goes on in marriage, parenting, and at the workplace—in all relationships between men and those we feel vulnerable to.

Often in the workplace those in power need to put down in others the unacceptable feelings that they can feel inside themselves. For example, a woman executive in a high-tech computer firm noticed that her male boss seemed upset at a meeting. They talked about it afterward and she found out that there was a management problem in the company. She offered solutions, and he picked up on them and carried them out. She was aghast weeks later when she got a negative performance review, in which he criticized her as "too protective." His disdain of her "protectiveness" was rooted in his own shame at the need to be "protected" from his own management difficulties by a more savvy woman exemployee.

THE FIX-IT INSTRUMENTAL STANCE

The *fix-it instrumental stance* in the face of interpersonal difficulties is another connective strategy men use. Faced with a child's wish for time together or a wife's demand for a fuller emotional response, a man may adopt a highly rational, problem-solving stance. By doing this the man finds a way to connect with his family that affirms his self-worth and gives him a way to "be there." However, this strategy doesn't really address the family's emotional needs, even though it effectively seals off his shame at being uncertain how to respond.

An engineer returned to his suburban house to find his wife upstairs weeping in their bedroom. Almost exactly a year earlier, the couple had experienced a miscarriage late in pregnancy. He put down his briefcase and went to her to ask what was wrong. She told him that her work as a reporter had taken her into a local elementary school that day, and the sight of the schoolchildren made her sad, reminding her of their loss. The engineer was caught by surprise at this grief, for he had buttoned himself up tightly as the anniversary of the miscarriage approached. He stood up while his wife continued to cry and went to the phone to call the family doctor.

"Can you talk to Mary; she's very upset," he pleaded. The doctor spent close to an hour with his patient, who then went to sleep and woke up the next day feeling resentful of her husband for not "being there." He was stunned.

"Wasn't calling the doctor the smartest thing to do?" he asked me.

In fact, that is how he had learned to treat profound grief—to find someone who could fix it by taking the immediate pain away. By taking action, he distanced himself from the situation.

Deborah Tannen, linguist and popular author, says that men tend not to ask their female partners about plans, while women will check in with their husbands.[8] She also observes that men tend to want to take action to solve problems while women want to talk about the problem and put it into words before "doing" something about it. This is a variant of the old folk wisdom that "men do, women are."

However, taking "independent" action to solve problems also helps us manage fears of being embarrassed or shamed, overwhelmed by feelings of anger, sorrow, or neediness.

The grieving wife confronted the engineer with his impotence ("I can't even keep my wife pregnant") just when he wanted to return to the peace and security of his house. Becoming instrumental puts all the feelings back in place.

"Sometimes I just want to bury what I'm feeling," he told me. But even amid his denial, the word *bury* resonates in our conversation, secretly expressing his sorrow about the lost baby. Talking directly to and comforting his wife would have exposed the engineer to too much feeling, too much sorrow, anger, and hopelessness. So he called in an authority to "fix" the problem. Taking action, becoming instrumental, is often one of the best ways to get away from profound feelings that threaten to overwhelm the self. However, the instrumental stance involves more than managing feelings. Often men's call to action carries a connective thrust.

In this family, the engineer's wife is really the emotional switchboard—she is the one who expresses lots of the feeling. She's been prodding him to express his grief about the miscarriage. She wants to feel that he still loves her despite her inability to have children, and she wonders if he blames her for the loss. He, meanwhile, feels swamped by the infertility experience, not sure what it all means, scared for his wife's health, and worried that she'll become "more and more depressed." The last thing he wants to do is get angry at her, or express too much loss. He already feels guilty enough, and doesn't want to "strain her anymore." He wants to make sure she's all right.

The bedroom scene was a continuation of an unacknowledged dialogue they'd been having for a while. Confronted by a wife expressing grief in a way that seemed scary to him, the engineer sprang into action. He called the doctor, which in his mind is what a strong man is supposed to do. It's as if he was saying to both of them: *I'm a take-charge guy, I know what has to be done, I can deal with this.* Comforting her himself would stir up too much of his own pain and his fear of helplessness. His phone call to the doctor asserted: *I am a worthwhile man who can get you what you need.*

Calling the doctor may also have been an attempt to get what *he* needed, symbolically. "Maybe fathers always absent themselves when you really need them," the engineer had once said to me, speaking of the distance between himself and his own father. Deep down he really wanted to be reassured by his own father that he was okay. He needed to find out from his father what was acceptable for a man to feel emotionally, yet their relationship was still enshrouded in silence during this difficult time. The phone call to the family doctor also gave voice to his deepest feeling: *We need a man in this house who can restore order, and fix the problems here. I've got a sad*

*wife, we've had these miscarriages that frighten and sadden me, and I
don't know how to deal with this—I need my father!* In this way,
the engineer's seeming remoteness and control were actually cries
for help—bids for emotional support for himself as well as his
wife.

Becoming an authority is another way to become instrumental
and to take action, thus allowing connection with others at moments when we feel really on the spot. By having the answers,
giving orders, being in control of a confusing and unclear situation, we can escape from the painful feeling of danger and vulnerability. We also find a way to be seen and valued by others, or so we
feel. Men's tendency to take charge is a wonderful and life-saving
gift at moments of mortal danger; but it can get us into trouble
when we're dealing with problems of love that require more subtle
wooing.

Abe is an executive in the hotel industry; he is in his mid-forties
and happily married to a woman with a career of her own. Abe and
Jean have two children. After several days away on a mid-winter
business trip, Abe returned home to their rural house in the New
England woods to find his eleven-year-old daughter and eight-year-
old son fixing dinner with his wife. Abe walked into the kitchen,
where mother and two children were clustered around a counter
cutting salad vegetables. Jean and the children looked up, saying
excitedly, "Hello, Daddy!"

Eight-year-old Ronald piped up: "Daddy, I missed you!"

Abe, standing across the room, looking at his wife and children,
replied: "Ah, good to be home. Didn't anyone notice the ice
buildup on the roof when I was gone?" He told the family why it's
dangerous when there is so much ice on the roof, talking about roofs
and collar ties and ice versus snow weight. His wife started to seethe
("Did you even notice that your son said he missed you?" she was
to demand later of her husband), and the kids turned back to the
vegetables. Then Abe became even more instrumental, planning out
loud, with gusto, how he would go up on the roof the next day to
clean off the ice and maybe Ron could help him, and wondering
how the woodpile was holding up, and suggesting they could have a
family day of cutting some wood for the stove. Jean, who managed
perfectly well while her husband was gone, became more and more
angry.

What was going on here? Would Abe really prefer to be on the
roof rather than in the kitchen with his family? I think not. But in
criticizing Abe, we might be overlooking the difficult task he faced

as he stood in that kitchen doorway. Abe's real task was to integrate himself into his family after a week away, to get his wife and children to attend to his needs and to refocus his attention on them and their needs. Jean and the kids have formed a little subgroup within the family, leaving Abe, the father, on the outside. What do they know that he doesn't? What have they done during each day of his absence? Jean is actually in a powerful position as the gatekeeper to Abe's information about their time apart.

Often fathers returning home from a business trip may wonder about their true worth to their family: Am I just the provider? The father may also experience a flood of contradictory feelings—wanting to be back in the bosom of his family and wishing he were free and independent, on the road still. In the transition from the public world of work to the private world of family, all the debts he owes his wife and family for being away may collide with his wish to be taken care of and to be close to his wife and children.

For many men, like Abe, this seemingly mundane task of reintegration taps deep questions about love. What are we loved for? we wonder. Can I be loved for being the father, just for being present, or do I have to perform and work hard and provide to be appreciated? These questions arise for men with women just as they do for men with children.

Abe's solution to the problem was to become the authority who can come in and give orders. He thus affirmed that he had a place in the family (he's the one who knows about ice and how to keep roofs clean) at the same time that he expressed his anger at the subgroup that had formed around mother. Breaking up that cozy family scene in the kitchen, giving his family orders, was Abe's way of saying, "I'm here, I'm home, Daddy's back." He couldn't allow himself to be in the spotlight without the accoutrements of authority: To reply to his son directly, to say "My son, I missed you too," would be to expose himself too much.

In setting himself up as the authority, in trying to be big, Abe undercut what he wanted, which was to feel needed and appreciated. He missed the emotional subtext and solved the wrong problem: He was fixing the roof when he ought to have been attending his own achy heart and the hearts of the people around him.

At work, too, men take an authoritative stance that protects them from exposure and uncertainty, but that also gets in the way of getting their own needs met. I once consulted at a small firm where the president was upset because he felt alienated from his subordinates. In particular, he wanted to work more closely with his male and female executives on gender issues in the workplace. So several months earlier he had called a company-wide meeting for all senior and middle-level executives.

"What a bust," he complained to me when we spoke. "I brought together everyone for the morning, had lunch catered, and tried to talk about where we are as a company in terms of gender issues, but it went very poorly. Hardly anyone talked."

I was impressed by this man's concern and decency, and wondered what had happened at the meeting.

"Well, I did some reading and gave a lecture on men's styles of administration and women's styles. I laid it all out on a board and said, 'Here's how things are, let's get that straight from the beginning and go from there.' So after I had these different styles outlined on the board I said, 'Okay, let's discuss this. Any questions?' "

"And?"

"The men seemed inattentive and the women seemed angry. I can't understand why it all backfired."

Maybe the problem lay in the fact that his insistence on being the expert made it difficult for his staff to open up their uncertainties and perceptions. The men likely felt competitive with the boss but were unable to express it, since the bigger and more "all knowing" he became the more puffed up his male subordinates became. And his female executives felt patronized and angry that he addressed their concerns like an authoritarian father. The boss's goodwill in opening up the area for discussion at all was completely forgotten. It's not what he said, it's how he said it. What was harder for this man of sixty years to do was to put aside the authority that he had held for so long and to say what he felt most deeply.

At one point he turned to me in exasperation and explained: "It feels like the women and men here are not sure of how to work together, and I want to talk about what unites and divides us these days."

"What if you just started with that?" I wondered, impressed at how direct and nonthreatening he sounded.

"Oh no," he protested. "What kind of boss would I be if I began with an open-ended question like that?"

For this man, bosses don't begin with open-ended questions; they don't stumble or admit ignorance and curiosity. He had wanted to help and nurture, but the only way he saw to do that was to lecture his "family" and become very authoritarian. His staff perceived him as judgmental and demanding, and everyone missed his yearnings to take care of and help those who truly did depend on him.

Good bosses, like good fathers and husbands, *do* begin with open-ended questions at moments of emotional challenge and stress, providing people an opportunity to feel seen and heard when they most need it. Often employees need to know it is okay to air in front of the boss their uncertainties, fears, hopes, and confusions about the changing workplace of business problems.

ABSTRACTION AND INTELLECTUALIZING

Finally, another strategy men often use to deal with moments when their love and hope leave them emotionally flooded is *to become very logical and controlled and "heady,"* cut off from their hearts. At these moments, the restrained, dry "headiness" is actually an attempt to connect, but it's easy to miss the heartbeat underneath the abstractions.

Here's an example. One day I was sitting on a couch in the lovely apartment of a fifty-year-old scientist named Isaac, who was telling me about his life. Beethoven quartets played on the record player in the background as this charming man told me about the deepest pain in his life. It concerned a letter he had recently received from a twenty-five-year-old son that forced him to reevaluate his worth as a father. The son was discovering things about himself in therapy and now felt compelled to tell his father how angry he was at him. "Growing up with you was like walking on eggshells," the son wrote. "I had to be constantly worried about you, wondering when you'd fly off the handle and explode in rage." The son went on to outline in painful detail how his father had messed up his life.

I've struggled enough with anger at and love for my own father to empathize with the son. But being a father myself, I thought about the mixed love and resentment fathers feel, the way our hopes and dreams are tethered to our children, the desperate way that many of us want to know that we're doing a good-enough job—and my heart also went out to Isaac.

"What's that letter like for you?" I wondered.

As Beethoven's controlled fury filled the room, Isaac began to tell me in even tones about the failures of science, particularly in the sixteenth century. Science was the root of the problem—it was an antisocial activity that had drained too much of his time, and this goes back to certain issues connected with René Descartes's view of the mind-body problem.

As I listened my mind began to numb over. I recalled Norman Mailer's description of the Apollo astronauts about to set off on the first moon landing in 1969, how they used phrases like "extinguishers of foam" to drain any feeling out of the event.[9] The astronauts explained technical details of their mission, but the true significance of the event was lost. As I listened to Isaac, the human feeling of his life felt similarly drained from our conversation. What did the failures of science have to do with this man's angry conflict with his son? Struggling to keep up, I momentarily felt like I was on "College Bowl": "For ten points, who was René Descartes, and what does he have to do with Isaac's fathering?"

I was tempted to give up trying to understand this man's heart. This is how men talk, I was thinking, like "extinguishers of foam." This man must not have much feeling about being fifty years old and having an angry son three thousand miles away telling him what an awful father he was and is.

But Isaac must have sensed my confusion, for with his own sense of urgency he leaned toward me across the couch. "Look, I desperately need illumination," he said. "I have lots of problems. But thinking about them is not the only way to solve them." Then he went on to tell me about Auden's poem "Musée des Beaux Arts." This poem, Isaac told me, is based on a painting by Brueghel entitled *The Fall of Icarus*. It concerned the same powerful legend we encountered before in discussing the troubled relationship between father and son. Icarus, the Greek lad who disobeyed his father and flew too close to the sun, melted the wax wings made by the father and plunged to his death in the sea.

"In this painting, you're looking down into a bay," Isaac explained, "and the water is beautiful and blue and there are some people tilling the soil on the side of a hill and there's a fishing boat with some people fishing. And if you look very carefully you can see the edge, the white end of Icarus's leg. He has fallen down. Nobody sees him. Nobody is paying any attention to him at all. One of the most heroic deeds, trying to fly. Ah! . . . Nobody, nobody knew that he had failed."

Isaac stopped then, and looked at me, the swell of feelings palpable between us. Auden, Brueghel, Icarus. The voice of the "College Bowl" announcer pressed me: "For fifteen points, what do these three figures have to do with Isaac's fathering abilities?"

Then a kindlier voice came to mind—a supervisor who worked a lot with men, who once said to me: "Sam, you think too much when you listen to men. Open your heart a little more and you'll hear what they're saying." He meant that I would get as abstract as they did, and miss the feeling underneath the "extinguishers of foam."

The key words in all this leapt to mind: *failure, heroism, unseen.* Isaac was trying to tell me about failure, and what it meant to him to feel that he'd failed. What it was like to work hard and try to live up and to try to justify your father's life and your own and then to find that you'd failed.

Suddenly I understood the art criticism I'd gotten earlier—the Brueghel picture and Daedalus and Icarus and the son's wish to use his father's wings to fly high and then the failure. Isaac was talking about his own hopes and failed dreams. The hopes and broken dreams of men.

Isaac was trying to tell me about feeling worthless: *I could just disappear beneath the waves; no one sees the heroism in my life and no one sees the failures.* He was dealing with the heroism of the father and what he must endure: the everyday separations from family in the service of work and providing that we take for granted in our society; the need to arm oneself for achievement; the letting go of softer sides of oneself in order to make it as a man; the opportunities for more direct love and affection that get lost in the silent imperatives of toughing it out and remaining stoic. Being a father and husband can be a little bit like going to the moon— seat of romance and the ancient mysteries of love—but having to stay in your space suit, a plastic sheath of silence and technology sealing you off from what you most yearn to touch. It's like applying extinguishers of foam to the most resonant experiences of life.

And he was speaking as well of the failures of fathers: our anger, our silence, all the missed opportunities in love and at work; the failure to achieve the great triumph, the Nobel Prize or whatever; the costs of being a father and husband.

What man can't relate to the human feelings of heroism and failure Isaac was giving voice to? But Isaac couldn't give voice directly to the feelings. He could talk about Brueghel, Auden, and Icarus, but to speak of his own sense of failure would be too pathetic, too unmanly and unfatherly. It would only add to the sense of failure and worthlessness he already felt as his son's letter sat on the desk near him. So he detoured into art and historical criticism, an analysis of the history of science, speaking in coded abstractions about his own pain.

No wonder his son feels unheard and is angry: He talks of feelings and gets an analysis of science in return. And no wonder the father feels unheard and is angry: He talks of failure and broken dreams and he gets an angry accusation from his son, informing him of the 101 ways he has failed.

So father and son fought and in that crucial way were connected, but the very anger that connected them also held them apart. Both father and son needed some forgiveness from each other and neither could provide it. Neither man was able to speak of the deeper connective yearnings each felt: the wish of both father and son to feel beloved of each other, to feel that they mattered to each other and could be "seen" and responded to by the other. They've learned "provocative" connection—angry letters, intellectualizing, accusations—but they haven't mastered more truly "responsive" connection.

Isaac is right, there is a heroism and failure in men's lives: the heroism of sacrificing connection in order to protect and defend those we love, of being able to get the job done at the cost of one's own dreams and yearnings; the heroism of going to work every day when we often prefer to remain in the cozy warmth of our families, of yearning for more from our fathers and mothers and making do with what we've gotten. And there is a corresponding failure in men's lives—missed opportunities for nurturance and care as husbands, fathers, friends, and lovers; ways in which we miss the deeper emotional subtext that is all around us; moments in which we absent ourselves, emotionally or physically, when we could be present and available; times when we fail to get more of what we ourselves need from life to feel really alive. How much of the heroism and failure in our lives is unchangeable and how much could be different? How do we mourn the past—our own past, that of our fathers—so as to be seen more clearly for who we are as men?

As I left my interview with Isaac, I wondered how fathers and children, husbands and wives, can get past the intellectualizing and anger and the use of external objects or actions to represent love. How can we reveal how extraordinarily important we are to each other? How can we mourn and let go of the impossible expectations of invulnerability and autonomy in our lives so as to be seen more clearly for who we are as men?

Isaac's pessimistic image of Icarus buried under the sea, the ultimate failure of men, is too gloomy. Men *can* also succeed in their wish to be more connected, nurturing, and caring. The problem is that many men facing the widening social and emotional challenges of adult life find that some of their most treasured male skills conflict with their desire to become wholer and more responsive people. "I know how to get things done," lamented one forty-five-year-old man. "I just don't know how to get what I want."

Often when I listen to men talk, or as I reflect on my own life, the words of poet Robinson Jeffers come to mind. "A little too abstract, a little too wise," he cautions. "It is time for us to kiss the earth again / It is time to let the leaves rain from the skies / Let the rich life run to the roots again."[10]

We become a little too abstract and wise when we strive so hard to be big and strong, when we want answers before we ask questions. We become the aggressor a bit too quickly. Anger and aggression in the form of verbal pokes, physical prodding, work, and our capacity for abstraction help us connect; they protect our self-esteem and help us feel more sure of ourselves as men. If we can be on top, if we can control feelings, if we can get the answers quickly, if we can be stoic and not need anyone else too much, then we don't feel too exposed, or inadequate, or fragmented, or overwhelmed.

But along the way we fail to learn or forget how to talk about vulnerability, sorrow, shame, how to heal wounds that continue to ache, how to draw others closer and not just drive them away, how to be more responsive to those we love. How do you speak of love and heroism and failure as a grown man and also *feel* like a man?

What does it mean to find a "rich life" again? Does it mean to take your family and move to Paris? To turn your back on all that you've accomplished as a man? No: I think the rich life we seek already lives within us. We can start to find it if we understand how we get flooded by shame, sorrow, anger, and love at intimate moments; if we discover how important a man's love is for women, children, parents, and friends; if we push back against the painful myth that men have little to offer each other emotionally.

For many men, growing older means wanting to return to or discover the richness of relationships, which they may have pushed aside in the rush to become a man. Adult life offers opportunities not only for wounding, but for healing as well—healing our relationships with the women we love, with our children, with our parents, and with our friends.

4

HEROISM AND FAILURE

RELATIONSHIP PRESSURE POINTS

IN MEN'S LIVES

"I've got a new plan," my friend Pete advises me mysteriously over lunch. He is a cardiologist, married, with two young children. A savvy, committed father, he's not the image of an overdriven man. We have a favorite topic at our lunches: Having achieved much of what we want—work, marriage, family—can we now enjoy it?

Often when we talk I'm amazed at how much self-reflection underlies Pete's confident, take-charge, "doctor" attitude to life. "Here I am forty-seven years old, and I've dealt with getting married, I've managed to pick a career and establish myself in it, and Joan and I have two great young children," Pete once said to me. "Back in college I'm not sure I would have predicted that I'd accomplish all that; sometimes I'm amazed that Joan married me, and how much my kids love me, warts and all."

Today Pete reveals his new plan as we munch on our sandwiches: "I'm going to cut back on my hours, spend Friday mornings home with the kids."

Wanting to spend more time with his kids has been on Pete's mind for a while, and it's not hard to guess why. Pete's father was a doctor also, a GP in a small country town. He was the hero of the town and had more time for his patients than he did for his family. As a child Pete idolized his father for the ability to take care of the whole town, but he also missed his father's presence on a daily basis. Then Pete's dad died unexpectedly of a heart attack at age sixty-five, when Pete was in college. His father had ignored the warning signs for years, reassuring his family that "doctors don't have time to get sick." Then he dropped dead walking to his office. Pete never had the chance to say good-bye.

Pete had many reasons for becoming a doctor, and one of them was the sense of connection that his work provided to his lost father. But it also tied him to some of the pressures his father had felt before him. "My kids are growing up so fast," Pete reflects. "I don't want to feel like I hardly knew them."

We make a pact, Pete and I: We'll meet in a month and see how his "plan" is going.

When the month has passed I'm eager to see Pete. We meet as usual at a favorite restaurant. The waiter has hardly taken our order when I look at Pete expectantly.

"I'm working fifty-five hours a week!" Pete exclaims with a befuddled tone. "I can't understand it: I'm working more than before we spoke—I've started to book hours on Saturday."

He gives me a progress report, sounding like the commander of an army in full retreat: "Let's see, I took Fridays off and for several weeks that felt good, but then the kids seemed less interested in the plans I made. I'd tried to schedule things and wasn't sure what would interest them, and my wife had the time free anyway it turned out and also I got this flood of referrals and started scheduling them in."

With a sheepish look, Pete concludes: "Maybe I really am my father's son: I just feel more comfortable at the office."

Here's a man who wants to make major changes in his life in theory, but in practice he doesn't know what to do. He takes time off from work but then feels exposed and unsure of himself in the family. On the other hand, he opens his schedule to make time for his kids on Friday mornings, but then he doesn't know what to do without the familiar load of work appointments; it's as if he feels stripped of his accoutrements of masculinity. He feels inadequate without the props of male power and prestige—the commute to the office, the patients waiting for him, the secretary.

Pete's attempts to stay home on a workday left him emotionally flooded with conflicting feelings of curiosity, joy, relief, fear, and shame, as well as competitiveness and anger when he feels he's not living up. A father sitting on the floor surrounded by children's toys and asked to "play baby" for the four thousandth time often thinks: *I'll just sneak off to the other room to return a few phone calls.* When he takes time to play Legos or go to the playground with his child, what father doesn't also think about the work he could be doing—the work his colleagues *are* doing—on that article, assignment, sale, whatever?

Spending Friday morning at home may even have stimulated Pete's memories of his own father's absence from his childhood. He's not sure what a father is supposed to do with his kids, and perhaps his wife or the baby-sitter can do it all just as well. It's difficult for Pete to access his yearnings for his father or his own enjoyment at being a kid because these are so tied up with grief at his father's absence. So it's easy to feel like a third wheel as a father, rather than a vital and important part of that Friday morning with his children.

It would be nice if Pete could talk with his wife about the difficulty he feels getting into the family, the tenuousness he feels in relation to her. But he doesn't have words for that. Pete feels a strange emptiness when he stays home. Inside, he's thinking: *The more I'm with you and the kids the lonelier I feel.* But how can he say this to his wife?

Pete is also trapped by his wife's very success as a mother. "Joan is so good with the kids," he says apologetically, "it's not like I have any complaints."

He can't find a way in. And indeed his work is important to the family: He earns more than she does—so providing becomes the major contribution he makes. It's as if Pete agrees, albeit reluctantly, with Margaret Mead's opinion that "fathers are biological necessities and psychological redundancies."[1]

Feeling exposed, inadequate, and emotionally flooded, Pete withdraws, gratefully, to the refuge of his office. Feeling more comfortable being in charge and knowing familiar answers, he goes back to being a doc on Friday mornings. He returns to a familiar way of connecting with his family—as the breadwinner and provider who shows his love for his family by how much he achieves at work. In doing so, he distances himself from those disavowed parts of himself—the little boy who wanted his father's presence more, the father who wants to take some risks to be more available to his children, the husband who wants to feel more available for and equal to his wife at home.

NEW MAPS FOR OLD ONES

Walking back from lunch with Pete I was reminded of the words of a man in a workshop. He had come to a weekend retreat on "Men and Intimacy" because he felt pained and upset despite his busy career and family life. I knew he must have problems as a father and husband that had led him to give up a weekend and pay the money to attend the workshop, but he wouldn't say much about himself aside from the outer events in his life and his career.

At one point, in desperation, I said, "I wonder if it's easier for you to talk about other people than about yourself."

"You mean like my feelings?" he asked. "For that I need a map, I don't have one."

"What kind of map?"

A tone of pessimism entered: "I'm not sure any map would help."

Then he started telling me about the movie *Platoon*, and a scene in which a boobytrapped map case blew up the poor soldier who was trying to open it.

He wasn't just being a movie critic. He was worried about what might explode in him were he to look at his feelings. This man was giving voice to the anger and exasperation that might ambush him if he were to open up. He worried about turning others in the group off if he attacked them, or about being humiliated by being asked to leave. Some men fear being swallowed up by their grief, others by their neediness, others by their ignorance or innocence.

In a deeper way, though, we all have faulty maps, maps that ambush us or lead us astray. We learn to think of work and the public world as the biggest challenges in our life, but we learn less well how to operate in the family and with those we love; we learn how to fight and defend ourselves when hurt but not how to draw others closer when we're in need of them; we learn how to protect and defend, but not what we have to offer in the world of emotions—how we're important as husbands, fathers, sons, and friends; we learn about the heroism of male achievement and authority, but not about the heroism of male vulnerability and uncertainty, and how to live without having all the answers.

Pressure Points. This chapter draws a map of relationship pressure points in men's lives—a map that I hope will be more accurate and detailed than the family maps so many of us carry around. Pressure points are normal, common points of transition and change in relationships—marriage, parenthood, career—that create internal struggles around intimacy and identity for men.

Most of the crises we struggle with as adults are not simply about which career to pick or whether to hold on to or let go of our work, or to stay married or not; they're not simply about money or a "mid-life crisis"; they're about deeper love and attachment dilemmas that often seem insoluble.

Seemingly intractable dilemmas of love often get woven into our careers, and it can be difficult for a man to feel fully satisfied at work until he comes to terms with the disappointments and failures he experienced growing up. So the pressure point I'm going to start with is that of work. As we grow and mature we encounter a widening set of pressure points: marriage, starting a family, being a father, and the aging and death of our parents. At each of these points we struggle with hope, love, anger, shame, and sorrow. Each pressure point along the map of manhood is shaped by the heroism of our attempts to live up to our responsibilities as protectors and defenders, a heroism that also envelops failure: the sacrifice and distortion of our wishes for connection.

The accuracy and detail of any map depend on the skill of the mapmaker. This is not a comprehensive survey, but rather an attempt to describe some key points that have helped me clarify issues in my work and my life. Our understanding of these points will shape the flow of the chapters that follow.

WORK AND LOVE: PROMOTIONS, DISAPPOINTMENTS, AND SECRET OBLIGATIONS

Career shifts and decisions are often times of hidden struggles with love and shame for men. For many men, career is the major source of masculine identity, and the man who questions his career commitment—or loses his job or is not promoted often—feels considerable fear and shame at the threat to his masculinity.

Beyond this, though, promotions and demotions at work often become pressure points around love. Promotions are right up there with getting fired in the list of major life stressors.[2]

Searching for Father at Work. Consider Tony, whom we met in the last chapter. At the age of seventeen, Tony had wrestled his dying father to the ground in a last desperate attempt to wring a sense of manhood from a father who seemed to be wasting away and who would ultimately leave Tony powerfully tied to his mother. Through his twenties Tony tried to find a father to replace the one he had lost, a father who would provide him with a sense of being a worthwhile man. Often he looked to bosses for this gift.

When I met Tony, he was thirty-eight and had become a financial planner in a large accounting firm in Seattle. Intelligent and studious, tall and athletic, Tony looked like a football linebacker; he struck me in both his looks and accomplishments as the sort of son a father might be proud of. But Tony didn't know that, and certainly didn't feel as if he were a man worthy of other people's regard and confidence.

Tony did tax and investment analyses, working in "the back room" doing research and computer support work for the firm's partners, who actually met with the clients. Tony worked hard and wanted to become a partner himself. After several years, he was in a position to become an associate in the firm. However, the boss wanted more than just a subordinate; he wanted to know that Tony could handle himself in the competitive world of bringing new accounts to the firm. For Tony, this business demand touched on powerful issues of manhood and shame.

The firm developed a plan for Tony to make a series of presentations about its services to large banks, hospitals, and other institutions. Tony procrastinated, never feeling ready. Much of his lack of confidence stemmed from his low assessment of his competence as a man. As he put it, "I don't want to go out there to a roomful of people and have to sell myself, or the firm." Every time he considered the prospect, he was flooded by a sense of inadequacy, some of which was rooted directly in the feeling that he had never really connected with his father.

The more exposed and inadequate he felt, the angrier Tony got at his boss. "Why doesn't he show me how to do it?" Tony asked at one point, giving voice to his secret wish: *Teach me how to feel manly.*

Tony didn't say this to his boss, however. Instead, he became more and more "chippy" with him, using his anger to cover up a painful sense of being scared to go out and sell himself.

Tensions rose between him and his boss. Tony didn't know how to defuse his anger, and he kept his fears to himself, because they seemed like proof of his own inadequacy.

One morning soon after arriving at work, Tony walked down the hall for coffee and met his boss coming out of his own office.

"Tony, what's holding up the presentation at the Commercial National Bank?" the boss inquired.

Tony tensed and replied: "I haven't been able to get it organized."

The two men stared at each other. Tony was too proud and afraid to say what he felt: *Can we sit down and talk? I feel scared. I want some of your power and strength.*

The boss didn't pick up these vibes. Preoccupied with other matters, he snapped impatiently. "Well, why the hell don't you get it organized!"

Tony, feeling challenged and on the spot, handled himself as if he was on the street. "You want it organized, why don't you do it yourself?" he said, echoing the insolent tone he used with his father that fateful day at the dining table. Tony used the same provocative connective strategy at two pressure points in the life cycle—in his family at adolescence, and at work as an adult. And the underlying message was the same: *Help me. Why don't you do it so I can watch? Let me learn from you!*

The boss, standing in the middle of the corridor, the rest of his staff looking on, watching this confrontation with an insolent subordinate, turned away without a word. And while Tony went to get his coffee, the boss went into the office of his VP for personnel and told him to terminate Tony's employment at the end of the week. Tony did not even get the usual two weeks' termination pay.

Tony was shocked: "I expected a gunfight and he told me instead to get out of town in one hour."

Instead of provoking a gunfight, Tony shot himself in the foot. In trying to get his boss to act like a father, Tony used a similar dynamic—provocation—and it backfired. He was envious of his boss, he wanted his strength, but he also wanted his boss to be like a good daddy who would teach him what he needed to know because inside he didn't feel like he really had the right stuff. So he was angry at his boss but also needy of him, in the same way that he was needy of and angry at his father.

Provocative anger covered the shameful feelings of need, of wanting to know more about what it means to be a man, of wanting a powerful father to teach and protect him, of carrying around the sorrow at all that he lost with his father. The cocky pose left him feeling safe from the worst fate: being unmasked and exposed as a mama's boy.

"If only men would learn to talk about their anger, not act it out," lamented a colleague of mine. "Men do have it tough—we are ripped off a lot emotionally, starting at an early age. Things would go a lot better if men talked about their need, instead of getting angry and alienating everyone."

What my friend forgets is that many of us, like Tony, don't have a language for talking about the shame, anger, and sorrow we feel. Tony hasn't had much opportunity to name and label what he's feeling, so as to make it more coherent and manageable. He hasn't been able to talk much about his loss of his father, the antagonism and love between them, the aching emptiness inside.

Naming and labeling feelings—giving them words—gives us a sense of internal coherence, instead of a vague inner sense of threat, of being unmasked and feeling inadequate.

Like a lot of men, Tony used provocative anger to cover his shameful feelings and to connect. Asking for help from his boss was like asking for help from his father: Tony wanted to get close but not at the cost of his self-esteem. The boss, not being his "ideal" father, responded to the put-down, not to the need, and he fired Tony. And Tony was shocked and further shamed because he had expected his boss to come through for him.

Listening to Tony talk, hearing the shame around his father's death, the fear that he's not really a man, and the speed with which his neediness turned to anger, I felt that what Tony needed was the opportunity to talk with other men about how difficult the father-son and mother-son relationships are. He needed to feel more accepted by men he respects and less isolated with his private story of failure and humiliation.

But Tony's maps of manhood right now don't permit that. He has learned to isolate himself when vulnerable, to get angry when needy, and to see other men as threats who might leave him feeling less like a man, not as emotional resources to help him deal with his low self-esteem and feelings of incompetence.

Mentoring: Becoming a Father at Work. And what of his boss? Tony's boss is not literally his father, of course, but in some ways he is a "father": He is an admired man from whom Tony wishes to find the affirmation he didn't get when he was younger. The older generation pays a price for not being able to decode these urgent messages from the younger generation and not being able to respond even if they do "get" it. Tony is a different and demanding "son," yet by striking back and putting down Tony, by hearing the challenge but not the wish, his boss has lost an opportunity to nurture the young and feel cherished by them.

The mentor phase of a career is not so easy for many men. Becoming a mentor means trying to help the young consolidate their identities in the world of work, helping them make that big shift out of boyhood into manhood. Many potential mentors face the challenge of how to handle the combination of competitiveness and neediness that the younger generation presents to them at work. These emotional tasks are rarely attended to in our current talk about mentors as "role models." This more restricted definition of mentoring offers older men less opportunity to truly feel generative, to learn a language of cooperation and nurturing instead of just practicing top-down leadership.

Daniel Levinson, an astute observer of mentoring, points out that the mentor-protégé relationship is really a "love relationship." The mentor may feel cherished and valued in ways he was never able to allow at home, as a father, husband, or son. Often, mentoring is an opportunity for a man to feel like a "better" father than he was able to be in his own family, where the intensity of the father-child bond so often leads to alienation or disappointment. Similarly, the protégé may also feel "loved" in ways that he was not able to find with his own father or mother.[3]

The good-enough mentor needs to be able to encourage mastery of the roles and skills demanded at work while also providing care and reassurance that cherished parts of the protégé need not be sacrificed in order to succeed at work. True mentors allow their protégés to feel they are their own person while also allowing a healthy emotional dependence.

The melding of both mastery and care may be difficult for a male mentor or protégé. The protégé is dependent on his mentor for validation: He needs to feel that he can impress and rely on the mentor without losing his self-esteem as a man or exposing himself to harsh judgment for acknowledging his need for his mentor's help, advice, or protection. The mentor too is vulnerable. He wants to feel respected, that he has wisdom to offer the young, and that he can allow his protégé to do better than he did. The mentor may not understand or have experience with the importance of emotional support and validation for the young. He may not have received that sort of mentoring in his own life. He may not be ready for the normal emotional dependence he feels on his protégé. Both mentor and protégé may quickly become judgmental or demanding of the other, using provocative connections because they can't find ways of accessing the shared vulnerability and need they each feel in the relationship.

When both mentor and protégé are males, it can be very hard for them to let their relationship mature from a dependent relationship into one of equality without anger or betrayal or put-downs coming between them. Daniel Levinson and others have noted how often the mentor relationship ends in difficulty and accusation.[4] This often happens because neither mentor nor protégé knows how to answer a basic question, one that many men ask of their fathers: *Does my life have to be similar to yours for me to be okay? Can you love me if I'm different from you?*

Bob and Nate, protégé and mentor trying to transform their relationship at work, offer an example.

Do We Go to War? Bob is a principal in a venture capital firm in Denver reflecting on the changed relationship with his own mentor. At age forty-five Bob has gone from being the protégé of the president of the firm, functioning as his assistant, to working more autonomously within the company, directing the crucial research arm of the firm, and being responsible for selecting potential companies for investment.

Now Bob finds himself wanting something different from Nate, his mentor. In the past he wanted to please and accommodate his boss, but now he wants his respect and some acknowledgment of his own power, and of his life decisions. Bob has structured his life differently from his mentor, spending more time at home with his kids and trying to be a more involved father. His boss, who had created the firm on his own, used to routinely spend ten-hour days at the office.

Bob wonders if Nate really values his choices and so does Nate: Does his beloved "son" Bob honor his values? Can Nate depend on this "son" to do his duty in the firm that he himself has built with such effort?

Over breakfast one morning on the eve of the Gulf War in a Denver restaurant overlooking the Rockies, this tension erupted in a discussion about war.

"What do you think we ought to do about the Persian Gulf?" Bob asks his mentor, as the coffee arrives.

Nate doesn't hesitate:

"I think we ought to bomb the hell out of them!"

Bob is aghast. "I disagree! The use of such force might have serious unanticipated consequences."

Then the two of them are off and running, arguing about making "hard decisions," about courage and sacrifice, about "standing up for what you believe," and being "tough-minded" versus "soft." Underneath the political debate, the two men are talking about how these issues affect themselves and their working relationship.

Bob was aware of the undercurrent to their argument: "I kept wondering what Nate thought of me, am *I* weak, am *I* strong enough? You know, in the world of business there is always this concern about whether you can make the hard decisions. Can you push the button when necessary, fire people during a recession, give negative performance reviews when warranted? Particularly given that I tended to give some priority to my family, I wondered if Nate saw me as 'soft.' "

Bob gives voice to the hurt a young man feels when his respected mentor fails to validate his work and family choices.

What Bob can't say to Nate is: *I want you to respect the choices I've made even if they are different from yours. I want you to know that I love you even if I'm different from you.*

Both men are also struggling with a basic tension around autonomy and connectedness as their relationship changes. Bob has autonomy and dependency split in his mind, assuming that if he is independent of his boss he can't also depend on him. "Since I've taken over the research position, I've wanted Nate to see more autonomous parts of me," he explains, "and I fear being cut off from him—that I'll be isolated, that to assert my difference from him means that I'll be abandoned by him." Many sons didn't feel that their fathers treasured their potency and power, and thus it can be difficult for them to know that the mentor who is both "father" and "mother" to them in the workplace may cherish their growing skill and competency. One universal question of sons to fathers that echoes through our lives as men is: *Can I be both strong and needy of you at the same time?*

Nate too mixes up autonomy and rejection. He sees the differences between himself and his protégé as a type of rejection. Some mentors separated from their own fathers in anger and alienation and so they inevitably see the normal transformations of the mentor-protégé relationship as building up to a fight. Here again is the "wounded father" within us, carried from our own experiences as sons into the workplace.

This "war" has a happy ending, as both men work to defuse it. To Bob's surprise and delight, Nate begins their next breakfast together weeks later by telling Bob about a difficulty with his own grown son and asking Bob's advice about how to handle the situation. "You've been able to think more about these family matters than I have," Nate says, with those words affirming for Bob the integrity of the choices he has made. Bob understands then that Nate is not as single-minded as he appears. Bob realizes that he needs to acknowledge the fears and hopes that he brought to the mentoring relationship rather than just assume that any difficulties were Nate's problem alone.

I empathize with both the mentor and protégé. Certainly the shift to being an authority who can "mentor" the young in a university setting has felt like one of the biggest challenges in my career development. For twenty years or so after college it seems the biggest challenge was to "make it" in the world of work by *achieving*. Then in my forties individual success no longer seemed the only or most satisfying goal, and I made a conscious turn toward relationships offering more nurturing possibilities, such as mentoring younger students. That was fine as a general goal. But learning how to deal with younger colleagues' demands on my time, their fears of failure *and* of success, finding ways to reassure them without taking over, and setting limits while also allowing others to find their way has become a much more difficult task than writing grants, giving lectures, and writing books on my own.

When it's just a work goal involved, there are familiar strategies to use: set goals, prioritize work to be done, get a team together, find ways to control your anxieties about failure, and get the job done. But when a protégé or younger colleague turns to me for a more emotional kind of support, the situation is very different. Recently I got a phone call from an older graduate student named Jean whose dissertation I am directing. Jean's accomplishing a difficult feat—in her forties, with a family to take care of, she's close to getting her Ph.D. It's been a struggle, and over the years she has come to depend on me for support and reassurance as well as direction about analyzing data. Today she's upset over trying to write a chapter of her dissertation. Jean's adolescent daughter went out on a date the previous night and Jean stayed up till she got home early in the morning; now she's exhausted from little sleep and also worried about the pressure the university is giving her to finish the thesis if she wants to graduate on time. "I'm at my wit's end; I don't know how I'm going to get this dissertation done," she laments to me on the phone.

Often at these moments, I hurry to find a solution that *will get the person off the phone so I can get back to my own work.* Then I realize that they don't want just a quick-and-easy solution. *They want to talk*—to feel heard, to know if their anger or fear or sadness or shame is appropriate, to learn how to deal with what they're feeling. Rushing them off the phone or giving them some instrumental solution (for example, "move graph thirty-two to page twenty-seven, and reanalyze the data on page ninety-nine") doesn't deal with the emotional subtext, which may simply be: *I need some recognition from you, or reassurance, or validation.*

Often, though, attending to the emotional subtext leaves me with a tinge of fear. How do I avoid getting drawn in over my head? I wonder. I fear that I don't really know how to reassure somebody rather than just tell him or her what to do. Unpleasant questions surge forward in my mind: Is this really important? Where's the pay-off to me in this?

That morning I turn off my computer and listen to Jean, and we talk about her schedule and time involved and it becomes clear that she will very likely be able to complete the dissertation on time. *What she wants from me is reassurance, that's all—she wants me to tell her that she can do it and that I have faith in her.* As I listen, there's a part of me that feels shy about being there emotionally for her. Internally, a part of me turns away. The calming, soothing voice she wants feels too much like a mother's voice. It's a voice that I'm not used to using, maybe one that I often can't provide to myself. Or to my family. I'm aware, reluctantly, as we talk on the phone that the part of me that turns away from Jean also turns away when my kids need me emotionally to be there for them.

On the phone that day, I know Jean needs me to give her something she can really hold on to, and to do so I have to take a risk and become vulnerable. What I said sounds so simple in retrospect: "Jean, I've worked with you for years and you've always been able to get it done, as a mother and as a student. Today you're overwhelmed, tomorrow you'll feel better, after you get some sleep. *I know you can get this dissertation finished.*"

"Really?" Jean asks, now shy herself.

"Really," I repeat softly and honestly.

Months later, bunched in with my other faculty colleagues, I watched proudly from my seat on the podium as Jean came up, filled with pride herself, to accept her diploma. When Jean really did graduate, on time, as she hoped, in some part because I had been able to mentor her through graduate school and the difficulties of her dissertation, I experienced a different kind of reward at work. I tapped into the deeper satisfaction of discovering that I also had care and nurturing to offer those who needed me. This lesson was one I took back home, feeling bolstered in my confidence in my "fathering" ability. Perhaps fathers don't *always* have to absent themselves, just as workers don't always have to be high-achieving lone wolves.

I suspect men are constantly taking lessons back and forth between home and work about what it means to be a good-enough "father/mother" to our protégés and our families. The rewards are great at both home and work. Chapters 5 and 6 explore these issues more fully.

Money and Love. Money may be the major way a man measures his self-esteem and his worth to those he loves. My discussions with men leave me feeling that this is still true, even in a time of changing sex roles. Many husbands and fathers still measure their self-worth in terms of their contribution to family income. Many of us grew up with fathers who valued money a great deal, particularly if they came of age during the Depression. Other men are haunted by memories of fathers who were not able to provide adequately for their families, or fathers who were worried about this.

So, many of us experience shame about our manliness when we feel we're not earning enough money. And "enough" is a difficult concept. When your major contribution to the household is providing and protecting, then how much *is* enough? Many men struggle with an open-ended sense that they should earn *more*: provide for their children's college, their own and their wife's retirements, a bigger home or apartment.

Work is still the major measure of men's performance, and the most obvious index of career achievement is how much you earn. In the race to feel comfortable about yourself as a man, it's hard to "get past the money question," as one movie producer put it. Many working wives don't understand their husbands' shame at not earning enough money even when there is enough income between the two of them.

Harry, for example, is a building contractor who feels some embarrassment about depending on his wife's income. Harry often starts fights that originate in his wish that Alice worked harder and earned *more* money and his shame at wanting that. Sometimes the fights are rooted in Harry's blind fury that his work doesn't pay better even though he very much likes being involved in domestic matters. Harry's struggle with shame is intensified by the fact that his own father was inept with money, an embarrassing fact that was never openly discussed in the family.

For men, then, work is often the center of their experience, a kind of second "home" where reside many of the hopes and dreams about themselves. For Tony and his boss, as for Bob and Nate, work is a place to continue working on the father-son relationship and on their self-esteem as men. For other men, such as Harry, work is a way to express their love and commitment to their wives and children, and to feel okay about themselves as men. Work is often a place where a man feels most valued and important as a man. A man may feel rather naked and exposed without a firm commitment to work.

Many men who leave their current work to make career changes, voluntary or not, feel like orphans, with no place to go. Career counselors can make the mistake of overlooking the shame that men feel when they talk about changing careers. "No man leaves his work, even of his own free will, without some embarrassment; like maybe 'I couldn't hack it after all,' " suggested one man who had carried out several career changes in his life.

Work is a "pressure point" for men because it expresses our hopes and dreams about love, and becomes the place where we try to master or compensate for feelings of failure or disappointment as husbands, fathers, sons, siblings, or friends. At times that is very healthy and adaptive. However, we may also cut off opportunities for healing in relationships by taking our wounded hearts to work and trying to heal them there, in privacy and isolation. And we become more vulnerable to sorrow, failure, and shame by trying to find at work what we ought to be looking for in other parts of our lives.

Let's now look at those other parts of life—marriage, parenting, and other intimate moments in the adult life cycle—and explore both the pressures and opportunities men experience.

FATHERHOOD

For many of us, fatherhood is the opposite pole from work. Moving between these poles can create considerable tension, as well as huge rewards if we can figure out how to do it right.[5] Chapter 6 explores fatherhood in detail. This section introduces several pressure points around fatherhood, and the way we often play work and fatherhood off each other.

Becoming a father is a normal, chronic emergency. The birth of a child changes the way we see things. At age thirty-one, Archibald MacLeish, future Pulitzer Prize–winning poet and playwright, gave up a promising trial law practice to explore the life of a poet. He had become a father, and was driven by the wish to see things differently. "I must go about looking at things, laboring to see them," he wrote to a friend.[6]

This labor to see things differently leaves many men at a loss. Life tugs at us in a new way but we have no language for talking about it. When they have a child, many men yearn to become as warm and nurturing as their mothers, or they feel they don't want to repeat the patterns of their own fathers, much as they loved them. So what do we do? With no language to respond to these new experiences, we often throw ourselves into working harder.

Other men want to have more involvement in their families, yet they are held back by internalized images of masculinity that emphasize a traditional male stance toward women and children. Some men feel considerable embarrassment and confusion at their own wishes to become more emotionally responsible; we lack clear images of the emotional contributions we can make to relationships as caretakers, not just as protectors and defenders. Often fathers don't know how to deal with the interlocked feelings of being displaced by the child and head over heels in love with him or her.

In the weeks before the birth of his first daughter, Tom, a thirty-eight-year-old taxi driver, found himself preoccupied with a key detail of his own past: whether his father was present at his birth. Tom knew his father as a rather aloof, preoccupied man, and echoed in the memory of his father was his own conflict about what kind of father he himself would be. "My father loved his cars; he had an antique car collection, and spent more time in the garage than he did in the house," Tom recalled. The subtext: *My father loved objects more than people; a man's place is in the garage, not the nursery.* After several months of agonizing about it, Tom finally asked his father whether he had been present at his birth. The answer disappointed: "No."

After the baby was born, Tom found himself stuck on the horns of a dilemma: He felt both tenderness and anger toward the baby. This mix of positive and negative emotions may come as a surprise to both men and their wives. *Like Tom, many men fear becoming like the isolated father they knew, without knowing how to be the tender father they yearned for themselves.* Silence and withdrawal from the family or angry arguments after the birth of a child may be signs of a man's struggle with shame.

"My father gave me a real gift!" exclaimed Tom one day. "He said to me, 'Times have changed so much since you were young. I worked the day you were born, but you have a chance to do it differently, and you're lucky—I envy you.' " This comment from his father gave Tom permission to feel more present emotionally. It freed him to draw on experiences he had as a teenager taking care of his older sister's children.

Wives may not be attentive to how inadequate a husband feels during the transition to fatherhood. After the delivery, one husband was fiddling with the diapers of his newborn when his wife lost her patience and reached for the infant, saying that she'd diaper the baby herself. A nurse standing in the room cautioned the new mother: "Give him time, let him learn. Consider yourself lucky—not all husbands are so willing to take responsibility for the baby."

Men often talk of their businesses as "my baby" and yet lack the ability to give voice to the creative and nurturing wishes that fatherhood evokes. *We have little vocabulary for describing the profound importance of fathers in lives of sons and daughters.*

Many men have only a dim awareness that their presence as fathers is important. Yet at each stage of a child's development— infancy, toddlerhood, school, adolescence, young adulthood, and beyond—fathers have vital contributions to make in the lives of their children.[7]

The adolescence and "launching" of children is another pressure point for men. Often fathers of teenagers don't know how to get out of the authority role that they and their family have cast them into, and with great pain they find themselves increasingly alienated from the very children whom they yearn to hold on to a little longer. At one workshop, a colonel in the armed forces talked about his struggles with his sixteen-year-old daughter: "She wants to travel across the country this summer with her boyfriend, and I don't know, that seems too much for her. But the more I put my foot down, the more she seems determined to defy me."

"Why stop her?" asked another man in the group.

"Well, I'm worried about how she'll handle things—it seems overwhelming. What will she do for money, what if she and her boyfriend break up, what about her safety?"

"Well, have you asked her that?"

The colonel looked astonished. "You mean have a dialogue with her?"

"Ask her about her plans, how she'd deal with these unexpected possibilities or unavoidable realities."

The colonel was so dumbfounded at this notion of talking openly with his daughter that he had to ask for reassurance. "You mean it's okay to ask her an open-ended question?"

His puzzlement felt palpable to me since I too struggle as a father with the question of where the boundaries of my authority lie, how open to be, how much leeway to allow my children, and how much restraint and containment to impose. Few fathers don't yearn for a richer, fuller relationship with their growing children; too many fathers feel stuck in an angry or forbidding authority position.

Many of us carry around a regret at not having known our children well enough, of having worked so hard while they were growing up, of never really having seen them for who they are. "There's a fundamental asymmetry in life," mused one father of teenagers. "When your kids are young, they want their daddies around and we are out working, thinking our kids will be around all our lives; as our kids grow up, fathers want to slow things down and spend time together, and the kids want to be up and away, fly the coop, thinking their parents will be around forever."

We speak of that late teenage process of separation as the "launching" of children, as if they were missiles. Yet often our hearts fly after our children, and this can be a time of silent grief and loss for fathers, embarrassing to them and unrecognized by the family.

What father, as his children gradually leave home, is not painfully aware of how fast they have grown up? As former U.S. senator Paul Tsongas once said, "No man on his deathbed ever lamented that he spent too much time with his family."[8] A man may feel shamefully aware of how little he invested in his family and how much he invested in work and wonder if the investment has been the right one. But it may be harder for a man to shift the balance of his emotional portfolio than his financial one.

Even when his investment in the home has been profound and strong, a father may struggle with the speed and intensity with which children separate. "No man ever had enough of children's gratitude or a wife's affection," one man said to me, quoting Yeats. The deeper, more painful feeling underlying this thought may be a father sense: *They matter so much to me, and I seem to matter so little to them.*

Often a father and child get stuck in a language of anger and disconnection, unable to find ways to connect as their relationship changes.[9]

One adolescent son left his father with the bitter words: "I'm glad to be leaving this fucking house. The only regret I have is I'm leaving these poor helpless children in your care." As the father and son fought and yelled, these words allowed them to verbalize what they hadn't been able to say before—how helpless both of them felt: the helplessness of the father to give his blessing to the child as he leaves; the bitterness between them; and the father's inability to get a blessing from his child, a blessing that would heal the wounds of the past. And don't forget the helplessness of the son: to get his father's blessing, to feel like a real man as he leaves, and to know that the sins of the past are forgiven.

Often the anger and hostility between father and adolescent child mask a fragile and delicate search for forgiveness and connection that neither party seems able to complete.

MARRIAGES AT MID-LIFE

There is often a larger *rearrangement of the family at mid-life* going on as kids grow up, creating another pressure point for men. This is particularly true for men in traditional marriages. The family itself is changing, as the wife goes back to work or starts to work now that the kids are older. The husband, whose intimacy needs were disguised by his role as the provider and protector, may be left shamefully aware of the loss of the family that he knew.

It can be very difficult for a man to talk about his interdependency with his wife as she becomes more autonomous. After years of seeming independent he suddenly is confronted by basic sorrow, resentment, love, and hope that he may have difficulty labeling, much less understanding. When a wife goes to work the husband may wonder if he's still important to her, whether he has anything to contribute to her, whether she still finds him interesting. The painful insecurities men experienced as gangly adolescents may resurface: *Do I have what it takes to hold the interest of a woman?* Once again, as when men's provider role is threatened, or when they try to become more active fathers, men are confronted with worries about how the women they love will react to them. A man may feel he's becoming a little boy again, wonder how much of this his wife can stand, and get very quiet or resentful. Some men become overdriven at work or drawn to affairs and other relationships outside the family as a way of sealing off the inadequacy they feel. In charming or seducing a woman other than our wife, we may restore our own sense of potency. In her arms we may feel the sense of warmth we have lost in the marriage, and the romance of an affair can make us feel truly needed and desired by another person. The adoring eyes of a lover affirm that *yes, we really do have value; there is someone who finds us worthwhile.*

When I first spoke with him, Tom was a thirty-eight-year-old lawyer, articulate and engaging, who had just done a remarkable thing: He had supported his wife's going back to graduate school, spent a lot of time at home taking care of the kids, and also become quite successful and prominent at work. Yet he also spoke of the "neglect" and the "minor depression" he felt since his wife went back to school and was too busy to be available in the ways she once was. Struggling to describe the experience of a changing family, he said: "It's kind of like the Budweiser rings. They have an image of integration and connectedness and it was like I was the center ring, holding it all together. Now it's as if all the rings are flying apart."

The mood of neglect and sorrow took Tom back to an early loss: the unexpected death of his mother when he was eight years old. His wish to hold on tightly to his wife reflected the hope of never having to endure that loss and separation again. Listening to Tom I was reminded of psychologist George Goethal's point that the separations and transitions of life are often more difficult for males than females.[10]

Such vulnerability felt shamefully unmanly to Tom, and he entered into an affair as a way of dealing with the fears raised by the increasing autonomy of his wife.

Yet Tom knew that much of the struggle lay within himself and his own vulnerabilities. When I reinterviewed him ten years later, the affair was over and he and his wife were still together. She had become a successful administrator of a public health agency. He revealed: "It is hard to talk about but the wish is still to cling to mommy."

There is an acceptance and coming to terms with loss in Tom's words. In the years since I had first seen him, Tom had gone into therapy, as well as found some close male friends. In therapy Tom talked about the death of his mother, the autonomy of his wife, and the growing independence of his teenage children. He and his friends swapped stories about how their families were changing and about the stress on them as well as their wives. "We all agreed that the traditional bargain we expected when we married—that the husband will protect and defend while the wife provides comfort and support—now seemed null and void," Tom told me with humor.

Through therapy and talking with his friends, Tom began to recognize his loneliness, to see that he felt lonely when his wife wasn't there for him and that loneliness could be tolerated and mastered. Tom also came to understand that the increasing independence of his family was different from the feeling of abandonment he had experienced after his mother's death.

Tom and his wife have worked hard to preserve the marriage, demonstrating that struggle is often healthier in a relationship than too much tranquility. Tom became more open with his wife, revealing his vulnerability when she seemed so preoccupied with her work. "I would tell her that I need time with her," he said. "We'd make time together." They also learned to fight together verbally, expressing directly the frustration and impatience each felt at the common difficulties of a two-career family at mid-life. Tom at age forty-eight is really coming to terms with separation and loss for the first time. When he tells his wife directly about his difficulties in coming home to an empty house, when he asks for more of her time, when he realizes that *she is still there for him even when she is more autonomous, when he finds that his children go off to college and still need and love him even as they become more autonomous,* Tom is learning that separations can be endured, that he will not be swamped by the loneliness he has hidden from all these years, and that he has continuing worth and meaning to his family even though he is no longer their sole protector and defender.

For a man in Tom's position, one of the most important things is feeling heard. Of course it's hard to feel heard if you're not talking. Men will speak of the house feeling "colder" since their wives went to work, and to compensate they'll start on some household or business project, searching for an action strategy to fill in the emptiness or need they feel. But the action may only remove them one step further from being able to express the nagging loneliness they feel.

As Tom's story reminds us, naming your loneliness and vulnerability is the first step in coming to terms with it and in finding new ways to connect with our families. For many men, the pressure point at mid-life lies in the challenge of finding a new kind of intimacy with those we love—and with ourselves. We shift from the protector/provider role as husband and father to a position of greater vulnerability, but also potentially much richer intimacy with our families.

INFERTILITY AND REPRODUCTIVE DIFFICULTIES

Inability to conceive, miscarriage, abortion, stillbirths, and other reproductive difficulties are experiences that often have a profound impact on men. As medical technology increases the options available to parents, more and more men find themselves strangers in the strange new world of reproductive and childhood medicine. And yet these men and those who depend on them and want to help them often have little understanding of what they are going through. Of-

ten the attention shifts to the woman and the man is left in the role
of protector/defender.

The husband struggles with loneliness, loss, anger, shame, embarrassment, and hope while also trying to "protect" his wife. Infertility problems plunge the husband as well as the wife into the abyss
of broken hopes and dreams. He may wonder if his wife will ever be
able to get pregnant. He may wonder who's "to blame," himself or
his wife? That's a no-win question. If it's "your problem" (for example, you have a low sperm count), then there's your own shame
at being "defective," as one man put it. If it's "her problem" (for
example, she has endometriosis or other difficulties with conception),
then the already vulnerable woman feels even worse about herself—
and the blame she heaps on herself leaves the husband feeling worse
about himself.

A man may wonder what "rights" he has during these experiences, particularly given the legitimate attention directed to his wife.
He may wonder what to do with his rage and shame, and may feel
that his emotions are inappropriate since his wife is already vulnerable. Often men withdraw and become silent during these times.

The husband may feel the loneliness that comes from encountering a new, unexpected problem such as infertility. He may have
few friends to turn to, or he may not know how to get help or support
since infertility is not a "manly" topic for discussion. Many men I've
talked to have wanted the reassurance of their fathers during infertility experiences. They'll express a wish to go and talk to their
fathers, but few men actually do that. Other men wonder if their
fathers still love them, given that they are "failing" at the manly
task of producing progeny.

The three miscarriages that my wife and I struggled with plunged
me into a feminine world of reproduction and also mocked the or-
dered, high-priority work world that I was supposed to function
within. As we tried to conceive over a period of several years, we
seemed to live increasingly in the obstetrics-gynecology service,
where female nurses and my wife talked with familiarity about a
subject that always seemed mysterious to me: the female reproductive
system. I learned about ovulation, the cervix, secrets of the uterus.
Often I'd look for a man to talk to who could legitimate the vulnerability I felt and who could understand my fear of not having a child,
my rage, and my feelings of loss as well as hope. The men I encountered most were doctors, who were experts at those most manly tasks:
being in control, answering questions, and providing techniques and
prescriptions to solve problems. The distance between their self-

composure and my desperate swing of feelings was often a source of shame for me.

This was a new kind of vulnerability for me, one that I couldn't control by *working harder or doing better*. Even as I threw myself into my work for distraction and relief, my swampy mix of shame, loss, fear, and hope bogged down my efforts to get back to "manly" tasks.

The husband may also be trying to deal with and manage his wife's rage, loss, loneliness, and *her* inability to talk about her feelings. A woman experiencing reproductive difficulties may turn against her own body and lose interest in the sexual relationship with her husband. The husband may take his wife's preoccupation and sexual withdrawal very personally, as sign of his failure. For a man, sex is such a crucial way of getting warmth and feeling intimate, and is so tied to his sense of manhood, that being unable to get close to his wife sexually may strike a profound blow to his self-esteem. Thad, for example, was quite supportive of his wife, Jill, around the time she needed surgery to correct a problem with ovulation. Both Thad and Jill hoped that the surgery would enable her to conceive. Thad worried about his wife's surgery and talked poignantly about how much his hopes for a child rested with the procedure. "It would be easier if I was the one being operated on. I hate seeing Jill go through all this pain." The couple could not have intercourse for several weeks after the surgery, and Thad felt considerable frustration and impatience at the absence of sex.

In my office one day several weeks after the successful operation, Thad, exasperated, exclaimed: "There's no sex in our relationship and it's getting to me!" He described a fight between them the night before. He had hoped to interest his wife romantically and she felt he was being insensitive. The supportive husband had become the demanding one. What became clear was that intercourse was the only avenue for him to get *close* to Jill and to feel some tenderness and warmth amid the loneliness of the experience.

Another man came into my office very relieved after making love with his wife the night before. This was the first time in weeks they had sex, after a diagnostic procedure for infertility. "It feels so great to get my penis back!" he exclaimed. He meant that it felt so good to feel *manly* again—not to feel emasculated, as he had during all those weeks, when his penis was useless and irrelevant, with no power or magic to it.

In addition to all this, there is the real or potential loss of a child that we may have difficulty acknowledging. We may be very much adrift in a sea of loss and love and vulnerability that feels foreign to us, yet undeniably real.

Bill Pauly's poem "Heart/Song for Christopher Raymond" captures the way fathers may be tethered to an imagined child, real though never met, who has been lost through miscarriage or stillbirth:

> Zero night
> for leaving,
> son, mariner
> on wish-
> bone chip
> of moon
> sailing home.
> Christopher,
> be well compassing
> oceandark
> your birth day hymn,
> starstorm
> in the eye.
> We sail, too
> Still. Born.[11]

In his novella *Swimmer in a Secret Sea*, William Kotzwinkle gives voice to a similar pain. This lovely story focuses on a pregnant couple who live in the backwoods during winter, the husband fretting endlessly over making sure he and his wife can get to the hospital, making careful advance provisions about starting the car engine, getting through snow drifts, and making sure he has covered all his bases as a loving husband and father-to-be. All goes without a hitch, only to have the baby stillborn at the hospital. The book begins with the protector husband, ends with a grieving father burying the body of his child and saying good-bye to his swimmer in a secret sea, the baby, now dead, who had been alive within the mother.

What is the secret sea; who is "Still. Born"? Don't we too take part in this experience as men? How do you grieve and grow through these times, acknowledge and speak of loss and love, left unspoken by generations of men? How do you connect with other men, master the anger and shame and sorrow?

Todd and his wife, Mary, both in their mid-thirties, have had an abortion and now Todd is putting in very long hours at the computer firm he works for. Mary, though reluctant, had wanted the abortion. Todd was more uncertain: "I've always wanted to become a father," he reflected to me one day, "but I didn't make a big fuss about it— I kind of let her decide." Yet he also recognized that he allowed the abortion to happen. Three years later, Todd has still not come to terms with the sense of loss he felt, and the "unmanly" feeling of having terminated a pregnancy.

"I think a lot about the baby," he says sadly, "but I don't know what to feel." Then he speaks of wanting to "bury" his feelings, and gets angry when I wonder about whether he imagines the fetus "buried."

Often the husband is the swimmer in a secret sea, his pain and loss opaque to himself and others. Beneath Todd's stoicism runs anger and despair at his sense of inadequacy: Real men are supposed to protect and defend women and children, and here "he" terminated the pregnancy. He's not sure what his "rights" are here at all—what he's entitled to feel, whether he's entitled to share in an experience that "belongs" to his wife. "After all, it's her body—she had the right to do what she wanted," he says defensively. Once again the language of rights and responsibilities protects a man from loss and shame.

When there are fertility problems or we have children with medical problems, it is tempting to withdraw into some part of life where we have control—our work, hobbies, other relationships—because the painful mix of grief, anger, and love we feel is too much out of control.[12]

THE AGING AND DEATH OF PARENTS

The *search for reconciliation and healing* in the parent-son relationship is often a crucial adult pressure point for men. Despite the fact that many of us thought that we became adults when we got our college diplomas, or started working, it's becoming clear that the process of separating from parents extends far into adulthood. The centripetal pressures driving the adolescent and young adult out of his family subside at mid-life and beyond to a search for reconciliation. Daniel Levinson, author of *Seasons of Man's Life*, believes that for most of us, real forgiveness and reconciliation is not possible until our forties.

Many men become the financial adviser for their elderly parents, or take care of instrumental issues like helping parents move to a retirement community. These practical concerns keep them from addressing the yearnings for greater emotional closeness, or from finding some forgiveness for the difficulties of the past.

It is this same need to be instrumental that we men have, and that our loved ones depend on us for, that leads many men into a peripheral position emotionally as fathers, husbands, and mentors at work, as well as with aging parents. The wife may become the social ambassador within the family, leaving the husband to struggle to find some deeper connection with his mother and father.

Many men want to be successes at work for their parents; they want to show their love for their mothers and fathers by constructing a big empire out of money, feeling like a big honcho, and yet they remain unable to display their love openly. "My father grew up during the Depression and became successful," reveals Bill, a counselor at mid-live. "He would come home when I was a kid and pull out hundred-dollar bills and wave them in front of me and say, 'Someday you'll know what this means.' " Bill doesn't make a lot of money and he is careful how he spends it. But he makes an exception of one item: a Mercedes 280 SL that sits in the driveway, looking somewhat out of place next to his more modest home. Bill knows why he has bought such a car: He derives a major source of satisfaction from the pleased expression on his father's face when he drives home for a visit. "Maybe some of it is competition, to show him that I own something fancy. But more of it is just that I want him to see that I'm his son, that I understand what those hundred-dollar bills meant."

What is harder to express is the *wish to give something back to our fathers.* In the display of the car, Bill is trying to give his father a gift, to tell him how much he loves him and appreciates the sacrifices he made. The grown son needs a way to express his love to his parents in order to identify the loving part of himself. Bill is really asking whether *it's okay to feel loving toward his father.* He can't express this directly so he buys a car that might please his father. And, too, the son wants to know that he is beloved of his father.

Bill is unable to really speak of love with his father, so he buys a fancy car as a symbol, with the hope of pleasing his father. Yet in buying a car that is out of character for him, he's not really true to himself. He distorts himself and gives a mixed message, looking like just a competitive show-off while actually trying to elicit a smile of love on his father's face.

The Lifelong Father-Son Dance. Fantasies about climactic "reconciliations" between fathers and grown sons may be misleading and miss the point. *Through our adult lives we often try to return to*

*father, literally and symbolically, for reassurance, support, and emotional
sustenance.*

A more relevant model here is the dance of separation-
connection that children do with mothers. The little boy or girl
leaves mother's lap to explore the world and then returns for "re-
charging." This process of swinging between separating and connecting is true of the adult as well. A similar, though hidden, process
takes place between grown men and their fathers at times of transition and change or emotional stress. Divorce, infertility, becoming
a father, the changing family, work successes and disappointments—
all of these milestones make men want to get reassurance from father
that they are doing okay, that they are "real men," that they are
still beloved sons.

Mothers and Fathers and Grown Sons: Gifts of Love. Grown
sons are often looking for a way to "recharge" with their mothers,
to give and receive love from them. Mothers can be more difficult
for men to deal with than fathers.

My father, at age seventy-seven, recently had major surgery for
an abdominal aneurysm, a stretching of the wall of a major artery.
"It's lucky we caught this in his yearly examination," the doctor
explained, his voice turning ominous. "If the artery wall should rup-
ture, there's nothing we could do."

It was the first time my father, in my memory, had ever been ill.
He seemed both befuddled and humbled by the reality of surgery and
the long process of recovery. I made time to be there for my parents
when he came out of surgery, and was shocked at seeing my father
barely conscious, sedated, with tubes attached to seemingly every
orifice. He looked up from the stretcher and smiled when he saw my
face, grasping my hand weakly. Weakly he spoke my name, then
reassured me: "Don't worry, I'm not going to die." He looked as if
he had been beaten up, and I remember thinking, *This is not how my
father is supposed to look.*

Over the weeks, spending time together in the hospital allowed
us both to see each other in a new light. I knew better than he how
to talk to doctors, and I took some responsibility for finding out
about his medical care, and provided reassurance and support. During one of my visits the doctor hurriedly swooped in to check on his
patient. He needed to examine my father's abdomen. Efficient yet
not unfriendly, the doctor carefully lifted aside my father's hospital
gown as we talked. The incision stretched from his waist to the top
of his chest. A neat row of thick dots on each side marked where

the stitches had been. "Geez, Dad!" I exclaimed, shocked by the concrete evidence of the surgery. As the doctor poked and examined the incision, my father turned to me. He was having some trouble talking because he had strained his jaw muscles tensing from the pain during one of the postoperative procedures. So he strained to speak to me.

"I didn't want you to see my scar," my father explained shyly.

"Why?" I wondered.

"Because you'll always be my little boy," he replied, taking my hand.

As I took my father's hand, I reassured him from the heart: "That's right, Dad, I'll always be your little boy." Yet I also knew that something had changed between us. In seeing my father's scar, I was no longer just his little boy—I was also a grown man. I was seeing his deepest scars, his helplessness, his dependency and fear, his need for me. With his openness he was allowing me to take care of him, even as he struggled still to protect and take care of me. I was grateful to him for these gifts.

All through my father's tribulations, my mother took care of him too. She, more than I, kept watch on the doctors, protecting her husband, and kept us all informed. When he struggled at home with a postoperative infection that the doctors had overlooked, my mother helped my father into a cab, supported him when he fainted on the way, and got him back to the hospital. When I returned from their home in New York City to my home in Boston, it was daily phone calls to and from her that connected us all, and that relieved some of my anxiety at being so far away. As always, she seemed the one who held the family together. Her steadiness truly recharged us all.

During that time I wanted to scoop her up, to support her, to talk of my love for and need of her. But that seemed much more difficult than getting close to my father, since it was fraught with the tensions of the mother-son relationship and with my fear of truly turning into a little boy. After one of the long Boston–New York phone calls, I finally was able to say to her, "I love you." She said the same, and we began speaking openly of love for each other. That felt like a true gift to me. I thought about the many men who do not get or give such gifts from their mothers, and about how much a man can suffer without some direct sign of love to and from *both parents* as he ages.

How Much Is It Worth? Small amounts of connection or words of encouragement from a father to a son can help restore flagging

spirits or relieve a sense of despair and loneliness. Yet often it remains difficult for fathers and sons to get closer because they lack
the words or resort to fighting. Here's an example.

As I was taking an elevator down to the ground floor after a TV
interview in California, a burly cameraman named Ted once played
Top Secret with me without the cards.

"I haven't seen my father in over two years. Things have never
been great between us," Ted confessed earnestly as we faced each
other alone in the elevator. Ted told me how he had left Brooklyn
for Los Angeles, in search of work in film. He was the first member
of his family to leave the cozy enclave of the family in New York
City. His father had taken the move hard, not really wanting his son
to go even as he was proud of the courage his son displayed in striking off on his own. The father had never been able to do that in his
own life. Two years later Ted was working in TV, proud of his accomplishments, but also wanting to see his father's pleasure in his
achievements, wanting to know that it was okay with his father that
he had been able to make a new life for himself in California. He
wanted his independence, but he also wanted to be able to return
home.

"He's seventy years old," Ted told me, "and next month the
whole family is getting together in New York on his birthday for a
celebration."

He paused, then asked simply: "Do you think I ought to fly back
for it?" The only noise was the hum of the elevator as it descended:
fifteenth floor, fourteenth, thirteenth.

"What do you want to do?" I inquired.

"I want to go, but do you think he wants me to?" The bell
indicated that we had passed the third floor.

"I'll bet he does, even if he can't say it," I ventured.

"You mean it's worth the air fare?" he asked, as the doors opened
on the lobby. He thanked me intently, and we parted.

Who's worth the air fare: himself or his father? What first struck
me about Ted's story was that Ted himself lacked a sense that his
presence was important. He was ashamed of the yearning to be valued by his father and asking about whether he should go to the
birthday left him feeling embarrassed.

Then I realized too that Ted was asking how much the visit
would cost him emotionally: Will he go all the way there and feel
rejected again by his father? A bad investment. Equally "unprofit-
able" would be to go and feel like *he* rejected his father by spending

the time in silence or false good cheer in order to cover the loneliness and alienation he feels.

At the deepest level, Ted was asking: *Is it worth trying to work things out with my father? How do I do it? If I go to New York and see my father, what do I do then? How do I make things better after just showing up? I don't want to feel a painful failure when I return from this visit to him.*

Ted ultimately did go to his father's birthday party. He wrote me months later: "I arrived home and my father was sitting in the living room. I was nervous what he'd say to me, and we didn't have real long conversations during the weekend. But there is one moment I remember. On Sunday, my father was sitting in his chair when I got up that morning. I leaned over to say hello. He put his hand on mine, clasping it tightly, and said, 'Thanks for coming.' " With those words Ted got a lot of the recognition he had been looking for from his father. And his father's kind words revealed a different kind of father than the judgmental, critical, "wounded" one Ted had carried around inside of himself.

"Reconciliation" with fathers means coming to terms with both the "wounded father" within us and the "real" father we encounter in our lives. Chapters 7 and 8 explore how both these processes of healing occur.

Pinocchio's Nose and the Transformation of Men. Ted's letter to me carried hope with it. After reading it, I thought about Isaac, the brooding scientist with the angry son, whom we met in the last chapter. He and his son had not been able to find a means of reconciliation, and thus both were denied the healing possibilities of seeing each other in a new light, of giving and receiving love directly. It was the absence of hope that Isaac referred to when he spoke of the myth of Icarus, the boy who tried to fly too close to the sun, ignoring his father's warnings and plunging to his death, unseen. The Icarus story is a despairing vision of men's ultimate fate, the lonely failure of private, self-contained dreams of great achievement and adventure.

But there is another vision of manhood, one that offers a more optimistic, hopeful outcome to our struggles—the story *Pinocchio* by Carlo Collodi. *Pinocchio* is the story of a boy who is created out of a discarded piece of cherry wood that cries in pain when cut. His "father," Geppetto, always yearned to have "a real son," but instead creates the wooden puppet. In a wooden way, Pinocchio tries to be a real boy, but he gets into all sorts of difficulties. As he starts out on his first adventure in boyhood, he ignores his father's warning and lies his way through a number of scrapes. Each time he lies, his nose grows longer.

Eventually Pinocchio winds up alone and entrapped in the belly of a huge shark. At this moment of despair, facing death, little Pinocchio feels his way through the darkness of the shark's belly and spots a "dim, flickering light in the distance." He gropes toward it and encounters "a little table, well prepared, with a lighted candle stuck in a green glass bottle; and sitting at the table there was a snow-white old man. He was eating some fish, which were so much alive that sometimes they jumped out of his mouth while he ate them." Pinocchio realizes the old man is his father, who had set out years ago to rescue his wooden boy, but had become lost. The son throws his arms around his father's neck, shouting, "Oh, Daddy! My daddy! Have I found you at last? I'll never leave you again—never, never, never!" The old man replies eagerly, "So my eyes do not deceive me? . . . You are really my dead Pinocchio?"

Together, the boy and his father escape from the shark's belly. But in order to do so, Pinocchio must save his father, who cannot swim. As they prepare to emerge from the fish's mouth to try to reach shore, the father protests: "It's no use, my boy. . . . A puppet like you, only three feet tall, could not be strong enough to swim if I were on his back." The boy takes his father's hand and reassures him: "Follow me, and don't be frightened!" The son instructs the despairing man: "Now climb on my back, and stick tight. I'll do the rest." The father consents.

"As soon as Geppetto was on his back, Pinocchio jumped into the sea and began to swim. The sea was as smooth as oil, the moon shone brightly and the shark slept so soundly that cannon-fire would not disturb him."[13]

Pinocchio saves both his father and himself. In the process, he turns from a wooden boy to a real boy when his fairy godmother smiles on him.

The story of Pinocchio seems to me to chart a process whereby a man moves from woodenness to realness. Many of us create falsehood in our attempts at masculinity, adopting behaviors that distort us. We often grow a Pinocchio's nose in our false efforts to express and get love. Bill, for example, who prizes the expensive sports car in his driveway, distorts himself in trying to express his love to his father. The story of Pinocchio reminds us of the crucial transformation that comes in our lives when we risk giving and receiving love directly. Not just as sons, but also as fathers, husbands, mentors, and friends. In doing so we grow from "wooden" to an authentic masculinity.

The Death of Parents. We continue to struggle with our parents even past their deaths. Peter Lynch, perhaps the most successful money manager of his time, walked away from his position as portfolio manager of the Magellen Fund at age forty-six. "I've been working six days a week since 1982 and for several months now I've been going into the office on Sunday mornings, too, and I've run out of gas. . . . It's time to do other things."[14] In the background of his decision lurks a key milestone from his past: His father was forty-six years old when he died.

Clearly the death of a parent doesn't end the relationship. Many men who come to workshops have fathers who have died, and they are still working on the relationship.

We may yearn to have our father see our children, wonder what he'd make of our lives; we may fear winding up dying young like him, or wonder what helpful advice he might have carried silently to his grave. Often a man carries around an unshakable loneliness because his father is not there to help him feel like a beloved son, or to offer at least "a second chance" at reconciliation. Often when a father has died, the grown son is denied the chance to give him "the gift" of pride in his son's accomplishments or the satisfaction of making amends for the pain and love of the past.

In his poem "Follower," Seamus Heaney evokes the grief, love, and shame that may be interwoven in the father's and son's lives. In this poem, Heaney remembers a heroic, silent farmer, a father and "an expert" at what he did:

> My father worked with a horse-plough,
> His shoulders globed like a full sail strung
> Between the shafts and the furrow,
> The horses strained at his clicking tongue.

Heaney recalls:

> I stumbled in his hob-nailed wake,
> Fell sometimes on the polished sod.
> Sometimes he rode me on his back.
> Dipping and rising to his plod.

He recalls wanting only to grow up like his father "and plough," as he followed in his father's "broad shadow round the farm." But the boy felt small and incompetent compared to his heroic father:

> I was a nuisance, tripping, falling,
> Yapping always . . .
> As the boy becomes a man, he laments a change:

> . . . But today
> It is my father who keeps stumbling
> Behind me, and will not go away.[15]

Heaney gives voice to the way our fathers can stumble behind us, as we feel profoundly burdened by the yearnings and obligations we feel toward them. We spend much of our adult emotional lives trying to come to terms with their stumbling, the failure and heroism in their lives, their absences, rejections, or inadequacies. In his evocation of the strong father who plows and tills the sod, Heaney also reminds us of the son's wish to be nurturant and fertile, to find within that manly, caring part of himself.

The poem also asks implicitly, How do we tolerate our own stumbling? Heaney captures the way a man's sense of being a hero, an expert, dwindles away as he ages. Here is a final, elemental pressure point for men in our age of changing sex roles.

IMPOSSIBLE EXPECTATIONS AND MEN'S LOSS OF THE HERO ROLE

A man once said to me that the worst thing about being a man in the modern world is that you can't be a hero anymore. It's tempting to scoff at such a statement, but there is a profound loss expressed in it as well.

The attempt to live up to impossible ideals of manhood is a factory of shame and sorrow and resentment for many men. Many of us today struggle to balance success at work and at home, striving to be available in both arenas in ways that our fathers were not, and feeling unsure of how well we're doing in either. As one lawyer said, "All day long I have to be very good at what I do in the office. When I come home with the kids, I'm often tired and spent and a lot of the time I feel I don't live up with them either." With our emphasis on performance, it's easy for us just to add on another set of "job skills" or "performance demands." We rewrite the "job description" of adequate man to fit our modern agenda of being "the ideal daddy" or "nurturant husband," and then feel inadequate and resentful when we fail to meet the new ideals.

Some men feel duped and judged falsely by the changing values of our day. A divorced father at mid-life with three daughters says, "Humiliation is the hardest feeling for me; I get so angry when I feel it." When does he feel humiliated? "Try not having custody of your kids when you didn't ask for the divorce and worked your butt off to support them when we were married and after the divorce."

Another, younger, man said: "You ask a woman out and you don't know whether to offer to pay for her dinner or not. It feels like I can't do anything right with women these days." These sorts of difficulties may violate a man's internal image of masculinity as totally cool, confident, and self-possessed.

Today all of us, men and women, are struggling to make difficult choices without easy answers. How do we men temper our perfectionist images, our internal demands for expertise and competence that get in our way when we try to approach those we love as real people rather than heroes? Much of the second part of this book traces the grieving involved in reclaiming a real sense of self in an age without easy definitions of what it means to "be a man."

"It occurred to me that loneliness wasn't being alone—it was being unable to say the things that were important to you," says a character in the novel Good News from Outer Space.[16] It's not just saying what our hearts feel, it is also feeling heard. Men don't get that feeling of being heard in our society: We stifle our cherished hopes and deepest pain, and those we love may not hear our coded language of love.

Men today, like women, are struggling to find viable roles that allow them to combine loyalties to the past and to the future. Often that means overcoming a social failure of imagination about men, and allowing men to grieve for the past—their love for their fathers; the differences and similarities they feel as fathers, husbands, sons, and friends; the everyday heroism and failure in their lives.

A Roman poet once urged his compatriots to remember: "There is room for courage in the bedroom as well as the battlefield, my friends." There is indeed room for and need of courage in dealing with sexuality. However, there is a deeper bedroom courage still: the courage to understand the fears and opportunities that love presents to us as men.

Men learn a different kind of courage: the courage to be stoic, to endure pain and suppress needs, the courage of the doomed fathers on the Titanic to let go of those they loved and endure their loss. But another kind of courage allows us to connect with others, to face our fears and needs and see ourselves and others more clearly.

PART TWO

STURDY
CONNECTIONS

5

CONNECTING WITH

WOMEN

MOTHERS, WIVES, BOSSES,

AND FRIENDS

Max looks across the restaurant table at his wife, Linda. She looks lovely in her new dress, and he's realizing how little time they get together, with two young kids and both of them working. Tonight the kids are home with a baby-sitter, and they're in a favorite Mexican restaurant.

While they wait for their order of nachos and beer, they've been reviewing what they call "the agenda"—all the little household things that never get talked about.

"By the way, Max," Linda drops casually, "did you notice the upstairs bathroom light has burned out at home?"

"Hmmn," says Max.

"Will you have a chance to fix it soon, honey?"

Don't 'honey' me, thinks Max. *I can hear that tone in your voice: There's more I should do.*

"Sure, honey, some time," Max replies.

"You always say that, dear," Linda says nervously, looking at her water glass. "I don't want to start a fight, but it feels like I'm always responsible for these household fix-it things." She doesn't say it, but she thinks: *And I hate feeling like the man in the family.*

"Well, I'll get to it." *Why do I have to pay attention to all this stuff?* Max wonders. Max, a real estate salesman, does a quick mental calculus of the pressures he is facing. *I'm trying to sell that factory over on Route 3 and the boss is leaning on me and I've worked all day to support the family and I've still not done enough.*

Linda presses on: "It's not like I want to think about this all the time—I have enough work to do studying for the nursing exam. You're probably going to say I'm bitching at you again."

Yup, bitching again, Max thinks. *What am I saying? Bitching—I love Linda. What a creep I am.*

"You know you're not so bad at changing light bulbs," Max encourages Linda.

"Of course not," Linda acknowledges, "and I know it's often more convenient for me to do it, I'm around the house so much. That's not the point. There's a part of me that wishes you'd do it— that you'd be more of the man around the house."

"I am the man around the house!" protests Max, uneasily. He imagines himself in a skirt.

"I agree—it's just that I take care of so much of the home repairs. I mean, you're great with the kids. It's just that sometimes I just wish there'd be a more manly presence around tools and all."

Max thinks of the last time he did change a light bulb. One of the bathroom ceiling bulbs had burned out and Max had stood precariously balanced on one of the kids' stools trying to coax four minuscule screws out of the socket so as to remove the glass fixture cover. Standing on tiptoe, he had almost fallen into the tub. Finally the screws had yielded, and he changed the bulb. But as he pirouetted around wooing the screws, Max had a confrontation with John Wayne right in his own home. He even contemplated asking the two workmen replacing shingles on the house next door for an estimate on changing the bathroom light bulb.

Max looks around the restaurant. All the other couples seem to be having such a great time. He wishes some other husband and wife would have a fight, so he'd feel less alone.

Max decides the best defense is a good offense:

"Why do you nag about this?" he demands abruptly. "The bulbs will get changed."

Matters descend, as they often do, into gender stereotypes.

"Nagging!" Linda exclaims. "I'm just trying to keep the household in order."

Max is on a roll: "You just can't let things be, always a woman trying to control the house."

"Well, you're a typical man! Sitting here wanting to be taken care of." Linda pouts. "Jewish husbands just don't like to do heavy lifting."

"I don't mind heavy lifting—I just wish you'd give me room to breathe." *I can't stand Linda's anger; it scares me.*

"Well," Linda wonders aloud, "how come you have such difficulty talking about housework and who does it? Look at you, getting all angry and starting to sulk; it makes me feel bad."

Talk of my feelings, talk about my inadequacy. It's impossible to be a man today.

"Can't we just let the bathroom light off the agenda tonight? I'll get to it. I promise." Max holds up his fingers in a Boy Scout oath.

"Yeah, sure. I know I don't feel comfortable not cleaning up and taking care of things. You know, a mother's task. At least my mother." Linda laughs ruefully. "I'm not a shrew about all this, am I?" she asks shyly.

"No, no," Max responds, taking her hand. "And I'm not a lazy husband, am I?"

"No, sweetie, you're just trying to live up to impossible expectations. Just like me." She laughs again, taking Max's hand in hers.

"It sure is different than we expected, being parents and being married."

"Yeah, maybe we're lucky it's only taken us fifteen years of marriage to realize that," Linda observes.

Max brings out his deepest question, trying to make a joke of it: "So you still love me?"

The waiter appears with the nachos.

"I sure do, sweetie."

"And I love you," replies Max. "This is what we need to be talking about, not who's going to fix the bathroom light."

"I can just hear the violins playing in the background," a friend of mine exclaimed with disdain when I related Max and Linda's story to him. "Too lovey-dovey." Perhaps their story appeals to me precisely because we need to understand more about love and what is *not* being said between men and women. There are lots of things men and women need to tell each other these days about need, trust, and love—topics that may be harder to broach than fashionable issues of "power" or "divisions of labor" or "role sharing."

The traditional bargain in a marriage was that the husband provided and worked hard in the real world of work, while women were the emotional caretakers in the family who provided rest, relaxation, support, and confidence boosting in the home. Today, with women working and men trying to be more responsive in the home, both sexes struggle to live up to impossible expectations.

For men, today it often comes down to a conflict between home and work, competition and nurturing, self-possession and responsiveness, being "real men" and "new men." Sometimes we succeed, and sometimes we fail. How do men and women forgive each other, and themselves, when they don't live up to expectations?

This chapter explores how men's grief, shame, and anger obscure our love for women, and how our wish to be supportive of women and supported by them comes under pressure during a time of changing sex roles. Around women, men often feel a poignant sense of powerlessness rooted in their lifelong sense of exclusion from the "feminine" world of feelings. Yet men contribute in vital, emotionally important ways to the success of a dual-career marriage, to a wife's sense of satisfaction with her life, and to the ability of women to move confidently into the workplace. Understanding our contributions to women offers us an opportunity for greater empowerment around our own nurturing and life-giving capacities as men.

Obviously there are many different facets of women's nature, as there are of men's. This chapter focuses on the *hidden emotional expectations* that women and men have of each other that provoke strong reactions in each gender. My intent is to present a way that men and women can "mother" and "father" each other, at home and at work, providing each other some of the emotional sustenance that both sexes are too often denied because of gender stereotypes.

Power As a Red Herring. "Why talk about men's feelings; men have all the power in the family, and at work," a woman once cautioned me. Although it's often true that the traditional male role—earning the primary income, or being the authority/disciplinarian—gives men a sort of central power in the family, many husbands struggle with an internal sense of powerlessness in dealing with the emotional agenda of the family.

As we've seen in earlier chapters, control and power needs often are symptoms of battles with shame—efforts to maintain face or puff ourselves up when we are feeling small and inadequate and diminished. Men, as well as women, who become physically or emotionally abusive, or preoccupied with control and power, usually start from a feeling of being unheard, unseen, or otherwise diminished. Often the only advantage men have in dealing with women, children, or other men is their power to intimidate. This in itself can generate shame and a desire to control or dominate.

Let's explore first the vulnerabilities men face in connecting with women, then the crucial contributions men and women make to each other's well-being.

WOMEN ROLLING THEIR EYES: HOW MEN ARE OFF BALANCE IN THE FAMILY

Women have a hard time accepting (and men have difficulty coming to terms with) the power they have in men's lives. The first person we love is a woman, women are often the emotional tutors for boys and men, mothers often are the "affective switchboards" who link up members of the family, and women become the audience and ultimate reward for much of men's achievement in the real world. The writer Tobias Wolff's description of the street corner balance of power between early adolescent boys and girls continues to echo in the consciousness of grown men: ". . . they were girls, and empowered by the fact to render judgments on us. They could make us cringe just by rolling their eyes."[1]

Who's rolling their eyes at men today? Many men feel judged and rejected by their working wives. Even if they support their wives' decision to work, they may feel disappointed or disoriented by some of the consequences of her autonomy. First of all there's the *loneliness* that comes from having a wife with commitments out of the family. According to the old formula, if you're smart, or tough, or a gifted athlete, then you get the girl. And she provides welcome relief from the difficult and trying demands of making it as a man. Today, many men work hard, but they may not feel like they've gotten the girl, because the girl is also working hard and not able to focus her attention on him in the ways he expected.

"I always expected any wife of mine would work, I just never expected it would be like *this*," exclaimed a man to me once, describing the sense of abandonment he felt when he came home and found his wife still out at work. Such an experience may confront a man with his hunger for connection and companionship that had been masked in the traditional marriage.

Men will feel *envious* of a wife's success, her ability to go back to school or to make it in the workplace. A man may feel that his sense of himself as the authority in the home is called into question by a wife who also understands the workplace. My wife, Julie, went back to school for her M.S.W. at age forty, while pregnant with our second child. Listening to her stories of the camaraderie with fellow students, the long lunches and intense classroom experiences, whetted my appetite for closer friendships and a less lonely, work-centered existence. I found myself resentful as well as proud of her friendships and accomplishments, and sometimes ashamed of my envy.

Given that Julie was entering a field similar to mine, I also found her questions about what this theorist meant or what to do in that situation to be a mixed blessing: Sometimes she'd ask me about things I knew and I would wax eloquent, but often I had less idea than she and my sense of my own expertise felt suddenly fragile. At such moments I'd confront the age-old husband's dilemma: If I'm not an authority what do I have to offer my wife?

Wives who work, then, may unknowingly engender a sense of inadequacy as well as pride in their husbands. Another source of shame for a husband, whether his wife works or not, may be her different way of handling feelings in the family. Men often feel *ignorant* in dealing with women, particularly given the woman's emphasis on expressing feelings. We often don't see ourselves as important as sources of emotional support and empathy for our wives.[2] And when women ask us to be more responsive to them, either at home or at work, we frequently end up feeling vulnerable. Women's affective orientation can leave a man feeling as if things are tilted against him. A thirty-eight-year-old minister in a vital, healthy marriage told me at length about his efforts to support his wife's career. He took obvious, justified pride in the resiliency of their relationship, yet as he described his family he made his wife sound like a live-in therapist:

"My wife asks me what I'm feeling about something and I tell her, 'It's okay with me.' She says calmly, 'That's not a feeling.' " He chuckles at his bemusement.

"I try again: 'Sounds good.' Still not a feeling. Another try: 'I like what you said, or I don't like it.' Finally I get to my own feelings."

Men have had good reason through history for putting aside their feelings: They're the ones who had to fight the battles and defend the castle or hearth. Yet must the woman always be one-up on feelings? A savvy, intelligent book editor, struggling with marital difficulties, once exclaimed to me: "No wonder many men close off in relationships: Emotions are a battle they will lose." Rather than being a way of understanding each other, emotions may feel to a man like a competition or struggle in which the woman is calling the shots. The wife then becomes the critic or judge of our adequacy.

Here's an example:

"I had just come home from work," reported Sal, a thirty-eight-year-old police sergeant in Baltimore who had been trying without success to have a child with his wife. "There had been a shoplifting incident at a local shopping mall with several teenage boys involved. There had been a lot of yelling and finger-pointing between the kids and the security guards and I had spent a lot of time telling people to cool it and keeping things from getting out of control." Sal is good at his job, which often involves mastering fear and being able to command respect.

Sal got home and found two messages on his answering machine. The first message was from a couple who, like Sal and his wife, had been trying to have children. It told them the good news that they were pregnant. "The second message was from my wife at her job, asking me to call her, which I immediately did. She asked me what I felt about the first message."

"I'm not sure," I replied.

"She said: 'Well, why don't you take a minute to think about your feelings about the phone call.' "

Sal's tone changed. " 'The hell with that,' I yelled. 'I've just walked into the house after hours of people yelling at me, now you want me to tell you exactly how I feel about a pregnancy we're not having?' "

He explained to me: "It felt as if I was on her timetable, having to immediately shift gears, with no sympathy for what I had been through all day. Now I had to just feel things on demand."

Sal *is* in touch with certain basic and strong feelings, about his marriage and the pregnancy difficulties they're experiencing. But he's in touch with them in a different way than his wife: He strives for control while she asks for expression. The difference between these styles creates problems. It's not that men don't feel, it's that men often manage feelings in ways that wives don't understand. And by putting the burden on Sal, his wife seems pretty clearly to be avoiding her own need to say how awful *she's* obviously feeling.

In different guises many couples struggle with precisely this issue: how to support and encourage each other when trying to live up to difficult—and markedly different—ideals and expectations as men, women, husbands, wives, fathers, mothers, and workers? Often we find ourselves battling with each other at precisely those moments when we are trying to connect.

What makes it even harder for men to open up to women are the deeper expectations rooted in our struggles with our mothers. Men don't like to think about how much women evoke the wish for and fear of mother within. And we all fancy that we have outgrown childhood images. Yet women evoke mother for men, just as men evoke father for women.

Let's explore how adult struggles between men and women, at home and in the workplace, are shaped by the feelings we have for these lost parents.

MEN AND THEIR MOTHERS

The kids were in bed; best of all, they were even asleep. My wife and I sat wearily in our kitchen, contemplating those precious two hours between their going to sleep and our going to sleep.

The phone rang. It was my mother, calling from New York.

"Hi, Sam. How are you?"

I felt the familiar warmth and invitation to talk. There was something I wanted to say to my mother, but I couldn't really put my finger on it. We exchanged brief pleasantries, then my mother asked a familiar question: "Is Julie there?"

The two women were on the phone for the next half hour, chatting like mother and daughter about clothes for the new baby, about an upcoming family reunion.

I felt a twist of envy and of loss. How many men lose their mothers to their wives? Much as I love the fond connection between them, I was aware that somewhere along the line I felt, at age forty-two, that I'd lost my mother, the same mother who had been my major ally in adolescence.

When I was a teenager there were many evenings when my father sat downstairs glued to the TV, with my brother for company, while my mother and I were together upstairs talking over the day's events. Those conversations with my mother helped me through some hard times in high school: fears about stuttering in class, lack of confidence and adolescent shyness.

I learned many things from my mother. Whatever skill I have as a listener, as a therapist, feels rooted in those long conversations during my adolescence. I learned that there was consolation and comfort in connecting with another loved one about seemingly insoluble human problems, that changing how you looked at a problem was sometimes a better solution than trying desperately to "fix" it.

A lot has been written about the intensity of the mother-daughter bond; but the bond would have to be pretty intense to match the incandescence of the feeling between mother and her firstborn son.

Listening to my wife talk to my mother on the phone that evening, I wished I could connect with my mother in the old way again. Yet now a mother's comfort seemed inappropriate. It had for a long time. What I feared most from my mother was her power to evoke my own need for her.

The worst thing in the world is to be a "mama's boy." But where does that leave men who still do love their mothers as well as the woman in their adult lives, and who want to have vital relationships with them as they both age?

And what is the connection between the first woman in our life and the ones that follow: our wives, colleagues, and friends?

Relationship struggles with women are often rooted in men's unfinished attachment struggles with mother—their simultaneous desire to be close and to separate. Men love and fear their mothers, and they have to deal with mothers in order to deal with women, just as women have to deal with fathers in order to deal with men. Both genders have work to do.

As we saw in Chapters 2 and 3, boys have to separate from mother in order to establish their gender identity. Often our earliest renunciations of mother and our struggles to develop a trustworthy sense of father make it difficult for us to accept our needs for "motherly" support and nurturance as men. We also tend to suppress the ways that we are like our mothers.

The result is that men often hide their wishes for support and confidence boosting from their wives, or they fear a woman's anger and scorn so much they withdraw from the relationship. They fail to learn how to provide the kind of manly support women need in a time of changing sex roles, or they get stuck in envy of women's options in life.

By mid-life many men fall into detached relationships with their mothers. Some glorify their mothers as "wonderful" in a sentimental way. Others become caretakers of their mothers, making minor repairs around the house or taking care of finances, with little emotional connection.

Usually the relationship between adult son and mother has a "secondhand" quality. The wife becomes the social ambassador, the emotional switchboard who keeps the husband connected to his parents and in-laws.

But powerful feelings about mother often live beneath the surface. "I went home for Sunday lunch recently," said one forty-year-old truck driver. "We were sitting around the table talking and my mother was walking around offering us all muffins and bagels and coffee. At one point she reached down to stroke my forehead, just the way she used to when I was just a kid, and when she put her hand on my brow I jumped back as though I had been shocked."

Another man who resisted telling me about his mother during our lengthy interview described his struggle in this way: "Whenever you ask about my mother I feel like a drunken soldier with a tattoo on his arm that says 'Mom.' I feel like: 'Don't mess with my mother.'"

As discussed in Chapter 2, these images reflect the wounded mother inside men—our internal sense that getting *too close to mother is dangerous*, that in her presence we will quickly lose our adult self or our feeling of being a "real man." Men struggle with the fear of being too like mother themselves, or of allowing themselves to be mothered too openly by the women in their lives. Many of us have an image of women as providing nurturance that we can only receive at our shame or of women as scornful and demanding beings who have the power to reduce us to little boys; both of these are rooted in our need for and love of our mothers.

Some men feel so needy of women, having never gotten enough from mother, that they harbor an impulse to sacrifice all to keep the love of the women in their life, and feel considerable shame as a result. Other men may not feel "manly" enough inside because they have identified too strongly with their own mothers: Unable as adults to hold the love and attention of women, they see scorn and their own shame reflected in the eyes of the women around them. Other men may have felt too tethered to a mother who was not emotionally trustworthy, or whose attentions were elsewhere while they struggled for emotional sustenance; when they became adults, these men see women as "dangerous."

There is great sadness and shame in men's wishes to hold on longer to their mothers. Men often have no way to speak of their love for and fear of their mothers.

In the life of every boy there is a moment when he realizes he can't depend on mother as he has in the past, and many of us don't know how to deal with that recognition. I think the mother wound inside men lies in the recognition of their need for mother and their inability to express such yearnings. For me, the recognition came at age sixteen when I was driving into the Bronx one day to pick up my father from work.

THE RECOGNITION

The windows of our light-blue Ford station wagon were open because it was a warm summer day. This was a big day; I had my learner's permit, so was allowed to drive on the Cross-County Parkway down to the Bronx as long as an adult was in the car. My driver's license felt like a truer marker of emergent manhood than had my bar mitzvah three years earlier. Driving in the car with my mother was more familiar to me than driving with my father; all those years she had ferried me to doctors' appointments, the orthodontist, and on other errands. Now I was driving her, and I felt a mix of pride and embarrassment at driving my mother around.

We went across the Grand Concourse, its trees beginning to bloom, and down to busy Fordham Road, where my father's carpet store was located. Shoppers were taking advantage of the beautiful weather, and the streets were crowded. No problem for me; I navigated the big Ford wagon through traffic and nearly up to the front of the store. I could see the signs my father had printed up, advertising sales on broadlooms and linoleum, remnants of all kinds available. Somewhere behind the big windows filled with merchandise my father was hard at work, selling to customers and managing salesmen and deliverymen.

I spotted a space in front of the store. Not a huge space but big enough to berth the car if I worked at it. Parallel parking was always a big deal on the driving test; it ranked right up there with starting your car on a hill.

But I was the man of the car, and I was going to do it. My mother sat next to me, looking into the store, wondering where Louie was. I lined up the Ford next to the car in front, eyeing the guy sitting in the driver's seat. He stared out the open window, an unlit cigar jutting out of his mouth. Perhaps his wife had gone in to pick up a package while he waited there. I inched backward and started to turn, feeling like I was trying to wrestle with *Queen Mary* into this space. Suddenly the guy came to life, yelling as they can yell only in the Bronx: "Hey, watch where you're going, kid!"

Fearful of scaping his car, I slammed on the brake, tires squealing, car bucking. I checked the mirror. No damage.

My mother admonished him, instantly: "You don't have to yell at him."

There is both a whine and immense power in her voice, the voice mothers use when defending their children.

The guy clamped down on his cigar and looked off into the distance. I parked the car.

And I was frozen with shame. In my bones, without words, I realized my dilemma: *I am too old to rely on my mother for protection.* Inside the store was my one safety: my father. My father knew how to drive just fine. He probably knew how to deal with loudmouthed bullies; but he was inside the goddamn store attending to some customer, not to his son. That's where he stayed: inside the store. I didn't know how to get him out of the store, I didn't know how to get his protection, and I probably didn't want it.

What was in my mother's tone that shamed me so? It was the combination of scorn and vulnerability. The scorn, which she might not even have intended, conveyed the vileness of manhood. *Don't you humiliate my beloved son.* I might as well have knickers and an ascot on. The prince, above reproach from the world of men. That scorn remains with me even now, leading a part of me to turn away from the loutish devalued cult of manhood.

At that moment, I recognized both how much I appreciated my mother's protection and how humiliated I was by it. I realized that I could no longer rely on my mother to fight my battles. From now on I would have to fight those battles myself.

There was also vulnerability in her voice that day, the vulnerability that many women must feel dealing with cigar-smoking men: Could she make her admonishment stick? What if I had to rise to her defense and this cigar-chomping lout turned out to weigh three hundred pounds and be nine feet tall?

Then I'd have to get my father.

Deep down I probably yearned for my father's protection and guidance that day. If Father had come out and stood up for me that might have been okay—at least better than hiding in my mother's skirts.

I loved my mother for standing up for me, but I was also angry at her: In my need for her was also my shame, and in meeting my need she also made me resent her for it.

And I suspect I have felt resentful of every woman I have loved: For every woman, like my mother, evokes my need and shame at the same time.

CONSEQUENCES

One result of the growing boy's conflict between the need for protection and the need for independence from women is that many
men carry around a little boy inside them whom they cannot admit
to. There are many times in all of our lives when we feel enormous
stress and want just to crawl into mommy's lap. After a hard day at
work perhaps, or a hard time at home with the kids; times when we
feel nearly drained and wish someone would mother us. Yet many
men are so humiliated at their wish to be mothered that they get
angry and provoke fights when they feel most in need of help and
support.

This becomes a major source of friction in many marriages. Often
a husband wants from his wife what he got from his mother, and the
wife doesn't want to or can't give that to him. The wife may be
drained herself, or she feels the "mothering" in the marriage goes
all one way, from her to him. It is a mark of maturity on the part of
a man or woman to give up the wish to be *passively* mothered—the
yearning that the other person read your mind and know what you
want without your having to ask for it or take responsibility for
wanting it.

Again, we need to free the idea of "mothering" and "fathering"
from gender and realize that it is something that both husbands and
wives provide for each other and for themselves.

Often we're trying so hard to prove our manliness that we can't
ask for support and help in legitimate ways. Instead we become passive or childlike. Jake and Marilyn are a good example of this. Jake
is a husband under a lot of pressure at work, worrying that he isn't
doing a good-enough job supporting his family, and feeling the responsibility of trying to be a good-enough father and husband and
employee all at the same time. One evening Jake arrives home with
an aching back. He's been working so hard that he feels out of touch
with his wife and kids, trapped in his bubble of male adult responsibilities.

I'd love a moment of touch and contact with my wife, he feels as he
enters the door of the house. He wishes his wife would rub his back
and in that way provide some support and reassurance. But when he
enters the familiar scene of his family, he thinks: *I can't just ask
Marilyn to rub my back. I can't tell her how overwhelmed and discouraged
I feel today.*

In any case, there remains so much household work to do—
putting the kids to bed and picking up after them—that neither hus-

band nor wife has "mothering" each other on the agenda. So instead Jake looks at the garbage that has to go out and mutters, "Damn, my back hurts." *I wish Marilyn would offer to rub it* is what he's thinking.

Screw your back, I've been working all day too is what his wife is thinking. *Just take out the garbage!* However, she doesn't say anything.

Getting no response, Jake gets annoyed: *She doesn't even listen to me!* So he goes to the refrigerator and gets an ice pack and lies down on the couch, emphasizing: *This is serious.*

Marilyn puts the kids to sleep and cleans up the house while Jake sits there hoping she notices how sore his back is and ashamed of himself for not really being able to get what he wants: *Please give me some comfort and support.*

An hour later Marilyn comes downstairs understandably furious at Jake, who sits there needy and ashamed and angry. The last thing anyone is going to do is rub backs and restore hopefulness.

Marilyn *might have* given Jake the comfort he yearned for if he had found a mature way of asking for it. But in other marriages, the wife may have trouble even permitting her husband to be less than heroic. A wife may not want to hear her husband talk about wishes for motherly comfort and help and reassurance that have been tossed aside in the rush to become a man. After one man talked movingly about how much he missed his mother, his wife, who had listened with all goodwill, blurted out: "I always wanted you to show your feelings, but not like *that*." Wives may have trouble when husbands seem too needy or upset; who will protect and defend if the men are vulnerable?

Yet I suspect most women would trade men's heroic image for the direct and honest expression of feeling.

The Mother Inside Us. We can rage at or cry about fathers because that is appropriate, man to man; but man to mother smacks of "wimpishness." However, it's important for our own healthy development as men to come to terms with what we learned at mother's knee, or in her lap.

Many men who complain of feeling dead-ended at work or who say they're having a "mid-life crisis" are actually struggling to return to interests and enthusiasms that they learned from their mothers: artistic creativity, playfulness, a more nurturing attitude toward people. One now successful artist had struggled for many years as an unhappy lawyer. In talking over his life with me he recalled sitting as a young child with his mother on a hill in the backyard of their suburban home while she showed him how to draw. For years his love of painting had seemed "feminine" to him until in his forties he began to sort out what kind of work he truly loved.

Nurturing young children may also make men feel overly feminine, overly identified with their mothers. Robert, for example, is a thirty-eight-year-old father of a newborn who struggles to spend time with his family and to feel competent in the home. Despite the fact that as a teenager he regularly took care of his three-year-old sister, he displays remarkable shyness about becoming more responsive and involved as a father. For Robert, his more "feminine" capacities are a source of great shame, since they were very much tied to his mother without much legitimation from father.

Like Robert, many men who are trying to become more involved emotionally as husbands and fathers sift through their memories for images of mother or tenderer parts of fathers.[3] These images can serve as important guideposts—if we're lucky enough to find them and embrace them without shame.

WOMEN'S COLLUSION WITH MEN

Women's need to be the caretakers of relationships dovetails nicely with men's need to be taken care of. As one savvy woman executive said, "There's a price we pay when our husbands become more involved in the family—we lose that sense of being the Good Mommy for everyone."

Often men feel little freedom to participate fully in the family.

It may be that since a woman's sense of self is so embedded in the context of relationships, she can't feel good about herself unless she is helping or taking care of someone or controlling the emotional give-and-take.

It may also be that some women need to demonstrate their own superiority at home to protect their identity. Even for women who are successful at work the feeling of being in control of family life may still be central to self-esteem.

I often hear mothers with grown children wonder how they can bring their husbands and the kids together? They'll report that they've "tried everything" to help the father and the kids spend "meaningful time together" and "still nothing happens." Often mothers don't realize that by trying so hard they have taken over the whole connective ritual between father and family, allowing their husbands, who are already unsure or passive, no way in. Such a mother can't get out of the "gatehouse" role.

For men it can feel as if women are sacred keepers of the hearth, family representatives of the household gods, the fount of secret domestic wisdom. Women have great power and authority by virtue of this "gatekeeper"/family arbiter role. It can be a way of keeping men, even children, at bay; it can be a way of putting down men even as they seem to be trying to do good. The feeling they convey to their husbands is: *You may be a man but you don't know how to diaper a baby correctly, you can't iron right, you don't know how to really clean a kitchen, so why don't you just move along back to that male world of yours?*

Such an attitude on the part of women does not arise from ill will. Rather, it is routed in women's sense of rejection from the world of men and in their earliest experiences with their fathers. Just as men disconnect from women rather than show their love of and shame about their mothers, so too women often hide from men their love for and shame about their fathers. There's a difficulty for women in giving dad his due, and a related need to protect mom. This conflict in the lives of women makes it hard for men to understand how important they are to women as emotional providers. Let's explore the importance of male affirmation and support for women, beginning with the first man in a woman's life—her father.

THE WOUNDED FATHER IN WOMEN'S LIVES

Daughters have a legitimate and appropriate need for their fathers. Women struggle with feeling beloved in the eyes of their father just as men do, and men need to understand the father archetypes in women's lives.

"I wish my father were alive to see what I've accomplished," a successful career woman remarked wistfully on her forty-second birthday. Her father died when she was twenty. "He always stood behind me growing up as I tried to be a different kind of girl, and I think about him almost every day."

Where's Papa? Discussions of the pivotal role mothers play in their daughter's lives are pervasive in recent theories of women's development, but the role of fathers in their daughters' lives is largely ignored in the professional literature.

Yet we know fathers are very important: There is a wound being masked here. In her studies of successful women, Lora Tessman found that fathers are very important, and that women engage in a lifelong process of coming to terms with them. Tessman shows how a father's emotional engagement with his daughter helps shape her confident vision of happiness as an adult, as well as her goals in regard to work and love.[4]

Dianne Tennis, a minister, writes that one of the reasons many women resist the "feminization" of the church and maternal images of God is because it strips them of the feeling of being beloved by a paternal, fatherly God. In her article, "The Loss of the Father God: Why Women Rage and Grieve," Tennis writes: "We want the reliability of a Father God because we have scant experience of a reliable man. We mourn the death of God the Father because He is the one available Father who is reliable."[5]

Women often struggle through adulthood with their love of and disappointment in their fathers. In her poem "The Interpretation of Baseball," poet Carole Oles awakens from a dream and takes the time "to study who was missing from the dream ball club that paraded through the dark." She recalls the childhood days with her father in the bleachers at Yankee Stadium, "where you took me at seven though I was not the son whose heart, that sly courser, unseated him. / He was the one you saved your prize for, / the baseball Babe Ruth signed."

Oles laments the missed connection between herself and her father: "At the game you tried to show me what you saw / but I was gabbing about something else: / another hot dog, how many more minutes."

She summarizes the daughter's poignant search for connection: "It took time, Father, to see / you swinging, connecting."[6]

Connecting with father, and with other men, can be a painful process for the daughter. The woman may miss the man's uncertain, mysterious ways of trying to show himself to the woman he loves, to include her in the world he loves, and to understand her love.

As author Mary Gordon notes of her troubled relationship with her father: "In the end, I named my son for him. The decision was like him: paradoxical, vexed, troubling, but finally a source of an uneasy joy."[7]

Tooting the Horn. A grown daughter may feel painfully divided between wounded images of mother and father. One successful woman painter uses a vivid image of a train to describe the pain of her family: "Mother shoveled the coal while father drove the train and tooted the horn." Mother is defeated and crippled, while father is exhibitionistic and voracious. He is the forbidden, exciting one; mother the needy, engulfing one. Some daughters feel that father has usurped mother's place in her affections just as he has drained mother of her energy. The daughter may want to be loyal to mother but also want some of the joy and challenges that father had in his life. The girl who observes mother becoming depressed or dissatisfied as daddy climbs up the ladder of success may feel a lifelong resentment of men and a simultaneous attraction to their prerogatives. She may want to be a good mother and a helpful wife but also run the business or give the orders in the workplace. The conflict between wanting the glory of driving the train yet also wanting to be home, shoveling the coal, can be a source of considerable pain.

"The major conflict of women of my generation," says a forty-two-year-old fund manager on Wall Street who is also a mother and wife, "is that we all want to be home *and* successful too."

We can forget as men, if we ever knew, the conflict women have, before they even married us, between wanting to toot the horn and shoveling the coal. A woman who feels she can't drive the train without guilt may start to resent her husband and feel angry. When her husband becomes the target of this conflict, he is likely to retaliate, saying, "I haven't had it so easy in my life either," and so they are off and running. Neither knows how to "mother" and "father" the other through the normal grief and pain that both genders experience in a time of changing sex roles.

The fallout from the breakdown of the traditional family and the shift to the two-career family creates major issues in women's lives, and therefore in the lives of the men who live with women. Both genders are torn between competing visions of themselves. Similar issues probably arose between our parents, but they remained hidden behind the more limited roles open to men and women in the 1930s and 1940s and 1950s. Today's men are better off in that our wives are not sitting home depressed by the washing machine. But we stand to lose if we personalize all the new stress on our wives and then get angry and walk away.

A female executive at a major high-tech firm observes that "many women feel shame about still wanting a father figure; it's unacceptable to be seen like that at all. It's not politically correct. You can be accused of wanting a 'sugar daddy.' Sometimes just wanting to find a male mentor can be viewed as that."

Often women and men adopt the same destructive strategy: fighting with the opposite sex to mask shame and need, instead of finding ways to nurture each other. Here's another example. Recently I invited a bright, older graduate student into a class I teach on "Managing the Work-Family Relationship." The student, who at mid-life was trying to combine a family with a professional commitment, was researching a Ph.D. dissertation on the internal conflicts successful women feel.

She arrived at my class that evening to talk about her area of expertise. The class, composed of about half men, half women, was a friendly, chatty group. The graduate student began to talk about how little support women get from men and, to illustrate, she presented a couple in which the husband seemed deaf to his wife's pain. The class then began to dissect the couple. The temperature rose. The women started to steam and get angry while the men hunkered into defensive positions. The next thing we knew we were embroiled in a heated discussion of men's work commitment versus women's family commitment, as if each gender faced only one set of issues.

Polarized, men versus women, we completely lost the original topic: women's conflicting loyalties to work and family.

After class the graduate student and I walked out together, on the way to our cars. "That was interesting," I observed as we left the building, "but I thought you were going to talk about *women's* conflicts about success, not about couple conflicts."

She looked sheepishly at me. "Yes, you're right. I don't know what happened, I just found it very hard. It was all those men—I felt too ashamed to reveal all the uncertainties that women struggle with these days in front of all those men."

In other words, she was embarrassed at revealing to men that women don't have it all together. Reflecting on the student's comments I realized that both sexes struggle with their dependence on one another and with the difficulty of revealing their wounds to each other. The student couldn't talk of the embarrassment of interviewing women who are successful but not happy; revealing this "female struggle" to men was too much. So the class went from being a group discussion to a battle between the sexes. But underneath the anger is the shame and embarrassment of showing wounds.

In work with couples, psychologists often see a wife get angry and impatient with a husband who is confused about how to respond or what his feelings are. He feels ashamed but willing to struggle and she gets angrier. He feels as if she "jumps down my throat," telling him how unavailable and unresponsive he is. Her history with her father comes back to haunt her; her intensity is often fueled by a deeper sense of rejection and shame at the hands of men, of all the times she felt abused or emotionally ignored. He meanwhile gets scared, unable to legitimize or tolerate his anger, as he's flooded by his fear of women's anger, dating back to mother. *"We call them bitches because they scare us,"* remarked one high-powered male executive to me in a moment of candor.

These gender issues are often transplanted to the workplace. Both men and women at work struggle with internal wounded mothers and fathers in dealing with each other, just as they do at home.

WORKING TOGETHER

The presence of women in the workplace often puts us back in touch with our shame and grief, undermining the ways we as adults have walled ourselves off psychologically from our needs for mother and "mothering."

An executive told me that after his last performance review, when he was criticized by his boss, he left the office and felt upset. His best friend in the department, Betty, a fellow executive, came up to him and asked how it went. "I acted very frosty," he told me. "I just didn't want to talk to her—I just felt a jumble inside and needed to wall her off." This man had an easier time relating to his male colleagues. "With the guys we could get angry and feel like victims or aggressors, but with Betty it felt too much like I'd be leading with my hurt."

The presence of women in the workplace, then, can undermine men's traditional defenses of toughing it out or connecting via anger and challenge. "It's like running to mommy and saying, 'I have a boo-boo,' " concluded one man accustomed to working with women.

Men, too, may be confused by what they perceive as women's emotional orientation in the workplace. A female executive exclaimed: "It's like men go brain-dead when you try to talk about the feelings involved in our daily work."

She went on to describe a moment recently: "I was talking about the loss to my boss after three executives had left in the past six months. I said, 'It's sad,' and he said, 'Sad?' almost as if challenging me. He just didn't get it that there was some loss there. He doesn't attune to the social and psychological effects," she concluded emphatically.

Yet the boss told me a different story. "Sure I'll miss them, yet I've spent my life learning how to be independent and in charge; it feels like the women often are asking me to play team work and all, but what will I lose if I show my feelings too much?"

In fact, the female executive is quite competent and successful, and her more relational style is just one aspect of her and of what she brings to the workplace. Her worries about the three executives who left do not negate her ability to make the "hard" decisions. Often, though, we men worry that compassion will impinge on our ability to be effective; we fear that if we show how much we care we'll be seen as just a "bleeding heart."

This woman's boss is giving voice to a question: *How can I be an authority and also remain open about my feelings?* Many of us formed our images of authority as children from observing men, perhaps our fathers, model authority in hierarchical, dominating relationships. These are still powerful images: the take-charge guy who has the answers, not open to questioning and not displaying too many feelings. Just outside the Hotel Thayer in West Point stands a statue of General George Patton, World War II hero and West Point Academy saint, with an inscription of hard-won words of advice to generations of soldier-leaders: Never Take Counsel of Your Fears.

Some men do not see anything wrong with public threats and humiliation as a management style, even in the family. That, after all, is how they have experienced leadership in their own lives. One executive and his wife came in for counseling largely because his wife was fed up with being yelled at in the home. When asked about his verbal intimidation, this man was startled: "I do that at work and everyone likes it. You mean *you* don't?" When he learned that his wife *really* didn't like or respect being yelled at, he learned to do things differently, listening and suggesting more. It was almost as if he were asking: *If I don't act tough, how do I command respect?*

Certainly there is an element of identification with the aggressor in many of our styles of leadership and authority as men. A man once said to me, "I was chickenshit as a kid, but somewhere along the line I learned that if you picked up a stick and started to swing it, other kids would get scared." He was the head of a company and talking about leadership.

We learn bravado and intimidation. Men may be used to such styles, or numb to them; women feel hurt, angry, or abused. Men may feel dumbfounded and embarrassed when expected to act otherwise.

And as men we learn to do the work in spite of our anxiety: We behave as if feelings are not a source of information but rather one of distraction that we must hide or control. We didn't get much legitimation for our feelings so why should we attend to them when women are present? Women's attention to relationships and emotions may leave a male manager, like a husband, hopelessly adrift in a foreign, feminine world over which he has little control and for which he has little use.

ROMANCING DADDY IN THE WORKPLACE

Women in the workplace also put men back in touch with an early shame of feeling inadequate in comparison to women.

In one office where I consulted, a tiff broke out between male and female executives over a comment made by a male vice president to a rising female executive.

As the woman, whose name is Peggy, explained, "I am so pissed at Ted. He came into my office after I got a project assignment that was very coveted in the firm and asked me if I was romantically involved with the boss. And he asked with this smile on his face!"

Peggy is indeed competent on her own, and may one day be the CEO of the firm. Yet the boss, who has several daughters of his own, does take a "paternal" interest in Peggy and feels proud of his ability to foster the career of a woman. Unlike Peggy, Ted has never been able to find a mentor easily. By attacking Peggy, Ted is asking how he too can be noticed and nurtured by the boss. Many men spend most of their lives looking for an older male figure who will help mentor them. Many of us don't find such men.

Ted was jealous that Peggy found a mentor to help in her career. Then why did he ask if she had a sexual relationship with her boss? Because Ted unconsciously assumed Peggy was using physical intimacy to gain emotional intimacy, an ancient equation in men's minds. Ted's envy was likely fueled by his perception, even though innacurate, that Peggy had an avenue for connection with the boss that was unavailable to him. Like many men, Ted couldn't conceive of intimacy without sex, and his confusion of the two in the workplace may explain why he has remained aloof from mentoring relationships. It may also limit his ability to mentor younger women.

Charming Daddy. The feeling that it's easier for a woman to woo daddy almost torpedoed a seminar I once gave, because I was so slow to recognize the men's feelings. Several men invited me to give a graduate-level seminar on "Current Issues in Gender Studies" at a university. Students, both male and female, signed up in advance.

One of the men, Dan, helped organize and publicize the event, and contributed considerable effort to making it happen. When the first session began, several of the men seemed clearly uncomfortable, and about midway through the session, unable to ignore an awkwardness I couldn't name, I asked the students what was going on. Several of the men were furious. Sheepishly, they directed their fury at me:

"How come you allowed women to attend this seminar?"

Dan seemed the most embarrassed: "I like women, I don't mean to appear weird, but I thought this would be a seminar for men only." We were then able to have a good and open discussion of "the issues": the men's fear that the women would no longer respect them as "real men" if they were too open about their feelings, their worry that they'd spend more time protecting or trying to impress the women than thinking for themselves.

The discussion was very productive and eye-opening, except for one thing: Nothing seemed to make Dan feel less angry at me for my "betrayal," as he put it. "I helped you organize this seminar," he said peevishly, "and you didn't tell me women would be present." Finally, Dan revealed the bottom-line intimacy issue. He remembered going on family outings and being ignored by his father, who was charmed by a younger sister.

"We'd drive places on Sundays and she'd wind up in the front seat talking with my father, while I spent my time in the back seat with my mother."

Now he again felt betrayed by a "father": He had gone to all this trouble for me, a man he admired, and I hardly seemed to notice him. He feared once again having to take a back seat, that I'd be so charmed and preoccupied with the women that I would give him no help, acknowledgment, or support.

There's a wound there that men may fear showing to women: feeling inadequate or deprived of father's love by a charming woman and wondering how to be manly about it. Men who feel supplanted by women in this way are often unsure whether to reveal vulnerabilities or paper them over.

Often battles for support and connection in the office and workplace are rooted in family battles about who is the most loved. It's important that we don't get so stuck in misleading notions that men "have all the power" that we overlook the heartache men can carry to work with them as well.

What does it mean to try to heal these wounds and conflicts as an adult? What does it mean for a man who loves women, and a woman who loves men? Let's examine how we can become good-enough mothers and fathers to each other, at work and in the home.

MOTHERING AND FATHERING EACH OTHER
IN A MARRIAGE

A manager tells me that his wife "nags" at him to be enthusiastic at job interviews because her father was always depressed. He has to stand up for himself to get her to calm down. "I am not your father!" he exclaims. Yet he *is* fathering her: calming her anxiety, explaining himself, acknowledging the parts of himself that are like her father, and identifying those that are different. By taking this active, reassuring role, he feels some empowerment in the relationship. He asserts himself as her emotional equal and claims for himself the right to speak with confidence and authority to her.

Ideally, fathers should demystify masculinity for daughters, but they often don't, and thus we need to do this as grown men. Women, like men, carry around misconceptions about the other gender. Men have a responsibility to say more about what they're experiencing.

Calming a wife's anxiety is being "fatherly" to her; attending to her emotional needs with empathy and warmth is being "motherly." Both roles are open to men—and to women—in good relationships. Let's look a little more closely at what it means to be fatherly and motherly to each other.

A husband's enthusiastic response to his wife's accomplishments and successes both at home and in the workplace is very important. The husband often has the ability to do two things crucial to a woman's self-esteem: validate her competence *and* confirm her femininity. He reassures her through his attention, regard, and words of support that she doesn't have to sacrifice either her womanliness or her competence in order to be successful. Often daughters dearly wanted to hear that from fathers and they didn't.

Empathy is a crucial ingredient between men and women today. Empathy refers to communications that leave us feeling heard and understood. People feel valued and treasured when they feel *heard*. How do we feel heard? When feelings and difficulties are legitimated and acknowledged by others. Often it's important just to acknowledge the difficulties of managing all our commitments and of living up to sometimes contradictory expectations for ourselves. Sometimes it's more important to say "I understand" or "No wonder you feel that way" than to try to "solve" the problem for the women we love.

The feeling that her husband is supportive and understanding is one of the most important elements in a woman's marital satisfaction and absence of role conflict.[8] "Spousal support" refers to a combination of attitudes, feelings, and behaviors that communicate understanding and love. Debbie Delafield, in her doctoral dissertation on self-esteem and career satisfaction in women, distinguishes between cognitive empathy and affective empathy. Cognitive empathy refers to communicating positive attitudes and beliefs, such as a husband's saying, "I believe that women should have equal opportunities to those of men and if you want a career, you should have one." Affective empathy refers to emotional communication, a feeling one has been understood with the heart as well as the head. An example of affective empathy might be a husband's reassurance: "I can understand that trying to work in a man's world can be frustrating, challenging, exciting, and demanding."

Empathy was *not* flowing from Allan to his wife, Janet, the night she came home at her wit's end. Allan, a very successful businessman, could not understand why his wife wanted to get an M.B.A. and go to work as a financial analyst. They were both in their forties, and the kids were in college. One year as Christmas was fast approaching, the kids were scheduled to come home for a visit, and there was a heavy workload at the mutual fund where Janet worked. Janet was looking forward to the visit of the kids, having the house full of their energy again, and was arranging a large Christmas meal and party while she also worked late into the night to monitor the stocks she was responsible for at the fund. About 10:30 one evening the week before the holiday, Allan and Janet were sitting in their kitchen having a cup of coffee when Janet said how frazzled she was at "all the items on my list, everything I have to get done."

Allan responded: "Well, you don't have to work, you know." With this phrase Allan wiped out all of Janet's yearnings to be both a good-enough mother and a career person, refusing to hear or legitimate her struggles with conflicting parts of her life.

Moments after Allan's comment, Janet cleaned up the coffee dishes and went to bed, withdrawing from her husband. The next morning Allan, in an attempt to recoup, encouraged his wife to hire a housecleaner for a few days to help "cross a few items off your list." But he missed his wife's deeper wish: that he be there to listen to her struggles with the competing expectations in her life, and that he affirm her importance to him as a wife and mother and careperson. That Christmas was chillier for these spouses than either would have liked.

Husbands, too, need both cognitive and affective empathy from their wives. Like a wife, a husband wants to know that his partner believes in him and can understand the complex pressures he operates within. It can be very important for a husband to hear that his wife values his attempts to spend time with the family, and that she believes in his active participation as a father and a nurturer. Yet it is also important that she understand that trying to operate in what has traditionally been the woman's world of family can be frustrating for a man, and that trying to be a good-enough man in today's world can at times feel like a no-win situation. Each of the roles men play today—provider husband, worker, father—can pull at and contradict the others, just as they can for women.

As men we often understand and empathize with more of what our wives experience than we say. We often take for granted what women struggle with in the workplace, for example, because we've gone through it ourselves and assume that's part of the world. A man knows what it's like to feel like an imposter, to feel unsure of himself in the world of work. Women often attribute detachment or stoniness to men when our silence really indicates that we take for granted that certain difficulties are a part of life.

Wives feel supported not only when they've been heard and attended to but also when there are active efforts to provide *behavioral support*. In other words, as one woman said, "It's nice when my husband listens, and it's even nicer when he takes out the garbage too."[9]

When a man needs help from his wife, he can make her feel powerful, needed, and important if he comes to ask for it directly. But if he doesn't ask directly, he diminishes and disempowers her in a way that sets up attachment battles. Ted and Linda provide an example. At a time when Ted faced frightening surgery for a chronic back problem, he struggled with how to get help from his wife.

Ted recalls the time right before the surgery: "I was scared and ashamed and really pretty out to lunch for the weeks that I was trying to decide whether to have the surgery, and which procedure to go with. During that time I went around trying to hide my fear, resenting Linda for asking me to help out with the kids, but also not able to tell her how worried I was about the surgery, and the time away from work and the family."

The two skirmished for several days until Ted finally directly told Linda that he was "scared and upset and I needed her to listen to me and not have so many opinions."

Linda responded: "It was awful until Ted made clear how badly he felt. He was clear and direct." And that made all the difference.

Decoding the Messages: Meaning More than We Can Say. As men, often what we do or say does not accurately reflect what we need or want. We speak in codes. Sometimes neither husband nor wife reads the code of each other. For example, when the husband feels vulnerable he starts a fight. Or when a husband needs to "lick his wounds," as one man put it, he withdraws, getting preoccupied, or quiet, or wanting to be alone. He needs to soothe himself in a private, solitary way in front of the TV, at the bar, or elsewhere, and thus restore his self-esteem.

Or a man may assert his independence when he feels too needy. It's as if he's saying: *You won't love me if I'm not in charge and earning your admiration.*

We often become instrumental when we are worried about our wives or children. The code here is: *Let me take care of you so I don't have to worry about whether you'll be ground up at work, or able to take care of yourself at school.*

Men may fear being abandoned if they are too fragile, and will distance themselves from their wives rather than look "pathetic."

Husbands and wives can help each other by not boxing the other into a corner. Asking if a husband feels "on the spot" or "too exposed" in the middle of a "hot" discussion may help. It can be helpful to remember how awful not having the answer or not feeling in charge can be to a man. Ask yourself: How would *I* talk about matters when I feel self-conscious or vulnerable? The answer may be a helpful guide for a wife to what a husband needs, or is feeling.

It's often helpful, too, for both husbands and wives to remember to be "motherly" to each other. We become "mothers" for our spouses when we attend to their unspoken need for a gentle touch, or offer a kind word of reassurance, providing the warmth that comes from feeling heard and attended to, often in small ways. All adults need to feel "safe" and enfolded and reassured at moments when they lack confidence or hope. Often "mothering" is the first thing to go in busy marriages, as couples become very good at a "corporate" or "managerial" style, getting the kids to school, managing two careers, but have little time left to nurture each other.

MOTHERING AND FATHERING EACH OTHER IN THE WORKPLACE

Mark, an engineer and director of a division at a large industrial firm, recognizes the talent of a female associate who has a young baby at home. Mark encourages her even more by promoting her. One day, when Betty wonders out loud if she can really live up to the demands of the job with a new baby at home, Mark replies: "Betty, you're so good that someday I'm going to be working for you. I look forward to that day."

Many women treasure the male mentors they've known, just as men treasure their female mentors. Let's examine what's involved in each gender's affirming and supporting the other at work.

Women as Mentors to Men. Daniel Levinson reports that women can be vital mentors for successful men: "A relationship with a female mentor can be an enormously valuable experience for a young man, as I know from my own experience," Levinson writes.[10]

A female mentor may help a man acknowledge and gain perspective on his difficulties combining roles and different parts of himself. She may help put male behavior, particularly male aggression, into perspective for the younger man. At a university where I taught I was lucky enough to have a woman mentor, Alice. In my first year I encountered some severe criticism from an older male faculty member, whom I shall call Alfred. He approached me one day to chide me about not covering enough material in one of my courses. It soon became apparent that he didn't really know what I had covered in my course, but instead was basing his opinion on a preliminary course outline he had seen.

I was furious, but stowed my feelings, unsure what to do. I brought the incident up one day with Alice. I felt hurt, wounded by Alfred's criticism. Was he right? I was aware of an undercurrent within myself that wished that Alice would take care of all this and confront the professor for me. "You and he need to talk this over," she suggested.

Soon after, I found myself having lunch in the school cafeteria with this man and Alice.

Alfred and I were sitting across from each other. I felt some safety from having "mother" nearby but also knew there was some work I needed to do with Alfred. Yet I might as well have been facing down the cigar-smoking lout once again. Part of me wished my "mother" would take are of this. *Why don't you confront this man, tell him he has it wrong?* part of me pleaded with Alice silently, as we all ate.

But Alice just engaged in some friendly banter with us. This time I was going to have to do it on my own. I knew I had to say something and I sensed that Alice was waiting for me to stand up for myself.

But I didn't know what to say, or how. I was caught in my anger at Alfred, and my fear of him. The time ticked away.

Finally Alice, probably sensing my paralysis, said gently during a break in the conversation, "Hasn't there been some misunderstanding between the two of you?"

Alfred looked puzzled. I had to take the plunge: "Alfred, I have a bone to pick with you."

"Oh?" To my shock he seemed interested and wanted to hear.

"I don't think you have an accurate idea what goes on in my course. Did you see the syllabus?"

"Well, no, I saw the description you wrote at the beginning of the semester."

"Well why didn't you ask me? To see the syllabus?"

Alfred looked at me, and apologized: "You're right; I should have asked to see it before jumping to conclusions."

Alfred and I then talked about my course. He asked about what I was doing, offered some suggestions, and seemed genuinely interested in what the course was about.

There was relief in standing up for myself, along with the realization that Alfred and I could confront each other without a real blowup. I sometimes fear that if men start to disagree and argue, blood will flow as the aggression gets out of hand.

I learned from my female mentor some self-respect that day—that it was okay to stand up for myself, that I could get angry without losing control, and also that it may be worthwhile to try to work things out with the older male generation. In some ways I said good-bye to the cigar-smoking lout that day.

Later Alice said to me: "You just were welcomed into the male fraternity; like two mooses stamping around and creating dust storms. A way of welcome, from the professor to you." She managed to say this in a kind way so that I didn't feel men were being put down. Really, I was being clued into an insight about how men connect. The professor's attack on me was as much of a hello as a pushing away, and Alice helped me see that.

Yet she also didn't let me off the hook: She helped me get into a situation where I could talk with Alfred but she didn't do my work for me. And by doing so, she defused the potential shame and humiliation of the encounter.

Our social image of mentoring involves an older man mentoring a younger one. Yet women can mentor younger men, just as men can mentor younger women. Many men dream of being mentored by a woman, and many harbor a yearning to find a strong and nurturing mother whom they can trust and depend on. This wish on the part of the protégé can make for a strong and resilient mentoring relationship. However, when a woman mentors a man it's important for both to remember that the relationship can bring up issues of shame and humiliation for the protégé—the same sort of shame an adolescent boy feels when trying to park the car in the presence of his "protective" mother.

Men as Mentors to Women. Mary, a successful female executive, remembered her male mentor in this way: "Solomon made me feel happy about myself. He kept it low-key—didn't rave on about me but he saw ways I was diminishing myself vis-à-vis others and he'd call me on it."

At age forty-three Mary was looking back on a relationship that had been ongoing for seven years. Now she and Solomon were nearly peers because she had shifted to a different part of the company and no longer directly reported to him as her "boss."

"Solomon left me alone to set my goals," Mary said, "but he spent time with me, drew me out, insisted I write down my plans for myself." There's a strong paternal quality to her reminiscences about him. When Mary said: "He didn't just tell me how great I was with little reality to it," I recalled the comment to the boy who replied to his mother's well-meant encouragement: "Oh, all moms say that."

An older male mentor like Mary's can offer a special kind of affirmation to a woman.

"Once I was thinking of applying for a more high level position," Mary recalled. "He spent an hour talking to me, let me get at it myself that I *wanted* that job. Solomon left me feeling intact, that my self-esteem was okay, that I was worth something, and that he didn't take over in my trying to make decisions. He valued me and let me think things through with him."

There is often a sexual charge to the male-female mentoring relationship, which can lead the relationship astray. It's not an acting out, but an element of a sexual intensity, of "love" if you will. Mentorship is a love relationship, and thus the erotic enters into the closeness.[11]

A problem for male mentor–female protégé relationships, or vice versa, is in knowing how to handle the sexual undercurrent. If things get too hot or one person takes advantage of the trust implicit in this relationship, then the mentoring goes astray.

Here's how one woman talked about her mentor, looking back on the relationship years later: "There was a definite sexual energy to our relationship that really helped it. Complemented on the relationship. Of course neither of us would act out on it, but there was this charge to it. We used to play off each other's conversations, like we knew what the other was thinking, and it was playful and fun and helpful in the workplace. Those qualities came out because of the sexual playfulness between us. Once we had to give a presentation to the board of a new company where he worked and I was nervous. I came in that day and he was across the room and we were going to make a presentation about how we did things back at the company where I now worked, and we had had no chance to really talk together about how we would do this presentation, no up front time at all. People were shooting questions at the two of us and we had to play off each other's communications and we worked so well. It felt as if I were at a cocktail party and wanted to have a good experience with a man, to impress the crowd with how well we got along. It always felt gracious, friendly, attractive; we wouldn't be undermining each other, sabotaging each other, trying to outdo each other. Rather it would be a way of setting each other up to have it come out well, and sort of complementing each other. That quality came out at the meeting, and we had that quality without there being any affair or playing out of it, just that energy."

Often we're so worried, rightfully, about sexual harassment that we can't enjoy that energy.

What made it feel safe for her? "Well, we all are aware of laws and limits, and if I said he was harassing me he would have been in trouble. But also this is a trustworthy person, we both knew that sex was not what the relationship was about. It was about competence and feeling good about yourself in the workplace."

For some male mentors sex and closeness may get mixed up and lead them to withdraw from or mismanage the relationship.

For female mentors, on the other hand, combining assertion and femininity can be a challenge, particularly when dealing with male protégés. A woman boss spoke about the difficulty she felt giving critical feedback to a valued male subordinate: "I wonder if he thinks I'm a bitch, masculine, unattractive, dikey. My femininity is important to me and if I'm perceived as a hag or bitchy, it hurts. I'm aware of pulling my punches with some men, coloring my feedback. I get intellectual, avoid the main point."

Fathering Women or Return of the Lout? Men, too, may struggle with anxiety about their assertiveness when dealing with women.

Once I was called in as a consultant to a corporate sales division with a woman leader named Marcie. Marcie, an established executive, smart and thoughtful, felt that the "upper echelon" of male and female executives in her division was not as productive as it could be, and that some of the difficulties were related to how the men and women were getting along. Could she buy a weekend morning of my time so we could "talk informally" as a group about gender issues in the workplace?

Concerned that her senior staff "get something" from this unusual activity of coming in on a weekend morning to talk about a difficult topic, Marcie reminded me several times to be at her company offices by 8:30 sharp Saturday morning so we could begin. A few days beforehand Marcie called to ask if I could come "a little early" so there'd be time enough for everyone to introduce themselves before getting started.

I agreed and once again tiptoed out of the house early on a Saturday morning, while the kids watched cartoons.

I arrived at the company offices to find a table full of food and about twenty of the staff, including Marcie, milling around and talking. The fruit and doughnuts and coffee were good, yet 9:00 A.M. arrived and we still hadn't got to talking as a group. Finally we sat down, forming a large circle around a conference table, and proceeded to start around the room with introductions. Clearly everyone felt the oddity of this event. Each person wanted the others to know something special about himself or herself. We learned about kids graduating from high school, deaths in the family, new plans and hopes people had for each other; the kinds of things not often talked about in the office.

This was important, worthwhile work of getting to know each other better as people. By the time we finished an hour had passed and it was ten o'clock.

Finally Marcie introduced me formally to the group. We were about to start talking about men and women working together when a man raised his hand:

"We've been sitting here for an hour. Could we take a brief break so we could use the bathroom and stretch?"

I noted that it was 10:15 and stole a glance at my notes to be covered. The pages seemed to have increased in size since I arrived. I recalled I told my wife I'd be home by 1:00.

Marcie looked at me uncertainly. The lines of authority were not clear here: Who was in charge?

Oh, go along and be nice, part of me urged anxiously. *But when are we going to get the work done?* I wondered. *Don't be so rigid!* the "nice" part of me argued back.

We agreed to take a break, but I felt a bit like a stodgy father trying to put a pall over the high jinks, or perhaps like a cigar-smoking lout of a man insisting on having his way.

Several people stood up from our table and proceeded to the

bathroom, others went into the hallway for conversation, some went back to the coffee and doughnuts. Once again the room looked like the waiting room at Grand Central Station.

During the break Marcie came up to me and whispered: "Can you stay a little longer than one? We can't get things organized here and I'm worried that we'll run out of time."

Thinking of my family waiting for me at home, my wife with things she needed to get done and expecting me back on time, I was tempted to reply: *Sure I'll stay, if you'll pay for my divorce lawyer.*

Then I realized: *Someone had to take responsibility for this event.* Marcie, confronting understandable staff difficulty around working together, had been trying to be the "good mother," making nice with doughnuts and coffee and light talk, not demanding too much of her staff, probably hoping they'd "be nice" too and start to get along. The stratagem clearly wouldn't work because these were not little children, and there were some real issues around gender that needed to be confronted. Being too "nice" can also be not nice, too costly.

"I think it's important that we get going, before we worry about when we're ending," I replied.

There was a pause. Marcie seemed to suck in her breath. *Have I hurt her?* I suddenly worried, wondering momentarily if I was a nasty lout.

"Okay, you're right," Marcie agreed, suddenly "getting it" as well. "I'll ask everyone to hurry."

Then she went up to a cluster of people and started talking to them. She slowly waltzed around the room trying to demurely get her recalcitrant staff to sit down at the large conference table in the middle of the room. Half the staff was hanging out at the bathroom, the other half remained clustered around the table of food; hardly anyone sat at the conference table where the "work" needed to be done.

The clock read 10:30.

We clearly had a rebellious family here, one without a father willing to create order and limits, and in retrospect I wonder if Marcie invited me because she felt like an overwhelmed mother struggling to pull together the children.

It occurred to me that I had to say something, display authority, or the meeting was doomed. Otherwise, like rebellious children who don't want to take their medicine (I was the medicine), the staff members would never sit down so we could begin to work.

There is a place for mastery here, I realized, a place for a "father" of either gender. I thought of my father, of so many fathers and mothers, who must set limits and model authority and take the flack. The father's dilemma: If he doesn't set limits, the kids will be angry, and if he does the kids will be angry.

I tried some ironic humor: "People don't seem reluctant to get on with things, do they?" I say to no one in particular. Then to my neighbor, a woman still seated next to me at the table. "Everyone just wanted to go to the bathroom at the same time."

Fortunately my neighbor got the joke. "Right, no reluctance. *Hey, will everyone please sit down!*" she yelled in an authoritative voice.

I then loudly asked the person at the front if she would close the door so we could begin. People came in and we did begin.

"If you hadn't said something we never would have gotten started," a man across the table remarked, with relief.

Marcie later thanked me for getting the meeting started. This struggle around "fatherly" authority and "motherly" nurturance is not gender-based. Many women are authoritative, and I've had experiences with "mothering" men who are trying so hard to be nice that their staff can't focus on the work goal.

When we demonstrate that authority and power can be life-giving and not just abusive, we are "fathering" each other and ourselves. That was the role I was trying to play in this particular group.

Once everyone finally came together at that Saturday meeting, we spent two hours as a group talking and doing exercises about gender differences in the workplace. This was a wonderful, open group, in which we talked directly about what it means to be a man and a woman in today's work world.

One man, a supervisor, reported feeling as if he couldn't do very much right as a man in the eyes of the woman he worked with. A woman talked about her sense of a "men's club" that the women couldn't penetrate. Another man picked up on the "club" image and said that he felt like "feminism" was a club that he was getting beaten up with, that he was always being judged as a man. Some of the men asked whether it was okay to have a woman friend other than your wife. The friendship and camaraderie they felt with women co-workers clearly strained their sense of loyalty to their wives. A woman supervisor talked about how put down she felt by a male executive who dismissed out of hand her interest in recent writings about women's managerial styles.

Then it got to to be 12:30 and one of the participants asked me: "We're almost out of time and I have all these questions. Could we take some time to ask what to do with all this?" So we talked about *being attentive to* and mindful of workplace battles that are shame-based and rooted in family dynamics; how men and women can feel *exposed or on the spot* and "seen" in ways that are painful and difficult to talk about, thus creating battles in the office that distract us from the deeper issues around self-esteem and love. One senior female executive, herself a mentor of men, was attuned to the discomfort of some of her protégés in both relying on her as an authority figure and in being close to her. We talked about the importance of women in men's lives, and men's desires to mentor and nurture. We talked about legitimating the anger, sorrow, and neediness both genders feel in our time of a changing workplace.

It was 12:45. We'd had a good, ground-breaking discussion in which some manageable strategies for "handling all this" emerged.

Then the mood was suddenly broken. A woman participant, Nancy, leaned across the table and said to me: "It feels like you're saying you just have to go with the feelings here, which is okay, but I wanted some tools, a toolbox."

A toolbox. I flashed to all the memories of men and women as children going to their fathers and saying in different ways: "Daddy, can we sit with you in your workroom, be with you while you work? *Let is into your toolbox.*" And all the times that daddies kept girls out of the toolbox—and boys too. Children saying to fathers: *"Daddy, I want some of the mastery you have,"* and fathers refusing to give it.

At first I felt criticized: *You're telling me I'm just touchy-feely, that I haven't given you any real competencies.* Then I remembered those memories and realized that Nancy was saying:

Don't leave us alone with these issues that are so scary. We've just begun to talk and now we're going to be alone. With a crunch I realized that I *was* the same old father: I promised so much, I offered new insights, just like a daddy who to the young child (still alive within us) seems to have so much magic in his toolbox but then leaves. *Daddy, you leave us on our own.* Daddy goes to work, puts on the TV, mother and father get divorced, while the kids want more from father. *I want you to play with us longer and instead you go to your things, to the workshop, to the newspaper, to the TV.*

This yearning and dismay were relived in the conference room of the company, childhood longings and resentments swirling around the Danish modern furniture and mocking the adult demeanor of us all.

It felt to me it was time to move past the anger and recognize the power that we all do have. So I said to the group, "I feel like I've just given you a box of tools and you don't want to take them."

Then Nancy replied: "It feels like you're daddy and have all this information about the workplace and you're about to leave us." In affirming this longing for father, the group was already beginning to take responsibility for being "fatherly" to each other, beginning to talk more openly about and accept the realities of working together.

What Marcie's group needed was someone willing to help them open up and talk about difficult issues of gender, expectations, and the changing workplace. This meant someone needed to be the focal point for the tension, saying to the group in an encouraging, non-coercive way that they could begin to talk about scary topics and master them, even that they had the skills to do so *on their own*. Marcie was trying so hard to be the "mother" who makes everything okay that she couldn't put her foot down and bring the family together. "Father" had to do that. "Mother" Marcie was soothing and giving, keeping everyone inside an illusion of closeness while "Daddy" Sam came in and raised tensions and forced people to look at their differences and expectations.

This is not a knock on women. A woman boss can be "fatherly" as well as motherly, like Alice, my female mentor, who helped me face Alfred the professor and find ways within myself to work things out more fully with him. In the workplace, as well as the family, we need both the "motherly" and "fatherly" functions. If "father" sets limits too arbitrarily, too abusively, then no one is safe. And, if things are too "squishy" or touchy-feely then no one is safe either. Fathers and mothers hold each other in check and complement each other; together they make family members at home and at work feel safe, needed, supported, and carefully guided.

It may be that we need to rediscover the art of being a nurturant father, at work and at home. Often when they are "fatherly" men get afraid of women's anger, just as women get afraid of looking "unfeminine" if they assume the fatherly role.

And we need to remember that there *are* men who have kept parts of mother alive within themselves. Despite all the theories of "disidentification" with mother and men's supposed "renunciation" of the feminine, there are many men who can draw upon memories of a mother's love and use the memories as guides to how they want to act as adults. For some of us mother had to be so repressed or denied that nurturing is problematic, but for others mother remains available once we feel manly enough to return to her.

Julie finished talking to my mother on the phone the other night. She was about to hang up when I interrupted:

"Wait. There's something I want to say to her."

My wife handed me the phone.

"Hi, Mom."

"Hi," she said with an uncertain tone. I wasn't feeling very confident myself. It is unusual for me to get back on the phone. I've gotten it back, now what do I do with it? I thought.

"Just wanted to talk a little more. How are things really?"

So we talked about thoughts of retirement, which was on the minds of both my parents, the drain and pleasures of work, the shock of aging. "I turned around and I'm in my late sixties," she told me. Tell me about it, Ma. Only yesterday I was twenty-one and now somehow my fiftieth birthday inches closer and closer. She told me about the pleasures and pain of using her senior citizen card, of getting on the bus in New York City and not wanting to admit she qualifies for the elderly fare reduction but not wanting to pay full fare either.

Then she paused.

"Oh, Sam, it's nice to talk with you like this."

Yes, Mom, it is. Her tone expresses the same ease and comfort she provided me all those years. Now I am providing it to her. And I realize she needs me too, that something was lost for her as well in our letting go of each other years ago, as necessary as it was.

Then I know what it is I want to say to my sixty-eight-year-old mother: Thank you. I love you.

6

CONNECTING WITH

OUR CHILDREN

FATHERING SONS, FATHERING

DAUGHTERS

Ralph is a fifty-year-old businessman lamenting how distant he and his teenage daughter have become, and what a loss this is for him.

"She's fourteen going on twenty and I know she won't be living in our house all that much longer, yet she accuses me of not being interested in her anymore."

The group of mothers and fathers gathered to talk about parenting listen carefully. Ralph is an engaging man, heavyset and friendly. He's a busy salesman, on the road a lot, yet he calls home devotedly.

"No matter where I am I call in the evenings." His tone emphasizes fidelity as he speaks of being connected to his family by the phone lines.

"I always ask about Darlene when I call."

"Ask who?" inquires another parent.

"My wife."

"Why don't you ask your daughter?"

"Well . . ." Ralph starts to reply, clearly confused, as if he had never thought about that question before.

"My wife usually answers the phone and I ask her about things. She tells me what is going on and I leave messages for the rest of the family with her. By the time my daughter gets on the phone there doesn't seem much to say."

He stops and thinks, then asks shyly: "Do you think it's important that I talk more to her directly?"

Ralph's question reflects a crucial failure of perception that direct interest and attention from him are vital for his daughter, and that asking about her is not the same as talking to her.

Then Ralph protests: "But she's into boys, dating, dressing up. Teenage girl stuff that her mother seems to know so much more about."

He concludes: "She talks to her mother, not to me."

Then Alice leans forward in her seat, across the room from Ralph. Herself a mother of teenagers, she talks to us about how painful the withdrawal of her father felt to her as a teenager, how much time she spent trying to attract his attention—and always, always, feeling as if she failed.

Turning toward Ralph, she advises: "When you're a teenage girl, others may have information but fathers provide the affirmation."

Fathers provide both information and affirmation for their sons and daughters. The desire to feel affirmed and beloved by one's father is powerful in all children.

The irony about fatherhood is that we often withdraw emotionally from our young children or adolescents just at a time when they most need us. A father may get nervous around his daughter's developing sexuality and feel that mother "understands" daughter better, or a father becomes so interested in encouraging a son's autonomy that he overlooks the little boy's need to lean on daddy a little bit longer, or the father strives so hard to be an authority that he forgets to make sure to tell his kids he loves them, or he makes such a sacrifice in trying to be both a successful provider and a nurturing father that he feels constantly depleted and resentful in the home.

This chapter explores what it means to be a good-enough father to both sons and daughters, identifying the special, vital, *manageable* contributions that fathers make to families. Making connections with sons and daughters is unquestionably a struggle; and even the most well-meaning of fathers may at times agree with Oscar Wilde's wry suggestion that "fathers should be neither seen or heard, that is the only proper basis for family life."[1]

There is often a profound attachment battle going on for fathers and children, shaped by a cultural undercurrent implying that fathers are not really important emotionally to the family, by the fact that children are naturally ambivalent toward fathers, and by the father's difficulty in handling the powerful feelings stirred up within himself by his children. As fathers, men are drawn back into their own childhood struggles with their longings for mother and father, with their aggression, and with their self-respect.

Let's examine both the opportunities and the struggles that fatherhood presents.

THE LONELINESS AND SUDDENNESS OF FATHERHOOD

Tom is a high school physics teacher, six feet, five inches tall, with a deep voice. Speaking after class one day, alone with me in the room, he told me what he found most "puzzling" about being a father. "I can't believe that this little bundle has such massive power over me." He spread his large hands out before him, forming a cradle in front of us.

"My little girl for months hardly showed any acknowledgment of me, it seemed to hardly matter whether I was there or not. Yet she had the power to open a door right here in my chest and leave me wishing she would just crawl in so I could hold her here." He placed his hands over the front of his chest. Then Tom's eyes darted toward the classroom door, perhaps nervous about being seen in such a tender moment.

The strength of the love men feel for their children can be quite disturbing to them. Tom is speaking about the wish to feel nurturant, to be caretaking, to hold his child close to his heart. Men are used to loving from a position of strength, yet children lead us into a new kind of vulnerability: how to be emotionally close and responsive? It's one thing to be a Proud Papa or the hardworking Pater Familias who protects and defends in the traditional way that men express their love for their families; it's quite another to want to take a child into your heart and nourish and nurture it.

Such yearnings may feel feminine or unmanly, or inappropriate for the man.

Yet certainly that is what most of us yearned for as boys: to be the apple of father's eye, to feel strength and comfort from a father, sheltered and safe. Often those yearnings have been repressed or denied in our struggles to grow up and be men.

Fatherhood is a confusing swirl of feelings, of love and hate, of wanting to be tender yet also trying to embody authority, wanting to spend private time at home and wanting to live up and be a public success.

In his book *The Fragile Bond*, Gus Napier notes the "deep, sleep-walking trance" that fathering evokes in men.[2] Often the foggy feeling that comes when we are with our children, the ease with which we drift away emotionally, arises from the man's inability to recognize or understand the intense feeling that family life is evoking.

Bill, a forty-five-year-old father, took time from our interview to proudly show me pictures of his son and daughter, whom he spoke of with obvious delight. A busy lawyer, he wondered about how much time he spent with his kids: "My wife says I'm not involved enough. There is a way when we're all together on a family event that I seem to disappear emotionally from the situation."

He smiled, with a questioning look on his face. " 'Where do you go?' my wife often asks me."

To Bill's wife and kids, it seems as if he hardly was interested in them—his passion lay elsewhere. Yet Bill, gesturing with frustration at several thick legal files perched precariously on his desk, revealed a deeper battle:

"Often I'll be working here at the office thinking about how I'd rather be with my kids. I'll hurry to finish a brief, or get some work to my secretary so I can be home on time so I can see them." He stopped, momentarily confused, then continued: "Then I'll be at home, playing with my kids, and I'll be thinking about the work I ought to be doing, or how I'd rather be at the office. The past weekend I was taking my five-year-old daughter, Mary, to the children's museum and we were together having a great time and I saw how playful and relaxed she was and I remembered how little time my parents spent with me doing that. I loved being at the museum with her, but another part of me felt how little I got myself as a kid."

Here is a loving father who when he's home is confronted by painful and confusing feelings—remembering his own loneliness as a boy, feeling lonely now as a father, wondering how much to give to his kids. Resentment and love all mixed together bring on that foggy feeling and a desire to flee back to the office. Getting foggy and distracted helps Bill to sidestep confusing feelings: wanting to be available to his children, feeling resentful of them, wanting to live up at work, and wanting to spend more time at home.

A confusing pull of inner feelings is a normal part of fatherhood, and the conflicts can begin as soon as the baby arrives. Men will often attest to the love and debt they feel to their wives. But this can make it all the harder to identify the feelings of exclusion and ineptness that fatherhood can breed.

First it's easy for fathers to feel *on the outside looking in*. Your wife is breast-feeding or bottle-feeding, and there may seem like little to do. The sight of a baby nursing at mother's breast can put a man back in touch with his own wishes to be mothered and cared for, passively taken care of. The irony is that just at the time when mother and newborn are forming a cozy little bond and "nesting" back home, the new father is out working harder under the demand to provide more.

Also you're *testing the limits of your own ineptness*, often being judged by your wife. Robert told me at length of his wife's "mockery" of him when he tried to change his newborn son's diapers the first time in the hospital. It turned out that the "mockery" was her smile and suggestion that he "let me do it just to make sure." Robert's sense of being exposed and inept, and his fear that he really couldn't do this "parenting thing" as well as his wife, led him to feel particularly sensitive to her comments.

Parenthood is "a chronic emergency," especially with newborns. The new father is more *depleted* and faces a changed relationship with his wife. So he's resentful and hungry at the same time. For many men, the satisfaction of being the breadwinner and taking care of the family in the traditional way is only partial compensation for feeling inept around the baby.

In addition, the sheer intensity of the mother-child bond can lead the father back into shameful feelings of *competition with the newborn*. Soon after the birth of their first son, while his wife was still breast-feeding their infant, forty-three-year-old Todd became increasingly preoccupied with his work, and spoke of how little he got from his wife. At work Todd became infatuated with Ellen, a fellow lawyer in his firm. They'd have long talks and lunches at work, after which Todd marveled at what a better listener Ellen was than his wife, who seemed to have ears only for their baby. One day Todd walked into Ellen's office with a surprise announcement: He wanted to confess his love for her. Ellen became predictably flustered and upset, and withdrew, reminding Todd that he had a wife and family at home.

"How did things backfire so?" Todd wondered to me aloud.

"How are things at home these days?" I wondered.

"Basically I feel ignored by my wife. It's an old feeling—it's just the way I felt as a kid when we'd all sit at the dinner table eating and I was ignored by everyone. I could not get my parents' attention."

Remembering that his newborn son, breast-feeding, was continually "at the dinner table eating," I asked whether Todd felt left out at home now.

"Yes," agreed Todd, shaking his head sheepishly. "Maybe it's good Ellen put her foot down—now I can concentrate on finding a place for myself at home."

What made it hard for Todd to concentrate on his home life were the uncomfortable feelings of being angry and resentful of his wife and baby, of not being able to get enough attention, of feeling again like a lonely little boy left out of the family warmth.

Sometimes men will look within themselves and see only their father's anger. Rod is a father of several children who has kept his distance from his family. In describing fatherhood he told me about his own father, who "spent most of his time at home working in our backyard. He was such an unhappy man, he cut the grass every weekend, spent hours working on his garden and flowers."

Rod can only remember his father's anger: "Sometimes he'd yell at us to come out and help him. My brother and I would cut the lawn or clip bushes, but we never did enough. We hated it." Rod's father accomplished the difficult task of working year-round in the yard, despite New England winters. "He worked so hard on those flowers," Rod said sadly.

The yard, the place outside of, yet near, his family, became the emotional home for Rod's father, the place where he could channel both his anger and his tenderness. The love he lavished on the garden expressed his anger and exclusion from the family, and also his generative and caretaking side.

Rod fears repeating the angry and sullen image of his father in the home; and his fear makes it hard for him to explore either his angry *or* his loving feelings. So Rod tends to keep buttoned up at home.

We grant more easily to women than men the difficult feelings aroused by being a parent, feelings reflected in phrases like "postpartum depression," "maternal overload," and "the empty nest." Men too struggle with these feelings, but they are often associated with shame and a sense of helplessness or not living up.

Becoming a father is not something that many men think about years before the event. Unlike career achievement or working, which we rehearse and practice for even as children, fatherhood is not a crucial part of our identities until we actually become fathers.

MILK FROM THE BULL'S HORN:
THE IMPORTANCE OF FATHERS

One reason fathers often disengage from their children emotionally is because they feel unimportant, as if they're just an "echo" of mother or "a fifth wheel." But so often this is simply wrong: A child *does* notice whether or not father is present, both physically and emotionally.

Fathers play a vital role in the child's normal drama around separation from mother; they safeguard and nurture their child's healthy self-respect, and they are the guardians and custodians of their children's healthy aggression and mastery.

Fathers are the bridge or beacon to the world beyond mother. They beckon to the child: *You can survive separation from mother.* What plagued many of us was the difficulty in letting go of mother, the fear that father was not trustworthy, that if we really put our trust in him he'd either humiliate or abandon us. He'd put up the newspaper or turn on the TV, or he'd tell us we were wimps. Not being sure if we could let go of mother, it became frightening to really hold on to her.

By standing outside the early mother-infant bond, which is so intense and "fused," the father serves as a reassuring figure who says: "You can let go of mom, there's a whole world beyond mother that is exciting and interesting and ultimately manageable."

The father beckons to the child at many different ages. For the baby who only has eyes for mother and is disconsolate when she leaves the room, for the toddler who wants to explore the world beyond mother's lap yet timidly wonders if safety lies only in her arms, for the school-aged child taking the school bus for the first time wondering if it's better to stay home with mommy, for the normal teenager tottering on the edge of adult sexuality and power— for all of these children, father's attention and interest are a bridge away from the comfort of mother toward the comfort and challenge of the larger world.

Most of us know the story about Jack and the Beanstalk. In this fable young Jack climbs up a magical beanstalk and steals various treasures from a menacing giant who wants to kill him and eat him; once he barely escapes through the help of a kindly old lady who hides him in the kitchen of the giant's castle. *Jack and the Beanstalk* is a favorite story in part because it captures some of the mixed feelings children have about their fathers, their fear of them and their wish to transcend them, to steal power from them. Bruno Bettelheim describes this story as a "battle for dominance between son and father."[3]

These are indeed crucial father-son themes. Yet there is another "Jack" story, less well known, that reveals another side of the father-child relationship. *Jack and the Bull* tells the story of a young boy who is exploited and cast out by a mean family of women. Hungry and dispirited, Jack comes upon a bull in a field who sees his plight and advises him to "unscrew my left horn." Scoffing, the boy does so and, amazingly, finds warm, fresh bread; from the right horn flows an endless supply of milk. The powerful, wise bull and the young boy become friends and set off on a series of adventures; the boy rides joyfully on the bull's broad back, drinking his milk and eating his bread. Before the bull dies and the boy becomes a man, the bull teaches the boy a series of lessons about courage, strength, and tenderness. As the story ends young Jack finds a happy life on a farm with a kindly old lady who becomes a mother to him.[4]

The story of *Jack and the Bull* captures the importance of the nurturant father who can complement mother, balancing the normal and expected difficulties in the mother-child bond with his own masculine warmth, tenderness, and wisdom.

The nurturant father is a steady, dependable one whose son or daughter can count on his presence and emotional support. Many men find it difficult to provide this fatherly presence to their children: Their hearts are tested by the trials of fatherhood and they are not ready for the poignant mix of dependency on their children and rejection by them that fatherhood brings. We struggle with our own neediness and have difficulty seeing or responding to our children's need for us.

Certainly I wasn't prepared for the separation-attachment struggle I experienced with my own children.

IN AND OUT OF THE TRASHCAN

One day—though certainly not for the first time—my three-year-old son threw me in the trashcan and then pulled me out again, in the symbolic way that all children act out their feelings over and over again with their fathers. Perhaps the event is so vivid still in my mind because it was public and embarrassing. One beautiful New England fall day, the sun shining, the air snappy and energetic, my wife and I were driving together through Cambridge to pick Toby up at his preschool. It was his first year there and being reunited with our boy at the end of his school day was an exciting moment for all of us.

The preschool was housed within a large stone church. Julie double-parked our car along the curb, while I went to get Toby. A long concrete walkway led to a wooden fence, behind which lay the play yard where the kids gathered, awaiting their parents.

As I closed the fence gate and walked toward the busy knot of teachers and children, I felt that wonderful fullness of fatherhood: that I was able to make things happen for my son and my wife and my family, and that on top of that I was a father who participated in the life of my son. Here I was coming to pick him up, just as I often dropped him off in the morning. Capable provider, enabling daddy; I was a legend in my own mind that morning.

I spotted Toby over by the climbing structure, talking to a buddy about superhero supremacy in that poised way three-year-olds have. Who's more powerful, Superman or Spiderman? The familiar pleasures of childhood conspiracies and buddy talk washed through me.

Then Toby saw me, and his face beamed. He ran down the walk toward me. I noted the smiles of several teachers. Toby was scooting toward me, I was kneeling down to catch him . . . and then he ran right past me as if I were a statue and motored gleefully up to the car yelling, "Mommy, Mommy." Behind me was the car with its passenger door open and my amused wife leaning across the front seat hugging her son. I stood up and turned around, dusted off my knee, and walked back down the path alone. I wondered if it was possible to look as if it hardly mattered to you whether your son noticed you at all when you picked him up at school.

A kernel of indignation rose within me: *I'm the father, not the son. He's supposed to need me, not I him.*

(Later that night when I sputtered, "It's as if he didn't even see me," Julie knew to hold my hand and reassure me: "He needs you as well as me, and once we're past this mother hunger, the tables will be turned." She was right.)

As I buckled Tony into the car seat, he grabbed my hand playfully in his, snuggled it up against his chest, and looking me directly in the eye said in his most comforted dreamy voice, "Da, Da," reminding me that in truth the family was not complete for him until I was there as well.

It's easy to retreat to a stony or aloof posture rather than to acknowledge that need for our children and to remain constant for them. All fathers confront the temptation to become remote providers or cold authority figures who give their kids a good home or drive them where they need to go but who forget the importance of the nuzzle on the cheek, the tender word, and the loving gaze.

One of the lessons of parenthood, true for fathers and mothers, is not to take what happens with our children too personally. We need to see their testing, rejections, anger, and surprising mood changes less as a comment on us, and find a way to provide constant, enduring love no matter what. Fathers have to woo their children, and if we want to seem strong and without need then we will try to rise above that. Yet the wooing is exactly what our children want: to feel they are irresistible to us, and treasured by us.

To woo them, though, you must remember the natural ambivalence kids may feel to fathers, the way fathers can become larger-than-life figures children want to get away from or assert independence from as well as be close to. As symbols of autonomy, protection, and strength, all fathers stir up mixed feelings in those who depend on them. Let's explore the confusion a father may feel as children strive both to prove their independence and linger longer in his lap.

Constancy. We take the constancy of mothers for granted, yet we overlook the importance of father's constancy in the life of the child. The mother's ability to remain available emotionally to her children amid the "dance of separation" that all children perform is vital. Yet so too is the constancy of the father, and many fathers do not realize this: They mistake the child's need to idealize and dethrone them as evidence only of distance or antagonism.

No matter how small or inadequate a father may feel, he is still larger-than-life to his young child. Our size, depth of voice, the fact that we work outside the home and seem "heroic" or exciting to the child, all work to lead the young to want to wall us off, defeat us, get some emotional space from us. Even in today's world of working mothers and work-at-home fathers I suspect that most fathers still have this heroically masculine, romantic aura for their children. A father may not understand or easily tolerate the child's need to get away from the lap—to assert his independence and not be a baby, and then the confusing way a kid will want to come back and be "held" again—emotionally and physically.

This is true for teenagers as well as for young children. One reason adolescence is a troubling, difficult time is that adolescent boys want to put distance between themselves and their fathers and then return to them again as children. The yearning to remain a little boy around strong men and not have to enter the adult world is so strong that many adolescents struggle with fantasies of homosexual submission to fathers, of fathers co-opting them, or taking them over. "Homosexual submission" is a scary phrase but it refers simply to the adolescent's fear of his own wishes to remain submissive to and dominated by a father who will in return offer protection and stability. The adolescent is really doing a dance around father with both his passive and aggressive wishes. The adolescent's cry to his father "I don't have to accept your authority!" or "Get off my back!" is often not really about authority per se but an attempt to sort out his own limits and strengths in relation to this powerful man whose opinions and love he secretly cherishes.

The teenage daughter is also "trying out" different combinations of assertiveness and femininity, carefully gauging and watching father's reactions as keys to her own self-esteem. Her ways of dressing, her bookishness or lack of it, her flirtations with boys, are often experiments in holding on to her father's love and attention even while protesting her independence and disinterest. The daughter in this way tests out what styles of adult femininity her father will affirm and value.

The challenge for the father is how to leave the door open for his young child or adolescent, rather than to buy too quickly into the message that he is unwanted or only seen as an authority.

One twenty-year-old man I worked with in therapy spent most of his time trying to prove his independence from his parents, particularly his father, who he never seemed able to satisfy. His hero was Henry David Thoreau, who lived a lonely life of independence at Walden Pond, outside Concord, Massachusetts. One day this man came bursting into my office for his appointment eager to reveal a fact he had never known about his hero:

"Did you know that Thoreau every day walked home into Concord to have lunch with his mother!" And with glee he reported to me an observation attributed to Thoreau: "The best place to live is on your mother's doorstep."[5]

This man then began to talk about how much he also yearned for some guidance and help from his father.

THE FATHER'S LOST CHILDHOOD

Most important, in becoming fathers we confront our own boyhoods and our own fathers. Rather than sorting out this internal struggle many fathers retreat to a distant, remote posture of authority or preoccupation with "manly" affairs. The irony is that the real "wisdom" of fatherhood—the milk and the bread we have to offer our children—lies in remembering what we most sought as children.

"It's easier to feel like a boy again with my two-year-old," says thirty-three-year-old Mark. " 'Are you a baby?' my little boy asks me when I'm down on my hands and knees playing with those Matchbox cars with him. It's like I'm a kid again."[6]

Boundaries between ourselves and our children get blurred in fatherhood. We begin to see ourselves in our kids. I hadn't remembered what a happy childhood I had until I had a son. When Toby was born the doctor handed him to me in the delivery room and I held him close to me and did a sort of jig. My first words to him as we danced were: "We're going to have a lot to talk about, you and I." Already my own boyhood was dancing before me. The endless afternoons of softball, friendly competition with buddies. Things that I lost in becoming a responsible adult.

Yet there's a burden here as well: the wish to make Toby's childhood a "better" version of my own. It took me a while to realize I had to separate him from me, to see that he isn't me. It's a constant effort not to impose my needs on him, not to want to reclaim a lost youth through him or force him to have a certain kind of childhood.

As we stood together in gym watching our young kids do the balance beam and tumbling exercises, a father once said to me, "Every time Joey slips and falls I see my own clumsiness when I was a kid, and I want to look away."

We may see our own shame and grief in our children's struggles, failures, and we want to look away, and thus become detached. Or we try to take away their failures and thus become demanding and pedantic authorities. We lose the ability to stay with our children emotionally.

It was this blurring of boundaries between themselves and their children that may have led several fathers to admonish the teacher of their sons' play group not to let the boys dress up anymore in girls' clothes. The three- and four-year-olds loved experimenting with different outfits, and the teacher lamented the loss for all the kids. One of the fathers explained his position: "When I was young I was severely teased by other boys for playing with girls' clothes and I'll not let that happen to my son."

Here the father, with all good intentions, is distancing himself from his young son's world of childhood fantasy in an attempt to safeguard his son and himself from shame. He's actually creating shame by trying to protect himself from it.

THE FATHER-SON DIALOGUE
AROUND SHAME AND TOUGHNESS

There is often a "gender anxiety" in boys, a concern with living up
that seems to reflect a collusion between father and son. Boys so
fiercely want to live up, to feel like young men in their father's eyes.
And fathers are often so anxious that their sons live up and be tough
and strong that they become overly stern and withholding or judgmental. A major dilemma for fathers and sons is how to help a son
feel tough enough without also leaving him ashamed of his tender
capacities and yearnings.

This doesn't mean fathers should turn into mothers, or that we
need to "feminize" boys. It's a valuable and important task for a
father to help his son to learn strength, to accomplish goals, and to
meet personal challenges. However, it's also important that a father
support the boy's sense of self-respect and wholeness as a person.

That's why it's important to *tell your children you love them*. "I
don't understand why my kids say I don't love them," exclaimed a
bemused father. "If love is defined by what I do, of course I love
them." Kids need to hear they are loved, at all ages.

Fathers often have difficulty telling their kids they love them.
It's often easier to be an authority than to say "I love you." But we
fathers have a need to and right to make clear our love for our
children. Our culture often makes it hard for us to do that, and
sometimes kids in their need to prove their independence may seem
not to want to hear it, but the expression of love from father to child
is a treasure that builds the youngster's self-esteem.

Standing by your child, particularly at moments of failure, is also
important. One father with several grown children summarized the
most important lesson he'd learned as a father in this way: "Be there
for your kids when they've lost a game, not just when they've won.
There's so much competition among boys as they get older I've
learned that it's particularly important to be available and supportive, to take time with my kids when they fail, not just when things
are going well."

Often fathers don't *understand the value of saving face* when dealing with kids. We want to cure a problem, or can't tolerate our
child's struggle, so we want to take it away: But we don't see that
children want our support without feeling taken over by us.

"Tell me a moment you are particularly proud of as a father," I
asked fifty-year-old Arnold, a father of a young son and daughter.

He paused to think, and then told me of a recent time when his eight-year-old son was trying to swim across the lake near their summer house. Arnold vividly described a moment of high drama. His son intended to show his mastery of swimming, and having an audience was particularly important. With his family lined up talking on the shore, the son suddenly announced that he was going to swim across the lake.

"My first reaction was to forbid him," said Arnold. "It wasn't a huge lake, more a big pond, but he had never done it before. But I could feel this performance was important for Mark. So I said, 'Okay.' "

Halfway across Mark tired, and the father, watching from shore, realized that his son didn't know how to pace himself in the water. He needed help.

"I didn't want to jump into a boat and pull him out of the lake in front of everyone. So, I quietly said to the others standing around on the shore that I thought I'd go for a swim myself. I swam out to my son, who at this point was beginning to thrash around quite a bit."

Arnold smiled, recalling the scene: the son's attempts at mastery, the father's wish to help without undercutting.

" 'Hi,' I said. 'Can I join you in the swim?'

" 'Okay,' Mark gurgled with relief.

"Then I suggested we tread water for a few minutes, just to get our bearings. My son gratefully agreed. After we both rested we set off, and I purposely set a slow pace so he could keep up. We rested several times in the water and got across together. When we got to the other side, the whole family applauded what Mark had done."

Compare Arnold's story to this father's very different response to a son's difficulty with swimming. "When I was thirteen years old and at boarding school we had swimming races for parents' weekend," recalled thirty-two-year-old Ralph. "I could hardly swim and didn't want to race. I found my father and pulled him aside and asked if it was okay if I didn't race. He yelled at me that he was paying my tuition and I would damned well go out there and compete. I did it, felt like I was close to drowning, and hated him all the way."

Many of us kids, like Ralph, learned mastery only through being shamed. So as fathers we identify with the aggressor and too quickly become judgmental authorities who demand performance without helping our children master their sense of inadequacy or fear.

With daughters, we may struggle to allow them mastery and competence. We may shame them for not being soft enough. "I read a

lot as an adolescent and loved to argue and debate about books,"
reported Sally, a successful forty-year-old career woman. "I know my
father loved to talk with me about current events and books I'd read,
but I think he also felt that my intelligence was not really womanly.
Once when I was about twelve, I was telling him proudly about a
school report I had done and he suddenly turned to me and said:
'Gee, you know, you have shoulders like a bricklayer!' " Sally was
still pained by the way her father had shamed her by implying that
despite her competence she was not really very feminine.

Often we get so stuck in the authority role as fathers that we
don't give our children a way to draw us closer without feeling they
have surrendered. Because of men's preoccupation with power, and
the sense of the father as the strong one with all the answers, many
times fathers loom too large in front of their children. We have
difficulty getting into a healthy, less threatening role with our kids
because we are trying so hard to live up ourselves.

Sometimes our kids will teach us about mastering shame and
forgiveness, if we will only listen.

One Thanksgiving my wife, kids, and I drove to my parents'
house in New York City for the holiday. Things went very well—
until it was time to leave. After several days of being coddled and
indulged by grandparents and parents alike, both my usually polite
young children turned into colicky newborns. Leaving set the tone:
Both Toby and Emily refused to say good-bye to their grandparents.
In front of the house they yelled about who got to sit in which seat,
they fought over comic books, and they hardly noticed their grandparents waving as we drove away. The whole way home I fumed and
lectured them on "good behavior." By the time we reached the
Massachusetts Turnpike I took us all for a long journy on the guilt-
and-shame train, making all the usual stops: How could they not
even say good-bye after all the nice things their grandparents did?
and so on. My own disappointment was mixed in with my outrage:
I wanted my kids to be cute little charmers so I'd feel like a "good
son" who could produce the perfect grandkids for his parents.

The more I got up on my high horse, the more Toby undercut
me. He had all the seven-year-old's complete repertoire of tricks for
dealing with parents: hands over his ears, humming loudly while I
talked, looking out the window, taunting me. The message was clear
even if I, caught in my dream of All-Moral-and-All-Teaching Dad,
was deaf to it: Give me some space, back off, let me sort out what
I'm feeling. Even as I lectured him, painful images of my own father

expressing outrage when he was disappointed in me came flooding back. His major way to deal with inadequacy and disappointment was to get more and more puffed up. And there I was now, doing the same thing.

Finally we arrived home, all of us ready to explode out of the car. Toby ran into the house without a word. As I finished bringing up the luggage, he offered an invitation, in a casual yet friendly voice:

"Dad, want to play a game?"

Sure, how about Hangman? I thought, sulking about my own impotence to bend my children to my will. Luckily, though, I accepted his invitation.

Toby ran to the "play drawer" where games are stored. There were a lot of games in there, but he was clearly looking for one in particular. Finally he pulled out a board game we hadn't played in a while, a slide-and-pursuit game that involves playing lots of tricks on your opponents.

We set up the game, and as we played I noticed he was soon in my lap, holding my hand, talking eagerly about how he was going to beat me, and how I might beat him. The competition connected us.

"This is fun, Dad," he informed me, clearly reaching out to me.

It certainly was. *But am I too lenient?* I wondered, feeling myself unstiffen. *What about the apology?*

The cover of the game stared up at me from the floor. Then I noticed the name of the game we were playing: Sorry.

Was this apology, unspoken but clear, as good as the verbal one I demanded? It felt so, because the alternative was too shaming. The apology I demanded felt too much like asking for unconditional surrender, forcing humiliation on a child trying to preserve his boundaries and self-respect.

Fathers, too, can model a less shaming, more forgiving stance and thus temper the son's need to live up to impossible ideals of manhood. Fathers can do this by *acknowledging their own mistakes, detoxifying error* and uncertainty for the young boy. Fathers will thus convey the important message that failure and need are acceptable parts of being an adequate man.

In her book *On My Honor* Marion Bauer offers a vivid example of a father truly helping his teenage son cope with loss and shame. In this story Joel's best friend, Tony, drowns while they are both swimming in a treacherous river that they had promised never to go near. Tony had "dared" Joel to swim in the river while out bike riding far from town, and against his better judgment Joel accepted the challenge.[7]

What gives this tragedy great poignancy is that Joel intuited Tony's challenge beforehand, and had asked his father for permission to go bike riding with the secret hope his father would say no. Instead, to Joel's shock his father somewhat distractedly agreed, asking Joel only to promise not to go swimming. The son's wish for a face-saving excuse from his father went unheard.

So Tony disappeared in the river and Joel in panic fled home on his bike, trying to keep the tragedy secret, professing ignorance of Tony's whereabouts. Finally, that night Joel confessed the circumstances of Tony's death to the distraught parents and ran up to his room, slamming the door. He sat there in the dark, feeling the sharp lash of shame and guilt, wishing for his own death.

Joel's father, standing downstairs, was understandably stunned. His son's disobedience had resulted in another child's death. His own son, thank God, was alive. But now Joel's father faced the agonizing question of what *he* should do.

Joel's father appeared quietly in his son's room, sat down near the bed, and began by apologizing to the boy. His son was astonished: "Why are *you* sorry?"

"I misjudged the situation. I'm sorry I gave you permission to go."

Then the father also acknowledged the son's vulnerability, and how sorry he felt about this: "And . . . I'm sorry I wasn't there to help you, that you had to be so frightened and so alone."[8]

I will admit to being stunned at the father's words. At first I was indignant and skeptical: What about punishment, morals, the boy broke a promise, there was a death, we need justice here! Then I found myself close to tears. The father didn't tell his son that he was a bad boy and now needed to be punished, he didn't emphasize distance between them by saying something like "This must be hard for you"; instead he "joined" emotionally with his son. The father acknowledged *his* error (that fathers make big mistakes too, not just sons) and he legitimated sorrow and vulnerability (how awful it is to be "frightened and so alone").

The son, in a whisper, asked his father to "make it go away." The father confessed his limits: "I can't," and he told his son the truth: "It's going to be a hard thing to live with, for both of us. . . . But there is nothing else to be done." Finally, comforted by his father's compassion and his honesty, Joel's grief emerged and he began to sob, his head settling onto his father's chest.[9]

The father broadened the agenda for the son, finding a way to legitimate and talk about the son's need—his shame, loneliness, and grief—in a way that didn't just confirm his self-hatred. The father, in other words, was protecting his son's self-esteem just at the moment when it was most under assault.

The tears I shed sprang from the wish that my father had done the same for me, helped me get off the hook at times when I felt most shamed and exposed. I wished he had helped me learn that failures, even horrible ones, can be acknowledged and mastered, that shame needn't fester within oneself, that tears need not always be kept inside and comfort denied.

It's much easier being a father in a book than in real life. Could I ever give those gifts to my children? I wonder. This is not to say that fathers need to be paragons of restraint and self-perception; we all botch up at times. Yet it certainly seems that fathers play a crucial role in managing their children's self-esteem at these moments. "My mother always forgave me," exclaimed one man. "That felt like her love for her little baby. What I really wanted was to feel like my father understood how bad I felt and still respected me."

The son, especially, looks to the father for confirmation of what men feel in moments of need, failure, humiliation, and self-doubt.

Fathers, though, in trying to safeguard their children's self-respect, engage in an internal confrontation with their own fathers.

THE FATHER'S CONFRONTATION WITH HIS FATHER

As fathers we often measure ourselves against an internal image of what a father *should be*, an image we formed as children from observing our fathers. This internal struggle with our fathers can make it difficult for us to see our own children clearly.

Men often talk of their own fathers as heroes or devils, and so it can be painful and uncomfortable for a man to be just a human being for his son. A lot of us didn't see our fathers struggling with failure, admitting error, accepting comfort in difficult times, or when we did it seemed so extreme and disturbing as to be a source of shame for us. Men will talk about how their fathers were able "to tough stuff out," or how they "worked so hard all those years without needing anything from anybody." Or men relate the contrary image:

"My father wept endlessly about being fired" or "He worried constantly about money, there was no way to help him."

When a man perceives his father as too heroic, he may not associate comfort or support or a "joining" emotionally with fatherhood and may not be able to give them to his own children. Or a child's need for an emotional response may shatter the father's wish to live up to the heroic image he has of his own father. When a child needs his father to acknowledge that he too makes mistakes or to understand how awful it is to fail, the father may not be able to respond because of a need to be the kind of invincible hero that his own father seemed to him. It's as if he feels: *My father was a hero and if I don't act the same way then am I really a man?* On the other hand, when we see our fathers as failures themselves, then our children's needs and failure become a source of shame for us, and we become angry or withdrawn: *My male lineage is unmanly, so my son's need is confirmation of my shame.* Out of these images of our own fathers come what has been called the "punitive superego" of men, the tendency to search for punishment in times of failure or grief or disappointment, to think in terms of good and evil when confronting simple human needs for love and attention.

Psychologist Martin Silverman talks in a paper titled "The Male Superego" about the "harsh, merciless" quality of the consciences of many boys. "A not inconsiderable number of boys do not advance far beyond this en route to adulthood," he notes.[10] Superego development doesn't stop in childhood, but continues into adulthood. My hunch is that father and child together can help each other learn a more tender vision of manhood.

THE FATHER'S WORLD

Children want and need to feel access to their father's world. As children reach the ages of five to eight they turn to fathers as a bridge out of the family and into the world beyond home, what Erik Erikson calls "the industrial world."[11] Erikson describes middle childhood as a struggle with industry versus inferiority, in which the young boy and girl look for confirmation of themselves as tool users, as beings who are valued in that traditionally masculine world of activity.

Children want access to their fathers' world of activity, and to feel that their fathers are comfortable in their own childhood world.

Father's attention to the young child's world affirms his son's masculinity and his daughter's femininity. How many of us grew up thinking that masculinity was something we had to *achieve*—by our performance in school, on the football field, by impressing our peers, or by "scoring" with girls? The father's ability to welcome his son into the world of masculinity by taking an interest in what he does and loving him passionately reassures the boy that his masculinity is something he *already has*, not something he has to achieve.

And a father's loving attention to his daughter's interests affirms her femininity as something naturally within her, not as an attribute to be achieved by being "cute" or "charming."

Father is the first man a girl loves. He helps his daughter feel that she is valued by men. Father's affirmation of both his daughter's competence and her femininity is crucial to her ability to feel both womanly and successful. "My father taught me that men can be kind," summarized one successful lawyer, who is also a mother and a wife.

"I didn't feel that I was any less a girl because I was smart," recalled Jane, a thirty-five-year-old mother. With a fond expression, she went on: "And I'm sure the fact that my father loved to talk to me about books we each read, as far back as I can recall, helped me realize that."

The poem "Carpenter" by Arthur Smith illustrates the joyful presence and mystery the father provides for the young child.

In the poem, a boy returns home one dark, cold fall afternoon amid the "red glow" of leaves in the gutter to find his father in the garage, "bent over frozen lumber, working." He remembers the "whirring" of the table saw, the sun "like ramps of yellow glass on the roof." While the father works at the saw wordlessly:

> I was on my knees
> piling the shavings,
> gathering nails
> and marbles of pine sap.

The boy is sustained and exhilarated by the father's wordless presence.

> When he was done,
> high on his shoulders
> I went flying.

Then the father returns his delighted, reassured son to the world of mother:

> Into the warm house,
> into the bright kitchen we went
> where the smell of doughnuts
> hung from the ceiling.[12]

The feel of father's shoulders makes the doughnuts smell sweeter. Fathers can swing their children on their shoulders by telling them they love them, by inviting them into the father's world, and by spending time in their world.

There's not a lot of reinforcement for fathers to welcome children into their world. For example, many of us these days make a special effort to work part of the time at home. A father working at home usually makes children curious, which in turn may lead them to become disruptive. The child seeks attention and distracts dad, who then feels torn in several ways: wanting to play, wanting to get work done. There's often that lingering sense: *I should be working.* Men not accustomed to being pulled in several directions may feel resentment as well as joy at a son's or daughter's overtures.

It can be easier to wall them out, or to continually give the kids mixed messages: *It's great to have you around, but you're always in the way.*

"I realized one of the most important things about being with my kids is to focus on them when I'm with them—not to try and do two things at once," advised one father with a home office.

A father's participation in a child's school is another important way to enter his or her world. It will also help children in both the early and later grades realize that school is not just a women's world but is an activity valued by men as well.

One man, who often dropped his son off at grade school and made a conscious effort to spend time in the classroom, recalled the hurt he felt upon receiving a classroom newsletter thanking mothers for their recent contributions to the classroom. Every mother was mentioned by first name; not one father appeared on the list. When the father asked about this omission, the savvy, good-willed teacher expressed shock. "Gosh, I didn't think to include the fathers," she explained with dismay. The culture makes it harder for fathers to feel good and appropriate about providing firm shoulders for their children. A society that tells a father that he has little to offer his children emotionally undermines his desire to enter their world.

There is another way in which fathers provide strong shoulders: by helping to contain and safeguard the healthy aggression of their children. It is often the father's difficulty in dealing with aggression—both his own and his children's—that leads him to withdraw psychologically. Let's examine the struggle around aggression between father and child.

DEALING WITH AGGRESSION—THEIRS AND OURS

Buying My Son a Sword. Several years ago I went to the discount toy mart with my young son to buy him the item he had been talking about for weeks: a long gray plastic sword. We had gone to several toy stores in search of the treasure, without luck. Evil-looking Uzi submachine guns, yes; nasty rubber hunting knives by the score; but no swords. Finally, our persistence paid off.

Toby ran through the aisles of the store with a righteous zeal. To my amazement, he ignored the piles of toy armaments, helmets, "laser tanks," and miscellaneous rocket ships in search of the sword.

I participated in this quest with mixed feelings. The aisles of the toy stores seemed a dark imitation of the world around me, filled with violence, weaponry, and the mindless glee of destruction. Masters of the Universe stared impassively at us through cellophane wrapping, and Inhumano, The Evil that Lurks Within, lay scheming on the shelf as we passed.

My wife and I had at first banned fantasy play with toy weapons. We tried to channel Toby into other pursuits. But at the supermarket he would relentlessly search out the toy section and come running to us like some demented general imploring the congressional Armed Services Committee: "Would you buy me this?" In his hand he waved a secret-agent cap pistol, a cowboy six-shooter, or one of those spring-action jobs that shoots little plastic balls.

"No guns," we said. Books, yes; games, yes; dump trucks, okay. Yet far more powerful forces were at work here than we had bargained on.

One night at dinner, Toby suddenly began chewing frantically at one corner of his slice of bread. He was hardly interested in the tomato soups in front of him, but he burrowed into the bread like a starving mouse. He ate an entire quarter of it, then placed in it front of him, staring thoughtfully.

"Look, you've made an L," I remarked cautiously, pointing to the bread.

No, he signaled, shaking his had, his eyes never leaving his new creation.

Toby picked up the slice with his hand in the crotch of the bread and pointed the barrel at me. "It's a gun!" he exclaimed with glee. "Bang, bang, bang." He sprayed whole-grain bullets all over the room.

I didn't have to conduct a body count to note that a lot of those imaginary projectiles flew in my direction.

"Look, Dad, fire comes out the end, then bullets." Where Toby had learned the fine details of gunpowder explosions was beyond me, but this sealed my belief that there was a secret underground of three-year-old knowledge.

Shortly after that, we relented and bought Toby a blue plastic pistol, which he promptly dubbed his "pew-pew" gun in honor of the whirring noise that accompanied the blue sparks. Now we were in search of a sword, which my wife and I had come to feel was a necessary prop for Toby's boyhood drama.

The good news for dads caught in this pursuit is that our sons can be provocative guides back into that world of playful, rakish aggression many of us left behind in our rush to be "good boys." Sword fights with our sons and joint alliances to slay the evil dragon often have the intoxicating air of a forbidden pleasure, even if a wife looks on with disapproval (or relief—for many wives are happy to let their husbands take over this role with their sons).

"Our kids will tell us what they need, if we listen," a psychiatrist friend, speaking more as a father, once told me. Soon after our trip to the local arms market, my son went to bed early, exhausted and sniffly with a cold. The sword he chose lay forgotten downstairs in the family room. I tucked him in and kissed him good-night as he coughed and sneezed. Turning off the lights and quietly padding out of the room, I heard him cry out. His words were muffled, and I was concerned; it sounded to me as if he was saying his throat hurt. I sat down next to him, and he repeated himself dreamily, his words now firm and clear:

"I want my sword with me!"

Toby's words that night convinced me that unless I was willing to enter into his fantasy world of aggression and power I was going to miss a crucial way of connecting with my son. And I was to learn, as many fathers do, that coming to terms with my son's aggression, helping him master those normal turbulent inner impulses, meant coming to terms with my own. Perhaps we both found our swords together.

Being a father means doing a continual dance with the aggressive wishes of our children, their impulses to power, mastery, and control. This is especially true for boys, who seem to be biologically "programmed" to be more aggressive than girls—with culture then reinforcing genetics.

How do we do justice to the healthy masculine needs of our sons in this time of gender consciousness? For we are increasingly aware of the dangers of boys and men who are trapped in a macho ethic— who are overstimulated around aggression and whose major way of relating to others is by "coming at 'em."

However, many males struggle with the opposite problem: inhibited aggression and lack of self-confident masculinity. Such men are very frightened of conflict, don't feel confident setting limits and disciplining their families, and pose as if they are without anger. Robert Bly touched on the inhibitions of younger males when he commented on the curious life-preserving but not life-enhancing quality of many New Age males.[13] By construing masculinity as dangerous and potentially destructive rather than life-giving, they cut themselves off from the positive aspects of assertiveness and they curb the energy of their creativity and boldness.

Defusing the aggression is one of the first tasks when working with men in groups, in business, in teaching, and in the family. Usually men have an underlying fear that their competitiveness and distrust and shame will get out of hand and we'll all wind up wiping each other out. "You've got to get across early to check your guns at the door or the meeting won't get anywhere," a colleague advised me one day.

The concept of "father hunger" describes a cluster of difficulties in young children, usually boys, that include low self-esteem, intense yearning for a male figure to relate to, and difficulties with the control of aggression.[14]

Many men have shameful memories of their aggression getting out of control during the normal struggles of boyhood. "My older brother and I were alone in the house one day," recalled a forty-three-year-old building contractor. "I was about eight and he was twelve. We were down in the basement and he started teasing me in that way older brothers have, and I remember getting madder and madder. Finally I waved my penknife at him, and it cut his hand. It really turned out not to be a severe wound, but there was blood all over and we went running upstairs yelling, with his hand bleeding."

Particularly painful for this man was the absence of his father as a figure who could help him learn to control his impulses and feel less shamed of his wish to wound his older brother. This is not to say that a better father would necessarily have averted the slicing; accidents happen. But if this man felt that he had a father he could turn to and rely on, the memory would not carry such symbolic importance. The contractor has had a habitual problem displaying his anger or strength. Wondering if his opinions and attitudes will hurt people, he has kept his penknife sheathed most of his life.

When it comes to handling childhood aggression, it seems as if half the parents want their sons to be Rambo; the other half, Alan Alda. Both approaches can lose sight of a crucial task for sons: developing a confident and trustworthy sense of masculine strength and aggression, what Yeats has referred to as "the fiercer life." The father is a key player in this struggle, particularly with his little boy or girl around ages three to five and again with his teenager.

SLAYING DRAGONS: THE SWORD WORK OF FIVE-YEAR-OLDS

Amid all the yelling and imaginary death and destruction in children's dramatic play with weapons there is an underlying drama around the child's sense of power, confidence, self-esteem, and strength.

When three-to-five-year-old boys talk of sword size, they are really talking about penis size. When the young brigand swings his broad sword, it is as if his penis has grown several feet. Swinging it at dad can be particularly intoxicating. With a sword, the little boy achieves a momentary equality with the big guys around him.

A friend is peeing with his little boy; they are both standing over the toilet when his son looks up to him and says in a conspiratorial tone: "Dad, someday my penis is going to be as big as yours." There is awe and hope for the future in the statement and the trust that the father can handle a son with a penis "as big as" his. Aggression in fantasy allows the son to make contact with and master his love and fear of his father. When my son thrashes away at me with his sword, I know my place; he needs to defeat me and be defeated. There is both consolation and mastery in this.

Speaking as a confessed arms merchant, I admit to a fondness for toy swords. No child's arsenal is complete without them. (Many different sizes, colors, and shapes are available.) Families should make sure to have at least two, so that fathers and sons or daughters can joust together.

Swords offer more possibilities for close physical contact and interaction between father and child than do guns. Unlike gunfights, in which the antagonists are physically separated, a duel of swords joins them. My son and I touch even as we aggress. "Sword playing," says one father, "is a form of wrestling."

One evening my son, at age six, invented a new form of aggressive contact to unite us, a sort of wrestling and sword play combined. Standing on his bed, Toby instructed me to hold out my arms and grab his. Facing me, his hands joined with mine over our heads, he growled at me and demanded I growl back at him. Then he laughed and, swinging our arms together, he started to dance. We laughed and danced, then he pushed me away and growled at me. I did the same and we snarled at each other for some seconds before Toby laughed with delight, pulled me toward him and we were back to dancing. And so the ritual went on. Aggression, tenderness, always connected, always apart; distance and anger and love swirling around and being mastered.

The hunger of little boys for this aggressive-playful contact with their fathers is palpable. One mother expressed it perfectly when she referred to her three-year-old son as a big puppy. "When his father arrives home from work each evening, Danny leaps on him and demands that they roll around on the floor and wrestle for fifteen or twenty minutes." The mother confided, "His father gives Danny something I just can't." Then she added sheepishly, "Or maybe I just don't want to." Lots of girls also love this kind of rough-and-tumble play with dad.

Swords also echo ancient mythological images of masculinity. In the *Odyssey*, for example, Hermes instructs Odysseus in the joy of showing the sword, holding it aloft to catch the glint of the sun, not as a destructive act but as one affirming his proud masculinity.

Am I saying that we are supposed to applaud our sons while they blast each other with laser guns or pretend to hack up baby sister? Of course not. The key, as a wise parent once counseled me, is "not what your child is doing but how you respond to it." The challenge for the parent is to find ways of setting healthy limits and helping children come to terms with their aggression.

Limits help the child sort out when he is playing and when he is not. Limits help him learn that there are real consequences to real aggression. Finding out that there is a difference between whacking the pop-up Mickey doll and poking a friend can be one early lesson in empathy.

THE FATHER AS GATEKEEPER TO HIS SON'S HEALTHY MASCULINITY

Sword fighting and developing a healthy and playful sense of masculinity are not tasks that can be left to the mother alone. The nurturing and protecting of a young child's self-esteem is a task for the whole family, and fathers play a crucial role in the process.

Let's consider the father's role in safeguarding his boy's self-esteem. So much of the young boy's life is spent within the world of women, first with his mother and then with child-care providers and teachers at school. It is certainly not an indictment of women to say that they may project their own fears and anger about adult male aggression onto boys and then inhibit them from coming to terms with their deepest impulses.

In studies of mothers' play with their infant children, reported by psychologists Carol Malatesta and Jeannette Haviland, mothers had different ways of keeping baby boys and girls happy. The mothers tended to downplay the boys' emotions, particularly the negative ones, by not matching their expressions. Mothers, however, tended to match the expressions of their female babies, which brings them closer.[15]

So who fulfills the boy's need to have his aggressive impulses validated and contained? Fathers can step into this role, providing an empathic response to their son's aggressive overtures.

The wild-child energy and boisterousness of young boys often raises the hackles of women teachers. A male elementary school principal observed that, in a classroom, "the girls were all doing their projects and the boys were running around doing their various boyish things. The teacher, exasperated with the horseplay, lined the five young rogues up in a row and pointed at them.

" 'Stop,' she said. 'This is not a laughing school!' What makes it so poignant is that she is an excellent teacher."

Fathers are the gatekeepers to their son's healthy masculinity. Boys need their fathers, and they need them for different reasons than they need their mothers.

Over the childhood and adolescent years, the father can do several things for his son: help limit and set boundaries for the child struggling to learn self-control, as we talked about in the section on dramatic play; as the child ages, particularly into adolescence, the father can help him learn healthy male aggression and create a dialogue around love and hate; and he can become an interpreter to his wife for the son's normal struggle with aggression.

The husband can explain and validate the boy's struggle with his mother. A mother may see in her son's loudness or rough play the beginnings of adult male violence that needs to be purged. Mother and son may then become locked in battle that the husband can help to defuse. He can reassure his wife about the boy's struggles to master his aggression. Sendak's story *Where the Wild Things Are* is a helpful way to consider the boy's struggles to master his anger, as is the TV show *The Hulk*, in which the main character changes from a rational scientist to a raging brute when frustrated. Fathers can find many other examples on TV, the radio, and the news to use in talking about the meaning of violence and anger.

To be there for his son a dad needs to acknowledge these issues within himself. It's important for the father to look at the shadowy sense of resentment and anger that he has carried forward from his own childhood, so as to better understand his son's struggles.

THE UNSPEAKABLE: OUR RESENTMENT OF OUR FAMILIES

Max, a thirty-eight-year-old father of a baby, is the owner of several pharmacy stores. He tells me of the pride he feels at the birth of his son, Sean, and how competent his wife is at handling this major transition in their lives. He keeps stressing his wife's "competence," but doesn't speak very much of affection between them. He presents images of the mother and son doing this and that; Max's presence as the father is nowhere to be found.

Max, speaking very abstractly, says, "I feel some resentment at the situation, not at any of the people involved."

When I suggested that it is "hard for new fathers; we don't talk a lot about how left out they can feel," Max responded with relief and confusion:

"Is it hard for other fathers too?"

He then spoke of how painful it felt to be angry and impatient with this baby he also loved.

Often men feel considerable shame at their resentment of their children, and withdraw from the family because they want to turn away from these unpleasant feelings.

After all, we're supposed to love pregnant women and new mothers, politicians pat new babies, and fathers are supposed to protect and defend the family.

Yet there is a normal dark side to fathering, as there is to mothering. What is the father to do with his resentment of his children? What do children cost their fathers in terms of career success or personal goals? What about the advantages he provides them that he may never profit from or be thanked for? How do fathers deal with the normal resentments created in the past, what Jung calls "the shadow" that follows every man around?

Each stage of fatherhood brings resentment as well as love. Many of us are used to controlling our environment, approaching matters rationally, and being authorities. Yet the child can wrap us in a control struggle within seconds. We find ourselves struggling to change diapers on a writhing baby *now, not later*, or locked in conflict with a school-age child who is determined to finish his Nintendo game before leaving for school while we hold his coat and worry about being late for our first morning appointment (*C'mon, Dad, I'm getting my highest score ever, I can't rush now*), or trying to hold on to a teenager who seems so rapidly growing beyond our control, teasing us with drugs, sex, and rock 'n' roll, while our hopes seem like a perilous kite blown about in a hurricane.

Many of us feel an incohate anger at what we had to give up as kids in order to live up as men: moments of tenderness with mother, times we didn't want to tough it out, wishes to be passively taken care of. Children parade all those yearnings in front of us, and many of us get considerable pleasure in seeing our children blossom, yet we also feel the pressing resentment of our own lost childhood. A father may want to take off his armor, put down his shield, and not know how to do that, and then feel angry or resentful at his entrapment.

As I awaited the birth of my first child, I felt shocked at poet Reg Saner's description of the "small, thick hands" of a father whose "anger has made my own hands tremble, passing it on." The years of being a father have helped me understand more about that anger.[16]

It's important to remember that *being mindful of these feelings within ourselves, acknowledging them, is not the same as acting on them.* Abusive and angry fathers often have little inner capacity for acknowledging their anger. Whenever anger wells up inside them, they act on it beause only by acting can they tolerate their anger. It's not that nonabusive dads don't feel angry at their families at times, it's rather that they are more able to identify their anger and resentment at their children and talk about it with their partners, friends, or helpful professionals. Nonabusive dads thereby find support, get information as to how to handle difficult moments of parenting, and find nondamaging outlets for their aggression through sports, work, or hobbies.

Honor Your Own Aggression Toward Your Children. Children and teenagers stir up our aggressive wishes. So much of the media hype about "Homemaker Daddies" presents images of gushing fathers and cute babies or of teenagers and fathers who are "just pals" that many men today don't understand that it is also normal to resent, even at times hate, their children. From day one our children permanently change our lives, get in the middle of our relationships with our wives, and create constant dilemmas about balancing work and family. No wonder fathers, like mothers, sometimes contemplate how wonderful life would be without their kids.

Many fathers need to know that it's okay to envy or resent the child or wife they also love.

THE FATHER-TEENAGER DIALOGUE AROUND LOVE AND HATE

"Dad, how come car engines don't explode?" I asked my father as we were driving home from his store on a cold winter Saturday evening. I was fourteen years old. My father used to take me to the Bronx to spend Saturdays working with him in the carpet store he owned. Those were special times together when I felt I had my father all to myself.

My question was not only an abstract discussion of automotive mechanics. With all the gasoline and spark plugs under the hood, what kept it all from igniting and blowing us to smithereens? There was an edge of concern in my voice. My father explained to me patiently about pistons and drive shafts and the cold, hard steel of the engine.

Often abstract questions mask deeper human concerns. The possibilities of more human explosions haunted me. What junior high school student isn't fueled by explosive forces? The forces building up inside me—wearing braces, my father's financial struggles in his business, my mother's working, dealing with a younger brother eager to surpass me, discovering girls, and belonging to the male peer group—were the typical issues of boys my age.

Yet how do you talk to your dad about love and hate? *"Gee, Pop, let's skip the car engines—do you ever feel like exploding?"* My father seemed so in control on the one hand, with his business suit and tie,

the boss of his store, the driver in the car, and yet he had a smol-
dering quality under the surface. Best not to get too close to those
kinds of questions. Besides which, I wasn't so sure of my own smol-
dering quality.

Children tend to approach their mothers with questions about
emotions and fathers with requests for facts.[17] Fathers tend to talk
about changing flat tires, mothers about mending broken hearts. Yet
perhaps the researchers have missed something. Sons may feel most
comfortable bringing emotionally charged topics to father in a disguised form. Just as my questions to my father about why car engines
don't explode had a hidden emotional agenda, so other young men
may approach their fathers indirectly for "information" about broken hearts and human frustrations.

Let's look at other ways that fathers can connect with their teenage sons and daughters.

Open-ended questions are often helpful ways to create a dialogue
with a teenager.

One father described how a casual, open-ended question helped
get at the emotional subtext of a difficult situation. "My fourteen-
year-old son had been talking about how to deal with bullies in
school, and his grandfather had been urging him to 'punch back
when someone starts intimidating you.' I wanted to argue with my
father that this was a terrible idea. Instead, though, I said, 'Well,
that's always an option, but how else could Jim handle the situation?'
My father backed off, and Jim started talking about trying to look
tough, and how scared he was of not being accepted by the other
guys. We then had a really good talk about the prices of trying too
hard to live up to other people's expectations." Then the father
added, with a touch of irony: "We all had something to contribute
about that topic."

*Remember that adolescents are often struggling for father's love and
seek it by challenging themselves or their fathers.* Underneath a lot of
adolescent testing and aggression there may be a yearning to feel
really beloved by father. What the teenager is really saying is: *Look
at me, appreciate my growing strength and power!*

All teenage boys want to outstrip and outdo their fathers. That
is part of the adolescent's burgeoning manliness and struggle to come
to terms with his power and strength, both physically and emotionally. But the adolescent also needs to know that his father can take
it; that dad can deal with a teenager who feels like he's king of the
world. Too often fathers withdraw when their sons become teens

and the boy internalizes the shameful message: *I was too strong for dad; if I'm too strong my father will collapse or disappear.*

Ivan Turgenev's classic novel *Fathers and Sons* offers a fascinating study of the consequences of a father's withdrawal in the face of the son's assault. Bazarov, the nihilist, outstrips and demeans his father, who seems almost afraid to express any affection lest he "annoy" his son. The father's surrender and withdrawal counterpoints the moral decline of the son, who becomes more and more weighed down by his despair and empty success. Perhaps if his father had been stronger, more willing to stand up for himself and "wrestle" with his son emotionally, Bazarov would have found something to believe in.[18]

The biblical story of Jacob wrestling with the angel is a central metaphor for many men. Jacob's wrestling with the angel in a time of despair gave him renewed courage and strength, as well as inflicting on him a lifelong wound.[19] Sons often want to wrestle with their fathers, to feel confronted and contained and loved by them. We don't want to feel defeated by our fathers, or victorious over them, but we do want a response from them, even if we can only get a response by wrestling with them. Struggling with a strong figure can tell us who we are and help us feel rooted in ourselves.

Some fathers need to overwhelm their adolescent sons; they cannot tolerate the growing potency of the teenager, perhaps seeing their own mortality or decline in the burgeoning potential of youth. What father at times doesn't look at his growing son or daughter and see "an instrument that would grow out of bounds"? in the words of poet Alvaro Cardona-Hines.[20]

Our adolescent sons, filled with possibility, remind us of what we haven't achieved and of our eventual displacement. A twenty-three-year-old man recalls the humiliating experience of sailing with his father only five years ago: "I had been sailing with him for years and when I said that it felt like I could navigate the boat he sent me below and told me to get paint and repaint the bathroom. The better sailor I became, the more like Captain Bligh he acted."

Don't abandon your child to others to deal with his aggression. Judo and martial arts teachers, private schools and camps certainly have their place in helping sons learn a confident sense of personal discipline. However, too often the karate teacher or private school headmaster becomes a surrogate father for a boy who feels humiliated by the sense that his own father has sent him off to learn from someone else how to be a man. One forty-year-old man who went through a prestigious private school remembered: "I couldn't get rid of the feeling that I was sent away as punishment for the tough times that my father and I had, that my father couldn't really deal with me."

Don't box your kids into situations in which one of you has to win. Teenagers are very vulnerable to feeling shame. Find ways to keep doors open and to be responsive to an adolescent son's testing and need for you. A sense of humor can help: "I feel like I'm manning an information booth in the midst of a tornado," is how one father of adolescents described his family life.

THE FATHER-DAUGHTER DIALOGUE AROUND LOVE AND LOSS

Fathers play a crucial role in the lives of their daughters, both in the process of healthy separation from mother and in developing a healthy sense of self-esteem. There is a special "twist" to the father-daughter relationship, different from father-son interaction, that creates particular difficulties and opportunities.

Mothers are, of course, vital in the lives of all children, yet many grown women carry around a sense of disappointment in or rejection by their fathers, which can open a lifelong wound to their self-esteem.

What makes it difficult for fathers to engage emotionally with their daughters, to really connect with them?

For some fathers the birth of a daughter brings with it the sense of *the other*. Before the birth of our second child my wife and I didn't want to know the sex of the baby; we had liked the surprise when our son arrived. It had taken Toby twelve hours to emerge into the world; we had anticipated a similar experience the second time around.

But our daughter, Emily, would have none of that; she was born within an hour of our arrival at the hospital. A daughter? All along I had really anticipated another son. As I took Emily in my arms in the delivery room, I was speechless. No jigs this time. With a second child you know the specialness of the gift you've been given. You feel a deeper appreciation, and perhaps a deeper dread. But I was also frightened. How does a father deal with girls? The disappointment I felt was bred of the difference between us: It was hard to imagine her as an extension of myself. I had no sisters, so having a daughter was like entering foreign territory. And it aroused a certain fascination: I had fathered a girl; I was the father of a daughter.

Within a year, I was so in love with my daughter that I could acknowledge the disappointment and fear I felt then. There was a special thrill in seeing my daughter take on the world, in seeing her hardiness. For a long time I was constantly dancing around my son as he played with Emily. She would crawl on the living room floor while Toby jumped around her like a bronco. "Whoopee," he would snort; and she'd push up onto her knees and smile at him. I'd be up and out of my chair like lightning, as if refereeing a Mike Tyson fight. I was torn; I didn't want to interfere with their play. After all, this is what you want—brother and sister playing together. But I didn't want Emily permanently rearranged, either.

Toby would grab her hands and start throwing her arms up in the air. The ref knew an illegal hold when he saw one, and he'd move in to separate them. "Wait, honey," I'd say to my boy. But he hardly heard me; he was having too much fun pummeling his sister. I'd hear her laughter but it didn't register.

Once I pushed his hand away. Suddenly, her little hand slapped mine. As if to say no, no, she shook he head in the determined, no-nonsense way she used when I offered her a spoonful of food she didn't like.

With a shock I realized she was telling me to leave them alone. She was enjoying the gusto of her play with her brother. I took my injured pride back to my chair and resumed my session with the newspaper. But I am proud of her, of her spunkiness.

Since her birth, I've felt more allied with girls than ever. I'm not just a male, I'm also the father of a daughter. "I feel like I finally understand feminism after fathering daughters," confided a thirty-seven-year-old father of several young girls. "I look at my kids and wonder what sort of prejudice they'll encounter as they grow up."

One day at our neighborhood playground a little girl, about two years old, toddled up to Toby. He hugged her and then picked her up. She squealed with delight. The referee was about to move in again when the girl's mother, sitting nearby, smiled and said, "Oh, don't worry about her. She has two older brothers and knows all about little boys. She loves it and can take care of herself." Hooray for girls. Hooray for girls who can take care of themselves around boys.

Having a daughter gives a man entry into a world of femininity. Just changing a little girl's diapers helps to demystify the female body. Although our cultural stereotypes hold that all fathers want a son, there are certainly many exceptions to this. One forty-year-old father of a girl told me, "Being an older father, I wasn't sure I wanted to take on having a boy. The boys in Anne's preschool are all playing warrior games. Anne roughhouses too, but not like the boys. I really delight in her ability to focus her attention and carry out projects. She's also more cuddly and snuggly."

Another father tells me how much he adores his daughter and loves to watch her play dress-up or play with dolls. "I don't play all that much with her," he says, "but I love to be around and watch their fantasy play."

Such attention from a father is crucial to a young girl's self-esteem. The roots of a woman's self-confidence lie in a little girl's knowledge that her father loves her for who she is and what she does. Tessman finds that early attention and positive reinforcement from fathers are linked to the grown woman's capacity for achievement and career success.[21] Little girls literally throw themselves at their fathers, and a deep psychic wound can open when a father does not respond.

Some fathers may run up against the dilemma of supporting a daughter's femininity and competence at the same time. The very entry into the world of femininity they offer may be too seductive. Or we may want to keep our daughters cute and charming to protect them from the harshness of the world.

If fathers feel a duty to "toughen" up sons, they also feel a responsibility to "protect" daughters, to keep them soft. We may see in the daughter our own lost "femininity," the tender, expressive, or playful parts of ourselves that we lost in the transition to manhood.

The very strength of the feelings fathers have for their young daughters can lead them to withdraw. "I was kissing and hugging my two-year-old daughter in the supermarket checkout line the other day," said one father, "when I stopped and momentarily wondered what the women in line were thinking about this. Did they imagine I was a seductive father?" Although we have begun to pay much needed attention to the problem of sexual and physical abuse, we pay less to the more common tragedy that occurs when a daughter cannot spark her father's attention and love, or when a father's fears lead him to erect walls between himself and his daughter.

And of course there *is* a normal emotional seduction between father and daughter; a response that is different from that between father and son. The father and daughter are often spared some of the natural competitiveness of the father-son bond. The fact that fathers and daughters are the opposite sex is both a special opportunity and a potential source of tension. Daughters may seem at times like better companions than wives; fathers in turn are the men daughters can first practice flirting with. We may become fascinated by our daughters' love of us, at times thrilled by it, just as they become thrilled by their capacity to charm us. This normal father-daughter romance may feel too intense for either father or child, leading one to withdraw from or degrade the other in ways that can be mysterious and hurtful.

Many fathers of daughters express relief at having had a girl, and being spared "the burden" of raising a son. "Within a week of getting Sally home as an infant, I was changing her diaper, and this overwhelming feeling of understanding passed over me—that if this was a boy I would be uncomfortable, I would feel threatened, I would feel competitive and inadequate to bring him up," recalled John, now aged forty-five with a teenage daughter. He went on: "All this flashed through me with the feeling that it was a girl and I felt totally at ease and comfortable and I knew I was going to be able to do it. That was a remarkable experience."

"What would it have been like with a son?" I asked John to imagine.

He was quick to respond: "I would have had to confront my father's inadequacy in trying to raise a boy and help him with all I struggled with."

With a daughter a father may feel less need to live up to painful ideals of manhood; he can feel freer to be playful and relaxed with his little girl.

Some fathers, though, feel disappointed at not having a son. "No one to carry the family name forward, no one to play football with," lamented one father of twin girls. A father may not know how to connect with girls. He may not see tossing a football around as appropriate play for girls, and may feel shut out of the feminine world that seems to interest his girls.

The very bond of flirtation and specialness between father and daughter can lead to pain and difficulty. The father may come to depend on his daughter for comfort and soothing that he wishes he got from his wife, or that he can't find elsewhere.

This bond may become particularly painful during the daughter's adolescence, when each confronts the task of letting go of the other. Often fathers become protective in a withdrawn, distant way—setting rules, criticizing a daughter's behavior or judgment—as a way of dealing with the powerful feelings of loss involved in the "launching" of their daughters.

"My daughter will never date until she's twenty!" one father said to me, half seriously. Can you imagine a father saying that about his son? Of course not, because men can identify with their sons' sexual conquests. But daughters are different. Many fathers want their daughters to have full lives and be vital, competent adults. They talk of how good it feels to see their daughters get good grades or be talented artists or dancers. But they draw the line at sex or romantic relationships. "I've always assumed my daughters will have careers," one father tells me. "It never occurred to me that either of them might be only a homemaker." But this same man is involved in a bitter struggle with his teenage daughter about dating.

Is it possible that we have worked out our attitudes toward our daughters' competence in this feminist age, but not about their sexuality? "I've finally figured out that a father's mission is to protect our daughters from birth until age fifteen," one father says to me.

Protect them from what? From men, the father explains. "We've all been teenagers, and every teenage boy I've known has been obsessed with sex in a way women are not. Boys have sex on their brains from age ten to thirty every minute of the day."

Having a daughter can put a man at odds with his own masculine identity. Suddenly, his own sex becomes the enemy. Men seem like predators, with only one thing on their minds.

I think men's preoccupation with protecting their daughters has more to do with their fear of forbidden fantasies, their love for their daughters, and the difficulty they have in letting go of their daughters on the verge of womanhood.

The reality is that although we want our daughters to be strong and competent, have their own careers, and be free, we don't want them to be free of us. We fall in love with them, and then they desert us for another man.

The Disney studio's treatment of the fable The Little Mermaid is instructive in this regard. In this story, Ariel is the mermaid daughter of King Triton, the Lord of the Oceans and Ruler of the Deep. When she falls in love with a human—Prince Eric—who lives on land, her father is furious. He tells her how awful life is on the surface, that she is to have no further contact with her prince, and forbids her to leave their underwater kingdom. Ariel defies him and makes a deal with the evil sea witch, exchanging her beautiful voice for a pair of legs. (One needn't be Freudian to wonder about the symbolism of what is happening below her waist, as her finny fishlike bottom becomes a lovely pair of legs.) After a series of high adventures, both Ariel and her father are saved from the sea witch, Ariel wins her prince, and the two are to be married. King Triton finally recognizes that this is to the good. Turning to his trusty counselor, the crab Sebastian, he reveals his true pain:

"There's just one problem," Triton confides dejectedly.

"What is that, Your Majesty?" inquires the crab.

"How much I'm going to miss her," is the resigned and honest reply. The father's struggle is not around men, or sex, but around loss and love.

Alex, a fifty-year-old college professor and father of a college student, attests to the same issue in "real life." He speaks movingly of his worry about "smothering" his daughter as she graduates college. He is mourning the loss of the person with whom he shares books, the person he talks to and confides in. She is for him still a fragile being whom he wants to protect, and whenever she goes out he anxiously inquires about how she'll get home safely late at night. But underneath this demanding kind of protectiveness the young woman feels her father's lack of confidence in her ability to be independent. His daughter sets limits on Alex, reassuring him that she knows how to take care of herself. His vulnerability seems the hardest thing for him to verbalize, the sense of loss that he feels in having his ally, this "better wife," leaving the house. As Alex talks he struggles to find a way to be available to his daughter without smothering her.

Just as it can be hard for a father to affirm his daughter's autonomy, so too it can be hard for him to affirm her sexuality. Fathers may need to put down or diminish a daughter's femininity in order to protect themselves from the attraction they feel. Or they may have difficulty in acknowledging the way a daughter disappoints them.

Mothers are gatekeepers for the father-daughter relationships, as they are for the father-son bond. The mother may encourage or discourage the continuing engagement between father and daughter in the way she responds to them.

"When my son turned twelve I turned to my husband and said, 'Now he's yours,' " remarked a friend of mine whose son and daughter are now grown. "I just felt he knew more about dealing with teenage boys and sexuality and all."

"And what happened when your daughter reached her teens?" I wondered aloud to her.

"Oh, that was different," she replied. "My daughter was mine."

Part of the attachment battle between father and daughter is to find a place for their bond amid the continuing importance of the mother-daughter relationship.

Particularly as the daughter becomes an adolescent, it may be difficult for a father to develop or sustain a relationship of intimacy with his daughter. The father may believe that since the mother "knows" more about the sexual and social questions that the developing daughter faces, he should "give her over" to his wife.

The daughter may then feel she has lost her father's interest just at the moment when she needs it most. Fathers need to remember the importance of affirming their daughter's sexuality and femininity, no matter who provides the "information" in the family.

The intensity of the cross-sex bond means too that daughters will have mixed feelings toward fathers: wanting to draw them closer and to be daddy's little girl without losing or alienating mother. If there is a sense of deserting or betraying mother by attaching to father, the daughter may feel bitterly torn. Once again fathers have to find a way to be constant and available in the face of the natural ambivalence their daughters feel toward them. A father must accept his daughter's occasional aloofness or her need to provoke fights or to be with mommy and not take these as signs that his continuing attention and support and availability are no longer crucial to her.

There will come a day—thankfully still far in the future—when an exciting male will make my daughter laugh with joy. And I suppose I'll try to block that, just as I tried to protect Emily from her loving brother. And I hope my daughter's no, no, to me will again be firm and clear. I hope I'll have the good sense to know what to do. I suspect I will. She's already begun training me.

For now, letting go is still far away, and I can enjoy being alone with my daughter. Recently, we were together in the house for the morning. It was time to dress her. She was up on the changing table and I reached for a familiar sweatsuit, but my eye caught something else: a flowery yellow sundress with little rabbits on it. I realized that I had never put a dress on Emily.

The dress slipped over her diaper. I brought the straps over her shoulders and buttoned the whole thing. There were even little panties that snapped over her diaper. She looked breathtaking.

I put her toys on the floor, and we played together happily. She was, as usual, quite interested in her brother's collection of superheroes, which I helped raid. As we contemplated Ming the Merciless and his buddy Garax the Robot, my wife walked in. She looked at Emily and said, "That's great, dear, but you've put on her dress backwards." Well, no problem. Emily and I have lots of time to work all this out.

THE UNCERTAIN DANCE OF FATHERHOOD

Fatherhood is a continual dance with uncertainty, a swaying back into the boyhood of our lives to find the responsive father within ourselves and a swing forward into the future as our growing children confront us with new issues, new aspects of ourselves. At times we have to set limits, at others lose limits; at moments we have to be "motherly" and supportive, at moments "fatherly" and affirming of mastery. Often we need to be both.

There are few simple, easy answers, and often the uncertainty of being a father can be the hardest part of the experience. We wonder whether we are doing right by ourselves and our families; we wonder about our children, our parents, our own childhoods, our fitness to be parents.

Let's take a look now at how men can nurture both the healthy boy and the strong-shouldered father within by coming to terms with their parents.

7

BETWEEN MEN AND

THEIR PARENTS

HEALING THE NORMAL WOUNDS

OF MANHOOD

DRIVING WITH MY FATHER

My father and I are alone in the car, hurtling north on the highway, when an unasked, unwelcome question pops into my mind:

"Dad, do you ever think about your death?"

I should have said *the* unwelcome question, for I often find myself preoccupied by thoughts of my father's death when we are together.

The fall foliage, glorious color anticipating the gray of winter, dances past the car window. We are driving up to New Hampshire together, to meet my mother, wife, and kids for a family weekend.

For as long as I can remember, my father has turned into a vagabond as soon as he gets behind the wheel of a car. He loves the mobility, the freedom to go anywhere, the escape from earthly responsibilities and worries about "the business." Wonderfully oblivious to his son's ruminations about death, my father is ecstatic about the open road.

"Oh, Sam, it's great just to drift along, you and I on the highway," he says with real pleasure.

I am decidedly more earthbound. Pretty little New England towns whiz by: I feel haunted, almost paralyzed by *the question*. For years I've wanted to talk to my father about death; to what end I'm not at all clear. It's rare for the two of us to be alone together; in fact, I partly arranged our trip so that we might have some time "to talk."

I decided to take the plunge, momentarily closing my eyes as if I'm about to dive into cold water:

"Dad . . ." I strive for a matter-of-fact tone, as if starting a talk about football scores. "Do you ever think about dying?" The question tumbles out of my mouth; I feel the shame and embarrassment of a twelve-year-old asking about sex. I've uttered the horrible "D" word. Will my father be angry at me for asking?

He looks askance at me, his eyes leaving the road, and there is a note of irritation in his reply. "Why do you ask?"

Have I broken a taboo—a taboo that forbids us to talk about mortality, that prohibits us from questioning the cozy fantasy that mommy and daddy will live forever? For a frantic moment unpleasant possibilities spring to mind: Does he wonder if I "know something" he doesn't—that he is ill perhaps? But he is not ill; he is in great health for a man in his seventies.

Does he imagine that I am ill? That I think obsessively of death? That I'm suicidal?

My embarrassment pivots on the fact that I know I want something from him, something I can hardly name. Futility engulfs me: Why try so hard for these "talks"? We've said it all to each other. Over the years we've talked about how absent he was from my life because of his work; we've forgiven each other for the wounds of adolescence.

I even have it on tape. The producer of the *Today* show approached me when I was promoting a book to ask if my father could appear with me on the show to talk about the father-son relationship. *Go on TV with my father? What would he say, how would he act?* Yet when our host asked my father in front of the cameras what it was like to be a father, he replied directly and compellingly: "Well, when Sam was young, in the 1940s, it was a different world; men weren't expected to be present in their families. I worked the day he was born and worked most of the days he was young. I missed out on a lot and Sam and his generation are trying to do it differently and I hope they succeed."

He's said it to me privately too, talking in a heartfelt manner about his preoccupations with work. And he takes time with his grandchildren now.

Yet still I hunger for something from him, I hunger enough to interrupt his foliage reverie.

His slight tone of annoyance at my question makes me rush to reassure him. I once again take a visit to the Lost Canyon of Inarticulateness.

"Just wondering," I say as casually as I can. "Do you ever wonder what death is like?"

I don't speak of what else is on my mind. That at times when the telephone rings at home at night, a bitter fear crosses my mind: *It's Mom calling to tell me that Dad has just died.* (It's my father's death I imagine; my mother seems timeless.)

My father and I look directly at each other, momentarily ignoring the road. It certainly would be easier if one of us *did* die; then we wouldn't have to suffer through these talks.

My father looks relieved that I haven't any bad news to spring on him. Generous man that he is, he strives to answer my question.

"No, Sam, I don't think much about death." He looks out the window, as if uncertain whether to say more. Then:

"Here's how I think of it: As far as I'm concerned, I'm going to live forever, and if I'm wrong, the moment I find that out, it won't matter to me."

He laughs. I laugh. We laugh together.

A joke, I think. I want to talk of eternal questions with my father and I get a joke.

I'm seized by a wish to grab my father by the neck and wring an answer out of him. How messy: The car would swerve, and while my father tried to steer around the fall foliage, his forty-five-year-old son, fingers locked around his throat, would be shrieking: *Tell me! Tell me! It took me thirty-five years to marry and thirty-eight to become a father and now I want to know what it all means. What do I mean to you? Do you know how important you are to me? We need to talk about all this before you die.*

Then I realize what I want from my seventy-five-year-old father: I don't want to be left alone without the answers. I want a father who can keep me safe and strong, teach me all I need to know to be a good-enough man. A father who can counterbalance and affirm all that I got from my mother. I think I'm going to have to settle for something less from him, and maybe something more. Maybe then we can forgive each other.

We chuckle some more about his joke, glad to be in each other's company, and as our eyes meet, silent together, I can see the essential loneliness of men.

Men and their fathers are often trying to find a way to heal the wounds and find some reconciliation as they age. In this chapter I want to explore what reconciliation with parents actually means in a man's life, how it happens, what gifts parents and sons have to offer each other, and at what price. I'm going to use the stories men have told me as ways to understand how we may go about the task of reconciliation with parents.

I'm going to focus on fathers, often the forgotten participants in men's lives, and then examine how coming to terms with fathers also means facing the crucial role mothers play in men's lives. I'll consider as well the profound sorrow, love, and protectiveness men feel toward their mothers.

"I wish we could have just said we love each other, just have said it directly," lamented a forty-six-year-old son about his father. "If only, just once, my father would tell me he loves me," ruminated a grown son.

"I think of my father every day, even though he died over five years ago," a talk show host tells me during a commercial break. He doesn't say this on the air, publicly, but saves it for a moment of relaxed private connection between us, as we chat during commercials for fast-food restaurants. "I just imagine him saying good things to me, enjoying the success I've had over the past few years. He never knew about it, he died before it happened."

We are so quick to think about alienation and hostility between fathers and sons—oedipal rivalry, competition for mother, unwillingness of either generation to give way before the other—that we can overlook their poignant search for connection.

The adolescent and young adult impulse toward separation and distance often gives way at mid-life to the yearning for reconnection, a wish to take care of "final payments" with parents. As they age, fathers often feel a strong desire to sort out the past with their children, yet they feel stumped about how to draw their children closer. "Kids don't realize that as fathers age the most important thing is *forgiveness*," advised a seventy-three-year-old father at a workshop, lamenting his son's refusal to join him there.

When men get together to talk about themselves and their lives, the talk often turns to fathers. "My father is a big mystery to me," confesses one fifty-year-old man. "He'd go out to work in the morning at six A.M. and return at six P.M. I hardly ever saw him." Men often talk about their fathers in a halting way, as if revealing a still-tender sore. They bring up father and then change the subject, or circle around the topic of fathers, leaving it and coming back to it. As one man talks, others will get lost in their own reveries or momentarily leave the room psychologically, silently making lists about errands they need to do, or protesting aloud, "What's the purpose of talking about fathers and mothers?"

Often the process of coming to terms with father and mother extends over a period of years. Reconciliation is rarely accomplished by one quick fix.

THE WOUNDED FATHER AND THE REAL FATHER

Fathers are the first men in our lives, and our first and strongest vision of masculinity. Sons look to fathers for affirmation, for information, and as reliable allies in the struggle to come to terms with mothers. Our identities as men are often tied to a sense of shame, anger, or grief about what happened between our fathers and ourselves, and the way we confront opportunities as fathers, husbands, friends, and workers is often pegged to the relationship with this first man in our life.

A group of men in their mid-forties is playing Top Secret, the game of memories with index cards. Each man writes down a particularly embarrassing moment with his father; the cards are collected, shuffled, and redistributed anonymously. Then each man reads aloud a shameful memory:

> When I was a boy and went to Sunday school, I had to wear a tie that I could not tie. My father would have to get up in the morning and tie it for me. He was irritated and rough in the process, causing me to feel stupid and inadequate and unloved. . . .

> At age eight or nine, my father was driven home intoxicated. His brother brought him home. My mother had been trying to protect me from knowing this, but through the evening her anxiety was rising to fever pitch. I picked up on her anxiety and felt very ashamed that my dad was out of control due to his drinking. . . .

> Seeing my father hit my sister in the face with a paint brush. He lost control and lost some respect from me. I was twelve. . . .

> Being spanked so hard by my father that I lost control and wet my pants. . . .

I refused my father's invitation to go watch a football game with him. He was hurt by that and went by himself. I stayed home and watched TV. . . .

I met my father one day on the street after he had moved out. It was cold, cold. He was dirty and his clothes disheveled. He said he had been robbed and asked me for money. I answered that I had none, although I did have some. I felt no compassion.

These memories reflect each man's image of a wounded father, rather than the reality of the father. When we are little, we usually know little of what our fathers are actually feeling or hoping. Instead we fabricate an image of our fathers, drawn from crucial and often painful moments, based on inadequate cues, quick glances, tones of voice. All children take such looks, tones, words, and actions very personally, interpreting events egocentrically.

As boys we often "misidentify" with our fathers, and construct an inner image of our own manhood around moments of shame, grief, and anger. Fathers are especially likely figures for these normal childhood "misidentifications" because they are absent so much, because there is so much intensity around fathers (who may strike a young boy as particularly heroic or judgmental or as a dismal failure), because often fathers assume (or are given by their families) only an authoritarian role and forget about the importance of a tender touch as well, and because of the normal "male clumsiness" around love.

Our own sense of self and our manhood is then linked to this "wounded" vision of our own fathers. There are many different kinds of wounded fathers in the lives of men.

Shaming Fathers. A man whose father shamed him when he could not tie his own tie may feel shamed and then get angry as an adult when confronting knots he cannot tie with his children, wife, mentor, or employees.

Fathers who seem too heroic to be real can also leave the grown son struggling with shame, grief, and anger if he fails to live up to this heroic image.

Shameful Fathers. When a man struggles with the shame of a troubled father—an alcoholic or overly needy man who seems to his son like a failure—he is speaking about his male lineage: *When men* *in my family get out of control, awful things happen.* His own ability to deal with the out-of-control parts of himself then becomes a painful source of vulnerability and anger. He may strive to redeem his own father, at the same time fearing to confront his own shame. Sometimes men have great difficulty even acknowledging that there is a problem or need in their lives for fear of becoming "pathetic" or too "needy."

Angry Fathers. Fathers who are abusive or angry can leave their sons quick to anger when vulnerable out of a misidentification with the fathers' rejection and rage. The man may greatly fear acknowledging his tender wishes and longing. In his poem "Passing It On," poet Reg Saner recalls a father who recently died, and who still lives within him:

> I was three and already
> my world shook with you.
> Now I'm what's left. The eyes
> I have are yours, your mouth.
> That trick of your upper lip—
> and those slurred l-syllables
> you still slide
> into a few of my words.

He recalled the "red fist" of his father's heart that

> I've chewed
> and gagged on, till I'm bled out and odd of it.

The anger is passed on through the generations:

> Already I'm hurt
> by my son's look—the way
> his eyes beat and grow secret
> under this strange love
> shaken into me.[1]

We all pass on some of the hurts—as well as the heroism—in our fathers' lives. Until men can come to terms with the shame, anger, and grief they carry around, they will find it that much harder to respond to their wives, children, bosses, and friends. We men must learn to express not only the hurt, but also the love in our hearts.

One way in which this happens is by grieving for our fathers. To do this means to explore and understand the heroism and failure in our fathers' lives, to see them more clearly. This means beginning to see them as real people struggling with pressures of their own, rather than as larger-than-life heroes or demons.

In "Father's Song," a love song about coming to terms with his father, singer Fred Small resolves: "Once more before he dies I will hold him in my arms without flinching."

Without flinching.

Fathers and sons flinch from one another because we get overwhelmed by sorrow, hope, anger, and embarrassment at our need for each other, because of the common myth that grown men have little to offer each other, and because of the ease with which men and their fathers get separated emotionally from each other in the family.

Kevin, whom I've come to think of as the Guerrilla Fighter, struggled with all these.

FLINCHING: THE GUERRILLA FIGHTER

"I finally got something from my father," confessed Kevin, a lanky forty-one-year-old teacher in a conspiratorial tone.

Kevin's father died when he was three; his brothers and sister were older and felt less "cheated" by the loss than did this youngest boy in the family who had little opportunity really to know his father. Kevin grew up with the humiliation of being one of the few boys in the community who had no father, relying instead on the fathers of friends to teach him about Little League and school affairs.

Kevin's mother never remarried, carrying a torch for the husband she had lost at the relatively young age of forty-five. Kevin became very bonded to his mother, the sole parent left, the essential parent whom he learned to protect.

Kevin told of a searing moment in his childhood: "One night when I was about seven I couldn't sleep and walked downstairs looking for my mother. I found her crying, holding a picture of my father. I turned around and went back upstairs. I never asked directly about my father again."

His father remained a sort of picture on the wall to his boy, a successful businessman fondly remembered in town, a man who had "died too young" from a heart ailment. Through his life, Kevin had learned to stiffen himself to his yearning for this father, gone but not forgotten.

Kevin married, became a father himself, and became quite good at the college teaching he did. But what haunted him was a simmering anger and sorrow, rooted in the feeling of never having really gotten what was rightfully his: a father to lean on, to support him, to help him in his need to separate from mother.

He came into counseling because becoming a husband and father often tapped both his anger at and yearning for his own father. "I feel too careful around my wife since she became a mother, trying to protect her and also angry at her. I feel the same way with my kids—I give to them and think about what I didn't get."

One day Kevin learned that his childhood home was being sold. This loss raised a number of painful questions for Kevin: Would he ever really feel like his father's son? Would he ever really feel like a man, given how distant he felt from his own father?

"I want something from him," Kevin mused one day.

"What do you want?"

Kevin thought of something concrete, an item he treasured: "A sword, the one my father had from World War II. It was a part of his army uniform." And it was visible in the picture of his father that his mother had held in her night of tears when Kevin was seven. The sword had been left behind in the basement after the house was sold.

"I used to look at that sword and think of my father: his strength, how handsome he looked in his army uniform."

Perhaps the sword could hang in his own house?

A new family was moving into the house shortly and it would be simple to ask for the sword. Except Kevin would not do that. He procrastinated, said he wasn't sure he could ask the new family for the treasure. He talked about the new owner, a father himself, and it was clear that there was something too "hot" in asking for fatherly attention from this man. The same old question lurked beneath Kevin's procrastinating: Can I be my father's son, comfortable in his memory, or do I feel like an orphan without even the memory of an available father?

So one night Kevin drove his station wagon three hours to the suburban family home, now being renovated by the new owners and still unoccupied. He pulled over to the side of the road across the street, put on camouflage clothes, darkened his face, and waited in his car. Past midnight, dressed like a guerrilla fighter, seeing no cars on the road, Kevin quietly opened the car trunk, got out a ladder, and scooted across the road. He quickly jumped the fence. With screwdriver in hand, he opened a window and silently climbed into the empty house to retrieve the dusty sword.

The next day, tired but victorious, he triumphantly told me of his exploits. There was one problem, though: He had to hide the sword in *his* basement since he didn't want to have to tell anyone how he got it. The birthright from his father remained hidden away.

At first I was shocked. Here he had taken the risk of trespassing, hidden from a police car as it passed, and committed theft. Why didn't he just ask for the sword that was rightfully his?

Then I realized: Kevin felt overwhelmed by the hunger he felt for his father. After a lifetime of proving independence he was deeply aware of wanting some sign of recognition from a father, even one who was dead, and of limited time to get it.

Grief and Father Hunger. For Kevin, to go to his father is to tap into the grief and sorrow of all he missed when that vital man in his life died too young. Many men have spent so much time proving they can make it without fathers who were absent, preoccupied, or otherwise unavailable that trying to connect with other men opens up deep wellsprings of grief. It can be hard for a man to acknowledge that pain.

Our grief also may reflect our wish to be rescued. In speaking of their disappointment in their fathers, men are often giving voice to their wish to have a man available, someone bigger and stronger who could come along and make things right, give us the right stuff at last, make us powerful and strong men like the stuff of our fantasies. Often men need to know that the yearning for a strong father is okay, and that some of our resentment of fathers springs from our own need. If we feel too ashamed of yearnings for a father's protection and comfort, then we can't talk about it. We can't forgive our fathers their failures, or ourselves our own.

We all yearn for protection. Men spend so much time taking care of other people, but who takes care of us?

In *Bonfire of the Vanities*, Tom Wolfe presents a wonderful portrait of this wish in the fateful recognition that his protagonist, Sherman McCoy, has at mid-life. Sherman McCoy, a wealthy investment trader, finds himself trapped in a spiraling web of lies and deceptions involving a mistress and a fatal car accident that threatens to overturn the foundations of his privileged life. Hounded and cornered as the truth is about to come out, Sherman desperately turns for help to his father, the aged "lion" of a Wall Street law firm. Wolfe's novel is a poignant study of shame and silence, and McCoy at this point is desperately seeking relief from a chain of events he cannot control and in which he is truly innocent, at least in part. As he walks into the law firm to see his unsuspecting father, Sherman remembers: "What bliss it had been, as a boy, to go visit Daddy in his office. From the moment he stepped off the elevator on the eighteenth floor he was His Majesty the Child."

Now Sherman confronts the wish for a protector, a shield against the humiliation and destruction about to descend upon him. But to find that protector he must show his need for him, something he has never been able to do. "Several times, in that glorious office, they came close to sitting down and having a real talk. Young as he was, Sherman had perceived that his father was trying to open a door in his formality and beckon him through. And he had never known quite how. Now, in the blink of an eye, Sherman was thirty-eight, and there was no door at all. . . . In his entire life he had never dared embarrass his father with a single confession of weakness. . . ."[2]

Sherman's father asks his son how things are going and Sherman confesses it all: that he's about to be arrested for reckless endangerment while driving, that there's a mistress, that he is losing his high-paying job.

His father responds by swinging into action, thinking about lawyers, offering to find him "the very best representation available." The only problem is that Sherman's father offers his son the names of "two old federal judges who were either retired or close to it." He buzzes a secretary to call these men, and, busy with work, she puts him off. Suddenly, his father looks rather lonely, old, and tired to his son.

"And in that moment Sherman made the terrible discovery that men make about their fathers sooner or later. For the first time he realized that the man before him was not an aging father but a boy, a boy very much like himself, a boy who grew up and had a child of his own and, as best he could, out of a sense of duty and, perhaps, love, adopted a role called Being a Father so that his child would have something mythical and infinitely important: a Protector, who would keep a lid on all the chaotic and catastrophic possibilities of life. And now that boy, that good actor, had grown old and fragile and tired, wearier than ever at the thought of trying to hoist the Protector's armor back onto his shoulders again, now, so far down the line."[3]

Sherman leaves the office, turning down his father's offer of money, unwilling to burden the aging man with further battles. In *Bonfire of the Vanities*, the discovery of his father's aging and limits is part of the process whereby Sherman McCoy comes to accept his own aloneness in the world, and to take active steps to regain control of his life. A crucial step for all men in coming to terms with their fathers is recognizing their fathers' limits and fallibility. In doing so, however, we face the anxiety of letting go of the personal myth that there is a powerful father "out there" who will come to help and protect us, if we only wait long enough.

Anger. Sherman may have felt like His Majesty the Child with his father, but Kevin, whose father died too young, never did. Kevin, in returning to his father for the gift of the sword, is also flooded with anger for all that he didn't get from his father. Breaking into the house is an expression of his wish to vandalize his father, to hurt him and get even. Many fathers and sons get so overwhelmed by the anger they feel toward each other that they have to withdraw to stay safe, to avoid the fear of hurting one another. Anger may be the only way left to fathers and sons to communicate.

Often at workshops for men and their fathers I'll start with an exercise in which men pair up to role-play a father and son. The task is to begin a father-son dialogue starting with the accusation that one teenager once made to his father:

"I'm glad to be leaving this fucking house! The only regret I have is leaving these poor helpless children in your care."

After completing the exercise some men say, "Yes, that's just how I left and now I don't know how to go back." Others say they couldn't imagine saying that for fear they or their fathers would wind up destroying each other; others speak of how awful it felt in the role-play to be a father hearing those words, how accused they felt and how much the urge to strike back rolled around with sadness and disappointment.

Often neither father nor son knows how to talk about the central word in the accusation: *helpless.* The father is helpless to feel admired and cherished by the son, while the son is helpless to get his father's blessing.

Often fathers and sons need to learn how much anger between them is a normal, almost expected, outcome given the pressures men operate under—the difficulty a father has in letting go of his son, the hopes and dreams and sorrows that are glued onto his son's life, the way we mix up our sons and ourselves. And for the son: how difficult it is to ask for your father's attention, to declare your independence from him and still feel as if you can hold on to him when you need him.

Shame. At the deepest level, Kevin doesn't want to take the risk of being turned down. Here is a powerful roadblock between father and son in working out their shame, anger, and love: *Both sides are* *scared they'll be rejected if they turn toward each other.* Kevin doesn't want to ask the new owner of the house for his father's sword because he doesn't want to get turned down again, the way he felt continually turned down by his father's absence from his boyhood.

What is the wound that father and son inflict on each other? It opens from the difficulty fathers and sons have in communicating that they are beloved to each other. Men and their fathers often avoid each other out of shame—they need each other but they don't know how to close the distance between them. Men I've known have missed family celebrations or anniversaries, kept conversations at surface levels, or spent time around their fathers but not *with* them because they cannot tolerate the shameful sense of diminishment they feel in their fathers' presence. Why, these sons wonder, must *they* be the one who takes the first step in trying to right an alienated relationship? The wound remains unhealed until both father and son can take these steps together.

THE WOMAN ON OUR SHOULDERS: LOVE BETWEEN MOTHER AND SON

Kevin has to claim his father's love like a thief in the night because he wants to protect his mother. To really go to his father in memory, to imagine himself beloved by his father, and to feel the right to ask for his father's sword, means to risk wounding his mother. Some men imagine that they are putting mother down or declaring her not good enough if they show a deep need for their fathers.

Men often don't claim their birthright with their fathers because they feel caught between mothers and fathers. Sons may act as surrogate husbands to their mothers—"better" husbands than their fathers—and carry around that shame. Many of us as boys, sometimes even as men, did prefer our mothers to our fathers, finding mother to be the one who listened more fully to us, to be more exciting and emotionally rewarding or available. The normal romance between mother and son is a powerful one in the lives of both participants. But when the time comes to resurrect our fathers, we fear their final accusation of our betrayal of them. For Kevin it was almost as if he imagined his father staring down from the picture on the wall and saying: "You little mama's boy, hiding in her skirts, you're not man enough for me to come back from the dead for!" In other words: *You're not worthy of my sword.*

For Jim, an unmarried business consultant, the fear of wounding mother was quite real. Jim grew up in a household with a family secret: his father, mayor of the town he still lives in, was an alcoholic. Jim's father died when Jim was in his teens, yet no one in the house could talk of the cause of his death. Jim at age forty carried around a painfully wounded image of his father's last year, in which his decline was obvious even if the reasons behind it were not. As a teenager Jim struggled with the humiliation of having a father on various kinds of medications, "acting weird." Jim's own sense of himself was very much tied to having a father who had failed and fallen apart toward the end of his life. Jim spent many years trying to console his mother for the loss of her husband, attempting to replace the lost father.

Finally, at age forty, unable to himself marry, struggling with low-paying jobs, Jim needed to know the truth about his father's illness. Had he died of kidney failure? Was he an alcoholic? These were the questions he needed to answer before he could get on with his life, "and truly lay my father to rest." The medical records were available to Jim at a local hospital, but he would not get them without his mother's permission. Legally he was entitled to see the records, but emotionally he was blocked from going to the hospital and asking for them.

One day near the anniversary of his father's death, Jim and his mother drove to the gravesite. Walking through the tree-lined cemetery, one arm supporting his mother, Jim summoned the courage to ask the unaskable:

"Mom, I want to get Dad's medical records from the hospital."

Moving the scarf on her head so she could see her son better, Jim's mother answered: "Let your father rest in peace, will you!"

Jim never asked about his father again, and continues to be haunted by his father's decline, unable himself to rest in peace.

Jim's story illustrates the way in which some sons are prevented from coming to terms with father by their fear of hurting mother, and by their need to protect her.

In one weekend workshop on "Men and Their Fathers," as we regrouped after Saturday lunch, Michael sat with an agonized look on his face. His look seemed out of place, given our camaraderie and the openness and hope many men were feeling as they talked about the topic that always seemed taboo growing up: "My father," as one man put it.

Michael was clearly involved in a painful inner struggle. He had talked movingly during the morning session about the absence of his father from his life, and he began to see the pain he and his father shared: how welded to his work his father was, how much he had been excluded from the family because of his mother's importance to the children and her expertise at being "a mother" in the family, and how much grief and loss was buried in his father's silent, stoic demeanor. Michael began to feel much closer to his father, and his angry alienation began to melt into a deeper understanding.

Then after lunch, Michael shifted uncomfortably in his chair and said: "All during lunch I've felt troubled. Here we are talking about fathers and ourselves, but it feels to me as if my mother is sitting on my shoulder the whole time, saying, 'What about me?' "

Michael was giving voice to his mixed love for and fear of his mother. He worried that by reconnecting with his father he might in some way damage or lose the woman he most depended on as a child, and still loved so deeply as a man.

It can be very difficult for men to talk about their love for and fear of their mothers. Men may fear their mothers' retribution for opening up family secrets, for losing their love, or for damaging or hurting them by what they say or do. Men who were swamped or overwhelmed as children by mothers who were overly dependent on them emotionally may feel *responsible* for their mothers' emotional well-being as adults. The bottom line is that struggles with mother often leave men feeling like little boys, fearful and unsure. Father stuff is manly and you can wrestle with dad, but mothers are more swampy and all-encompassing. Wrestling with mom can be particularly scary, leading to hidden taboos and attractions too seductive to name. One man, angry for years at his father's absence and "emotional neglect," described his father as "like a dragon, scaly and tough to fight with," but his mother was "like a fog, it's hard to describe her."

What emerged for this man was that his father was a lightning rod for the family anger and hope, that by virtue of his daily work and vital energy, he offered a vision of hope to the son who was left behind with mother, having to take care of her and overly dependent on her. His anger at his father masked his profound sense of disappointment that his father hadn't helped him cope more directly with his mother. For many of us men it is safer to get angry at father than to be angry with mother.

Mother love is crucial for children; its absence or loss can leave the sort of "hole in the world" that Pulitzer Prize–winning author Richard Rhodes writes so movingly about in his memoir of his childhood without his mother, who committed suicide when he was an infant.[4] The early experience of mothers' emotional importance often hinders men's ability to see their mothers clearly and separately as they both age. Our very lives depend on our mothers when we are first born, and for many men their emotional lives continue to be tied to their mothers throughout their development. Particularly given father's physical or emotional absence, many of us as boys depended heavily on mother's comfort and reliability, the way she could restore or take away our self-confidence with the tone of her voice, a few words, the expression on her face. The fear of damaging mother or being abandoned by her, in either case of *losing her*, is very strong in grown men.

Michael's question about his mother opens the way for all the men in the group to talk about their love for their mothers. Each man takes an index card and writes down what he would most like to say to his mother at this time in his life.

How much I loved my mother singing me to sleep: "You are my sunshine". . . .

I love you very much. I am scared that when you die, I'll have to face all the pain around Dad's death too. . . .

Slow down, Mom. Get to know Dad a little better. He doesn't have long to be in this world. Sit down and talk to him. . . .

I'm a grown man with my own family and responsibilities, not a child anymore. . . .

Accept me as who I am without judging me. I need you . . . Never forget that I love you. . . .

Several of the men reveal the shame of feeling too bonded to mother, cut off from father:

Since I was the oldest, Mom shared many of her frustrations about Dad with me. It was too much for me!!! It made me feel bad about him. . . .

When I was twenty I wanted to learn how to drive. My mother prevented my father from teaching me. She was too afraid to risk it—possible damage to the car. . . .

I was about eleven. I was feeling affectionate and playful and chased her around the house. She fell and started crying about what a rotten life she had. . . .

Once at the dinner table, my mother and father were talking about an unmarried girl they knew who was pregnant. My mother turned to me sharply and said, "If you ever make a girl pregnant, you needn't bother coming home again." At that time, I had never even had a close relationship with a girl. Kissing a girl caused me anxiety enough. I felt ashamed and betrayed that she could distrust me so much, just because I was male. . . .

I screamed at my mother in front of my family for trying to run my family's life and I had to be separated by my wife. . . .

Mom died early for our long-lived clan of heart disease. We didn't appreciate how ill she was; Dad tried to care for her himself, and didn't let on to the gravity of her illness. My sister and I felt somehow cheated that we didn't know and weren't there for her in the end. She slipped away without being noticed, after doing so much for us all.

Even though many of the men are revealing painful, ugly episodes with these stories, the strongest undercurrent is men's love for their mothers. When a man says that his mother took out many of her frustrations with his dad through him, he is also saying how hard he worked to heal his mother, to make her less frustrated and demanding. When a man remembers a mother's distrust, he is also giving voice to how much he wanted her to love and trust him, how important her responses were to him, how much he wanted to elicit the gleam of love in her eye. A man who felt cheated by his mother's secret illness and her too-early death is expressing the loss of his ability to say "I love you" to her, and to see her recognition of his love.

In this way men are honoring their mothers and the parts of themselves that are rooted in their love for her. It can be an uneasy love, though, as we speak of "disavowed" parts of ourselves that are like our mothers, or loyal to her. Talking about our mothers, holding on to them emotionally, without flinching, can bring forth the same kind of shame, anger, sorrow, and love that trying to connect with our father does. In order to explore their love for either parent, men need to know that it's okay to love both parents and to express their love for both parents. When love in a family becomes too "skewed" so that the child feels that he belongs only to one parent, then that child's sense of self is skewed too.

The sense of being the property of mother can haunt us into adulthood. When a man reconnects with his love of his mother, his yearning to heal or protect her, he can very quickly feel lost in the intensity of that yearning. There is a real fear of being smothered or overwhelmed by this emotional need for one's mother's comfort and protection. Often, however, our fear of our mother pivots on our father's absence. We fear mother's power because we don't have a reassuring internal sense of father's love and protection. We avoid being too emotionally close to mother because we weren't close enough to father. When all is said and done, the major complaint of many sons about their fathers often boils down to this: *They didn't save us from our mothers.*

This is not mother-bashing. Mothers can experience considerable pain at the wish to hold on to and let go of their sons. A son may bear the burden of a mother's hope for a better relationship than the one she has with her own husband, he may be her vehicle to redeem masculinity, or to heal the wounded father within her. Or he may be the vehicle for her to punish men and to revenge herself on the wounded father within. Carl remembers coming home from dates in adolescence to find his mother weeping on the couch about the maltreatment she received from her husband. Carl became painfully split between his loyalty to his mother ("Men are such brutes") and his loyalty to his gender ("I want to date women, not listen to my mother's pain").

Beyond this, a mother deeply loves her son as a child "of woman born," and she may struggle with the question of how to raise a being born of her body who is also her opposite, biologically and culturally. As Carole Klein writes in her book *Mothers and Sons:* "Mothers are told to remain emotionally involved with their sons so that the sons have enough psychological support to fulfill society's expectation of them. Yet as a woman embraces her male child, some voices will rise in ominous warning that she may create a 'mama's boy,' the ultimate crime. As a result, mothers often seem to live with their sons on the edge of pain, wanting to stay close, afraid not to pull back. . . ."[5]

The edge of pain around separation and loss may be very real for mothers as well as sons. The poet Adrienne Rich captures this in her image of fathers through history savagely crying to mothers: "My son is mine!"[6]

The pain of loss between mother and grown son, unable to re-unite across the chasm of biology and culture, may last a lifetime. Both are perched "precariously, on a fragile leaf," in the words of poet Eric Ormsby describing his relationship with his aging mother.

Yet for the grown son, the capacity to see women clearly— making them into neither needy dependents whom he must overpro-tect and "tame," nor into romantic angels whose love will save him from life—rests on an ability to come to terms with his love for, debt to, and anger at his mother. So too rests his capacity to hold on to the heroic qualities of his mother—her toughness, tenderness, and care—and his ability to offer those same qualities to himself and those he loves.

Often a man's relationship with his mother becomes more in-strumental and distant as the two of them age. Mothers and grown sons may be trying to connect but not know how to bridge the gaps between them. The very aging of a mother may leave a man helpless to know how to address his feelings for her. Finding his aging mother becoming "ever more fragile and precarious," poet Eric Ormsby writes:

> I love her now more urgently
> Because there is an unfamiliar and relentless
> Splendor in her face that terrifies me.[7]

Grieving for our mothers is similar to grieving for our fathers: It means coming to terms with them as real people, working on our relationship with them, and coming to terms with the depths of our need for them. We need to get perspective on our mothers and our fathers, to see them as people struggling with flaws and strengths, not as cartoon characters of ultimate power of judgment.

This process of coming to terms with parents is not a luxury, but rather a normal developmental marker of adult maturity. The quality of the adult relationship with parents, and, more important, the in-ternal image of them we carry around within us, are important pre-dictors of psychological well-being in adults.[8]

Let's focus in more detail on what is involved in the process of reconciliation between men and their fathers.

WHAT DOES RECONCILIATION MEAN?

We are not talking here about a heavy psychological airing out of all the dirty laundry in a family nor of a father and son becoming buddy-buddy in a superficial friendship, but rather about a father and son coming to see that the wounds of the past are healed and that there is some common ground and shared struggle between them, a mutual respect and appreciation. "Things are better with my father because now when I'm home with him it's no longer as if someone is running their fingernails on a chalkboard the entire time I'm around him," advised one man.

Reconciliation is rooted in the ability to gain perspective on the difficulty of the relationship, and see things less personally. What felt like a personal failure or attack or abandonment looks different when seen in its larger context. This happens in several different ways.

Getting perspective. Sons often need to explore their fathers' histories. The grown son can enlarge the narrow, one-dimensional image he had of his father as a child by coming to understand father as a real person, caught within the pressures and conflicts of the male role. Sons have described finding and reading the journals and diaries of their fathers. Often mothers have produced father's diaries for their sons years after the man's death. "I didn't even know it existed," exclaimed an older man obviously joyful to find his father had an inner life that included ruminations about him.

Talking to peers and relatives about one's father can extend our understanding. Business associates often knew the man better, alas, than we did.

A mathematician told me that when he was a teenager, his father seemed to disappear emotionally from his life. His father was never around and this was a deep wound for the growing boy. After his father's death, his mother gave the grown son his father's journal.

"I read to my shock that when I was fifteen my father was fired from his job for union organizing. He was so shamed by this he never told his children and then began to work three part-time jobs to support the family. He was working from eight A.M. to ten P.M. all those years. Seeing [what] my father struggled with makes me feel much more connected to him. I can see how similar he and I actually are."

Sometimes small pieces of information can solve larger puzzles. In exploring their histories, we may see new sides of our fathers, and come to understand ourselves better as well.

Because so many fathers and sons lack a common language for affection and caring, they need to develop such a language as adults.

One grown son was shocked to hear his father confess: "I never knew how to be both your father and your friend when you were young."

Small gestures, words, moments of shared perception can change a lifetime of alienation. "My father was dying in the hospital and I went to visit," one man told me. "I felt it would be the last time I'd see him. He had tubes coming out of his throat and seemed weak. All my life I had wished for more from him, and he never really took the time. When I walked into the room, he saw me and took out a pad he used to write on. He wrote:

" 'Sorry I can't talk, glad you're here.'

"It felt to me that he was saying that he was sorry for *all* the times we didn't talk. I've kept the note; it was very healing between us."

There may be only so much fathers can give emotionally. Some are inept, some pathological, others have aged and changed in ways that we don't see. What's particularly important is to "detoxify" the pain of the past by seeing that fathers and sons are not simply demonic or heroic figures, but that both are caught within larger personal, family, and social forces that create disappointment and sorrow as well as opportunity. We need to see that change is possible for both fathers and sons, that both may be trapped in outdated misperceptions that block the opportunities in the present. At root, the real work of reconciliation is *within ourselves*: seeing the past and present in a different light, getting past the normal blinders we bring to relationships.

COMING TO TERMS WITH THE FATHER WITHIN

Ultimately the task is internal: to see our fathers and mothers more clearly, to heal the wounds that come from misinterpretations and misunderstandings. If we understand their wounds—their shame, grief, and anger—then we can begin to understand how we share those wounds and pass them on in our own lives.

One of the most powerful moments in many men's lives comes when men give physical expression to their fathers' wounds. There are many ways to do that, and I have come to love the use of sculpting clay for its ability to evoke some of the most important and private parts of our pain as men.

SCULPTING OUR FATHERS

"Sculpt something that represents your father's grief," I tell a roomful of men. A fire crackles in the background; it is evening, after dinner, at a weekend men's retreat held in a lovely conference center not too far from downtown Chicago.

I have given each of the thirty-five men in the large, comfortable room a half pound of gray, wet clay. We sit at tables, in groups of five, most men looking curiously at the wet clay resting on top of old newspapers, the dated news stories a reminder of men's affairs out there in "the real world."

The men look apprehensive. I've just asked them to stick their hands into primordial ooze. We take our time, there's no rush. Each man plunges into the task and sculpts away.

One man holds up a clay heart: *He worked too hard all his life. He died when he was fifty-eight. He literally blew a hole in his heart.* Another man stands and shows us a clay fist, knotted tightly: *This is a clenched fist, tight and angry. My father never let up on himself or on us, and I am realizing that his parents pounded on him just the way he pounded on us.* Another man holds up a smooth, thick, square piece of clay: *A blank wall—I don't know anything of my father's grief. He was always in control, always perfect.* Several men shape the clay into phalluses: *My father's impotence in dealing with life.*

We begin to see our own wounds in our fathers, that we have identified with them and re-create parts of them even as we try to be different. Frank, who fashioned a clenched fist out of clay, is at the weekend because he hopes to find a different way to be with his children than the one he knew with his father. Max, whose father spent his life impotent and afraid, can't activate images of himself as a powerful and tender man. His sculpture? A wheelbarrow: *My Father spent his whole life working on the farm and got so little from his family.* Max thinks about the difficulty he has in being present with his wife and children.

Several men are crying; we all seem partly lost in dream images of our fathers.

One man reflects: "It's painful to think of my father as wounded and suffering and none of us knew anything about it; he kept all of that from us."

Yet as we get in touch with our fathers' grief, they become less "crazy" or mysterious. For some men, their fathers' sins become ones of omission rather than commission. Anger at father is replaced by a sadness at seeing father trying to connect, and lacking the skills to do it, of father trying to live his life in the best way he knew how. Men come to see themselves as both similar to and different from father, and having some choice in how they live.

You don't have to be a clay sculptor to explore your father's history.

Seeing yourself as having power, not just as the victim in the relationship, can be helpful. Often sons come in with a heavy agenda and talk *at* their fathers rather than listening to how much their fathers are actually saying when they talk about work, family, disappointments, and satisfactions, what they would do differently and what they feel most proud of.

In expanding our internal vision of our parents, we are also expanding our own possibilities and healing ourselves.

When men return home from a "Men and Their Fathers" workshop, they usually don't report enormous changes in their fathers or mothers, but over time they do find changes in *themselves*: how they see and understand who they are and who their parents are.

GARY AND HIS AGED FATHER IN THE GARAGE

"Growing up it was as if my father lived in the garage," Gary remembers, "working on his cars, spending more time with my brother there. I didn't much like the garage and didn't much like my father: he's a pretty angry, sarcastic, dominating sort." Gary, who works as a university professor of English, has chosen a very different life for himself. "Last year, though, my father turned eighty, and I wanted to go back to the farm, spend some time with him. So I took a week off and decided to stay with him and go into that garage. He still works there! We put engines in, took them out, tuned them up, things I've never been very good at.

"Two things happened, both of which I'll treasure. At one point I was trying to get a spark plug out of an engine and I couldn't do it. I got furious at myself; I couldn't even twist out a spark plug!

"My father leaned over and said, very gently, 'Here, let me do that—my fingers are used to this sort of thing.' I felt validated and seen by him in a way I had never been before."

When Gary's father leans over to his son with these words, displaying gentleness and tenderness, he is healing the son's image of his father and himself. The father is no longer just a critical judge who seems to say to his son: *You could never be a real man, you wimpy English professor.* Instead he forgives the son's incompetence and he tempers his harshness. Momentarily, Gary is a little boy being sheltered by his father.

"The other moment I'll treasure happened when my father started berating me as he always had, yelling at me for breaking something in the garage. I looked at him and said simply, 'Don't talk to me like that.' And he stopped! I have to say I came away from our time together pretty proud of the man. Eighty years old and still handling cars like a twenty-year-old. He's quite a guy."

By asserting himself in this way and by remaining open to his father's willingness to change, Gary heals his own self-esteem and raises the image he has of his father. Gary has insured that he no longer feels scorned and rejected by a man whose validation truly does matter to him.

Healing wounds is not always accomplished so effectively. One man I know wrote his father a letter listing one hundred things his father had never done for him, and then was upset when his father never replied! It can be important to be clear about goals in these matters: Are you talking to or writing to your father in the hopes of fighting old battles one more time, or of finding a way of healing old wounds?

Perhaps fathers are fated to let their sons down, and vice versa. We want so much from them—to show us how to live as a man, to deal with women, to feel okay about ourselves, to pass on the sacred vows of masculinity (whatever they are)—and yet many fathers are just trying to get out of life alive.

When there is too much alienation and distance, grown sons have little opportunity for a healing of the image of their fathers. If we fail to see a different side of our fathers as they age and mellow, we remain locked into a cartoon image of them that hampers our own growth as fathers and men.

TOM'S DISCOVERY: A FATHER'S SECRET
AND THE HEALING OF SELF

Sometimes a father's death frees us even as it wounds us. When I was interviewing men who changed careers I met Tom, who had left a painful career as a lawyer to pursue a successful career as a visual artist. At age forty, Tom was active and hardworking, teaching painting and exhibiting his work. Yet he lamented one prize that eluded him: His father had never acknowledged his new career and the difficulties involved in his changes at mid-life. His father was a banker and Tom felt his father always valued him less than an older brother who became successful in business.

The feeling of never really having gotten enough punctuated Tom's life. In his first marriage he never felt truly appreciated, and after the births of his children he didn't feel much emotional satisfaction in being a father. Deep down, Tom struggled with a nagging sense of worthlessness: Could he ever do enough to feel really cherished? The one person he most wanted to feel good enough for was his father, who never gave him a blessing.

Despite his success at work throughout his thirties and forties, Tom struggled with this question: *How did I get this feeling that I have to be a terrific painter? Why do I have to push so hard?*

I went back to see Tom when he was fifty, and he told me sadly that his father had died since we last met. "There was this odd occurrence. Soon after my father's death I was reminiscing with my cousin, who told me a story his father, my uncle, recently told *him*.

"Seems my uncle had been present when my father asked my mother to marry him. Here's what my uncle saw and heard: One day my father went up to my mother's father and asked for her hand in marriage. Grandfather asked what his plans were.

" 'Well sir, I want to be an artist,' my father told him.

"Grandfather was a rather crusty Victorian gentleman who often spoke in an ex-cathedra fashion. He responded sternly: 'Well. You can be anything you want, but you can't be an artist and marry my daughter—you won't be able to support her.' "

Tom was shocked and relieved and hurt as he began to intuit that his own life was partly a living out of his father's failed dream. There was grief and a wound in his father's life that had never been shared.

Tom told me that his father "watched me change out of law into something more risky or more difficult to pin down without ever sharing anything of his own about that struggle."

What Tom didn't get from his father informs what he does with his own children.

"I have tried to change that with my own children. Be more of a person to them and less like a sort of figurehead. To tell them how I feel sometimes. *I'm trying to live out something I would have preferred.*"

Tom offers an important lesson: how healing it can be for us to give to others what we didn't get. As he puts it, "I'm trying to shift out of being a parent into being able to enjoy my children as people and really listen. And I discover the main thing is that they want to hear what I feel and think. They want to hear it and I'm trying to pull away from the way my father did it. I'm trying to be a full partner in conversation."

Then Tom offers an important observation: *"The struggle for me partly was to realize that they are interested in what I thought."*

In struggling with his father's remoteness and pain, Tom is able to cherish himself and see that what he has to contribute emotionally to a family is valuable and worthwhile. Most important, Tom shows us that even when a father is no longer alive, it is possible to do work on the relationship. New information about his father changes Tom's image of his father and himself, and in giving to his children what he wished for from his father, Tom is healing his own image of himself.

I realized some of the importance of taking the time to find one's father emotionally after listening to Arnold's story of how he handled his father's stroke. It was a moment that allowed him to reconnect with his father in the absence of his mother.

TIME FOR CHILDREN: ARNOLD AND HIS SICK FATHER

Doris Lessing once observed: "We use our parents like recurring dreams, to be entered into when needed; they are always there for love and hate; but it occurs to me that I was not always there for my father. . . ."[9]

Throughout adult life we pick through our memories of mother and father in times of personal change as ways to understand who we are. Often we struggle with an attachment battle with the self: Do we listen to our hearts or not? Arnold is a fifty-year-old real estate developer in a high-powered western company. He is married to a businesswoman, and they have several children. I met Arnold because he is part of the Adult Development Project, a study of men now at mid-life who graduated Harvard in the mid-1960s.

When I first interviewed Arnold, at age thirty-eight, he didn't get around to telling me about his parents until near the end of the interview, and then it was mainly to say: "I've never been close to them at all. I've disliked my father for years and I'm just all alone." He was resentful of how he was raised by his father: "He still doesn't know very much about what it is like to be a child. He's very intolerant of children being children." He ended his description by saying, "I make every effort to stay as far away as I can," laughingly indicating that one reason Harvard was so attractive to him as an undergraduate was that it was three thousand miles away from home.

Ten years later, Arnold, now forty-eight, is talking about his parents within the first five minutes of sitting down with me. Sitting behind his corporate desk, he reflects, "I've become much more tolerant of them. When I'm visiting the old reactions come back and they are very familiar, but I can deal with them more appropriately." His words are not unusual: A deepening understanding of father is often part of the grown man's maturation.

He then tells me about the impact that his father's stroke had on him five years earlier. In his mid-seventies, his father had gone into the hospital for minor surgery and was recovering when he had the stroke. Arnold was involved in some intense real estate negotiations, yet he dropped it all to fly to his father's bedside. "I was working two hundred hours a month and for a while I had been doing hundred-hour weeks, and my wife and I had some trouble and then my dad had his stroke and it was an important time in the structuring of a deal. But when I got the phone call that my father was in the hospital I immediately made airline reservations and told the managing partners in the firm that I was going home for a week because everyone was telling me that my father was going to die."

Arnold was walking out the door of his office for the airport when his phone rang. "It was the managing partner," Arnold told me, "a very tough, nasty guy who makes as much money as he can and damn anything else." Arnold related the conversation:

"You can't go home now!"

"My dad is dying; I'm going to see him."

"This is really a shitty thing to do."

"I told him I was going home, had left memos for my staff, and that he could fire me if he wanted to."

"Turns out he forgot about it completely when I returned, and everything went along fine."

What was most important was what happened with his father. His mother went off on a well-deserved vacation, and it was just Arnold and his father, alone together for the first time in decades.

"When I was out there staying with my father, that was very important. He can't remember that period now but I helped him a lot. I had to bathe him some, take him to the bathroom. He doesn't remember it now but *it was important for me to do it and it had a real effect on my feeling about him*. I was able to keep him comfortable and kept him away from his tendency to be picky and enticed him into some very happy moments together." Arnold's sense of himself and his father changed as he saw a more responsive and playful side of the man.

Most important, Arnold found that he had something to give to his father, and that his gift was treasured. So Arnold's sense of himself was expanded: He went on to describe being more emotionally available and more able to cajole his teenage daughter out of her hard places now that he'd found that part of himself with his father.

Arnold's story helps us see that men grow and learn by giving. They can reconcile with parents by offering themselves in new ways. Sometimes *being with* and *giving to* our parents or our children are just as important as what we say to them.

CLAIMING OUR BIRTHRIGHT

Men's attempts at self-exploration can at times have a comic aspect, but underneath this I think there is a real purpose that has to do with claiming our birthright as men, claiming what we are entitled to by our very existence. Often we are struggling to claim a birthright from our fathers: a fuller sense of masculinity as strong and playful, boyish and fatherly at the same time.

Finding the birthright means feeling a satisfying sense of masculinity, feeling like a beloved son and an adequate man. Instead of having to prove our manhood all the time in work or toughness or distance, we learn how to combine both strength and love.

So Arnold, struggling with ambition and the need for recognition, begins to accept the playful part of himself, the one that wants to be home more with family, spend less time at the office.

"Maybe it's this competition I had with my father," he reflects, "some sort of proving who was right. My father was always very stubborn. He liked to debunk things. We had the first TV on the block and we'd watch 'Superman' and my father would sit there dismissing what happened. I was always being told to have adult approaches to things as opposed to childish approaches."

We internalize our fathers, we become the wounded fathers we lament. If he had to be right, and not childish, then we do too: no little boys allowed. In seeing fathers age and mellow, some of those wounds become healed within ourselves: We have less need to always be on top, to always be right. We can remember the child who was awed and passionate and loving, and nurture him within ourselves and others.

ACTIVE, HOPEFUL MEMORY:
THE DEATH OF A FATHER

Men search for this birthright even after their fathers have died. Jim
at age fifty felt rather distant from his father, feeling his sisters were
more favored. His father had died several years earlier, without the
words or gestures of acknowledgment that Jim had yearned for. There
were, though, two special links with his father that he treasured still
in memory. Jim struggled to claim both.

"When I was a young boy, I got very interested in what
my father collected: Indian arrowheads. Where we lived on the
Cape there had been Indian camps and there were Indian grave-
sites around, and my father showed me and I really picked up his
interest in that. We'd be looking around and talking and sometimes we'd find something very special, and he loved it and I did
too." Jim's hands danced in the air as he spoke of those trips.
Here is where he felt safe and alive: searching for things with his
father.

"Over the years we accumulated a wonderful Indian arrowhead
collection, which we kept in the living room of our house." Jim's
voice grew thick as he spoke of this connection to his father.

"After he died, everyone in the family wanted the arrowhead
collection, and I wasn't sure whether to ask for it or not. My brother
wanted it and I said why not?"

Despite the seeming ease with which he gave the collection away,
his disappointment and pain were palpable as we spoke. Would he
ever be able to feel like a beloved son to his father?

As we talked, we walked down to see the pond on his rural farm.
Watching me carefully, he told me about "a strange coincidence."

"Soon after I bought this property I was picking up some flat
rocks for a wall I'm building. One day I was down here after it rained
very hard. I was looking for rocks for the wall and it hit me like a
flash that right in front of me were some flat rocks. I started looking
for points, arrowheads. And I picked up five in an hour."

He laughed, shyly confessing: "It was like such a strong connection to my youth, to my father."

Pointing to a spot across the pond, he spoke of the "second
coincidence." He had given his father a woodcarving of an otter
that he had himself made. This was another special connection; his
father loved otters. Again a gift was lost as Jim allowed the woodcarving to stay at the family house when it was sold.

"The next day after I found the arrowheads, I'm looking across the pond and an otter comes out of the bushes and looks at me then ducks back into the reeds.

"It was all so coincidental, but I felt as if my father was saying hello to me, telling me that it was all right. There's something about this pond; it makes me feel so much more rooted here."

Jim reminds us that men can transform their relationships with their parents in *their memory*, in how and what they choose to remember about their parents. Jim works hard to retrieve the loving connections with his father, actively transforming his relationship with the man.

Ultimately reconciliations with parents are disappointing as well as empowering, because we rarely get all we hoped for from them. We seek a blessing and permission from our mothers and fathers that in the end we can only give ourselves. We yearn to feel, like Kevin, that we mattered to our fathers, that our love can be heard and legitimated by our fathers. We want to be able to express our love for our mothers, and to be able to freely express the parts of ourselves that are like them. We yearn to know that our capacity to love matters, to know that we matter as loving, responsive sons.

That may not be something that a parent can provide to the grown man; it may need to be found elsewhere: in our children's smiles, in our wife's joy at feeling supported and loved by us, in a friend's willingness to rely on us in a moment of need. These adult moments are restorative of the holes in ourselves. When the loving parts of ourselves are affirmed by others, we see that we matter and are worthwhile, that our ability to be emotionally present is cherished. In these moments we see a different vision of ourselves "mirrored" back to us, a vision that heals our childhood wounds.

Grieving for mothers and fathers may not be something that men can do on their own, individually. A man may be locked in by family taboos, or by explosive feelings, the shame and loneliness may be too much, or a father or mother may be unavailable in reality or in memory. How, then, are grief and shame healed, anger tempered?

It may be that men need to do some of this healing together, finding in the shared safety and challenge of men's groups and men's friendships a new and sturdier vision of manhood than that rooted in childhood wounds. Here is a dilemma for men: Our traditional ways of "working" on our problems—in isolation, in private—may not be of use now. We may need each other as men. Healing the pain of the past may be a gift that men can offer each other.

Let's explore how men's friendships can heal the wounds of growing up, how men can become mothers, fathers, and sons to each other, creating an enlivened, powerful, and tender sense of masculinity, even as they sometimes inflict further wounds on each other.

8

AT A MEN'S GROUP

WHAT MEN HAVE TO OFFER EACH
OTHER AND HOW THEY BLOCK IT

RACING WITH THE INDIANAPOLIS 500

It was a rainy spring day when I arrived in Indianapolis to lead a weekend men's retreat, open to the public. The weather in Boston had been damp and it was no better in the Midwest. The conference organizers were waiting expectantly at the gate. Throughout our planning for this event, the organizers and I had worried whether enough men would attend to cover expenses. When we last spoke there were thirty-five participants, not bad for an event that took up a weekend and cost more than two front-row seats to a Broadway show.

The welcoming committee, three men and their families, formed a crowd, making me feel too much of a celebrity. The tallest man there, with a gray beard, was a local Episcopal minister. His wife and eight-year-old daughter had come. "I won't be seeing them all weekend and they wanted to meet you," he explained in a confidential tone that sounded as if he were about to leave for the Russian gulag. I received a friendly handshake from another one of the organizers, an internist whose fiancée was there. I was later to learn that his father will not speak to him for marrying out of the faith. Standing in back, away from the gate, was the third member of the organizing

275

committee for the retreat, an administrator from the local hospital. He was separated from his wife.

Friendly, good-hearted hellos greeted me, but nonetheless there was an underlying gloominess. Are they disappointed in me? I wondered. I knew I was supposed to contain magic, and perhaps already there didn't seem enough of it. How many people came? is often the first question people ask about men's events. No one wants to be the only person at a party, of course. Yet there's more at work. There's safety in numbers, and also legitimacy. The larger the number then the lower the embarrassment. If lots of men do it, then it must be okay; I'm not deviant.

We moved, herdlike, into the huge parking lot and located our cars. All the men piled into one. I sat in the front, with the minister driving; the doctor and administrator were in back. Before leaving, the minister kissed his wife and daughter good-bye with some affection. "It's hard taking a whole weekend off; I know I'm going to owe something when I get back."

The administrator, who was the first to contact me about coming to Indianapolis a year earlier, related to the others how amazed he was that this event was finally going to happen. He had read my book, and called me up. As he spoke his voice had a tone of amazement at his power—the magic of being able to summon me here for this weekend. "Here I am a little guy from Indianapolis, and I called information and got his office number, and dialed the phone and Dr. Osherson picked up the phone. And I asked him whether he'd be interested in coming and he said yes and told me how to organize these weekends and here he is."

Magic. The power to produce someone big and powerful. We talked sympathetically about his wife who had left him. How embarrassed he felt that he couldn't make the marriage work; how estranged from his own father he felt. Why wouldn't he want to borrow some male magic? I could hardly begrudge him the wish to steal some power from me.

But how powerful was I? This was the question that swirled around us in our crowded Chevy, the question that couldn't be talked about. How many men will come and what will happen to them when they arrive?

We had all talked over the agenda beforehand. I would give some talks about the normal difficulties between fathers and sons, and then, using case examples, role-playing, experiential exercises, contemporary poetry, and music, we would explore how the father-son bond had shaped our identities as men and discover some of the paths to resolution of the wounded father men carry around within them.

Men's groups are particularly important because they provide opportunities for male closeness that are difficult to find in everyday life. They provide us an opportunity to experiment with new ways of listening and talking, building communications skills; to listen to each other and to ourselves without judgment; to provide support without trying too quickly to provide "answers." There are different kinds of men's groups. Some groups that have received a lot of media attention recently focus on mythic, "wildman" aspects of masculinity to develop more productive self-images. Drumming, reciting poetry, and chanting are de rigueur at these events. The groups I lead are organized in a different way. I do some teaching and educating about the core issues of shame, anger, sorrow, and love that men struggle with growing up and as adults. But the most important work of the weekend, I've come to believe, is the opportunity for men to explore anew, or for the first time, the inner terrain of their own feelings about themselves and their families through structured exercises such as Top Secret and through group discussion.

As we drove into Indianapolis I was aware that none of my fellow carmates had attended such an event before. This kind of retreat is an unusual one for men to attend: There is no specific work goal, but rather an emotional agenda. Will I shame them? Will I turn them into women? Will a riot ensue? Or an orgy? After all, in Leonard Michael's book *The Men's Club*, the group ends by attacking a refrigerator as an expression of men's rage at women, who seem to have all the goodies. There's no denying that all have fears and expectations about what's going to happen to us on our weekend together.

We whisked into downtown Indianapolis and exited the freeway to outsmart the late afternoon rush hour traffic.

"There's the Market Square Arena," pointed out the doctor, giving me a brief tour of local points of interest. I recognized the name from telecasts of basketball games of the Celtics playing the Indiana Pacers. Then with a rush I remembered that this was the home state of Larry Bird, the star basketball player of the Boston Celtics.

"How far away is French Lick, Larry Bird's hometown?" I inquired.

Smiles of recognitions.

"Not too far, about forty miles."

I was seized by a wish to go visit him. Invite him to our event:

Larry you've gotta have unfinished business with your father. All the sports magazines talk about it. Difficult family situation; basketball became a safe haven for the unhappy teenager. Maybe I could convince Larry Bird to take a fresh look at the past with a group of men he doesn't know. Maybe we'd even become friends, talk about life, shoot some hoops together. Gee, if I could get Larry Bird to come to this event, what a coup that would be for me!

The administrator plunged me back to reality; he was talking about numbers again. "Too bad we don't have just a few more; maybe some men will register this afternoon before we start."

"Of course we're competing with the 500," the minister advised.

"The 500 what?" I asked.

The Indianapolis 500, of course.

If you're not from Indiana or in love with car racing, it's hard to understand what an event the 500 is. My informants told me about it:

"The whole town goes gaga, even driving in the streets is more dangerous, everybody thinks they're in the Indy." We passed through downtown Indianapolis as this intense description of the Indy gripped us. We were all talking about it with great excitement. I was surprised at my interest. Five hundred miles around a track that is only two and a half miles long; the cars do zillions of circles. "It's amazing, hard to see the whole thing. Spectators have whiplash, the cars go around and around so many times you have to keep craning your neck—the speed is unbelievable."

"Ah, but the noise," interjected the minister, with a gleeful expression on his face. "It's like aircraft. Those engines have over two hundred horsepower, and no mufflers."

We sounded like a bunch of adolescents. *Awesome speed, man. Frigging unbelievable machines.* The race talk, like the basketball talk, calmed me, and it must have calmed my compatriots. A familiar comfort: talking with the guys about sports. Felt great.

And there was more.

"Is the pigpile still there?" asked the doctor.

"Sure is," said the minister, who explained: "That's the center circle where all the bikers go. Bring in cartons of beer. I was there once and all these people had taken off all their clothes and were dancing around, the men and the women. What a scene!"

"Well there won't be women at the weekend retreat," said the doctor. All laughed.

"Maybe we're the Indianapolis 35," suggested the minister. Then on a reverent note the administrator added: "I wouldn't want to be in the pigpen when the pileup occurs. Remember those crashes? Some great drivers died awfully young."

The names of youthful dead heroes were solemnly recited; we were preoccupied with speed and death. I even remember one name: *Billy Vukovich*. Died at the Indy 500 in the 1950s. Did he die plowing into the pigpile amid scores of naked men and women drunkenly dancing to their own music?

A typical male event: loud, fast, and someone has to die. So, I wondered, who's the great driver who's going to crack up at the Indy 35? Did each man in the car with me imagine that he was going to be the one to crack up the weekend event? Or was it me: the Harvard psychologist, the hot shot who might not be able to drive this event, after all? I had to admit it, there was my fear of men here, of failing in front of them. Perhaps my compatriots *wanted* me to crack up the event. It's often more interesting to see an "expert" fail than succeed. Who wouldn't be curious?

Each of the men at this upcoming event in Indianapolis is a competent, talented man in his own right. They've struggled with marriages, careers, parents, many of them are fathers. They've worked hard as men to establish with others that they can get the job done and take on manly tasks. Yet in coming to this weekend they are acknowledging that they don't have all the answers and that some part of their lives is not working as well as they'd like.

In that sense, these men are self-selected for psychological health; they recognize that something is wrong and they are taking appropriate steps to make changes in their lives. Yet their very acknowledgment is also a big admission for a man to make, and can be a major source of shame and anger.

For each man who comes to a weekend event, there is not only hope in my magic but also suspiciousness of me: Will I heal them? Expose them? Or worse: Will I corrupt them?

In *The Bacchae*, Euripides's classic Greek story of male arrogance and rationalism, the god Dionysius entices a skeptical King Pentheus to secretly observe women's mystical rites of passion and faith. Dionysius convinces Pentheus to dress up as a fox and climb a tree to spy on a group of ecstatic women followers of his cult. Pentheus, caught up the tree by the crazed women, is literally pulled limb from limb by his entranced mother.

I wondered dimly if these men imagined me as an Ivy League, bespectacled version of Dionysius, about to entice them into some bizarre, primitive rituals that would ultimately destroy them, strip them of their manhood, turn them into women.

Sometimes I wish I had that ol' Dionysian magic. I could cast some charms for protection from the anxiety I commonly experience when I go to a men's event: Do I have the right stuff? How well will I perform? When I go into a roomful of men, everyone looks so stolid. Men, my old competitors. Don't want to fail or trip up in front of them. Can't be humiliated.

Sometimes I thank my lucky stars for the early education I had in mastering shame, covering it up, gritting my teeth and getting through, buckling down and getting the job done even if your insides are turning to Jell-O. There are definitely advantages to having a callus form over your wound. Here's to male stoicism, and our ability to put feelings aside and get the job done.

Images of races sprang to mind as we took a sharp turn on our "shortcut" through the downtown area to our suburban retreat site. Would the weekend be a race? A race to solve everyone's problems and quickly? Men often came into these events with impossible expectations of resolving ancient struggles with fathers, mothers, wives, children, or bosses. Some men anticipated a weekend of "hard work" and emotional exhaustion. Yet perfect solutions are rare and men typically found themselves moving in and out of the room psychologically during the weekend.

I pictured myself trying to stay ahead of this group. Racing ahead of them out of town. Maybe I'd be raced out of town: the eastern city slicker who didn't attract more men to this event.

What about my wish to be one of the boys? I was tired of races—I'd had enough of them in my life. Now I was in my mid-forties, a father of two children, happily married, able to make a living. I wanted to stop feeling alienated from men, to return to the fold. After what seemed like a lifetime of feeling primarily allied with my mother emotionally, I wanted to hold on to what is best about that but also be able to tap into my affection for men.

We wound out of Indianapolis and came to fields with spring crops coming up. We turned around the corner and there was the retreat center, sitting high on a hill with a beautiful view of the surrounding country. As we pulled up to the front door, we came upon a cluster of men standing and talking at the entrance, waiting to register.

"Well, here we are," said the minister cheerily, and he went to talk to the crowd at the door.

We unpacked the luggage. The minister returned, obviously buoyed: "Ten more men want to register. That makes forty-five—things are looking good!"

Walking to the door, I was filled with a familiar sense of comfort and gratitude for the opportunity to spend a weekend with a group of men, talking about men's lives and feelings. There is comfort in being with a group of men. It harks back to those wonderful days of early adolescence. Playing baseball, hitting home runs. Tackling friends on the football field. Wondering about girls.

Power, mastery, love, sex. All those things that stumped me as a kid, that got mixed up with guilt and shame. Now I'm grown up, still trying to sort it out. Here's a chance to sit and talk with other men about how it's gone for them.

Here's our chance to learn it all over. Maybe this time we'll do it right.

SIMPLE GIFTS: WHAT MEN OFFER EACH OTHER

Men have enormous gifts to offer each other, yet often we remain disconnected by the competitiveness, distrust, and shame we feel. Male friendship stirs up deep longing and hope, but also the suspicion that we have little to provide each other emotionally.

This chapter explores how the normal, healthy adult relationships between grown men can foster personal growth and mastery of shame, grief, and anger; how it can strengthen our ability to be tender, supportive, and direct with women, and allow us to feel greater vitality in our lives as fathers, husbands, and sons to aging parents.

I'm going to draw primarily on the healing aspects of men's groups that focus on father-son issues, but I believe that the dynamics of connection and hiding, of growth and betrayal, apply to most groups of men and most friendships between men. Whenever possible, then, I will draw on the stories men have told me about their friendships with other men, the gifts they have received and the betrayals they've experienced.

First let's explore why male friendships are important and how friendships between men die. Then we'll take a look at what men's groups offer and how an unusual moment of experimentation in such a group changed my perception of men.

BEING TOUCHED BY ANOTHER MAN

When I talk to men about their lives, I find that some of their deepest feelings are reserved for moments of real intimacy with other men. Much as men want and need other men, they both treasure and feel uncomfortable with moments of genuine contact with another man.

An example is Jim, a partner in a large midwestern law firm. He has never been in a men's group, and is an unlikely candidate for one: He doesn't spend a lot of time with other men, has worked hard to obtain a lucrative partnership in a politically well-connected firm, and spends most of his free time at home with his wife and children. So I was surprised at his answer when I asked him one day in his office to tell me about a moment in the last year when he felt particularly moved emotionally.

Jim looked down at his hands to reflect, then told me about the day eight months earlier when partnerships were announced in the firm. "My friend Bob was denied partnership," Jim said, and he looked me straight in the eye to describe what happened: "What happened to Bob felt very unfair: He worked as hard as I, except he has a sick child at home and made very clear his limits on what he would choose to do. He didn't accomplish any less than me, but he did tell the senior partners on several occasions that he couldn't come in on weekends for case meetings.

"So he got a bit of a reputation as a black sheep in the firm and was denied partnership. Instead, he was asked to stay on as an associate. This was a real blow to him.

"By some strange occurrence I didn't find out about this until late in the evening before we were supposed to go to work the next day. I called him immediately and he was very upset, I could tell he was close to tears.

"So I offered him a ride in to work the next day. I drove and he talked: He told me about his son's illness, and the job, and he cried some. There we were driving down the expressway, talking about stuff, and he's crying.

"I pulled into the firm's parking lot, and we just sat there in the car for a while. I took Bob's hand and just held it."

This moment of real connection with another man was the memory Jim treasured most from the past year.

"What happened then?" I wondered, picturing the two men huddled together in the cramped sports car and feeling very moved by the scene.

"Some people came into the parking lot, and it felt a little odd to be sitting there like that with Bob, so I said, 'It's time to go to work.' And we did."

We're so used to seeing men as competitors, judges, or potential threats, that it can be difficult to see or hear the vital importance of receptive, comforting attention between men. It can be very important for men to feel "held" by other men, and I don't mean necessarily physical holding. Holding can be emotional, without physical touch; a friend can use words or gestures to indicate you are being seen and valued. You can feel held by being listened to closely and responded to in a way that legitimates what you are feeling.

Often we get nervous thinking of feeling "held" in any way by other men, since it can raise concerns about homosexuality and dependence. Too much connection seems "effeminate." However, being held by another man has little to do with sexuality and much to do with self-esteem. Often we don't understand this and we perceive a threat that blocks us from deeper connections with our male friends.

ODD FEELINGS: CLOSE ENCOUNTERS OF THE MANLY KIND

What can men contribute to each other? What gifts are overlooked or absent from our friendships?

Self-respect and Feeling Validated. Men have the capacity to legitimate and validate another man's struggles.

"I had taken my Subaru into the garage for some repairs," said Hal, who has struggled most of his life to feel manly enough in the eyes of his father, a man who loved to fiddle around with car engines. "I was trying to explain to the garage owner what the problem with the car was." Hal and the owner were standing together near the repair bay, while the owner wrote out a work order for the mechanic nearby. "I couldn't explain it and the owner wasn't getting it and suddenly I must have said something that sounded stupid because one of the mechanics said, 'Sounds like it's Hal again with that car of his.' I suddenly felt naked, like there I was again, a little kid who didn't understand about cars.

"The garage owner smiled, and said out loud: 'Oh Hal, they're just giving us a hard time again.'

"I felt so appreciative of the owner for speaking of us—I felt less alone and inadequate in the men's eyes. Suddenly it was okay, damn it, that I didn't know much about cars."

Here is an older man restoring a younger man's self-esteem by "joining" him and acknowledging that it's okay not to know, to be uncertain.

Will, a thirty-eight-year-old man in an ongoing men's group, provided another example. After bitterly describing yet another holiday visit to his aged father who failed to acknowledge him, Will demanded angrily:

"Do you know what it is like to want a response from someone you love and not get it?"

"Yes, I do," responded Frank, a man with several teenage children. He told Will about the pain and sense of rejection he felt from his children, and Will seemed shocked. "I had never heard a man I respected talk of feeling ashamed and embarrassed—it's the first time it ever felt manly to me." Will gained from Frank's words some self-respect for his struggles, as well as a perspective on and deepening understanding of what fathers feel. Will could hear from his friend Frank something that fathers and sons have much more trouble saying directly to each other: that silence can imprison men who care about each other.

Containing Anger. A soldier returns from Vietnam and can't get started again back in this country; he has too much pain and rage at what happened over there. In desperation he writes to a friend two thousand miles away, in Memphis, Tennessee, a childhood buddy he hasn't seen in eight years. He writes because he's close to the edge, and knows it. They agree to meet at a certain spot and time in Memphis. His friend waits on the street corner nervously; then he spots his old buddy. They look at each for several seconds, then embrace, and his friend's first words are: "Let's go raise some hell."

Which they do, and after the drinking and carousing and joking and teasing, the veteran begins to talk to his friend about the past, and to mourn his losses. He speaks of the almost unendurable pain of the war, of the buddies who died, of the part of him that died over there.

He's able to unlock the process of grieving because his old schooltime buddy has helped him contain his rage so that it doesn't spill over and destroy him and those he loves. The woman he loves has been able to offer him comfort and sympathy, but the man's fear and shame of his own anger has nullified what she can do. "Part of me was afraid of hurting her whenever we were together if my anger spilled out. When I saw Bill, my school buddy, I knew that he could take my rage, that there was little chance of wounding him like I might have wounded Jill."[1]

Many of us, not only vets, struggle with rage and anger at the burdens of manhood, what it costs us, and worry about whether that anger and resentment will wound those we love or wound us: drive them away, make us seem unworthy in their eyes, or force us to flee from our own sense of shame. Male friendships often offer men a chance to both express and master their rage.

Companionship and the Joy of Conspiracy. Often men need simple words or gestures from each other; it's not aggression we want to contain, it's just our need for companionship, and the brotherly camaraderie we lost in becoming men.

When I was moving out of my part-time office into one of my own, a simple offer from a friend made all the difference in my mental anguish.

I had shared an office with Ellen for several years, each of us half-time, and we had gotten along well. Except that Ellen had decorated the office, and my suggestions were not always appreciated. She had a very clear idea of what pictures to put on the wall, how many plants to have and what kind they should be, and what kind of furniture we should have. When a full-time office came available in our building, I signed a lease for it, then became panicked about whether I could furnish it myself—whether I could really pick out the kind of carpet, chairs, desks, plants, and pictures that would make for a pleasing, warm office.

At the age of forty-two, this seemed a ridiculous struggle: How could I not know how to furnish my office? The struggle was really around autonomy and self-sufficiency. The emotional subtext was: *Can I "make it" without mommy's support and guidance?* Those were the feelings that made it hard to talk about and deal with what seemed like a simple, everyday move. So I walked around for weeks in a state of panic about the move that no amount of rational discussion with my wife, my friends, or my colleagues could dislodge.

At lunch with my friend Steve about a month before the move, he asked how I was.

"Okay. Or maybe not. This move . . ." I replied cryptically.

"Your office?"

"Yeah," I said, immobilized by the dread I had been struggling with for weeks.

"Moving offices is hard," Steve commiserated. He then proceeded to lead me back through a discussion of all the "angles," trying to show me that I didn't have to "worry"; the rent was reasonable, I was busy enough to pay for it, it "made sense" to have my own office at this stage of my career.

My spirits sank as I trudged through yet another "rational" problem-solving discussion. *I just had this "reassuring" talk with my wife last night and it didn't help,* I wanted to scream at my kind, earnest friend.

Just eat your sandwich and drink your beer, I felt inside. *It doesn't help to talk,* advised a cynical part of me.

But then what does help? I wondered.

"It's not a rational problem," I blurted out loud to Steve. "I know about all the angles."

"So what's the problem?"

Oh hell, might as well be out with it.

"It's got to do with Ellen, and leaving the office that she's set up. All the furnishings, and I just don't know if I can set up my office like hers. This feels ridiculous: I resented the way she took over the office when we shared it, but I don't know if I can make it on my own without her."

"I know what you mean." Steve smiled. "I share my therapy office at the university, and my office mate, Marilyn, decorated it so that I can hardly recognize it."

"I feel overwhelmed," I replied, "just at going out and doing all the work. Strange as it seems I don't know if I can match carpet and furniture and I want help and I don't want to ask Julie because she is so busy right now with graduate school and I feel lonely."

Secret's out; I felt better just for having said it: *I feel lonely.*

Steve smiled and his reply was direct: "I'll go shopping with you; I like to pick out office stuff."

His offer felt both liberating and frightening. I was amused at the thought of shopping with Steve, asking his opinion, feeling less alone and more confident about my decisions.

We joked about shopping together.

"Let's tell the salesperson that you're my shopping consultant," suggested my friend, whom I'd never known to pay much attention to personal fashion.

The idea of two men shopping together raised a familiar anxiety, which Steve expressed in a joke: "Let's say we're looking for furniture for our bedroom."

"Ach, what does it take to furnish a therapy office?" I asked. "All you need are two butterfly chairs and a hammock."

"How about if you pay me ten percent of the cost as a retainer?" needled my friend.

"Forget it, but I will pay for this lunch," I countered, actually quite grateful for his offer of help.

Two conspirators: just like me and my buddy Eric, both ten years old, whispering and making plans together after school.

Ultimately, Steve and I did not go out shopping together. As I contemplated his offer, familiar feelings surfaced of not wanting to depend on another man. *Don't become a little boy around this man, don't be too needy.*

On the other hand, Steve's offer was a kind of gift to me. By offering companionship he legitimated my anxiety; by naming my fear and joking about it, he made it less oppressive and dominating. Soon after, still chuckling, I went out and bought some office furniture, and made the move. My friendship with Steve has grown over the years and I look on that lunch and his offer as one of the bedrocks of that friendship.

I've also come to understand and respect how much love and affection between men can be communicated by the friendly joshing and verbal swordplay that characterize much of men's time together. And I've lamented the dilemma that creates: How do you get close and lean on each other when you're connected by a sharp poke or point?

Getting and Giving Information. Where do men find out what is appropriate for a man to feel when wooing a woman, when becoming a father, when mourning his parents, or when facing his retirement and his mortality? Women have numerous rites of passage and time-honored support groups—from bridal showers to quilting bees, from volunteer work to corporate lunches "for women only"—in which they exchange survival strategies and emotional support.

Men traditionally have tended to live their lives more in isolation, and the difficulty of finding out the emotional content of life's ordinary pivot points has been very costly to men: How do you juggle work and family? How do you deal with an angry and needy child? An angry and needy wife? How do you manage a lifelong relationship with parents instead of just "separating"?

Men are good at exchanging nuts-and-bolts information, but often they are more curious about the richer, more textured exchange of feelings about shared struggles and common pain. "I grew up without a father and until the weekend event I hadn't known that you could have a father and still feel so fucked up," recalled one participant at a men's weekend, several years later. Here is a guy who for forty-odd years felt that the absence of his father was the unchangeable mystery of his life, now seeing that fathers are a dilemma for many men, and that there are many options for how to respond to that dilemma.

Insights about fathers can work the other way too. "Thank God I chose the father I did, after hearing other men talk about their fathers," recalled one man humorously. It's in fact striking how many men leave a weekend event with a deeper appreciation and love for their fathers, more aware of the pain and complexity of being a father and a son.

My impression, both professionally and personally, is that we often want to talk with each other about nagging dilemmas of love that have no easy answers: for example, what is it like to be a grown man still dealing with the competitiveness and love between siblings; or how come child care and career don't fit together as easily as we expected them to when we got married, or how much money is enough to earn for your family; or when and how do you decide to give priority to other parts of your life than just work? Any point of transition—marriage, infertility, parenting, career change—can make a man want and need contact with other men who have gone through the same thing. Usually the desire to talk with other men bumps into a shyness, a reluctance, a fear of losing control, a belief that it's not manly to open up a heartfelt question without also having the answer.

Men often need to form a broader view of men, a view that comes from seeing other men listen attentively, respond appropriately, confront and cajole each other. "This weekend opened my eyes to a world that I never knew existed," related one fifty-two-year-old man. "The men's event was so good because we could have lots of feelings without resolving them immediately. It was important for me to see that men can stay with discomfort: We are so quick to change the subject, move onto something else more manageable, go in and solve it. Here I could see that it was better if you don't solve things too quickly, that confusion can be productive, and that has really helped me deal with those I love. I have less tendency to come on as an authority with all the answers and drive everyone away."

FEELING INFANTALIZED: TAKING THE BURDEN OFF WOMEN

Men as friends, colleagues, and mentors may be able to legitimate issues of vulnerability, shame, grief, anger, and hope for each other in ways that are difficult for women. When a man turns to a woman he loves or depends on for emotional help, there is often an undercurrent of being infantalized, feeling like a boy turning to mother for help. Deep down he feels he is not really manly when he turns to women for help. In talking to men about getting help and dealing with shame, I'm often struck by how men feel shame and anger about asking for help from women.

This doesn't mean that women can't be of help to men, but rather that men may have an even greater role in fostering each other's normal emotional growth. Men validate getting help, listen with a sense of "I've been there too," and provide a sense that need, yearning, loneliness, receptivity, and nurturing are part of the male agenda too. Understanding what men can offer each other in this way can take an enormous burden off a wife as the sole container or support for a needy husband.

"I feel there are just some things I can't get from my wife," says one man. "I know all this women's stuff, I was raised by my mother, my wife is very important to me, but I feel like I don't know men's stuff. In the men's group I'm in I feel at least they're my kind."

My kind.

It's hard to hear that phrase or talk about men's need for each other without wondering if this is just another excuse to exclude women. I'm aware of hundred of years of history in which men have retreated to their clubs, their offices, and their wars in part because they couldn't deal with women. And I'm aware that women have been the source of much of the most important learning I—and many men—have done about relationships and love.

There is a valid need for men to be able to find a place to talk without worrying about having to posture for or take care of women. However, it does become an excuse to exclude women when men cannot take the next step and find a way to talk honestly to women and include them in their self-exploration. For me it feels valid and important to find time to be with my male friends, but not if it feels as if I am excluding my wife emotionally. There's a rule of thumb I apply to myself: Have I told my friends something I wouldn't be comfortable telling my wife? I don't tell my wife everything I say to my friends, but if there are "secrets" I'm keeping, it becomes important to me to find a way to talk with her about them. One veteran participant in an ongoing men's group counsels: "It is also important to recognize that your wife/lover may not understand your desire to share your feelings with other men. That desire initially may be perceived as threatening to a relationship. I found it important not only to listen to my partner's concerns, but also to share with her how the group was contributing to me. She gradually discovered that my participation in the group was actually contributing to our relationship.[2]

One of the strongest reasons men are drawn to each other, and want time to themselves, derives not from a distrust of women but rather from the wish to return to the male chumship they lost in growing up. Let's explore this topic now.

MEN'S GRIEF AND THE LOSS OF THE MALE CHUMSHIP

For many of us, there is an early separation from men that is quite painful in our lives. We wanted to connect with our fathers more, we wanted to connect with our teenage buddies more, with our brothers perhaps, yet the bond between boys so quickly gets converted into competition and bravado and establishing our turf that we lose that boyish connection. As we reach our teens, much of that psychic energy goes toward women.

Some men feel they never really knew a dependable man, since their fathers were absent or gave them over to their mothers. Most often, though, there was some connection with father or friends or a surrogate father that gave the boy a hope and a yearning for still more connection. Men will often talk of their alienation from other men with an air of disappointment and loss; our anger at our sex often smacks of a broken heart rather than having never known or loved men.

Psychiatrist Harry Stack Sullivan has written at length of the importance of the preadolescent "chumship," which is later replaced by the heterosexual bond. Sullivan notes that the specific new interest in a "particular member of the same sex who becomes a chum or a close friend" is unlike the kinds of closeness that have come before in the life of the boy: "This change represents the beginning of . . . love. In other words, the other fellow takes on a perfectly novel relationship with the person concerned: He becomes of practically equal importance in all fields of value. Nothing remotely like that has ever appeared before. All of you who have children are sure that your children love you; when you say that, you are expressing a pleasant illusion," Sullivan argues provocatively. "But if you will look very closely at one of our children when he finds a chum . . . you will discover something very different in the relationship—namely, that your child begins to develop a real sensitivity to what matters to another person."[3]

In these nonsexual chumships of preadolescence, Sullivan argues, boys are exploring the nature of love. We may underestimate the pain involved in letting go of the male chum and the burden that it puts on women to soothe our grief.

"I did have a special buddy in summer camp during my junior high school years," remembered Matt at age forty-five. "His name was Edward and we used to practice baseball for hours together. Each summer we'd see each other and renew our friendship. One year I saw him at a camp reunion during the winter in New York City. All of us from our bunk walked around the city together, just talking and having fun. People said we were the fastest walkers in our bunk!" Matt's voice betrayed sadness: "As we got older we just drifted apart." He concluded: "By the time you're an adult, it's easy to think you're always in competition with men, for the attention of women, in sports, at work; I miss the kind of boyish energy Edward and I had together."

Many of us lose the ability to ask questions of, and depend on, one another as men. And we carry around a nostalgia for a lost youth that adds to our sense of grief as men, and probably also to our anger at women: *We gave up the "chumship" for you! We gave up the attachment to boys for the ability to be sexual.* Perhaps now men can have both: loving men and women, honoring both friendship and sexuality.

For many workshop participants, the best thing about getting together with other men is the simple horsing around with the guys. "One of the best moments at the men's retreat," writes a forty-five-year-old doctor, "was the Ping-Pong table and the games we played during the breaks and late at night—I hadn't felt that camaraderie with men since I was a child. It was this reconnecting with boys' play, a time when I was not suspicious of other men, a time when I felt comfortable with my pals, with the guys. The weekend together made me yearn for those sorts of relationships again."

Mick Fedullo's lovely poem, "In My Brother's House" captures the special bond between men. A man reflects on the fact that:

> My brother
> understands me
> at times so well
> I can see myself
> running to hide
> In his mouth when
> he is silent.

Fedullo recalls the attic in the house when they would play as children:

> We knew
> that there the secrets
> of the house
> revealed themselves,
> and there, we too
> could be understood.
> Secretly, we
> would pluck one wire
> on the inside
> of the dusty, ragged
> piano,
> and that note
> spread, circled us
> as though we were
> a fire, around which
> the ritual of love
> was being performed.

Now the grown brother returns to his sibling:

> Unlucky in love,
> I have come to talk
> with my brother, and
> before he says a word,
> in the quiet as he hands
> me a drink of bourbon,
> I hear that note
> again and feel at home.[4]

Feeling at home does not always come so easily to men—or to brothers. There is often tremendous resistance to really connecting with other men. "I want to connect with other men. But you know it's like my father," reported one older man. "In the last years of his life he put up a twelve-foot wall around our entire property. And I feel like when I get near to men, the walls go up." Another man wrote that his time at the men's event "scared me pretty badly."

The walls go up.

I know that one of my first reactions to spending time with a male friend, or a men's group, is a sleepy tug away from doing it, a voice within that says: *Why bother? There's so much else I have to do, why take the time?*

Many men share this resistance. Research on men's lives reveals that male friendships are often noteworthy more for their absence than their presence. In their careful study of friendship through the life cycle of five hundred men, Michael Farrell and Stanley Rosenberg found that while unmarried men in their twenties reported both having friends and seeing them regularly, there was a "distinct pattern of change" as men marry and age: "Marriage tends to diminish male friendship commitments, and movement into middle age leads to even more isolation from friends." Even when friendships between men persist, Farrell and Rosenberg note: "Intimate discussions are less likely among friends after marriage, reaching their lowest point as men cross the threshold into early middle age."[5]

Stuart Miller, in his heartfelt book *Men and Friendship*, talks about "the death of intimacy" among men. Miller chronicles a two-year period when he searched for deeper friendship with old acquaintances, "a quest so difficult that sometimes I doubted the very legitimacy of the enterprise."[6] Most of his time is spent merely trying to pin his friends down for times to meet for lunch or dinner. There's a comical element to these efforts. His friends, though they appreciate his calls, are preoccupied with work, out of town when he's free, or they become uneasy when he suggests meeting more regularly. At one point, daunted by his struggle to connect with friends, Miller wonders if he has abnormal intimacy needs.

Miller, chronicling the loneliness he and many men face, shows how "modern mobility, which separates men from one another in the most cruel ways, combines with our individualistic ideology of personal growth to litter our past with dead friendships. We rush to fill a puzzling emptiness with the love of women and with notions of our growth into rational adults."[7]

On the deepest level, men approach each other very cautiously as friends.[8] What is it about contact that scares many men into putting up walls? Let's explore the source of this resistance to real emotional contact between men.

PUTTING UP WALLS

Our sense of shame, grief, and anger often drives us apart and creates resistance to real contact with other men. We get "flooded" by powerful feelings that make us want to shut down, fight with, or get away from other men.

First, we struggle with authority when we connect with other men. Men fear losing their *manly authority* if they go to another man for help, or if they acknowledge difficulty, or ignorance, or loss of control in front of other men. Often the first step in getting help or support is admitting there's a problem. Much as we don't want to let on that there is anything wrong, we have to force ourselves to cross that line and say, "I need your help, my kids are driving me crazy [or my wife is upset]."

When men get together their need to prove their manliness often collides directly with their wish to be seen and heard as a feeling person. In men's groups the participants may anticipate a grueling, difficult event. To be a "real" male event it must be difficult, maybe even deadly. An Outward Bound with some emotional high ropes work: We have to be up there thundering and charging and hanging by our spiritual harnesses or else this won't be valuable. An Indy 500 of the emotions in which we all need loud, supercharged engines. Men will show each other how big their engine is, so as not to be seen as unmanly in their pain.

At one weekend retreat a man told the group on the second day of his dream the night before, after our first meeting. He was five years old and refused to get on the school bus because he didn't trust the driver, whose first name was Sam. When the driver in the dream insisted on going in one direction, the boy got off the bus and pushed the wheels in a different direction.

For this man the fear of losing his hard-won authority and becoming like a little boy who would be forced to go to school and learn boring, unhappy lessons was so great that he harbored a hidden wish to resist the leader. Getting help and answers from the group leader was not worth the price of feeling infantalized. It was not until he understood his own involvement in the proceedings that he felt truly able to join the group.

Men have experienced so much hierarchy and authoritarian leadership in their families and schools and camps and factories and offices that they can only imagine a men's group structured hierarchically: If they're not the leader, then they must be the boyish little follower. This is a form of "the identification with the aggressor" dilemma many men struggle with: The choice is being the dominant one or the subordinate; there's not any middle ground.

This dilemma prevents men from turning to other men for help: The more like a little boy you feel then the angrier and more resentful you may feel toward the friend you've turned to for help and answers. So you want to get away or pull him down, but if you do that then your hope for help is dashed. Often truly intimate friendships can feel like no-win situations.

Mentoring relationships and other forms of male friendship often founder when men can't tolerate the hope and resentment that mutual and shifting vulnerability and interdependency create. The relationship breaks up when both parties can only imagine the other as either dominant or submissive. The protégé wants the mentor to be a "hero" but such wishes also arouse the protégé's competitive lust, to cut the elder down to manageable human proportions. Yet knocking down the hero only deprives the protégé of his fantasized protector and model.

One men's group had to struggle with a bottle of bourbon before the men could achieve more egalitarian camaraderie, in which each member felt like an equal, beloved member of the group, not like an aggressor or victim. In the second meeting the group bought a bottle of bourbon, partly to deflect and defuse the anxiety all felt. This turned the meeting into a drinking party, complete with antiwomen jokes and literal and metaphoric pissing contests. The men stumbled home through New York City streets and over the next several days the sheepish members exchanged phone calls to talk over what had happened.

"We talked with each other at the next meeting," recalled Dan. "I felt there had been too much drinking, and we all seemed to agree. Then we decided that we would not bring alcohol to the meetings anymore, and we haven't. But the amazing thing about that decision was first that I was asked what I felt, people listened, and then we all agreed without anyone being the leader, or having to vote. We knew what we had to do. It's nice to feel that things evolved organically rather than hierarchically."

"My family life was basically a hierarchy," remembered Jim, another member of the group who works as an architect. "Dad was the kind who, if he didn't get his way, would roar, threaten, or punish." Particularly important in Jim's family was the cocktail hour, which was the signal for intimate yet tense contact in the home.

A second reason men put up walls with each other is because they get flooded by *object hunger*—their wish for contact with other men—and then withdraw or act out. Attention from male friends, time spent together, the awakening of memories of being with buddies, of opportunities with fathers, can excite our deepest wishes for connection with other men, something often denied in men's lives.

There may be a wish to cuddle up in daddy's arms, or to depend on the strength and warmth of other men. The craving for contact may stir up fears of homosexuality.

Once at a week-long retreat the group of thirty men were sitting in a circle in our large, carpeted room and talking about the yearning for more contact with fathers. "The older I've gotten the more I've wanted to be with my father," mused one fifty-year-old man. A calm silence settled over the room. Yet the tension of the yearning felt almost unmanageable. Here were thirty men who had for years put aside their wishes for close contact with other men, beginning with their fathers. The silence was shattered when one man, an engineer from Boeing, suddenly jumped up and turned to the man next to me:

"Joseph, I want to wrestle with you."

Wrestle?

Joseph sprang forward into the middle of the circle, opening his arms with a deep smile. The two rushed toward each other, embraced, and rolled on the ground wrestling. The room came to life. Some men wanted them to continue wrestling; others were upset. A shy man wondered aloud what to do if someone asked him to wrestle.

A plaintive inner voice shocked me: *How come you didn't want to wrestle with me?*

An exasperated participant broke the awkward silence: "I don't believe this—we were getting somewhere a moment ago, people talking honestly about stuff men don't say much to anyone, anywhere, and now we're talking about wrestling with each other."

His exasperation was understandable and perhaps to the point: It *was* easier for the engineer to wrestle, disrupting everything, rather than to give voice to those shameful feelings: *I long to wrestle with my father.* And: *I long for real contact and reassurance from a man I trust and love.*

Male Friendship and Homosexual Panic. In D. H. Lawrence's evocative study of male friendship, *Women in Love*, there is a scene in which Birkin and his friend Gerald, alone together, strip in front of a crackling fire at night and express their aggression and love for each other by wrestling nude. In both the book and the movie version this is a very intense and unsettling scene.

Let's consider for a moment the interconnection for men between friendship, bodily contact, anxiety, and shame. In friendships between men, I think there often comes a moment when we want to feel really intertwined with another man, perhaps the way we wished for close, bodily contact with our fathers. We yearn to lean on another man, feeling comforted and supported by him in the same way we support others, yet that urge for connection also makes us ashamed and uncomfortable. We want to hide it, mask it, deny it, and get away from it. Anything but say it. The engineer wanted to hug and be hugged right there, right then, and perhaps he suddenly felt close to the edge of a bottomless pit of yearning to hug and be enfolded by another man. Perhaps it was the same pit I looked into that day my friend Steve offered to go shopping with me: at last another man penetrated my loneliness.

Many of us, both gay and straight, feel confused about "homosexuality" and connection with other men. When we want to be close, we worry we're becoming homosexuals or overly dependent. Or we deny those yearnings or keep them secret even from ourselves. One thirty-three-year-old man, firmly heterosexual, talked with me at length about his wish to feel closer to other men, how much he enjoyed his weekly basketball night at the local gym, and the painful lack of male friendships in his life. But when I mentioned his warm feeling and enjoyment of men, he rebuked me:

"I don't like to talk about affection for other men; that takes us into the queer zone."

The fear of being gay or sexually attracted to other men often underlies the "homophobia" that men display toward each other, their discounting and mocking of their very attempts to get closer emotionally.[9]

We often do feel a sensuous wish for contact and touch with other men, though such wishes usually go unnoticed and unacknowledged. This is not sexual in nature. We have so often felt other men pull away when we most needed them that the urge to get closer, to feel the skin, the touch of our fathers and of other men can feel very scary. A man once told me that his most vivid memory of his father was the smell of his cologne and the bristles of his shaving brush; the touch and smell of his father. Boys don't have a lot of time to enfold themselves in their father's warmth, or in the warmth of other men; our contact is usually from a distance, as our performance is appreciated with a pat on the back or a word of encouragement, or we greet and part with a handshake and a wave. No wonder we carry around a depth of yearning to touch and hold each other, or a curiosity about what that would feel like, and then worry about our sexual identities when we feel such yearnings.

For men who have conscious homosexual desires or who are openly gay, considerable distress can accompany attempts just to be friends with other men. As a heterosexual therapist, I find that when I work with a gay man, one of the common anxieties for both of us is that affection and warmth and emotional intimacy may lead to sexual intimacy. Often just bringing that anxiety to the surface together, talking about it, can help to dilute it.

Heterosexual men are protected and misled by the way in which sexuality and closeness and intimacy all become intertwined in our minds and connected to women. We need to separate sexual orientation and preference from attachment and connection needs. Men both gay and straight have needs for warmth and connection from other men. Turning to other men for help, support, or warmth is unrelated to sexual preference. Often men are relieved to learn that their wishes for close contact and warmth do not mean that they are gay. And gay men are often relieved to discover that emotional intimacy and warmth are separate goals from sexual intimacy with another man.

Unfortunately, it's usually at the point when men begin to acknowledge their warm feelings and desire for each other that they need to demonstrate their "independence." In one group the members agreed after several weeks of "getting together whenever we could" to settle on a meeting time: every other Tuesday at 6:00 P.M. The next meeting three people arrived at 6:00, another showed up at 6:30, another at 7:00, and the last member rushed in at 7:30. Everyone was busy, and each could plead work and family pressures, but one member probably put his finger on the truth when he observed: "Just when we affirmed we needed each other we start acting like we really don't need to be here." The demonstration of autonomy often dilutes the anxiety and shame over the hunger for connection.

Men's feeling of *tenderness* toward each other can also lead us to put up walls. Listening to each other stimulates our motherly yearnings and identifications, our desires to respond to each other directly. We want to say that we're touched by what we've heard, to be more responsive, to hold each other, or to talk about our own vulnerabilities. But that feels too motherly or feminine, and we then feel frightened of being too exposed or shamed by the other men.

Mark, for example, talked about how ridicule and devaluing of other men protects him from his own common bond with them. "Along with my wife's support, the men's group I'm in is the major piece of hope in my life right now. I go there knowing it's one place I feel understood. But each time I go I look down on these men. Like they're not savvy, they don't feel confident about their relationships, they worry their wives will leave them, or they have sexual problems. I have the same struggles, feel a lot for these guys, but then I look down on everyone else in the group."

Men also need to know that when another man shows deep

feelings or discusses problems, they don't necessarily have to attempt to "solve" them or take them away.

Abe arrived late the first night of a men's retreat, a rainy, cold evening. And he sat silently through the first day. He looked forlorn and upset, like a prodigal son returning, and no one knew how to include him more actively in the group. Midway through the Saturday session, though, Abe began to talk.

"It's hard for me to be here; I didn't know whether to come or not," he explained. "You see, my brother committed suicide just last week." Abe was the older of the two brothers, in his late forties, and the more successful, married and the owner of a hardware store.

"My brother was the black sheep of the family, never all that successful, and there are some family secrets that no one knows. I'm not sure what to tell the relatives." What emerged was how close Abe and his brother were, the successful and unsuccessful one.

The grief and shame and anger at this tragic loss seemed palpable as Abe spoke, yet he kept his feelings buried deep behind his manly facade of being the brother who takes care of others, without regard to himself.

Several men struggled with how to respond to Abe. One man, Jake, got up and hugged him, looming over the surprised-looking Abe, who remained sitting in his seat. Others offered instrumental advice and help, one man suggesting Abe find a support group "where he can talk" while others gave their opinions about what he should or shouldn't tell the family members.

While Abe clearly appreciated these offerings, they seemed to miss the point. "The hug seemed kind of invasive," he told the group, "like it got in the way of my telling people what's going on for me—it actually blocked me off from seeing anyone else. And advice I *don't* need right now, I feel just at sea with all these painful feelings."

What Abe *did* need was to feel heard and responded to.

Then Jake, who had returned to his seat across the room, wondered: "Maybe we were trying to shut you up, with hugs and advice—your pain about your lost brother seems almost too much."

Abe nodded gratefully.

Then Barney, looking right at Abe, said, "When my father killed himself I wasn't sure if I should go after him or not. He shot himself in the driveway of our house when I was fifteen. Now I'm forty-five but I remember part of me didn't know how I could go on without him, another part of me hated him for what he did, and deep down too I knew I had to somehow make peace with what happened."

Several other men talked about what it was like to face losses, failures, grief that seemed unendurable. No one any longer forced anything on Abe or suggested what he should do. Instead the men were responding to each other, saying: *I've been there too; it's okay to talk about this.* One man, describing the loss of a baby he never mourned for, started to cry.

In this way men "hold" each other, legitimating the expression of feeling, acknowledging wounded parts of themselves, and allowing each other to talk of pain that no longer has to be kept secret.

Finally, because many men have *disidentified with other men,* they need great courage to connect with men. They feel ashamed of their own anger or they fear the anger of other men, and so they keep their distance. In many men's groups the early meeting are all about current affairs, which is not because men don't want to talk of themselves. "Last week we met for the fourth time and talked about history," reported one man. "The JFK assassination, Vietnam, the Iraqi invasion of Kuwait, the War in the Gulf. You know, what men do in the world—we couldn't really talk about ourselves." Yet often world events serve as symbols and metaphors for internal struggles. Men use aggression, death, invasion, and wars in the world as ways to talk about inner aggression, their own anxieties, and shame about their anger. *How can I talk about how angry I feel, particularly when it feels like more of that "bad" masculine aggression? How can I reveal how scared of other men I feel?*

Often men need to know that it's okay to talk about their anger and that it is normal as a man to feel angry as well as hopeful. Often men hold themselves aloof from friendships, as they do with their families, because of shame about their aggression.

In one group Julio dreamt soon after an intense meeting of walking down a beach by himself and coming upon an older man, a teacher, who was showing some children how to take shells and make them into flutes. "The man looked at me kindly, invited me to join, and said, 'You'll never make music out of these shells with dynamite.' "

In reporting the dream, Julio was really asking about the dynamite inside: Could it be expressed? Would it destroy him or his connection to the group? Men will wonder if they can talk about their identification with a harsh or angry father, or whether they can reveal the part of themselves that paid a big price to become a man.

And, finally, *wives play an important gatekeeper role* in the husband's struggle to connect with other men and the tender, empowered man within himself. Often men fear alienating or wounding their wives or mothers if they take time to nourish the bond with other men. A wife's distrust or encouragement can be a powerful force in her husband's struggles.

Carl, for example, was very ambivalent about his attendance at a weekend on fatherhood. Despite considerable sense of loss and alienation with his own father, he felt guilty about taking seventy-two hours away from home. "Leaving my wife with the kids. Is it worth it to do this?" Carl wondered what he would owe his wife when he got home. Was this an "appropriate" way for a forty-eight-year-old family man to be spending his time?

After two days of talking and listening, he still wasn't sure he was "really here" at the event. Before the last morning session he went upstairs to pack. He returned a few minutes later and as the session began he started to cry, clutching something in his hand. "I have some work to do on my relationship with my father," he started to explain, stopping to compose himself. Then he went on: "I'm so touched by what I just found in my suitcase." As he spoke, bent over in his seat, he opened his right hand to reveal a gold ring. He stared dreamily at it, running it through his fingers.

"I was packing and reached into one of the pockets and found my wife had hidden this ring, wrapped up for me to find."

He stopped, wiping away tears with the other hand. "It's my father's ring from West Point. He gave it to me just before he died." Carl had kept this ring unworn in a dresser drawer for years. Freed up by his wife's gift, Carl began to mourn the father who had died ten years earlier.

If men put up walls, women can open gates by their support and encouragement.

As men free themselves from shame at their hunger, grief, and anger, they can begin to provide each other the validation, warmth, and support they missed in growing up. They can learn to play together in a new way and to grow. The walls begin to come down as they learn the emotional terrain of friendship.

LONESOME COWBOYS: THE HEALING SPACE OF A MEN'S GROUP

In his wondrous novel *Lonesome Dove*, Larry McMurtry presents the friendship between Gus and Woodrow, two former Texas Rangers in the 1880s. In the novel these two sturdy, aging men struggle with the end of their careers as rangers, the closing of the frontier, and

the demise of their heroic role in settling the West. Woodrow also
feels the pain of his love for his grown son, Newt, fathered illegiti-
mately. He has spent his life without revealing to the boy who rides
with him that he is his only child.

Gus and Woodrow and Newt carry out an arduous, heroic cattle
trek across the unknown country to Montana. Near the end of the
novel, Gus is killed by Indians and Woodrow drags his friend's body
behind him in a broken-down wagon a thousand miles back to Texas.
Before leaving, Woodrow puts Newt in charge of the ranch they
have settled. It's likely the two will never see each other again, and
as they part, both feel an ache in their hearts. But neither father nor
son speaks of that ache. Woodrow looks down from his horse at
Newt and hands him an old pocket watch in a thin gold case. Woodrow had carried it with him since boyhood.

"It was my pa's," Woodrow reveals, then turns and leaves.

"Dern, Newt," says an astonished friend standing nearby. "He
gave you his horse and his gun and that watch. He acts like you're
his kin."

"No, I ain't kin to nobody in this world," Newt replies bitterly.
"I don't want to be. I won't be," says the son fated to repeat the
solitary life of the father.[10]

There is majesty and heroism in the story of Gus and Woodrow.
Yet as one man said, "Woodrow dragged that body a thousand miles
but could never tell his friend he loved him; he rode to Montana
and left the farm to the boy but never told him he was his son. I
want to do it differently."

What are the possibilities for men who don't only go off on cattle
drives to find meaning, who want to be able to speak of love, shame,
and grief with those they love?

In answering these questions, I'm going to draw on my experiences in men's groups that focused on father-son issues. The examples of fathers and sons coming together to provide the nutriments
of emotional growth and change apply equally well to all male relationships—friends, mentors, buddies, colleagues.

As men we often need an opportunity to safely express the sense
of diminishment and defensiveness we have felt in our lives. We
need to acknowledge that it's not all a sign of personal failure,
either ours or our fathers'. The shame, sadness, and anger we carry
around inside us are parts of a larger male struggle with integrity and
honor.

HEALING SHAME AND DETOXIFYING FATHER'S LOVE

Men need a place where they can mourn the sense of failure they felt as boys, and the ways they worked so hard to elicit a loving response from father or mother. The Top Secret game, in which men write down their painful memories on index cards, provides a way of making shameful secrets public, and this very publicness and "bearing witness" allows men to heal some of their early shame and grief.

When we distribute the cards and each read aloud anonymously in turn without discussion, moments that men had mulled over in stoic silence or isolation are given to the group: Expressing them releases some of the pain they hold.

Mark, for example, had never told anyone except his wife about the frightening, painful beatings he received from his father as a child. He wrote about them on his index card, and when it was read aloud Mark found himself "overwhelmed and appreciative that another man was saying what I would have been unable to say to the group myself."

Individual stories vary. What's more important in a men's group is that vulnerability, disappointment, and needs for intimacy become topics that men can share; that each member of the group can see that other men—capable, talented men they respect—also struggle with shame, anger, love, and sorrow.

To "detoxify" our love of our fathers and our experiences as men means to see them less as our own personal failure, denied and shrouded in silence, and more as struggles we can name and label and share. This is true of most of the intimate struggles in men's lives: our feelings of failure or disappointment as fathers ourselves, the struggles we have with the women we love, our concerns about our sexual performance or our sexual preference, the dashed hopes and dreams of our careers. Each of these can become shrouded in silence. We "detoxify" our stories when we give them public expression in a relatively safe and trustworthy group of peers. Giving our stories shape and substance is the first step in letting them go and creating new ones.

TELLING OUR STORIES: WORKING THROUGH SELF-HATRED AND DEVALUATION

Many men think they have nothing to contribute aside from their performance, taking care of others through work. This is connected to our devaluing of our masculinity. We learn early on to diminish our *caring self*: We don't perceive that what we have to contribute emotionally is of value to others.

This is part of the male struggle with shame, rooted in what we did and didn't get from our fathers.

But when we come to terms with our fathers, when we confront their pain and failure in the company of other men, what begins to emerge is a fuller picture of father, not the kind of one-dimensional cartoon image that dominates our childhood perception of fathers. Underneath the failure, heroism, anger, or seeming indifference there were more loving parts that father couldn't express. We see our connections to him and also our differences, and in the process we expand our sense of our own possibilities.

Men's ways of loving, first embodied in the love of our fathers, begin to take on a different shape. "Hearing other men's stories," one man said, "I see it may not have been just my father's incompetence or sadism or disappointment, but also his *fear*: how left out of the family he felt, or under pressure to live up, so he would yell at me." Another pointed to: "How much men feel they have to be in control and perform. How much my father depended on me to do better in baseball than him, how sad he was in getting older and not being able to compete, how off balance he felt with women."

In men's groups the talk needn't center on fathers; they provide a convenient way to begin to talk about what it means to be a man, but there are many other starting points. What's important is to find a way to begin somewhere. Once we start the process of talking about our experiences, we can find the value of being listened to by other men and being responded to as a person.

For example, at the Indianapolis retreat, after the Top Secret exercise, I invited the large group of men to divide into smaller groups of about six and find a quiet, separate room to meet in at the conference center. In the small groups, each man was given five minutes to talk without interruption about himself, while the other members just listened. The man could talk as much or as little as he wanted during the five minutes. After each man's five minutes were up, the rest of the group members had two minutes to respond to what they had heard. The point was for each man, no matter how shy, to get the opportunity for some "air time" and to feel heard.

The effect of just feeling attended to by a group of men can be quite powerful. In one group, Pat began by saying: "I can't recall when I've ever had five minutes just to talk to other men without being interrupted, just for myself." He began to talk about his adolescent difficulties with his father, but soon he found himself voicing his fear of winding up in a similar situation with his teenage sons, and how lonely he felt trying to work things out with his boys. Over time, what became clear to Pat was that he was having a much more intense reaction to his oldest son's graduating from college than he realized, and that he needed to talk to his wife and his son about what this family transition meant to him.

Words and labels for what we are feeling are often tremendously reassuring. They give order and meaning to what's happening. But it's precisely those words for their intimate experiences that many men are denied, or fail to learn growing up.

Even the most intellectually accomplished man may feel goofy or out on a limb when trying to talk about love. As the morning wound to a close and we returned to our single, larger group, Russ shared a lament. "I hate talking about feelings," he reflected. "It's like playing with a Ouija board—it's scary what might pop up."

"I know what you mean," agreed Dan. "This feels very swampy, but it's very exciting. I never really knew that I *had* feelings—in my family the men weren't supposed to."

Over time, as we talked and reflected and supported each other, men began to identify and label feelings that used to feel overwhelming, out of control, or unmanageable. "When my father turned his back on me, I felt shame—I never knew it had a name," as one man put it.

By labeling and identifying feelings, we come in time to intuit that sadness is not powerlessness or that becoming vulnerable doesn't always mean being in danger. This is why it is important as a man to find a way to tell your story, as we do with the Top Secret game or the five-minute format. Expressing conflicts and stress reduces the sense of lonely isolation and shame. Finding the words and hearing others' stories bolster self-esteem. Psychologist James Pennebaker, summarizing his studies of the healing power of telling stories, notes: "Writing about traumas or other stressors has positive and long-term psychological benefits."[11]

We can tell our stories to ourselves, through journals, to friends of either gender, or in group settings.[12]

BELOVED SONS: MEN'S NEED TO LOVE

Most important, men need an opportunity to express their yearning to be loved and loving. Often this struggle crystallizes around the

wish to be a beloved son. The tender sides of men are not often
affirmed, particularly by other men.

Later in the day of our Indianapolis retreat, after we returned
from lunch and some time for reflection, we talked about what the
morning had stirred up.

The index cards were again distributed, this time for the Treasure
Game. "Write something wonderful that you received from your
father—something you treasure and hold close to your heart."

"Link by link, the men move along the iron chains of their
memories," one participant noted afterward.[13] The air seemed incapable of sustaining anything inconsequential. Each man labored in
silence. Then the cards were again collected, shuffled, and read
anonymously.

> My father once hid a small piece of paper in a little
> safebox I kept in my study. After his death I was looking in
> the box and found the paper, on which he had written:
> "Please keep among your securities the knowledge that I love
> and respect you and will always be proud of you. . . ."

Men have many treasures to share; each one plucks a chord in
our hearts:

> I was nine years old, and it had snowed the night before.
> A cold, cold day, my father and I went out with our tobog-
> gan, up to the top of a sledding hill near the house. I got in
> first, then he, and he wrapped his coat around me for the
> long, windy ride down the hill. Bundled up like that, racing
> along, his warmth. I've never forgotten that day.

> When my son was born, my father came to my house
> and put his arms around me. He hugged me and said: "Some-
> day you will hold your son like this, and I hope you feel as
> good about him as I do about you. . . ."

> Taking the time for what my father referred to as 'dad
> and lad' walks around the area where we lived. These were
> very special since they happened so infrequently. . . .

> A ring he got in World War II that he handed down to
> me. . . .

There is nothing I got from my father that I treasure. . . .

A love of music. . . .

I once came upon my father when he was crying. He didn't turn away from me and he kept on crying. . . .

My father taught me my trade, with which I make my living. . . .

I was rescued from being swept down river, during a Boy Scout outing, by my father. . . .

He once wrote me a letter, the only one I ever got from him, and signed it, "Love, Dad". . . .

In remembering dad's love, however buried or unexpressed, we reclaim a disowned part of ourselves: the one that wants to love and be loved.

Reading these memories aloud around the room, men became aware that their fathers—and therefore they themselves—were capable of deep feeling, often hidden away behind a protective veneer. We were breathing life into images and memories of ourselves and other men; we gained glimpses of love and protection and concern and affection. Beneath our daily acts, both routine and heroic, lived our love and our fathers' love. We came to see that a man could take time with his children; that a man might have deep feelings of sadness, joy, protectiveness; that men could shelter and protect each other without losing their manliness; that a father could be a source of sweetness and kindness, not just authority and rules; that a father's love for his children could be more important than his income; that expressing that love directly was important.

"I'm realizing that my father may have really loved his family and couldn't express it, couldn't say it," reflected Henry. "He worked all those years and acted angry or defeated at home, but when I remember how much he enjoyed reading comics to us at night, it occurs to me that he may have felt cut off from us. Now I wonder if I want the same thing to happen to me with my children?"

Bill, without a single memory to treasure from his own father, told us: "Even so, it feels good to hear what men are capable of, it opens my eyes." With these words Bill reminded us all that we are all fathers to each other.

Feelings can be spoken of, displayed openly, and taken seriously. Gradually, men will speak from the heart: *I loved my father.*

JOE'S CHALLENGE

In reclaiming our love for and disappointment in our own fathers, we're reclaiming the ability to speak of and feel love as a man.

"Why speak of love?" challenged Joe, as we were discussing the Treasure Game. His anger was all the more surprising since he had been clearly engrossed in the exercise. "Just last week my father was in the hospital after a heart attack. We never talked much, but this incident made it clear that I don't know how much time we have left. I visited him last Thursday and felt I had to say something. I sat on the edge of his bed and looked at him and said, 'I love you, you know.' He looked away and said, 'I know, I know, we don't have to talk of that.' "

Joe stopped, with an exasperated shake of his head. "Why say it? He didn't even know how much that cost me, how much effort it took to say that—I've never said anything like that before."

Here I go to my father, Joe is saying, *and I want his blessing so badly and he doesn't even know how much it cost me. I crawled to his bedside and put down my armor and he didn't put down his! Do you see how awful that is?*

"Maybe that's the point," Art gently suggested. "The gift is for you as much as your father when you say you love him. You're speaking of love, something you've never been able to do before."

Asking for our fathers' love connects to being able to say "I love you" to our wives, children, and friends. Joe was keeping his disappointment and need for love buried beneath the burning anger he felt at his father. Joe sealed off the boyish parts of himself that wanted to be loved and loving, protecting himself from sorrow and disappointment, but also keeping himself in a tough, armored posture toward those he loved.

Joe might not go back to his father after the weekend and try again, but being able to acknowledge to the group of men his love and vulnerability, as well as anger, allowed Joe to reclaim disavowed feelings that he had put in cold storage.

Men in this way can give to each other what they longed for from their own fathers: close, caring attention; a sense of being heard and validated. It's not the same as snuggling up against your father in his coat on a snowy day while tobogganing together, but it is a warm welcome from the male community that can provide a sense of being cherished and validated as a man by men.

MEN'S GRIEF AND MEN'S GIFTS

Often men's tender impulses toward their fathers starve for lack of nourishment. Not surprising: Men's tender impulses often remain unnoticed and unsupported. How to give expression to these more tender sides of ourselves?

Often our tenderness toward our fathers is mixed in with grief at the alienation we feel from them; it's hard to let go if you can't express the sadness about missed opportunities.

In Indianapolis we used clay to express our yearnings to take care of, nurture, and heal our fathers. We sat on a sunny patio outside the dining hall, relaxed in the warm spring afternoon. Small buds of flowers poked through the wet soil around the edges of the patio, challenging the masonry at the edge for room. The men were spread out around tables, six to a table, each man trying to become familiar with a large lump of clay in front of him.

"Sculpt a gift to your fathers; something you'd like to give him," I suggest to the wary group. We all soon warm to the task. A man massages the clay, rolling it out on the table. Another rolls it in his hand, warming it, making it supple. Another man seems to be wrestling with the clay. It's as if they have their hands on their fathers' bodies.

A man holds up a clay bowl: *I'd like to give him this to pour his grief into and share it with me.* A clay V for *victory: I'd like him to have a real success in his life, one that he would take true pleasure from.* A gift box: *I'd like to give him a nonsuperficial conversation.*

Smiling, a man holds up a clay sheet of paper with furrowed lines etched across it: *A college diploma—my father always felt uneducated.* A clay S for *sorry: I want to apologize to my father for conspiring with my mother against him in his own house.*

The sun is setting as we break for the day. The men are working more on themselves than on their fathers, seeing their fathers in a new light, separating psychologically from painful childhood images, allowing a fuller sense of maleness into their identities as men.

Some men hug as we leave the patio, ripe with our hope, sorrow, and healing. Others shake hands; some just nod to others as if to affirm each other's presence in an important day's work.

A few men sit in a cluster on the ground in the corner still talking; in the center of the patio several men, new friends all, are singing; some drive off to find what downtown Indianapolis has to offer. Most of us head for sleep, with some trepidation, knowing that the next day promises a different experience together. Our work on Friday and Saturday has been highly verbal; Sunday holds a different kind of event, one that few of us have ever tried.

We started the weekend as forty-five guys looking at each other warily. Over the past two days we learned to sit together and listen to each other. We connected via our stories about ourselves, and the tone shifted, becoming less defensive and guarded, and more open. Coming in with a desire for quick answers, being very rational and "heady," we found we were able to talk together about affection, shame, love, sorrow, anger. In my graduate training as a psychologist I had learned that it takes a long time for a group to become cohesive and to feel safe to the members. When I first started to offer weekend retreats, the time felt far too short for anything really "significant" to happen. Yet over and over I'm struck by the ability of men to connect with each other in meaningful ways on these retreats. Men paired up to talk over meals; small groups used our breaks to go on hikes, play Ping-Pong, or sit and reminisce.

But tomorrow holds something new, less verbal, more physical.

As I head down the hallway to the dorm, Chuck passes me and asks: "I hear we're going to do a sweat lodge tomorrow. What exactly is that anyway?" His casual demeanor is betrayed by a skeptical tone.

I wish I could tell him that I knew.

AT THE SWEAT LODGE

It was pitch-black inside the structure where I sat, my knees folded close to my chest. We were packed so tight that I could feel the presence of the thirty-four other men. Coughing, low murmers, and the touch of the guys on either side of me. Sitting in the sweat lodge, the thought occurred to me: *What am I doing here?*

Naked. Seven o'clock on a warm spring night, in an open field at a rural retreat center outside Indianapolis. It's strange how vulnerable men look without clothes on. We had all taken off our clothes in the field before entering the sweat lodge. Our penises and testicles hung limp, as if they were embarrassed at being caught nonerect. Taking off our clothes had the air of shedding a costume, or armor. Eldridge Cleaver—back in his fashion designer days—had suggested that men's trousers include a fabric "cup" on the outside to demarcate the groin area. Cleaver reasoned that if men thus advertised the size and presence of their genitals, they would be less concerned about proving their masculinity. The cup to end all wars.

As we undressed, Joseph, our leader, warned us about the sweat lodge. "Forget all the prayers you know: Jewish, Catholic, Protestant, or Native American—they won't do you any good." Since I'm not given to prayers anyway—Yom Kippur, five months away, would mark the twenty-fifth consecutive year I had not gone to temple on that most sacred of Jewish holidays—I wondered what experience could be so intense as to transcend prayer.

A sweat lodge is an ancient Native American ritual in which men of the tribe gather in a hot, steamy lodge to celebrate the male community through a ceremony of communion and initiation.

I was skeptical but curious. The group of men who had invited me to Indianapolis had suggested hiring Joseph for one day to conduct a sweat lodge as part of the retreat. It's always easy to agree to something months ahead of time, I lamented now: *You don't realize the full implications until you find yourself naked and defenseless in a field in the Midwest.*

My part of the retreat had been reflective and talk-oriented. I was asking men to do that most difficult of tasks: to put into words their feelings about their lives. Joseph, introducing himself, described the week-long trips into the woods he led for men, which he called "vision quests." To me, "vision quest" sounded like the name of an optical supply store.

Several men had built the lodge in the afternoon out of branches and saplings. The retreat center already had a sweat lodge. Several of us had walked through the woods to examine it. We, the sweat lodge committee, decided it was too small. It was also used regularly by a women's group that came to the retreat center. They probably wouldn't like us remodeling their lodge and enlarging it for ourselves. Through the woods we spied yet another sweat lodge.

"Another weekend group must have built it," suggested the puzzled director of the retreat center. Sweat lodges everywhere: Condo Sweat Lodges; Time Share Sweat Lodges; Sweat Lodges for the Newly Conscious Male.

So another one was built in the growing community of sweat lodges. The carpenters among us provided direction. "Feels good to let people know I have some competency, I feel so closemouthed in there," said one, pointing to the meeting room.

Four men served as fire tenders most of the afternoon, building the fire and heating the rocks. This project took hours because the rocks need to be red hot and cannot be heated too fast.

As the frame of the sweat lodge was finished, we searched for a cover. Blankets did the trick. How about the floor? "The dirt floor looks pretty hard," one older man observed. "Yeah, we'll be in there for over two hours," another man observed with dark foreboding. *Two hours?* I gasped.

Our intent was to spread grass over the dirt, but we wound up with a floor of pine needles. *Two hours on pine needles?*

Late in the afternoon, our leader explained our upcoming mission. The purpose of the "sweat," he said, familiarly, was to purge us of the pain of the past few days—the struggles with mother and father—and to set us on the road to male identity, a vision of ourselves.

I am feeling defensive: The struggles we had in the meeting room to talk, to stay with our angry, needy feelings, weigh on me. Do the men feel that our time together talking as a group didn't work?

No more talk this night: It's time for the sweat. The darkness outside is bracing, and we strip in the field near the sweat lodge. Black sky, all the stars visible. No moon, no clouds.

Do I become an observer or a participant? My heart longs to become part of a male community, even—or perhaps especially—if only for a short while. My friend Nick, a filmmaker working on a project about men and sexuality, tells of filming a men's weekend retreat on the subject and at the end, when each man talked of what the days together had meant to him, Nick—standing outside the circle of men, filming the testimony with a camera on his shoulder—started to cry because he hadn't been able to participate.

The male position: standing on the edge, looking in at the warmth. Like a kid on a snowy street with his nose pressed to the window of bakery, as one man described himself to me.

Standing in the field undressing, I felt at a critical moment of decision. Being the leader in charge, having the answers, is easy for me. Matters get more difficult when I'm invited in.

There is a competitiveness I feel with other men: that I have it worked out, that I don't need them. I can show men I hurt and talk about the pain, but the point is: *I don't need men.* That's my belief. Perhaps it is the expected baggage of an older brother dethroned in all the usual ways by a younger brother, or the accumulated detritis of the competition between men.

Yet I know too that I want to find men, that a connection with other men means more to me than ever before in my life. Women I have always relied on, perhaps I take my allegiance to them for granted—but I've wanted to find my way to men, to find what about them inspires me and connects me to them.

I hung my clothes from a nearby tree, trying to seem nonchalant about all this. Hey, I always hang my clothes off branches before I go to sleep. My pants and shirt hung limply from the branches, like dead people. Then they all fell off. I picked them up, arranged them on their perch again.

My glasses presented a problem. They would be a liability in my upcoming sauna; they were metal and would heat up, as well as fog up. But I had trouble leaving them behind. Not being able to see clearly frightens me. When the entire event was over, a man told the group: "The most difficult part of the evening was sitting in the dark, buck-naked, bunched in with men and wondering how far up my leg it was okay for another man's hand to travel." Constant vigilance is the price of manhood.

The stars sparkled as I removed my glasses, a spectacle I usually enjoyed. People who don't wear glasses don't know the pleasure of seeing light look the way it does when you're stoned, when you're not stoned. But tonight I didn't enjoy the sight; I felt defenseless. Piggy in *Lord of the Flies* comes to mind, the intellectual of the group: The planewrecked boys smashed his glasses and turned on him as the group degenerated from civilization to savagery.

I tenderly balanced my glasses on top of my clothes, then I joined the line of men snaking its way toward the sweat lodge. Part of me still clung to the hope that this would be nothing more than a glorified sauna: We would sit around as if we were drinking beer and reading magazines. It'll be a piece of cake, I imagined, grasping for reassurance.

Before reaching the lodge we passed the fire tenders, and what a sight they were: The only light was the illumination of the fire pit, an enormous bonfire heating the rocks, which glowed and twinkled before my eyes. I felt transported away from mundane images of men by the sight of the four fire tenders, large guys, who have been building the fire and raking the coals for the past four hours. The Greek god who tended the forges of the world was named Hephaestes, and he walked with a limp because he had been wounded when his father, Zeus, threw him from Mount Olympus in a rage at his mother's adultery. Suddenly I felt proud of this hardworking, self-sacrificing god!

We crawled on our hands and knees into the lodge, forming two concentric circles around the still-empty fire pit. The lodge seemed surprisingly small. It was too dark to tell who was on my right and left, but I could feel their presence, our legs touching. I felt the pine needles on my feet, and elsewhere.

"We've lucked out," the guy on my left whispered to me.

"We're in the outer circle; at least there's somebody between us and the fire," continued the guy on my right. I recognized the voice: It was Jim, who had been so angry at me the day before. "I am scared." He laughed, furtively.

"So am I," the guy on my left agreed quickly.

"Me, too," I added, sounding like one of the Three Stooges.

"Everyone take the hand of the person next to you," instructed Joseph.

"Why are you scared?" I asked my new friend, Jim, as we sat, our hands entwined.

"I did one of these last year, and it was awful—it got so fucking hot inside."

He joked, we joked. The guy on my left agreed, and I was left wondering how come those who knew the most about this event were the most nervous. Not reassuring. I was glad for the opportunity to hold hands; it felt less lonely.

We made some jokes about avoiding the imminent stampede for the door, trampling each other, when Joseph admonished us to be silent. Suddenly I didn't love the instruction to "stay with my feelings."

The hot coals were slowly handed in on a shovel, one shovelful at a time, glowing fiercely. They illuminated the room momentarily, then were placed in the central fire pit. Again the rocks sparkled in my eyes, and in the reflected light I saw the naked men in front of me.

Then the door, or actually the blanket flap, was closed and Joseph started pouring water on the rocks; huge clouds of steam poured forth.

We each spoke in turn the name of our fathers: "Louis Osherson," I intoned. The names of these men whom we had spent a weekend speaking of in alienated, hurt tones sounded different now. They had let us down and we had let them down. Now, each man enunciated the name of his father thoughtfully, carefully: One man named his father in Hebrew, another in Gaelic.

The heat was rising but it still felt manageable. *Still doesn't feel much worse than a sauna. Good entertainment*, I smugly admitted to myself.

Then the heat took over. More water on the rocks. This was no longer a sauna. It was very hot, the oxygen level felt like it'd sunk to zero with all these sweaty males. Some men started yelling. There was fear in the ol' sweat lodge tonight.

"Look to your fathers," Joseph instructed. "Invite them in, let them help you."

Invite my father in? That felt like going too far. Really. Depending on my father, the father of my memory? That touched a wound.

Serious yelling and protests now. Joseph poured some more water on the coals and the steam rose. I squeezed the hand of the guy next to me: Sharing the pain, being able to speak it out loud, felt wonderful. A community of men to hear it, without shame.

"Say whatever you need to. Find a prayer within you that gets you through," warned Joseph.

"So much, so much, so much," I heard my friend on my left moaning. His hand was gripping mine tightly. Together we would get through this. So much what? I wondered. So much pain, enduring so much pain all our lives. This sweat pain felt familiar in that way, a concrete representation of more hideous burdens. What was different was expressing it in a community of men without total shame. Yes, so much.

Joseph poured *more* water on the coals. I hated him, the bastard, for putting me through this pain. Peevishly I thought: *He didn't have to throw that last bucket on there; that was decidedly not necessary.* It was hard to breathe; we were using up all the oxygen with our moaning and yelling.

Images of cattle cars, the Jews being transported to the death camps in railroad cars. All the suffering, and we didn't have to be doing this, a middle-class tour of human suffering. The red coals, the steam, the darkness were frightening and disorientating. Many of the European relatives on my father's side of the family had been lost in the Holocaust; I never knew whole branches of the family, lost relatives. Had my father ever recovered? Had he ever found his way through the silent maze of grief and mourning?

"Walk down the stairs, toward the earth, go downward. That's what you must do," instructs Joseph. "Use your fathers."

I am overcome by a longing for my father, for him to help me through all this, all this male suffering. I hardly want to acknowledge this longing, it seems too childlike. So *unseemly*, in this room full of men. An image of talking to my father on the front seat of a pickup truck. What truck? Suburban businessman, at home most of all in New York City, he's never owned a truck in his life. I want to cozy up to my father, feel his strength. Oh the hell with it: with my daddy.

Christ changed our name for God. "How are we to refer to God?" He was asked.

"Abba," Christ replied, which literally translated means "Daddy." And in so instructing, he transformed our vision of God from the stern Jewish Yahweh, certainly a demanding, remote Father, to an image of the "Daddy" in whom we may also find some comfort.

That's fine for Christ, but is there any comfort with the daddy inside me?

The guy on my right, Jim, had disappeared; I don't know where he is, although his hand is still in mine, twisted somewhat. But his silhouette is no longer visible beside me; he seems to be lying down somehow, although I can't imagine how that's possible in this jumble of bodies. Is he dead? A momentary panic seizes me: Oh, no, I'm next. . . . Headline: FORTY-FIVE MEN FOUND DEAD IN SWEAT LODGE. Subhead: *Group apparently searching for their fathers.* I grip his hand tightly, and feel relieved when there is some response.

I want to get out of this sweat lodge, away from the heat and the suffering, and the panic. Someone does leave, stumbling silently through the blanket door. My pride is soon wilted in the heat. I turn again to my father, imagine him sitting right next to me. I feel ashamed that I am so scared and first I apologize to him.

"Daddy, I'm sorry I'm so scared. You may remember when I was so scared in Little League. The time I faked being hurt to get out of playing, all because I was scared of the hardball." For a long time we played ball with softballs, and those big padded grapefruits didn't worry me, even though they hurt if you got whacked with one. But Little League hardballs were different: Those suckers were major league baseballs. They were rock-hard and they shot toward second base over a rocky infield. Professional baseball players have a big advantage: groomed infields. Notice how carefully major league infielders inspect the field before and during games; they don't want the balls hitting rocks or skidding off wet grass and getting past them—or worse, hitting them between the eyes or in the teeth.

We kids did not exactly groom the field before playing. Those hardballs rocketed at me. Once I was backing away from a hard grounder coming right at me at my second base position, trying to corral the ball before it got me, when it hit a rock and whistled past my right shoulder and toward the outfielder, who caught it on the fly. After that I used my glove more as a shield. Best of all was when I cut my little finger in a minor accident at home and begged out of games for the rest of the year. What shame I felt, waving my wounded little finger, carefully bandaged.

Now I apologize again to my father for failing to be a brave son, and tell him how scared I am now in the sweat lodge.

Joseph persists in throwing water on the rocks. He seems a satanic character, gleefully making overwhelming clouds of steam. I wish I were dead. *Get out of here!* screams a voice inside my head. Several more men do leave.

"Go toward the earth, go down. That's what you must do. Downward. Use your fathers," instructs Joseph/Satan.

A stairway comes to mind. My father and I standing at the top of the stairs leading to the basement in the home I grew up in.

"Daddy, would you walk down those stairs with me? I need your help. I'm scared."

Down the stairs we start, our hands held tightly together. I am still incredibly hot. But my father's presence is soothing, just Daddy and me. In my mind's eye he looks as he did during World War II, as he did in a treasured picture of him I once found in our house: dressed up in his sergeant's uniform, smiling and confident, handsome and trim.

Yet on our imaginary stairway, trouble starts: My father doesn't want to stay. He isn't sure if he can handle this event. Too hot for him, and he is scared, and he is turning his attention away from me. The wimp! I need him and he buckles. All those times when I was a kid and his head was buried in the newspaper at home when I needed him. Didn't he feel like a real man himself? Perhaps he couldn't help me because he didn't have the right stuff himself.

A powerful urge to turn on my father, to get away from his weakness, overcomes me.

Then the realization comes: He needs me to ask him to stay with me! He does not know that he is important to me, and I feel the same lack of grit for my son: wanting to tiptoe away when I'm really called on. Do I have the emotional resources to be there for my son and daughter?

"Dad," I plead, "this is important." I have to really ask, no more beating around the bush.

"Dad, I really want you here. I need you."

I imagine taking his head in my hands, my palms on his cheeks, turning him to look at me. "Please stay." My hands seem to feel the soft, aged skin on his cheeks, pressing into them, holding his head.

Fortunately, he doesn't break my heart. Father and son go down the stairs together. We are holding hands and helping each other. I talk of being scared of the dark; he tells me of his fears, darker still, at age seventy-five.

More steam. The hell with getting into the earth; I have to get us both out of this steamy hell. We are both in a truck, and I am young, talking to my father. He looks wonderful and there was a time when I remembered him looking that way—the picture of him in the army, looking handsome, confident, and strong. As an adolescent I used to go and cry in front of that picture in the den of my parents' house, because by then my father seemed so weak and depressed and needy and disappointing.

Now he's there and we are talking, me as a young son and him as a young father, and it feels great. Both of those men are inside me: the talkative, curious ten-year-old and the strong, confident father. There is that part of my father too. These figures are alive within me.

For the first time without shame, I see my father's vulnerability and need side by side with my own. I resolve to remember the vulnerability and the strength in both of us, so I can respond more realistically to him, my family, and myself. With pride I realize, too, that I am going to make it through the physical challenge of this "sweat," a personal victory over my own fear and panic.

Soon we open the door again momentarily and there is fresher air and then there is no more water on the coals and it's time to leave. Will there be a mass stampede for the door, all of us clawing and pushing at each other to get out? No, we leave in an orderly way, each of us crawling through the entryway, helping each other. Images of death and birth, as we go through the entryway.

One forty-year-old man left the sweat lodge with a new treasure. "My father was so gruff and demanding," he told me over coffee a day later. "I was sent off to private school at age fifteen and it was pretty clear that I was sent because I was screwing up on my subjects in high school. But when I was leaving that sweat lodge I had this memory of something I had long ago forgotten. My father used to go sailing with me, just me and him alone on the boat a lot during the summers. I loved those times with him, how wonderful they were.

As I was crawling out of the lodge the name of the boat came back to me: It was the sloop *Friendship*."

Over breakfast the next morning I remembered the guy on my right. What had happened to Jim during the sweat; where had he disappeared to?

Finding him by the orange juice pitchers, I asked him what happened.

"Simple," Jim responded with a laugh. "I burrowed under the blanket wall and stuck my head out the edge." He laughs again. "I've done this a couple of times. I'd never have made it if I hadn't stuck my head out to breathe."

Over the past few years I've surveyed approximately two hundred participants in these weekend retreats, and over 95 percent of them rate them as "highly satisfying." The complaints are usually that the two-to-three-day format is too short, or that there were too many people (smaller groups would allow for ever more connection and intimate sharing), or that some men wished they could follow up more back home.

In 1990 I surveyed ninety men two to three years after the event. I wondered what long-term impact such a short event might have. Over 70 percent replied. Even several years after the event, 93 percent felt that the event remained a "very positive experience." Many indicated that they still thought about their experiences and the men they met there. Some friendships developed from the events; some men started or joined men's groups; others reported changes in significant relationships with wives, children, parents, or deepening friendships; and a few mentioned that things were going better at work now that they had sorted out their obligations and loyalties to parents and were no longer mixing up bosses and fathers or mothers quite as much.

There were few miracle cures, but rather small victories and changes that mattered a lot.

"My father has been dead for twelve years and I felt I had made peace with him before he died," reflected one man. "The workshop helped me make greater peace and understanding with him by bringing my attention to the small things we shared together as father and son. I try to carry this point of view about the seemingly unimportant times we shared and not just the larger issues. It helps me greatly to appreciate the small, wonderful moments with my children."

Another man wrote: "The relationship I have with my dad has improved; we have better contact and communication, a step in the right direction."

A father with teenage children whose own father died before the birth of his grandchildren, wrote that the workshop completed some posthumous intergenerational work that needed to be done. "My father died just after I was married and had a son. I never got to know him when I was in his 'old' roles of father/husband. The workshop tied the knot and completed the circle of the thread between my father and me to my son—as well as back to his father and down to my yet potential grandchildren."

Among the most important aspects of the men's retreats were the chances for connection with other men. "Without a doubt, the most important part for me was seeing other men express their feelings," commented one man. Another wrote that the most precious aspect of the weekend was "remembering the fact that I did it, and the memory of other men expressing their feelings is often helpful. It seems to me that we all have the same emotional physics governing us—only in different makeups." Often immediately after the event, men will feel that they have to digest what happened. "I need some time now to do some processing," as one man put it.

Over time men will feel that they haven't accomplished as much as they'd like in feeling wholer and more connected with themselves or those they love, but they know they have started a process they will continue to work on. "I approach this task in fits and starts," wrote Jim two years after his time in Indianapolis.

CREATING A SAFE PLACE TO TALK

A man doesn't have to go to a weekend retreat miles from home, or sit in a sweat lodge for hours, in order to find more intimacy in his life. Everyday friendships as well as local men's groups both offer such opportunities.

Consider the place and *the priority you give to male friendships.* For some of us it can be a major step just to make time for lunch, dinner, or a friendly walk with another man. Small things matter a lot, like being on time, or constantly cancelling plans because "something came up." It's always tempting to me to make plans to see my male friends a last priority, yet I'm often struck by how grateful I am that I *didn't* cancel a lunch date just to get some more work done.

Often too, we don't *nurture each other*, by making clear that we value the friendship, even if we don't see our friends as often as we'd like. Men's friendships are more sporadic, less verbal and continuous than women's.[14] So, it's even more important to be clear that you hold a friendship in your heart even when you don't see each other. Explaining why plans changed, expressing regret, and being clear about the wish to be together are as important as what happens when you are together. Men often forget that their responses have a big impact on their friends.

Recently I called a friend, really an acquaintance, I hadn't seen in a long time. I wanted his help to talk about a project I was working on, and offered to buy him lunch, though I felt unsure of how much of his time I ought to ask for.

"I appreciate your taking the time to do this," I said into the phone, feeling somewhat shy and formal. This is a man I like, and I wanted to get to know him better.

"Sam, it'll be good to see *you*," he responded heartily, and I was aware how much I relaxed internally at his words, and how much I was looking forward to our time together.

For men who want to *form a men's group* as a way to explore who they are, the most important question is: How do you create a safe place for yourselves? That is the first question each potential member needs to think about. What do you need to feel safe in the group? I've found it helpful to be clear about the time and the place the group will meet, to be specific about how long the group will meet and how often. By being clear about beginnings and endings, each person can feel that he knows more of what is expected of him.

Often men's groups begin by considering whether they want to have an appointed or a hired leader, whether they want to set an agenda or leave topics unstructured and open-ended, and whether members will take turns talking or leave it as an open conversation for people to participate in as they wish. Some groups also consider how their time together will be spent, whether they will restrict themselves to talk or find some balance between talking and other activities, such as sports, going to movies together, and so on.

Tom Landsberg, a veteran participant in men's support groups, has discussed these matters in an excellent brief primer entitled "The Creation and Nurturing of a Men's Support Group."[15]

I think that feeling wholer and more connected as a man today means being ambivalent and torn—like Jim in the sweat lodge, many of us are both inside and outside the tent at the same time. We are constantly presented with opportunities for gaining more wholeness and empowerment, and often we need to back away in order to move forward.

9

THE CONNECTED SELF

HEALTHY INTIMACY IN AN AGE

WITHOUT ANSWERS

ANDREW'S DILEMMA AT THE RIVERSIDE

Andrew is a forty-five-year-old banker, divorced and remarried, with several grown children. One day he described to me "a moment with my son Paul that left me so moved I can hardly explain." He went on: "Last month I was visiting Paul at college for the first time his freshman year, and he asked me one morning to meet him down at the river. He had gone out for JV crew."

Andrew and his son had struggled a lot together during the transition to college. Andrew had made considerable effort helping his son decide about college and deal with the normal mixed emotions about leaving home. "I wound up doing several of the college applications myself, because Paul wouldn't get them done." Now his only son was off to college, far from home, but would he be all right on his own? Would he find a place for himself, develop some competencies in this new, adult world? Those were the questions that had plagued Andrew as a college student himself, and they were of course on his mind during the daylong drive to his son's college.

Andrew's eyes grew eager as he spoke of that morning on the dock watching the crew practice. "Standing there with other parents, it was cold and I was waiting for Paul, when all of a sudden, several boats came up the river. I couldn't tell which was his. First came a boat with the oars pulling in smooth rhythm. It was the varsity crew and they looked beautiful. They were moving so fast and effortlessly through the water, I knew it couldn't be Paul's."

Andrew stopped, took a drink of tea. "Then came another boat around the curve. At first all the oars were askew, some in the water, some in the air, the boat wobbling. Was that his? I wondered."

Andrew's big hands hit the table as he exclaimed: "I would have been proud of him even if the damn boat capsized, but instead the coxswain started to give orders. It was a woman. All the oars went into the water and they started to pull in unison. What a beautiful sight! The boat started to fly through the water. All of them pulling together, rowing with such power and strength!"

Andrew's eyes teared as he explained the significance. "My boy had done it! He found out about the crew, decided to do it, and was obviously enjoying himself." Andrew knew then that his son had made it into college. The boy was going to be all right.

Then Andrew found himself the odd man out on the dock. "There were all these other parents on the dock too. We were all watching, sipping cider. I found myself wanting to cry, I was so moved. I turned to another father standing next to me, and exclaimed: 'Isn't it wonderful!' He looked at me and said: 'Yeah, the foliage is just great this time of year.'

" 'No,' I exclaimed. 'The crew, the kids.'

"The man then told me that he was in crew in college and started to critique their technique."

I wondered aloud what Andrew did then.

"Well, I had these tears in my eyes and didn't want to be inappropriate, like crying on the dock while all the other parents were standing there sipping cider and this guy was giving me a lecture on crew technique. So I went over to a corner of the dock where no one could see me and just cried a little."

There is a mismatch of feeling here, as Andrew's joy, relief, and sadness are not legitimated as appropriate. The fathers are, shall we say, out of empathy with each other.

Andrew's feelings *are* inappropriate, in that he is emotionally flooded in a social situation of restraint and decorum. Andrew is momentarily overwhelmed with joy, sadness, and relief at his son's struggles, echoing his own struggle to make it as a boy. Andrew's struggles with college left him with some painful memories of shame about his own competence and success.

In relishing his son's skill and effort, Andrew is actually doing important psychological work for himself: grieving for his past difficulties, letting go of them, and finding a new part of himself as a proud father who can enable his son to succeed.

The man who says "That's my boy!" is also affirming that he is the father of that boy, that he has a son who can, and therefore that he is a father who can. Instead of feeling like an inadequate man, he feels like an enabling father with an enabling son: It's as if the male lineage is redeemed, and he becomes wholer.

This chapter focuses on how men become wholer, at age forty, fifty, sixty, or later, coming through their wounds and tentativeness to get back in touch with the vital wellsprings of their lives. I don't mean we should strive to be masters of intimacy in some perfectionist way—it's easy to get so filled with performance expectations that "intimacy" becomes one more burden added to an already overloaded male agenda. Rather, it's a matter of feeling connected, more at home with those we love, no longer denying or distracting ourselves from parts of us pressing for attention and healing.

Most of us are both the men on the dock: the one with powerful feelings and the one ignoring them at the same time. Being a man today means living with an inner ambivalence: wanting to live up to our fathers, wanting to be different; wanting to be in the warm coziness of the family, wanting to be out of it. We spend much of our lives in situations where we don't know where to put our feelings, and so we often disconnect from them.

Often as men we learn to speak the language of technique, anger, of shame and withdrawal. When those we love, not surprisingly, don't get the message, we become isolated and lose an opportunity for connection.

How do we find ways to talk with others and ourselves about the inner landscape, to speak from the heart, not just the head, to talk of what we love, and not just the fall foliage? How do we as men reclaim a language that isn't angry or shaming?

First, we need to acknowledge the hope or desire to try to connect with parts of the self that seem not to fit the mold of manliness. Then we need to explore new parts of self. To do either of these means to take a risk.

THE RISKS OF SELF-CONNECTION

After a very productive time at a weekend workshop, a man wrote a letter of thanks, noting: "It took me a couple of years to take this risk."

What is the risk to men?

A man once told me that he had given up on being with his kids during the week because "I feel like I want to be of use; the only place I feel like I'm of use is when I'm in the office."

The biggest roadblock to men is often the resistance to making time for themselves and others. Often as men we work hard to fill time and then get really anxious when the work is finished. We substitute a project for simply being with someone, or insist on having a goal whenever we are by ourselves.

Loneliness. Connecting with the self can bring a feeling of utter aloneness. "I work fifty hours a week and want to take some time off, but I wonder what I would do," remarks Phillip.

There is a kind of terror of a vacuum for men when they are not "working." And I mean *working* in its broadest sense. Often we want to fill our time and that's good enough. After all, work is easier than relationships. Work often calms us, serves as a means of reducing our anxiety and sense of loneliness. Without it a man may feel naked or stripped of his traditional means of soothing himself.

Finding ways to "play" via journal keeping or in therapy, by taking time with friends, a wife, children, a men's group, may feel very lonely and awkward at first. Sometimes we need to pass through the loneliness before we can find these activities exciting and rewarding.

Inadequacy. Before the birth of our first child, my wife and I went through a series of miscarriages. Each of them was a powerful loss. My wife seemed better able to express her sadness and anger, and there was a lot of attention on her as the "poor woman." Yet I knew there were deep currents for me of powerlessness, the embarrassment of not being able to father a child, also the vulnerability of loving without being able to fully protect. To understand the impact of the miscarriages better, to grieve more fully, I took mornings off from work and for the better part of a year I stayed at home weekday mornings writing in a journal. Whatever understanding I possess about how I grew up as a man, how I learned to distance myself from what I loved, my need for my mother and father, seem rooted in those mornings of self-exploration.

But running alongside the excitement and sense of personal discovery was also a shyness and biting fear of inadequacy, intensified when I would see my neighbors resolutely, purposefully going off to work.

The loneliness and fear of inadequacy may be heightened by feeling out of step with your peers.

Goofiness. One night at a restaurant during my "journal" phase I saw a colleague from work at a nearby table. We stopped to say hello and the conversation turned to what we were doing. In an attempt to catch him up with my life, and feeling hungry for contact, I launched into an overpassionate discussion of my journal and the miscarriages and where I was in dealing with loss and loneliness. A righteous seer descending on the marketplaces of biblical Jerusalem likely had less intensity in his voice. Caught with a forkful of steak halfway between plate and mouth, confronted by more intensity than he had anticipated, my colleague gave me some advice with a wry tone: "Gee, Sam, sounds like you need a dog."

And he was right: I needed some comfort and warmth, but the put-down reminded me of my inappropriateness in "spilling" out my turmoil to a colleague, and carried with it a reminder of exposure. We really are both prisoners and guards with each other all the time.

Connecting with others as a man means feeling divided, and struggling with loneliness, awkwardness, and conflicting feelings. We stammer while we're learning to speak a new language of love.

LIFE ON THE LEDGE

If you're going to try to heal wounds with others or draw them closer, you may at first feel in new territory, out on a limb.

Wayne is a black executive in the steel industry. He has reason to be proud of his life, for he has struggled out of a difficult past. "My father was a very flamboyant type," Wayne told me, "and I learned about his death as a suicide over the radio when I was twelve. Then I had to go to school that day and face all my classmates."

Being a father was challenging for Wayne himself. Life has not been easy with his twenty-five-year-old son, Sam, with whom he's had a distant relationship. Smoke belched from the factories beyond his office window as Wayne told me about a recent trying moment with his son, who had been living in Los Angeles.

"I had sent him a note inviting him home for the holidays and got back a letter. He laid me out—telling me that I had been a rotten father, never there when he needed me, and now he was pissed off, and he had no desire to come home."

Wayne's initial reaction was to write his son off: "I was tempted not to respond and just let him miss the holiday with us." But Wayne didn't fall for the typical male way of starting a dialogue: leading with an attack, rather than a more vulnerable position.

"I wasn't sure what to do."

"What did you do?"

"I got on a plane and flew to Los Angeles. Even angry, I knew I wanted to talk with him, and the letter, angry as it was, meant to me that my son wanted to talk to me.

"But I wanted to do this right, not come on like gangbusters. This may sound odd, but I wanted him to feel some control, like he was on his turf."

Wayne did an unusual thing: He got into the one-down position. "My first reaction was, well, let him come to me. But then I thought: That's what I was doing by inviting him home. Instead, I wanted him to know that I saw him as a man, able to exist on his own, and that he was important enough to me that I would come to him."

He looked out the window as he told me how their meeting went.

"Well, he was shocked I'd come, even though I had called ahead. He gave me a tour of Los Angeles, and we talked, got angry, I told him about my past and my father's death and the impact it had on me.

"I've learned to take risks, like I did with my son. Things are better than they've been. We've gotten closer, I make more time for him. We still have a long way to go, but at least we're *somewhere*, not nowhere like before."

Wayne offered me an image:

"Feels like he and I are two people holding their hands out, me on top of the ledge, or it could be reversed. We're holding our hands out, and it's up to either of us to pull the other back. The anger is there, wanting to let the other drop out of sight. As our fingers come together there are question marks: What will we do? He and I have the power to rescue and redeem or to let each other drop. Ultimately I feel we'll come together."

MEMORY AS THE MAP TO OUR HEART'S DESIRE

Leaving Wayne's office, I thought about the redeeming qualities of fathering, of giving to others what you felt the lack of when young. In order to do that, though, you have to remember the times you actually got it—how good a father's attention felt, a mother's comfort, the thrill of acknowledgment, feeling loved and responded to. Pediatrician T. Berry Brazelton writes: "Parental love is possible only because it has its roots in *former* attachments."[1] I suspect this is true of all love. We constantly are using our memory as the guidepost to our heart's desire.

Our own memory can provide the "maps" for what we need and what others need from us. That's why it's important to return to our own history, to find the memories of love and affirmation, even when they seem too few to treasure. Journals, workshops, exploring family history are all ways of retrieving these maps.

Buried treasures. When men play the Treasure Game, writing down memories of fathers that they hold dear, they are creating new myths and potentialities for themselves. Matt, for example, is a forty-year-old married man who grew up with an abusive father. He remembers continual criticism, peppered by physical pokes and spankings from his father, a high school teacher. Matt carries within him the yelling and physical abuse he absorbed from his father. As an adult, he very quickly feels panicky in emotionally charged situations, anticipating anger easily and losing control. An excellent neighborhood soccer player, he was recently humiliated while refereeing his son's high school soccer game. A goal was disputed and several parents started shouting at him. He confessed, "I felt so nervous, sweaty, and upset I had to leave the field, asking another father to take over for me."

In order to break the cycle of "anger-victim" feelings that scare him in relatively benign situations, Matt needs to find some sweetness in his own inner world, rather than the harsh voices that continually sing there.

At a men's event Matt plays the Treasure Game, and a special memory comes to him:

"My father was a high school math teacher. When I was young he would often ask me to come sit with him while he graded exams. He'd get a chair, have me sit next to him, and I'd help him check off right and wrong answers. It felt great to sit there with my father, working together, often with his arms around me."

Matt listens to his memory read aloud, and hears what other

men treasure about their fathers. And Matt begins to retrieve the part of himself that sought connection; he sees his capacity for love, as well as his father's, both buried underneath the painful memories of abuse. He is thus enlivening new parts of himself, more masterly and also more loving. He takes these memories home with him from the retreat, works on them in therapy, and months later comes to a resolution:

"I hadn't seen my father in years, but felt that I needed to talk with him, try to put the past behind us in whatever way possible. I called him in the town near us where he now lives and invited him to lunch."

Matt does this carefully, choosing a neutral location where he anticipates that his father will be more relaxed, less defensive. When they meet they talk about what they are doing these days, less about the past. "I don't condone what happened," Matt reflected later, "but I'm less angry, seeing what he had to go through. I feel like I see us both more clearly now, without pity."

As men we often need to look inward, to attend to the memories and the treasures buried there, in order to enliven our self-esteem and self-respect.

A STATE OF MIND:
SHOWING UP OR DISAPPEARING

Wayne's description of being on a ledge with the son he loves applies to many of us: Do we rescue and redeem (each other) or let ourselves drop out of sight?

Mack, a stepfather and a college teacher, tells me of "the most important event of the past year": "Feeling connected with my step-daughter, who's now in high school and has had lots of struggles with her natural father. We've worked a lot over the past year, sitting down and talking with the kids.

"I decided we needed to have a family meal and the first night my wife and I started it, no one came, but I just let them know that I was there with their mother and they started to come home for dinner. No big deal but very satisfying." Mack put himself in the position of honoring the connection and their time together: *I am here for you.*

Mack is aware of a different way of being "of use" to his family than just staying at the office: He acknowledges that he and his child are important to each other's development, that it's important to be there. Listening to his story, I recalled Woody Allen's line: "Half of life is just showing up."

We constantly have choices as to whether to reach out or not, whether to rescue or drop ourselves and each other off the ledge. When we're out on a ledge, we feel exposed, and sometimes paralyzed. Sometimes it can feel better just to drop off the ledge, to let ourselves go or let the other person go, let him fall away into the abyss. Then at least we have the relief and satisfaction of putting an end to the fear, the exposure, and the agony of feeling suspended by those we love, even if the ending is bought at great personal cost.

It can be helpful just to be aware of both our wishes for connection and for disconnection. Psychologist Ellen Langer points out that "mindfulness" is an inner quality of awareness that breaks old habits, mindless routines, and stereotyped ways of thinking.[2] Rather than immediately trying to resolve painful tensions about seeking or avoiding connection, it can be a good starting point just to become aware of the splits you feel inside; sometimes solutions will flow out of that awareness.

How to become more "mindful" as a man of our struggles with connection? From what other men have told me, and my own experience, here are some ways that help.

The Eternal Mother: Honoring Our Own Needs for Connection. It's important to remember that you are often struggling with love even when it looks like you're withdrawing. It's precisely when you feel engaged in a battle with someone else, when you are puzzled by tension or boredom, that you may be struggling most with connection.

I have to keep learning *that* lesson over and over, most recently with my wife. It was during that time when I moved into my own office at work, freed from my office mate, soon after that rejuvenating lunch with my friend Steve.

I had finally gotten through my anxiety about moving to and furnishing my own office, and at last I was on my own. No office mates to mess up an office with their ideas about furnishings, but also no one there to provide support and camaraderie, either. One evening soon after the move, Julie and I are sitting down at dinner when she asks: "Where's that pillow that was on our chair over there?"

Feeling like a little boy who's just been caught by the teacher, I reply, almost mumbling: "It's at my office."

"What is it doing there?" she replies, irritated.

I get huffy: "Well, I wanted it for an office chair, for my patients to sit in."

I can tell her sense of order and organization is frazzled, and sheepishly I realize things have been disappearing from our house. Julie helpfully enumerates them:

"So. Now you've got our lamp from the living room, and the pillows from the den."

Uh-oh. The pillows from the den. They were among *her* favorites too.

"Why don't you go out and buy another pair for your office?"

She implies I'm lazy or stingy, that I didn't want to go to the trouble or expense to get new ones, so I grabbed those.

With a shock I realize the pillows were made for me by my mother, and the lamp was one that has always reminded me of Julie.

But I can't say *Because the pillows are my mother's, because they feel warmer, because they remind me of you, the light of the lamp.* I feel too much like a little boy wanting mother's warmth still.

So I sulk, and get angry, and counterattack.

"So big deal. We hardly use them. Why don't you just let me take care of this move, without butting in."

Now we're on the verge of a fight, and a cynical part of me recalls what a man said when I asked him not just what it was like to be a father, but how things were in the marriage:

"It's better to be busy with the kids than to have time alone with your wife."

Julie tries to get back in touch: "Why are you so angry at me when I'm just asking about the house furniture?" Her tone implies reconciliation.

Part of me will have none of it. *You just don't understand the psychology of sulking,* I muse. *When you're feeling vulnerable, get angry or sulk.* I don't know how to get out of this awful place, so I say that to her:

"First of all, I feel on the spot. Do you really want to know about the lamp and the pillows?"

She looks at me, then responds directly: "Yes, yes, I do."

"I'm not sure of this, but I think it's my way of feeling safe in the office, and warm. The pillows are my mother's, and the lamp is yours and it helps me get through a hard time.

"I know it doesn't make a lot of sense, I know I'm only moving one floor, but moving to my own office and leaving that shared one brings up all kinds of issues about being able to make it on my own.

Having the lamp and the pillows reminds me of you, my mother, my family—things I love and that give me courage.

"It's the kind of courage I had as a kid—the courage of the four-year-old, the seven-year-old taking on the world, able to go back to mother and father when he needs refueling but then going back out there. It's a courage I lost many years ago, when I got to my teens. . . . That's what the pillows and lamp are all about."

Suddenly I feel like a little boy, ashamed of what I've revealed.

"This feels embarrassing," I say.

"No, it's sweet—touching."

Often if we can explain ourselves, we defuse potential battles. We are so worried about proving our independence and autonomy from women that we don't know how to ask for help in ways that they can hear. There's a medical syndrome named Alexythemia, which refers to the loss of the ability to give voice to feelings, and sometimes it seems that's what men suffer from.[3] Yet we *can* reclaim this ability. A good starting point can be to try to remember that when you're in a fight with someone you love, it's usually about feeling safe, loved, affirmed. Sometimes, then, we can avoid the preliminaries (the fight) and get to the bottom line: *I'm hurt by you, or need you, or am afraid of you, or feel cornered by you, right now, and don't know how to talk about that.*

It can be hard to explain yourself, though, if you feel too much on the spot.

Recognize the Role of Shame. Feeling "on the spot" or in danger is related to feeling humiliated. Shame can be healed by making it public with those one trusts, in a marriage, in a group, to friends. The worst part of shame is not being able to talk about it, the secret of it. Finding the words to say it to others in a place that feels safe can be very liberating.

Remember That It Is All Right to Need Support as a Man. Often we don't know how to ask directly for the comfort and support we need, then we feel resentful and can't give them to others who want the same from us.

Al is a forty-five-year-old executive who told me about a moment when he felt most "human."

"I was in the hospital after a car accident, with an eye injury. Scary, and I was alone. My family had gone home for the night."

The next morning was to be an examination and Al was in pain. It was early in the morning, the time Napoleon referred to when he said we all need "two A.M. courage, the hardest to find."

"The nurse came in to check on me," Al continued. "She asked if there was anything I wanted. First I thought of drugs, doctors, but that wasn't it. I said: 'Would you hold my hand?'

"I didn't need physical help; doctors or medication wouldn't help. I said to her, 'This isn't a sexual overture,' which was funny since there I was all wrapped up in bed.

"It felt scary to ask for help from a woman other than my wife."
The nurse replied: "Of course I will."

Many men struggle with appropriateness: Is it okay to ask for what I need or to give it? It usually is. The need is not the issue—we all have human needs for connection, reassurance, support—but how you ask for or give it is the issue. Many of us are locked into childlike ways of asking for and giving help: demanding it without asking or insisting others take it without wanting. So that our attempts backfire and we feel more shame.

Men as Allies: Prisoners, Guards, and Liberators. Men are constantly looking for affirmation and reassurance from others that their tender, humane sides are okay. When Andrew was telling his tale of the riverside, he was also asking me an implicit question: *Are my feelings appropriate? Are they okay? Is this manly?* My response to him matters: By listening and laughing and affirming his joy and pride, I can enliven these feelings; by remaining indifferent or withholding a response, I can deaden them.

We lament the absence of male friendship, and men will talk about the way other men "don't understand." There is truth to this: Men put down signs of weakness or neediness from other men. And it can be painful to reveal sore spots and uncertainties only to have another man respond: "Yeah, well, what about those Red Sox!"

However, often there is more available from men than we think. Perhaps the research about the absence of male friendship misses the point. Male friendship may be more hit-or-miss, sporadic, less regular than the contact women have, and it may be less verbal. Men may "check in" with each other from time to time, or carry around treasured moments of real contact that provide essential support they need.

Mike is a divorced father who sees his two daughters on weekends, and he delights in the time he spends with them. Yet the pain of his divorce continues to haunt him, and he carries around the unspoken fear that he is not really a good-enough father. One day he takes his daughters fishing with his friend Bob, who is married, and Bob's two children. The two men talk about part-time work in the front of the boat while the kids fish over the side. The conversation then turns to the work of fathering. Mike jokes:

"I'm just a part-time father, not a real one."

The humor hides a serious question: *Compared to you, can I take myself seriously as a father?*

Bob responds simply and affirmatively: "You sure seem like a real dad to me." Mike reports later that he felt "liberated" by Bob's response. "I rarely feel really like a father, like that part of me is validated by other men, particularly since my kids are not around much during the weekdays. Bob's words got me off the hook of feeling so bad about myself."

Bob becomes a liberator, but he might just as easily have become a guard by putting down Mike or failing to respond to him. As men we constantly have choices about what parts of each other we enliven and respond to. Do we help to free each other or do we act as fellow prisoners and guards to each other? For example, with a friend at work who is also a father, a husband, and a son, we have the choice of finding a way to make room for those private parts of his life or just ignoring them by participating in the pervasive social amnesia about men's involvement in relationships. Do we limit our conversations with male co-workers, acquaintances, and friends to work, sports, and world events, or do we talk about our kids and families in a way that acknowledges those other parts of ourselves? The choice is up to us, and we exercise the choice in our moment-to-moment interactions with those around us.

Find Ways to Talk About Love. Even when they are not fathers, men have opportunities for redemption and greater freedom.

Marvin is a sixty-year-old consultant to a family-owned manufacturing firm. One day he watches while the father who started the business and his forty-year-old son, the vice president, fight. The fight is a typical father-son battle about autonomy and adequacy, expressing both men's wishes to be their own man and still be beloved by the other. "They're men—they have to parade around like two bull elephants trumpeting and bellowing, to establish how big and strong they are," Marvin recognizes.

He knows this, at age sixty, because he recognizes in them his own pain over the death of his father years earlier. Marvin knows from his own experience that sons get locked into angry struggles with fathers because they feel tangled in bonds of love: They can't leave and they can't stay close to the father they feel tied to. Without realizing it, Marvin becomes a more liberating "father" for the owner's son, with whom he has a friendly relationship. Marvin talks to the son, later in the day, alone in his office, and manages to communicate an important message in a nonchallenging manner.

"What," he asks the man simply and directly, "are you going to do about your anger?"

The son replies, "I've never been able to talk about the anger I feel at my father with an older man." Marvin and the son do not have a long talk, but the son acknowledges his anger as something he must take seriously: He feels heard by Marvin and this helps him separate from his father.

Another example. At a venture capital enterprise that has finally become profitable after years of effort by the founders, the executives are arguing about hiring. Several of the younger, newer executives want to hire a rising "star" who has developed some flashy techniques of statistical analysis of companies. The older, senior staff have become resistant, and the decision keeps being put off; résumés get lost, meetings are postponed until everyone feels frustrated and impatient with each other.

It's apparent that the tension is between the old-guard, senior staff and younger, junior staff. A common tension point in an organization—the old angry at the young for getting too "uppity" and not respectful of the past, while the young feel that the senior staff just want to cling to power. These generational struggles are not only about power but also about love and respect.

The older staff in this instance are resisting the hiring because they feel "this new guy doesn't share our values," and they complain that he's not "intuitive," doesn't go after companies with real value, "besides what the numbers just tell us." At a climactic meeting to resolve the hiring impasse, one of the most senior members tries to remind the group about "the basic values of this company, and why we started it."

The younger men and women get more and more restive, wondering why "the old folks" are going into this "story about the past," as one man said to me later.

It looks as if war is going to break out in the boardroom again.

Finally a young man has the courage to speak of love, not only war. "I don't know how to say thank-you for making this firm a success, and also to ask you to give me some power too."

The tension seems melted by this comment. One of the angrier of the "dinosaurs" among the senior staff replies, "What I most wanted was to be acknowledged. I don't mind if you younger folk want to do things differently—but I do need to know that you respect and affirm what we did in starting this place."

The staff in this firm were caught in an oedipal struggle: the old and young not wanting to give way before each other. Yet if you only attend to each generation's wish to defeat and vanquish the other, then you miss the fact that both generations also wanted to feel affirmed and "beloved" by the other.

The men in the firm were split by their inability to talk of the love, obligation, and competitiveness between them. What melted the ice was when one of them took the risk of doing something "inappropriate": expressing the impasse they had reached in which the younger generation's loving feelings toward their "fathers" were given no place.

The firm wound up hiring the new guy, but most important, both older and younger staff took care of the emotional issues that were preventing them from working effectively together.

Consider How You Approach Difficult Relationships: To Reconcile or to "Win." People often need to feel affirmed, not wiped out or defeated by you. La Rochefoucald's maxim is true of most people: "Many a man would rather you hear their story than grant their request."

Consider Max's experience with his aging mother. Max tells me about the most difficult part of the past year. "I have no memories of my mother for the first five years of my life. She was there, but I can't remember her. My grandmother dominated everything."

Max has been struggling with his wife, and commitment, and knows some of it has to do with the anger he feels at his mother.

"My mother was a blank. Where was she in my childhood? Living with another man? She gave me up to grandmother? Did I have any value to her?"

Max went to her house for tea one day, to take a risk. Teacups clinked gently as this forty-five-year-old son asked the question he had always been afraid to ask: "Where were you when I was a kid?"

His mother looked at him over her teacup and her voice deepened as she replied: "Finally we can talk!"

Max felt the tension drain out of him as he heard those words, and his next reaction was: *Let's go for broke.*

"You mean you don't hate me?" his mother asked timidly.

"I missed you more than hated you. I want to know what happened."

Max's confidence carried the day.

"When she saw that all I needed was a response she felt more comfortable. I found out about her baggage of low self-esteem and how little she could make her presence felt, and how she allowed her mother to dominate, to the detriment of her marriage."

Max and his mother both needed to be able to talk; what they actually said mattered less. They needed to feel that they mattered enough to each other to be responded to, to have their stories heard.

Often we approach other persons with whom we're having problems (a wife, child, boss, friend, parent) less to *hear* them than to *beat* them: We want them to admit they were or are "wrong," or to leave them aware of our pain, perhaps to make them feel the hurt we've felt at their hands. Or we want simply to shut them up so we feel less under the gun ourselves. I've heard many people say, when speaking of a relationship in trouble: "I just want him to admit he was wrong," or "I want him to see how much he's hurt me." When we say this, we're still trying to win, which is okay if that's what you want, but it is different from finding some common ground and understanding. Often the other person quickly feels boxed into a corner, in danger, and starts to fight back or withdraw.

It's important to be clear about your goals when trying to heal a wounded relationship: "Do you want to achieve a final victory over the other person, or to listen to and hear the other person, to begin to put your common problems in greater perspective? The latter is truly more difficult than the former, because it involves some restraint, coming down from the moral high ground, suspending judgment, and being willing to go beyond yourself.

Honoring Male Aggression. In today's social climate it's easy to feel shame and guilt about men's aggressive connections, about men's bitterness, and about the harsh milk of masculinity. However, it's important to also give the devil his due and honor the role of aggression in men's lives as an important face-saving device, as a vital way of connecting without shame, and/or a way of mastering grief and vulnerability. Nobody wants to be blindsided by put-downs or intimidation. However, verbal pokes or challenges, as well as confusing or irritating ploys such as changing the subject to sports amid an emotionally wrenching conversation, can also be attempts to make contact or reduce painful tension.

FORGIVEN DEBTS: WOMEN AS GATEKEEPERS TO MEN'S SENSE OF SELF

Women play a very important role in men's ability to connect with themselves and others. Women are often gatekeepers to men's ability to know what they feel.

A wife's words and actions can serve to set up barriers or provide a welcome to the father trying to find a place for himself in the family. She has the power to increase his awkwardness and sense of shame within the family by keeping secret from him what happened during the day or putting him in the authoritarian role so he can't make himself emotionally available to his children. And she has the power to enliven her husband's image for children and enliven his image in his own mind.

Simple comments matter a lot to fathers, as when a wife reminds her husband: "The children really enjoy being with you" or "They ask about you when you're not here."

It's a delicate struggle for women because often their attempts to bring men closer, as husbands and fathers, may end up driving the men further away.

A savvy career woman once said to me, "I don't understand why my husband and sons don't talk more. We went away together in the summer before our firstborn son left for college. I told my husband I wanted him to spend more time with all the children this vacation. So I called ahead and rented a sailboat for the day, drove them to the dock, sent them out, picked them up, even made their lunches, and still they didn't seem to talk much."

"How did you know?" I wondered, struck by how hard she was working to get the men "to talk."

"I asked them when they got back."

This thoughtful woman didn't realize that her presence loomed so intensely over the men in the family that they could hardly talk. Feeling like little boys sent out on an errand by Mom, the men could not talk about what it was like to be a man in this family.

Sometimes instead of always trying to "help" men, women have to learn how to be quiet so the men in their lives can talk.

At a seminar I saw just how difficult it can be for women to get out of men's way, and also the goodwill that can flow from and to men who *are* willing to ask women for the emotional space to sort out their struggles.

There were seven women and two men enrolled in a one-day seminar on "Work–Family Dilemmas of Contemporary Life." Though the women were very curious about what marriage and family life are like for men, they spent most of the morning session talking *for* and about men, reflecting on their husband's, son's, or father's experiences.

One older woman talked about her husband's life-long grief at his father's suicide, and how much that has affected his work decisions ("He tries so hard to never fail") and being a father ("He delights in his children in a way his own father never could"). Another younger woman spoke with great feeling about her husband's struggles to be successful at work and also be available to the family.

They were basically saying great things, and seemed to be *inviting* the men to talk. By telling their stories, it was as if they were asking the two men sitting in the seminar: *Talk about yourselves, tell us what it is like to be a man.* And they were doing this with considerable goodwill.

The men, John and Jonah, sat impassively. They seemed loaded with feelings but it was as if they were holding their feelings in tightly, to avoid falling apart in front of the women.

Jonah was divorced and as the day went on he found himself confronting the emotional reality that his father left him when he was a young boy, also through a divorce. He seemed filled with anger, grief, and loneliness. But he struggled not to become too much a little boy in front of the women. He wanted to impress the women, and there was competition with John, who seemed more "together." Jonah wanted to be a man in front of the women, yet he was also caught up in his wishes that they'd take care of him.

The women asked him questions, trying to get him to open up, then seemed frustrated and stopped asking.

After lunch the tension was high, and the women talked more. The one thing that no one mentioned was that John and Jonah had not once spoken directly to each other. They kept looking at each other, and finally John broke the silence, addressing a question to Jonah:

"How are you doing?"

"Okay," replied Jonah, sounding relieved that the ice was broken. "Part of me is not here, it's out on another planet. I have all these feelings, about my father, my kids. I want to touch the feelings and not get near them—angry at him, wanting him."

"Yes, yes!" exclaimed one woman.

Another woman added: "We need our fathers and they disappoint us."

There was a flurry of activity, as several of the women started talking. Someone else asked a question.

At this point the instructor commented that beyond everything else, "The two men were just now trying to make a connection and many of the women started talking."

Silence.

Jonah then said, "All my life I've used women as a way of getting close. I let them express my feelings, taking care of them. The hardest thing has been to get close to other men."

Many of the women seemed visibly relieved: "A man who can state his needs is such a relief. I've felt such a burden all my life of trying to take care of men when they won't also say what they need and want."

It was also a burden for the women to let go of the mothering role, and let the men find a connection, one that perhaps they didn't control. One insightful woman, a mother of several sons, exclaimed: "It's hard when men are acting like five-year-olds who can't tie their shoelaces, obviously needing help, not to go over and tie their shoelaces for them."

Being a man today can feel like learning how to tie your shoelaces all over again. Not real shoelaces, of course, but the laces that tie and bind us to those we love. To learn all over again how to tie those knots.

John and Jonah talked for a while about being a man, about fathers and fatherhood, marriage and divorce. Again, it's not the *content* that was important, it's not *what* they said to each other, so much as the fact that they were talking. It was the affirmation each felt from the other for being a man with feelings, including the kind of shame, sadness, anger, and hopefulness that doesn't fit the mold. What mattered most was the affirmation they felt.

Does it *really* matter? What difference do a few moments of affirmation from another man make in the life of a man? I am sometimes skeptical, until I receive letters like the one I had from Jonah a year later, saying: "The connection I felt in the seminar led me to go to talk to my father, for the first time in years. Not everything worked out as I hoped, but I could see that his wounds were much worse than mine. I spent a weekend with him and not everything was resolved, but things are much easier between us. And much of the shame I feel is less burdensome."

Finding a Safe Space: Tying Knots All Over Again. Men need a safe place to sort out what they are feeling. Otherwise how do they connect with disavowed feelings?

Many men turn to their wives to "mirror" back what it's appropriate for men to feel. That's okay, but often it puts a burden on the marriage, and perhaps there are limits to what women can affirm for men about manhood, just as women acknowledge that there are limits to the understanding that men can provide them. My wife is undoubtedly my best friend, and I've learned and grown with her in more ways than with anyone else. Yet when we struggled with the miscarriages, or when I try to understand how to embody authority and responsiveness as a father, or when I wonder how much work or money is enough, then I know that I also have to talk with other men. For me, the important struggle is to feel that I can rely on both my male and female friends.

From Anger to Healthy Sadness. Often men become the targets of women's sadness or disappointment. Both sexes need to let down their guards, take each other more at face value, learn to forgive each other. Here's an example of how this can happen. At a staff meeting at a corporation designed to talk about "Being Male and Female in the Workplace," thirty women and three men attended, even though the gender ratio in the company as a whole was much closer to fifty-fifty.

The women started to express their anger at men. "It's the same as it always was, the men are not here, not talking about power and other issues," reflected a woman executive bitterly.

"I started to get uptight and wanted to leave," said one man who was there. "I mean I didn't want to get into male-bashing yet again. I didn't know what to say, but I blurted out, 'Everyone is talking about being angry at men, but aren't you also *disappointed* that more men aren't here? Don't you want men here, not just to reject them, but because you need men?' "

There seemed a collective sigh of relief, and one woman agreed out loud: "Yes, it feels like I know how to make men uptight or drive them away, but not how to draw them closer."

The man went on: "So we talked about how women wanted to feel affirmed and validated by men and how hard that was to talk about—to feel feminine and competent, to feel independent and caring."

The men then talked about how odd it felt to come to this meeting without more men there. They discussed their efforts to be responsive to women's concerns and attentive to their own needs as men when such matters *seemed* to be a low priority for many of the men at the company.

The dialogue moved then from anger and accusation to grief and appropriate sadness at the difficulty of making changes as adults, changes in both families and companies. And the group talked about the pain men and women share when they try to live in tune with the social changes of our time yet continually feel caught up in pressures and images of the past. The meeting ended in a hopeful atmosphere. It was clear that both the men and women profited from the opportunity to express and grieve for the limits of what they can do as people, to recognize their inner struggles to be good-enough men and women, and to grapple with the fact that they live in a time without easy solutions for either gender.

This applies to marriages, too: Many men feel overburdened by their wives and take their criticism to heart because they can't see that women struggle with *their* self-esteem and grief too and that women also have felt shamed and diminished. Remember to honor your wife's struggles to affirm her accomplishments and not to assume that she has it all worked out. Don't make her into the mother of your dreams or nightmares.

Simone Weil once observed of women: "Men owe us what we think they can give us, we must forgive them this debt." Men become larger-than-life fathers and idealized figures for women. Both genders struggle with shame and grief. Both genders feel suspicious of the other when in danger of being humiliated or diminished. And both genders also wish to love and be loved by the other.

In other words: Don't always take a woman's attack or anger as all that she feels; often her hostility conceals a wish to feel loved and reassured and affirmed. Both men and women these days are seeking ways to speak of love, not just war between the genders. Neither gender has all the answers as to how to do this.

Small Victories, No Magic Answers. We're talking about small victories: changes in perspective, seeing things differently. Often we ourselves need to change, not the other person.

We work on our identities and intimacy in fits and starts. We don't reconcile things all at once. Many men attend to these matters for a while, then withdraw to digest and seek relief, then find another moment to work on connection and love.

It's never too late, as I saw from a father and son, one in his forties, the other in his sixties, who came together, in some desperation, to a weekend retreat on "Men and Their Fathers."

HONEST TALK

Chuck is the owner of a bookstore, in his mid-thirties, married with several children. He is a tall, gangly man whose intense look belies a deep friendliness. At age thirty-nine he found himself preoccupied by thoughts of a career change: He was considering becoming a minister.

Chuck intuited there were resonances between his own life and his father's. At age thirty-nine his father had made a career change, leaving law to become a minister. Chuck was twelve at the time, and his father's career move ushered in a period of profound loss for him. "For the next six years I got to see him on the weekends and summertimes as he pursued a theological degree."

Now a father himself, Chuck saw that he was repeating this process of loss and distance with his own children. He works long days managing a bookstore and yet he also feels like there is more he can get from his family. He wonders if there is more in life.

Trying to sort all this out, he wants to talk to his father. "Unless I somehow worked on the gap that had widened between Dad and me, there was a clear danger of repeating it." But how to bridge those years of hostility and regret? "His absence those six years had left the two of us pretty distant emotionally. Sure we could chat about our work, but my mother was the main contact person and the two of us rarely connected without her there."

And Chuck is aware that his father is aging, nearing retirement. There's no longer unlimited time. One holiday when he was out for a walk with his father, Chuck casually asked: "How'd you like to go to a conference on fathers and sons?"

Chuck picked a conference held at a spot that mattered to his father and himself, a religious conference center where the family had gone to summer camp and his father had studied.

"Sure," his father replied, and Chuck signed them both up for the weekend conference on "Fathers and Sons."

Signing up was easier to do than showing up. Months passed and neither man talked of the commitment. Each wondered if the other had forgotten. "With five weeks to go, Dad called to see if I still wanted to go." The minister had several members of the congregation planning weddings on that April weekend, and he proposed to his son changing their plans for the conference and conducting the weddings.

"I was annoyed and insisted we stick to the original commitment," Chuck recalled.

So, on a rainy April Friday afternoon, father and son drove through the spring landscape, hoping for some rebirth in their own relationship. Chuck found the drive "a homecoming for both of us: the first time we had spent an uninterrupted time together in years." Memories of family camps and teen weekends came flooding back: memories that had been blocked in the painful alienation he felt from his father.

In the car they talked about Ed's decision to go into the ministry. Chuck found himself envying his father's sense of direction and unable to talk about the pain he felt during those years. "As I had done so many other times," he recalled later, "I silently chose not to rock the boat, not to get upset and not to mention my own needs."

Chuck wanted to feel valued and worthwhile to his father and *heard* by him, to know that *his* suffering mattered as well. But he still couldn't say this.

At the weekend seminar we made our introductions and then began with a role-playing exercise about fathers and sons letting go in adolescence. There were about forty men there, in addition to Chuck and his father, Ed.

The group divided up into pairs of angry sons confronting their fathers: "I'm glad to be leaving this fucking house," the son yelled at the father, who then must reply in whatever way he could. All around the room men role-played being shocked, angry fathers, and angry, despairing adolescent sons. Chuck and Ed were a *real* father-and-son pair yelling at each other. "The anger spilled out between us," remembered Chuck afterwards. "It all came out."

Many of the "sons" had difficulty with the anger in this exercise: "I could never talk to my own father that way: I'd worry it would kill him," or they feared their father would raise the ante, strike back, perhaps kill *them*, or that he would just turn away and become withdrawn, "like he did when I was a kid, and said exactly those things to my father," as one man reported.

The men who were fathers spoke of their frustration at the sons' accusations: "There was nothing I could say. I didn't know how to get him to talk to me, I felt so helpless and got angry back."

That evening one father, struggling to hold on to his angry son, said in a heartfelt way to him: "Tell me about it." The genuineness of the response caught the angry son by surprise: "He touched me and cut through my anger. I didn't know what to say—and we wound up talking about my anger. We felt closer."

Another role-playing son: "I didn't want to hear him ask me to talk. I didn't want to get close, I wanted to be apart. Like when I was an adolescent: I wanted to get away from my father. Now I want to get close and I don't know how." This role-playing son indicated how grateful he was when his "father" responded that night: "Okay, okay, but I'm here when you need me. Remember the door is open." The son concluded: "That response made me want to cry. I'd like so much to hear that from my real father."

Chuck and his father found themselves reliving the pain between them. "This exercise prompted me to talk about the last time we had a blow-out," recalled Chuck. "I was in the throes of divorcing my first wife and my parents came to dinner, hoping to help us patch things up. My resolve not to go on with the marriage led to raised voices and an angry parting." The son felt judged by his father, guilty and ashamed. Like a lot of men, Chuck carried around the fear of failing in his father's eyes and so he fought and fought to get away from those judgments which left him feeling weak and inadequate.

After the role-playing exercise was over, Chuck and his father stayed up talking well past midnight. They sat on their bunk beds in the conference center dormitory, like two young campers conspiring to elude curfew, talking about the anger and shame that drove them apart.

As Chuck put it, "Now, some seventeen years later, we talked about how we each felt and, in quietly analyzing the reasons for the breakup, I noticed how unemotional I felt now and that I was finally letting go of the shame and guilt I'd carried."

The next day we talked in our group more about the normal difficulties between father and child. Then we divided into pairs and role-played Barry at age five, skinning his knee and being told by his father that he was too old for hugs.

Chuck becomes aware of his wish for his father's support and affirmation, a "hug" from father at a difficult time in his life. After lunch father and son walk alongside a river near the conference site, talking about their lives. Sunny hours pass, but Chuck finds himself in a familiar bind. "Dad talked all the way back about his recent experiences on the committee that dealt with the ordination of homosexuals in the Church. While I was interested to hear this, I was conscious that my own agenda—to deal with some of the feelings raised by the morning's session—was not being addressed."

So as they neared the end of the walk, Chuck asked his father about his childhood. They compared childhood memories—of being a son, of growing up. His father's openness astonished Chuck, who felt "awe at the parallels between generations. Things like the age at which my grandfather, my father, and I had left home, and how alcoholism had affected the second son in at least two generations. My grandfather had been a mechanic and a woodworker, Dad an admitted woodbutcher, and myself a bit of both." Chuck wondered if "some sort of inexorable genetic programming was controlling males in our family."

From their riverside conversation, Chuck learned something even deeper about his father and himself. His father talked openly and honestly about the impact on his family of his decision to enter the ministry at age thirty-nine. The father was harder on himself than the son was: "Whereas I had been ready to forgive him," Chuck said, "he was still working on the regrets he had, looking back at those absentee years." With chagrin Chuck concluded: "Again, I had to give him credit for wanting to face more negative feelings than I was prepared for." As with the anger role-playing, his father was willing to talk about the anger, while Chuck drew back.

That afternoon Chuck and Ed and the rest of the men worked in clay, first sculpting models of fathers' wounds. The sixty-five-year-old and thirty-nine-year-old sat together like schoolchildren, hard at work on the wet mud, trying to give form to the scars that affected their ability to father. What was their fathers' wound?

Chuck remembered: "Most of us had lumps in our throats as we worked the clay to represent whatever our dad's wound was—for some, the enforced manhood and tragic loss of comrades in the Second World War, for others a job or farm responsibility that left little time for the children."

Chuck found himself sculpting a cross that became a bird, representing the ministry, his dad's calling, and also a cross to bear. The cross they had all borne and that had come between father and son. The image also was hopeful: The bird was taking flight from obligations—"a freedom I hoped he would enjoy in retirement." If his father could enjoy his life, perhaps the son could too: if the father is freed, perhaps the son can be.

"I found myself filling up with tears and talked about the 'bogeyman' of fear of contact that used to keep me from contact with Dad. How many times had I chosen not to take a risk, played it safe, but cheated myself too?" Chuck stood up to give his father a hug, and his father responded—father and son embracing across the muddy table.

Each man modeled a gift in clay to give his dad. Chuck modeled a sunset to represent freer times as he retired. Ed modeled a pair of lungs to replace those clogged by the bronchitis that had killed his father. Both Ed and Chuck had known a childhood in which a father's absence came too soon.

As Chuck said later, "The simple truth that was gradually becoming apparent to all of us is that fathers are also sons. As we struggled to define the conflicts with our fathers, we began to realize that they, too, had struggled with their dads. For me, this was a powerful door-opener. I asked Dad how it had been to be Clare's son, and this became a bridge to exploring each other's lives."

Chuck began to understand his need to hear his father say he

loved him. "Every son hungers to hear the words: 'This is my beloved son, in whom I am well pleased.' " And as the current generation of sons become fathers, we are reminded to let our sons know
what we've been through with our dads.

"Just as it's difficult for dads to give up their heroic role as their
kids grow older and less gullible, it's difficult to realize that sons go
through a period of hating their fathers while they sort out their
sense of separate identity.

"And there is no made-in-heaven reunion guaranteed for those
sons who try to reconnect with their dads."

In fact, the reunion between father and son had a tinge of disappointment for Chuck, as he realized that his father would never
become the ideal figure of his dreams. Chuck recalled that at the
end of the weekend, "when I'd given Dad a hug that afternoon, he'd
quickly made a joke about my height."

Chuck ended with a word of advice: "Contact isn't limited to a
solitary incident. It involves a commitment to a continuing process
that includes forgiving myself even if Dad's not there or not able to
forgive me."

Not all fathers and sons need to have a direct, weekend-long
encounter to begin a process of reconciliation. In his autobiography,
Tom Watson, son of the founder of IBM, described a volatile and
difficult father-son relationship in which both of them tried to balance their deep love and involvement with each other. Letter writing provided an avenue for contact. After tremendous business
arguments, laced with personal tensions, father and son were not
ashamed to write letters and notes that expressed their love for each
other. One instance is particularly instructive. Soon after succeeding
his father as president of IBM, Watson found himself locked in a
major, public, verbal fight with his father at La Guardia Airport.
Tom soon after wrote to his father: "I began to think of our thirty-
eight years together. My main theme seemed to be to realize again
and again how very wonderful, fair, and understanding you have
always been to me. . . . What I'm trying to say is that I love and
respect you deeply and want to have a chance to try again to show
you."

Letter writing and sporadic contacts allowed these busy men to
work out a process of reconciliation and understanding. Peter Davis
points out: "Other fathers and sons can learn much from the tremendous recuperative powers in the Watsons' relationship."[4] In fact,
we all can learn from models of risky and creative openness that help

us span the chasms of anger, pride, and hopelessness that separate us from others.

BEING OF USE AS A MAN

What's important is to locate the part of the self that wants to experiment, to give to ourselves or others what we didn't get enough of as children. Often our hearts are very adequate guides.

As a man you feel every day a tension between how much to speak of love and how much to keep hidden.

In New Hampshire one day recently, I was sitting on the front lawn of a friend's sheep farm while my seven-year-old son, Toby, rode his bike in lazy circles near us. We were happy to be there, having just moved up for the summer. Toby had found a hill and was enjoying roaring down it on his bike.

We sat in the sunlit afternoon, crickets chirping, talking about sheep shearing, wool prices, and our dreams for the warm July–August days ahead. Toby zoomed downhill toward us, in his own dream, but as he made a turn, he skidded on a sandy part of the dirt road and totaled himself. A complete wipeout. Worse, as his bike went over, his handlebars swung up and the end of one bar caught him in the stomach as he fell. Down he went like a boxer who's taken a powerhouse right to the solar plexus.

My friends pass the sandwiches back and forth, and I hear a lament about the price of wool, and a new sheepdog they've gotten. We all see Toby's wipeout, but I *really* see it. The conversation about the price of wool hardly falters.

Our friend Karlene glances at my son, who is standing up bent over. She says, reassuringly, "Sometimes they get the wind knocked out of them."

Her tone tells me to relax and enjoy the adults' conversation, and I appreciate her well-meaning words. Toby's fall had left me gasping for breath.

But I realize there's a deeper ethic at play on the farmhouse lawn: *Let the kids tough it out, reward and praise their conquests, they'll master their pain.*

Is this their ethic or mine? It's an ethic I partly believe and respect. My friends have raised wonderful children. But a part of me rebels: My son is struggling by the bike, and all that's happened is that the wind is knocked out of him, but I can't let him alone.

Then there's the question of whether *I* should tough this out: I don't want to have to let my son struggle with this alone. Do I go help or not? I don't want to be overprotective, but I feel I should be there. Perhaps for me as much as for him. It feels strange to get up and walk away from my friends, but I do it. *Will they see me as a wimp? Toby as a wimp? Look down on us both?*

My son is bent over his bike, holding his stomach, tears in his eyes. He sees me and his stoic demeanor breaks down: He starts to cry. "Dad, I want to go home."

He means *home*—to the city. All the difficulties of the summer move flood out: missing his friends, his bedroom, his toys.

Enough's enough. I pick him up in my arms and carry him down the road, back to our cabin. Mom gives him an encouraging pat as we walk in the door. I go to put him down and he grips me harder.

Grabbing some familiar books, I head for his favorite morning relaxation spot: our bed overlooking the lake. Wordlessly, we climb in together and, cuddling close, we read about Aslan the brave lion who teaches courage. We laugh together. My arm is around Toby and we touch as I read. He has some warm milk with honey in it.

How much regression should I allow here? I shut off my doctor's voice.

We read for about half an hour. Then he seems less interested. He gives me a hug and sits up.

"What should we do now?" he asks with his boyish energy.

I'm still contemplating the return of his optimism and spirit, when he answers his own question:

"Where's my bike? I want to ride some more."

He jumps out of the bed, shows his mother where the handlebar poked him, and heads out the door for the road and farmhouse.

"You come too," he yells back to me, running down the sunny dirt road.

Julie winks at me from the porch.

The warm summer breeze tousles my hair as I walk down toward the farmhouse and my friends, while my son finds his bike.

NOTES

INTRODUCTION: TALKING TO MEN ABOUT LOVE

1. S. Osherson, *Finding Our Fathers: How a Man's Life Is Shaped by the Relationship with His Father* (New York: Fawcett, 1987); S. Osherson and D. Dill, "Varying Work and Family Choices: Their Impact on Men's Work Satisfaction," *J. Marriage and the Family*, May 1983, 339–46.

2. E. Erikson, *Childhood and Society* (New York: Norton, 1963); G. Vaillant, *Adaptation to Life* (New York: Little-Brown, 1977); D. McAdams, *Intimacy: The Need to Be Close* (New York: Doubleday, 1989).

3. N. Chodorow, *The Reproduction of Mothering* (Berkeley: University of California Press, 1978); C. Gilligan, *In a Different Voice: Psychological Theory and Women's Development* (Cambridge, Mass.: Harvard University Press, 1982); L. Rubin, *Erotic Wars: What Happened to the Sexual Revolution?* (New York: Farrar, Strauss and Giroux, 1990); L. Rubin, *Intimate Strangers: Men and Women Together* (New York: Harper and Row, 1983).

4. F. Wright, "Men, Shame, and Antisocial Behavior: A Psychodynamic Perspective," *Group* 11(4), Winter 1987, 242.

5. N. Chodorow, op. cit., p. 169.

6. These ages are similar to other surveys of men in men's groups. Barrie Peterson from Rockland Community College in Westchester, New York, completed a listing of men's groups in the metropolitan New York area, specifically focusing on personal growth and emotional support. He *did not* include in his listing those groups stressing advocacy, service, or sports, or those that are "in house" such as "the dozens of men's groups in Alcoholics and Narcotics Anonymous, the Father's Rights advocacy movement, the Roman Catholic priests' support system, or the hundreds of fraternal and service groups in community or religious settings."

Peterson identified eighty-six groups focusing on informal support and growth, as well as twenty-three sponsors of men's retreats and workshops.

Forty-five of those groups responded to a survey he distributed, which indicated that the average age of a group is 5.6 years; one of the groups had been meeting regularly for 18 years! The average age of the participants was forty-four, with the youngest participant seventeen and the oldest eighty-two. Most groups meet in homes weeknights weekly for two to three hours. Priorities are: emotional support, male bonding, social/recreation, and education. Topics most discussed are: personal problems, relations with women, sharing life events, career choices, emotional growth, family relations, sex, competition, and stress. See Peterson, B. "Resources for Men

Northeast: A Directory of 148 Men's Groups," available from New Views Educational Services, Inc., P.O. Box 137, Little Ferry, N.J. 07643.

7. In terms of different parts of themselves, this is a group well satisfied with their lives. Seventy percent report themselves successful at work, and close to that number feel their work allows them to express their special abilities and talents. Sixty percent of the parents report themselves as satisfied with their abilities as parents. In terms of marriage, about half rate themselves "highly satisfied," with the drop largely accounted for by the men in their forties struggling through the difficult marriage-family years of mid-life, when marital satisfaction usually drops temporarily, rebounding only after the kids leave.

Yet "satisfaction" scores don't seem particularly helpful here. The key point is that many of the workshop participants have accomplished the traditional markers of adult success as men, feel satisfied with those choices, yet they still experience a nagging sense of something not really being right, and of wanting to understand themselves better. In a sense they are struggling with what Erik Erikson referred to as the mid-life task of "generativity versus stagnation," trying to come to terms with the life-giving and generative parts of themselves. And they are struggling with the "holes" in otherwise satisfying lives—"holes" that open because of unresolved problems in relationships with children, parents, wives, and others.

8. S. Osherson, *Holding On or Letting Go: Men and Career Change at Midlife* (New York: Free Press, 1980).

9. G. Emerson, *Some American Men* (New York: Simon and Schuster, 1985).

1: SHAME IN MEN'S LIVES

1. Shame is a complex phenomenon, enjoying something of a renaissance among researchers and clinicians. For an overview of shame, see A. Morrison, *Shame: The Underside of Narcissism* (Hillsdale, N.J.: Analytic Press, 1989); D. L. Nathanson, ed., *The Many Faces of Shame* (New York: Guyilford, 1987); G. Kaufman, *Shame: The Power of Caring* (Rochester, Vt.: Schenkman, 1985); H. B. Lewis, *Shame and Guilt in Neurosis* (New York: International Universities Press, 1971); L. Wormser, *The Mask of Shame* (Baltimore, Md.: Johns Hopkins University Press, 1981).

For discussions of male shame, see F. Wright, op. cit., and S. Osherson and S. Krugman, "Men, Shame, and Psychotherapy," *Psychotherapy*, 27(3), Fall 1990, 327–39.

2. The importance of *size* stands out in two of the four components of traditional masculinity: "the big wheel," meaning that men should be respected for successful achievement, and "the sturdy oak," meaning men should never show weakness, as identified by Bob Brannon. See B. Brannon, "The Male Sex Role: Our Culture's Blueprint of Manhood, and What

It's Done for Us Lately," in D. David and R. Branon, eds. *The Forty-nine Percent Majority: The Male Sex Role* (Reading, Mass.: Addison-Wesley, 1976). See also E. H. Thompson, Jr., and J. H. Pleck, "The Structure of Male Role Norms," *American Behavioral Scientist*, 29(5), May/June 1986, 531–43.

Many of us who don't feel like "traditional" males nonetheless partly identify with these images and values.

3. S. Hoffenstein, "Proem," in *Pencil in the Air* (New York: Doubleday, 1947).

4. R. Weiss, *Staying the Course: The Emotional and Social Lives of Men Who Do Well at Work* (New York: Free Press, 1990), p. xii.

5. R. May, "Concerning a Psychoanalytic View of Maleness," in R. Friedman and L. Lerner, eds. *Toward a Psychology of Men* (New York: Guildford, 1986), p. 193.

6. R. Bly, "The Night We Missed the Wedding," in R. Bly, *The Power of Shame*, audiotape available from New Dimensions Foundation, P.O. Box 410510, San Francisco, Calif. 94141-0510.

2: DIVIDED LOYALTIES:
MEN'S LONELINESS AND THE MYSTERY OF OUR
PARENTS

1. H. Kohut, *The Restoration of the Self*, (New York: International Universities Press, 1977); and H. Kohut, *How Does Analysis Cure?* (Chicago: Chicago University Press, 1984).

2. R. Greenson, "Disidentifying from Mother," *International Journal of Psychoanalysis* 49: 370–74, 1966.

3. T. Bullfinch, *Mythology of Greece and Rome* (New York: Penguin, 1979), pp. 187–88.

4. J. Herzog, "Pre-oedipal Oedipus: The Father-Child Dialogue," in G. Pollack and J. M. Ross, *The Oedipus Papers* (New York: International Universities Press, 1989), pp. 475–93; J. Herzog, "Fathers, Sons and Fathering Daughters," in J. Kall, E. Galenson, and R. Tyson, eds., *Frontiers of Infant Psychiatry 2*, 1984, 335–43; M. W. Yogman, "Observations of Father-Infant Relationship," in S. H. Cath, et al., *Father and Child: Developmental-Clinical Perspectives*, (Boston: Little-Brown, 1982), pp. 101–122; M. Lamb, ed., *The Father's Role: Applied Perspectives* (New York: Wiley, 1986); J. D. G. Goldman and R. J. Goldman, "Children's Perceptions of Parents and Their Roles: Cross-National Study in Australia, England, North America, and Sweden," *Sex Roles*, vol. 9, 791–812.

5. H. F. Searles, *The Nonhuman Environment in Normal Development and Schizophrenia* (New York: International Universities Press, 1960); Collected Essays on Schizophrenia* (New York: International Universities Press, 1966).

6. Genesis 22:8, New Jewish Publication Society translation.

7. I. Gad, "Hephaestus: Model of New Age Masculinity," *Quadrant*, Fall 1986, 191(2): 27–48.

8. S. Gerhogoren, "Graham," and C. Wright, "Firstborn," in J. Perlman, ed., *Brother Songs*, (Minneapolis: Holy Cow! Press, 1979).

9. F. Small, "Father Song," *No Limit*, Rounder Records, 1985.

10. A. H. Malcolm, "Titanic Survivor Joins a Lost Father," *The New York Times*, 16 April 1982, p. A14.

11. S. Schama, *Citizens: A Chronicle of the French Revolution* (New York: Knopf, 1989).

3: ANGER AND OTHER ATTEMPTS TO CONNECT

1. In any group, be it a work group at the office or a holiday meal at home, there is a struggle for all members between connection and distance. You want to be a part of the group and feel like a treasured member but you also want to keep your distance and not lose your individual identity. Men and women struggle with this tension, but it may be that the genders express the tension differently. Women in many groups will start connecting by becoming verbal and linking up different members, searching for common causes and experiences. Often in groups, especially family gatherings, men start drifting to the periphery, looking as if they are disconnected, but they're actually trying to find a way to get into the group without feeling overwhelmed and shamed.

Often men get labeled the saboteurs of groups because their ways of connecting are not understood or validated.

For more on how men manage themselves and others in groups, see T. MacNab, "What Do Men Want? Male Rituals of Initiation in Group Psychotherapy," *International Journal of Group Psychotherapy* 40(2), 1990, 139–54, and S. Krugman and S. Osherson, "Men in Groups," in A. Alonso and H. Swiller, eds., *Group Therapy and Clinical Practice* (Washington, D.C.: American Psychiatric Press, in press).

2. T. Clancy, *Red Storm Rising* (New York: Berkeley, 1986), p. 500.

3. G. Rochlin, *Man's Aggression* (Boston: Gambit, 1973), p. 254.

4. A. Freud, *The Ego and the Mechanisms of Defense* (New York: International Universities Press, 1948), p. 254.

5. S. Heaney, "A Kite for Michael and Christopher," in *Station Island* (New York: Farrar, Strauss and Giroux, 1985).

6. C. Gilligan, *In a Different Voice*, op. cit.

7. S. Osherson and S. Krugman, "Men, Shame and Psychotherapy," *Psychotherapy* 27(3), Fall 1990, 327–39.

8. D. Tannen, *You Just Don't Understand: Men and Women in Conversation* (New York: Morrow, 1990).

9. N. Mailer, *A Fire on the Moon* (New York: Little-Brown, 1970).

10. R. Jeffers, "Return," in R. Hass, ed., *Rock and Hawk: A Selection of Short Poems by Robinson Jeffers* (New York: Random House, 1987).

4: HEROISM AND FAILURE:
RELATIONSHIP PRESSURE POINTS IN MEN'S LIVES

1. Quoted in J. Allen, *Picking On Men: The First Honest Collection of Quotations About Men* (New York: Fawcett, 1985).

2. B. S. Dohrenwend, L. Krassnoff, A. R. Askenasy, and B. P. Dohrenwend, "Exemplification of a Method for Scaling Life Events: The PERI Life Events Scale," *Journal of Health and Social Behavior*, 1978, 19, 205–209.

3. D. Levinson, *The Seasons of a Man's Life*, (New York: Knopf, 1978), p. 100. See also H. Levinson, *Executive: The Guide to Responsive Management* (Cambridge, Mass.: Harvard University Press, 1981).

4. D. Levinson, op. cit.

5. The positive impact of fatherhood on the emotional and social development of the father is becoming well documented. For example, Snarey, Pleck, and Maier studied a group of fathers longitudinally, from their young adulthood to mid-life years. They found that fathers' ability to enter more actively into fathering was very much related to their resolution of the mid-life task of "generativity versus stagnation." The more involved young adult fathers were with their children's social and emotional development, the more giving and caring the men were by mid-life.

The importance of fathers for children also stood out. Snarey and Pleck also found that fathers' family participation improved their children's lives as young adults, producing more confident, skillful boys and mature, autonomous girls.

Interestingly, Snarey and Pleck found that fatherhood did not seem to harm the men's work lives; in the long run, involved fathers were as successful in their careers as uninvolved ones. See J. Snarey and J. Pleck, "Father Participation in Child-Rearing: Consequences for Father's Midlife Outcomes," paper presented at the annual meeting of the American Psychological Association, Atlanta, Ga., August 1988.

6. "Letters of the late Archibald MacLeish," *Harvard Magazine*, January–February 1983, 85(3): 48A–48H.

7. See S. Cath, A. Gurwitt, and J. Munder Ross, eds., *Father and Child: Developmental and Clinical Perspectives* (Boston: Little-Brown, 1982); S. Cath, A. Gurwitt, and L. Gunsberg, Jr., eds., *Fathers in Their Families* (Hillsdale, N.J.: Analytic Press, 1989); R. Levant and J. Kelly, *Between Father and Child* (New York: Viking/Penguin, 1991).

8. Remarks at Parenting Conference, Wheelock College, Spring

1985. See also P. Tsongas, *Heading Home* (New York: Random House, 1985).

9. Tom Watson, son of the founder of IBM, provides numerous examples in his autobiography of moments when explosions between father and grown son were the only way the two could communicate caring. See T. Watson, Jr., with P. Petre, *Father, Son, and Company: My Life at IBM and Beyond* (New York: Bantam, 1990). See also Peter Davis's thoughtful review of this book in *Family Business*, September 1990.

10. G. Goethals, "Male Object Loss: A Special Case of Bereavement, Anxiety and Fear," *Psychotherapy* 22(1), Spring 1985, 119–27.

11. B. Pauly, "Heart/Song for Christopher Raymond," in *Brother Songs: A Male Anthology of Poetry* (Minneapolis: Holy Cow! Press, 1979).

12. The way we cope with infertility problems may be related to our social and emotional development. In one longitudinal study of how men coped over a period of four decades with infertility in their marriages, the investigators found that different "infertility coping strategies" predicted men's adaptation at mid-life. For example, men who used what they call "self-centered substitutes" (e.g., becoming preoccupied with themselves) or "nonhuman substitutes" (e.g., treating a car as if it were their "baby") for the lost child tended to have poorer life outcomes than men who substituted parentinglike activities with the children of others. See J. Snarey, et al., "The Role of Parenting in Men's Psychosocial Development: A Longitudinal Study of Early Adulthood Infertility and Midlife Generativity," *Developmental Psychology*, 1987, 23(4): 593–603.

13. C. Collodi, *The Adventures of Pinocchio.* (New York: Knopf, 1988), pp. 133–34.

14. B. McKibben, "Lynch Quiets Pressure Cooker," *The Boston Globe*, 29 March 1990, p. 20.

15. S. Heaney, *Selected Poems, 1960–1987* (New York: Farrar, Strauss and Giroux, 1990), p. 8.

16. J. Kessel, *Good News from Outer Space* (New York: Tor Books, 1989).

5: CONNECTING WITH WOMEN: MOTHERS, WIVES, BOSSES, AND FRIENDS

1. T. Wolff, *This Boy's Life* (New York: Harper & Row, 1989), p. 40.

2. M. R. Elman and L. A. Gilbert, "Coping Strategies for Role Conflict in Married Professional Women with Children," *Family Relations* 33, 317–27; C. F. Epstein, "Multiple Demands and Multiple Roles: The Conditions of Successful Management," in F. J. Crosby, ed., *Spouse, Parent, Worker: On Gender and Multiple Roles* (New Haven: Yale University Press, 1987);

J. D. Gray, "The Married Professional Woman: An Examination of Her Role Conflicts and Coping Strategies," *Psychology of Women Quarterly* 7(3): 235–43.

For a review and extension of this research, see also Joyce K. George, *Career Woman, Wife, and Mother: Factors Influencing Role Satisfaction*, doctoral dissertation, The Fielding Institute, Santa Barbara, Calif.: 1990.

3. B. Brazelton and L. Cramer, *The Earliest Relationship: Parents, Infants, and the Drama of Early Attachment* (New York: Addison-Wesley, 1990); L. Kaplan, *Oneness and Separateness: From Infant to Individual* (New York: Simon and Schuster, 1978).

4. L. Tessman, "Fathers and Daughters: Early Tones, Later Echoes," in S. Cath, A. Gurwitt, and L. Gunsberg, *Fathers and Their Families*.

5. D. Tennis, "The Loss of the Father God: Why Women Rage and Grieve," *Christianity and Crisis* 41(10) June 1981, p. 166.

6. C. Oles, "The Interpretation of Baseball," *Poetry*, June 1988, vol. CLII(3): 133.

7. M. Gordon, "David," in U. Owen, ed., *Fathers: Reflections by Daughters* (New York: Pantheon, 1983), p. 106.

8. C. Bird, *The Two-Paycheck Marriage: How Women at Work Are Changing Life in America* (New York: Rawson, Wade, 1979); L. Gilbert, *Men in Dual-Career Families: Current Realities and Future Prospects* (Hillsdale, N.J.: Eribaum Associates, 1985); C. A. Wendt, *A Study of Marital Satisfaction for Managerial Women in Dual-Career Marriages*, unpublished doctoral dissertation, The Fielding Institute, Santa Barbara, Calif.: 1983; R. Rapoport and R. N. Rapoport, *Dual-Career Families* (Baltimore: Penguin, 1971).

I am indebted to Debbie Delafield and Joyce George, both at the time graduate students at the Fielding Institute, for extending my understanding of spouse support, empathy, and marital understanding.

9. M. H. Davis, "Measuring Individual Differences in Empathy: Evidence for a Multidimensional Approach," *Journal of Personal and Social Psychology* 44, 1983, 113–26; G. A Gladstein, "Empathy and Counseling Outcome: An Empirical and Conceptual Review," *The Counseling Psychologist* 6(4), 1977, 70–78; P. Mussen and N. Eisenberg-Berg, *Roots of Caring, Sharing, and Helping: The Development of Prosocial Behavior in Children* (San Francisco: Freeman, 1977).

10. D. Levinson, *The Seasons of a Man's Life* (New York: Knopf, 1978), p. 98. Oddly, Levinson has little in his theory to legitimize female mentors. In his theory of male development, he relegates women's place in men's life cycle to his concept of the "special woman" who aids a man in his quest to reach his dream. Women thus become a sort of Dulcinea figure to the male Don Quixote in Levinson's view of the seasons of a man's life.

11. Levinson addresses this when he writes: "Mentoring is best understood as a love relationship." See D. Levinson, *The Seasons of a Man's Life*, p. 99.

6: CONNECTING WITH OUR CHILDREN: FATHERING SONS, FATHERING DAUGHTERS

1. Quoted in J. Allen, *Picking on Men*, op. cit.

2. A. Y. Napier, *The Fragile Bond: In Search of an Equal, Intimate, and Enduring Marriage* (New York: Harper and Row, 1988), p. xvi.

3. B. Bettelheim, *A Good-Enough Parent* (New York: Knopf, 1987).

4. D. Lipman. *Milk from the Bull's Horn: A Live Performance of Traditional Tales Interwoven with Autobiographical Stories*, audiotape, available from P.O. Box 441195, W. Somerville, Mass.

5. Thoreau's complex relationship to his parents and brother, and the struggle around autonomy he experienced, is vividly discussed in R. LeBeaux's book, *Young Man Thoreau* (Amherst, Mass.: University of Massachusetts Press, 1989).

6. Here again is the importance of active *memory* in a man's life. Remembering the lost treasures of our childhood—what we loved and lost or held on to as children—can become guides to what our children need. These memories are often lost because we want to close off the feeling world in an attempt to master our unruly inner life and be real men. As one person said, "Remembering what we loved is not the same as holding on to our childhood like a kid."

7. M. D. Bauer, *On My Honor* (New York: Clarion Books, 1986).

8. Ibid., p. 84.

9. Ibid., pp. 86–87.

10. M. A. Silverman, "The Male Super Ego," in R. M. Friedman and L. Lerner, eds., *Toward a New Psychology of Men: Psychoanalytic and Social Perspectives* (New York: Guilford, 1986).

11. E. Erikson, *Childhood and Society*, op. cit.

12. A. Smith, "Carpenter," in J. Perlman, ed., *Brother Songs: A Male Anthology of Poetry*, Minneapolis: Holy Cow! Press, 1979).

13. R. Bly, *Iron John: A Book About Men*, (Reading, Mass.: Addison Wesley, 1990); K. Thompson, "What Men Really Want: An Interview with Robert Bly," *New Age*, May 1982.

14. J. M. Herzog, "On Father Hunger: The Father's Role in the Modulation of Aggressive Drive and Fantasy," in S. Cath et al., eds., *Father and Child: Developmental and Clinical Perspectives* (Boston: Little-Brown, 1982).

15. C. Z. Malatesta and J. M. Haviland, "Signs, Symbols and Socialization: The Modification of Emotional Expression in Human Development," in M. Lewis and C. Saarni, eds., *The Socialization of Emotion* (New York: Plenum Press, 1985); J. M. Haviland and C. Z. Malatesta, "The Development of Sex Differences in Nonverbal Signals: Fallacies, Facts and Fantasies," in C. Mayo and N. M. Henley, eds., *Gender and Nonverbal Behavior* (New York: Springer-Verlag, 1981).

16. R. Saner, "Passing It On," in J. Perlman, *Brother Songs: A Male Anthology of Poetry* (Minneapolis: Holy Cow! Press, 1979).

17. P. Wright and T. Keple, "Friends and Parents of a Sample of High School Juniors: An Exploratory Study of Relationship Intensity and Interpersonal Rewards," *Journal of Marriage and the Family* 43(3), August 1981, 559–70.

18. I. Turgenev, *Fathers and Sons* (Oxford: Oxford University Press, 1991).

19. Genesis 32:23–33, New Jewish Publication Society translation.

20. A. Cardona-Hines, "Hearing My Son Play," in J. Perlman, op. cit.

21. L. Tessman, op. cit.; C. Rivers, G. Baruch, and R. Barnett, *Beyond Sugar and Spice* (New York: Ballantine, 1981).

7: BETWEEN MEN AND THEIR PARENTS:
HEALING THE NORMAL WOUNDS OF MANHOOD

1. R. Saner, "Passing It On," in J. Perlman, op. cit.

2. T. Wolfe, *Bonfire of the Vanities* (New York: Bantam, 1987), p. 447.

3. T. Wolfe, op. cit., pp. 449–50.

4. R. Rhodes, *A Hole in the World: An American Boyhood* (New York: Simon and Schuster, 1990).

5. C. Klein, *Mothers and Sons* (Boston: Houghton-Mifflin, 1984), p. 7.

6. A. Rich, "August," in *Diving into the Wreck: Poems 1971–1972* (New York: Norton, 1973).

7. E. Ormsby, "My Mother in Old Age," *The New Yorker*, August 28, 1989, p. 32.

8. S. J. Frank, C. B. Avery, and M. S. Laman, "Young Adults' Perceptions of Their Relationships with Their Parents: Individual Differences in Connectedness, Competence, and Emotional Autonomy," *Developmental Psychology*, 1988, 24(5): 729–37; R. C. Barnett and N. L. Marshall, "Adult Son-Parent Relationships and Their Associations with Sons' Psychological Distress," Wellesley College Center for Research, 1990; S. J. Blatt, S. J. Wein, E. Chevron, and D. M. Wuinlan, "Parental Representations and Depression in Normal Young Adults," *Journal of Abnormal Psychology*, 88(4), 1979, 388–97.

9. D. Lessing, "What Good Times We All Had Then," in U. Owen, *Fathers: Reflections by Daughters* (New York: Pantheon, 1983).

8: AT A MEN'S GROUP: WHAT MEN HAVE
TO OFFER EACH OTHER AND HOW THEY BLOCK IT

1. The Movie *Jacknife* offers a fictional example of a similar theme. Robert DeNiro plays Megs and Ed Harris portrays Dave; they are two Viet-

nam vets. Megs, Dave, and a character named Bobby were buddies in Vietnam, until Bobby was killed saving Megs's life. Fifteen years later Dave is haunted by the painful memory of his buddy's death. He works as a solitary trucker and has become an alcoholic, living with his sister, cut off from life. Megs seeks out Dave and helps him grieve for the past and restore his life. A mood of anger and explosive violence pervades the movie, reminding us how much tension surrounds the pent-up energy of men trying to come to terms with sorrow, shame, and anger. In a climactic scene, Dave explodes in frustration at a high school prom chaperoned by his sister, Martha, a high school teacher. He flees in drunken shame, while Megs takes Martha home. Dave returns home apologetically later that night. Martha, enraged and frightened, turns her back on him. The edge of violence lingers on in Dave's scowl, his menace. Megs, however, offers Dave his handkerchief to clean the blood off his face. He is forgiving, soothing: "She can't understand, she wasn't there." He talks about the plans he and Bobby had, "to go to Fenway Park for opening day, no matter what." Dave starts to cry. Megs cleans the blood off Dave's face. The scene ends with the two men hugging, mourning the losses and the shame they've experienced. Dave is joined and contained in his anger and sorrow by Megs, who has also "been there" as a man.

2. T. Landsberg, "The Creation and Nurturing of a Men's Support Group," available from New Views Educational Services, Inc., P.O. Box 137, Little Ferry, NJ 07643, or from Tom Landsberg, 21–6 Andover Circle, Princeton, NJ 08540.

3. H. S. Sullivan, Interpersonal Theory of Psychiatry (New York: Norton, 1953), p. 245.

4. M. Fedullo, "In My Brother's House," in J. Perlman, op. cit.

5. M. Farrell and S. Rosenberg, Men at Midlife (Boston: Auburn House, 1981), p. 195.

6. S. Miller, Men and Friendship (Boston: Houghton-Mifflin, 1983), p. 16.

7. S. Miller, op. cit., p. 30.

8. For a review of how men approach intimacy with other men, see R. A. Lewis, "Emotional Intimacy Among Men," Journal of Social Issues 34(1), 1978, 108–21; and R. Weiss, Staying the Course: The Social and Emotional Lives of Men Who Do Well at Work (New York: Free Press, 1990).

9. M. Forstein, "Homophobia: An Overview," Psychiatric Annals 18:1, January 1988; M. Forstein, "Psychodynamic Psychotherapy with Gay Male Couples," in S. Cohen, ed., Contemporary Perspectives in Psychotherapy with Lesbian and Gay Men (New York: Plenum Press, 1984). See also J. B. Nelson, Male Sexuality, Masculine Spirit (Westminster, Ky.: J. Knox Press, 1988).

10. L. McMurtry, Lonesome Dove (New York: Pocket Books, 1985), p. 922.

11. J. W. Pennebaker, M. Colder, and L. K. Sharp, "Accelerating the Coping Process," Journal of Personal and Social Psychology, 1990, 58(3): 536.

See also J. W. Pennebaker, *Opening Up: The Healing Power of Confiding in Others* (New York: Morrow, 1990).

12. Journal keeping is a way of interviewing oneself. For suggestions on getting started with and using a journal, see I. Progroff, *At a Journal Workshop* (New York: Dialogue House, 1977); and R. B. Kaiser, "The Way of the Journal," *Psychology Today*, March 1981, 64–76.

13. W. Eckenbarger, "Sons and Fathers," *The Kansas City Star Magazine*, September 23, 1990, p. 10.

14. For a review of differences between the sexes in the structure and meaning of friendships, see D. Belle, "Gender Differences in the Social Moderators of Stress," in R. Barnett, L. Biener, and G. Baruch, eds., *Gender and Stress* (New York: Free Press, 1987); and L. Rubin, *Just Friends: The Role of Friendship in Our Lives* (New York: Harper and Row, 1985).

15. T. Landsberg, op. cit. For more perspectives on the varying types of men's groups, see "Men in Groups," *Wingspan*, April–June 1991, 11 Beach Street, Suite 4, Manchester, MA 01944; J. Tevlin, "Of Hawks and Men: A Weekend in the Male Wilderness," *Utne Reader*, November/December, 1989; D. Gross, "The Gender Rap," *The New Republic*, April 16, 1990.

For further discussion about the structure and process of men's groups, see S. Krugman and S. Osherson, "Men in Groups," in A. Alonso and H. Swiller, *op. cit.* and T. MacNab, op. cit.

9: THE CONNECTED SELF:
HEALTHY INTIMACY IN AN AGE WITHOUT ANSWERS

1. B. Brazelton and L. Cramer, *The Earliest Relationship: Parents, Infants, and the Drama of Early Attachment* (New York: Addison-Wesley, 1990), p. 148.

2. E. Langer, *Mindfulness* (Lexington, Mass.: Addison-Wesley, 1989).

3. F. Lolas and M. Rad, "Alexythemia," in S. Cheren, ed. *Psychosomatic Medicine*, vol. 1: *Theory, Physiology, and Practice* (Madison, Conn.: International Universities Press, 1989).

4. See P. Davis, "How Father-Son Battles Helped Shape Today's IBM," *Family Business*, September 1990, 14–16; and T. J. Watson and P. Petre, *Father, Son, and Co.* (New York: Bantam, 1990).

INDEX

ABOUT THE AUTHOR

Samuel Osherson, Ph.D. is a practicing psychotherapist and a research psychologist at the Harvard University Health Services, where he specializes in men's adult development. He is also on the faculty of the Fielding Institute. He lectures extensively around the country to professional and public audiences. He is the author of *Finding Our Fathers*, as well as articles for many newspapers and magazines.